W9-CCG-219

The Henrici Harmonic Analyzer, a symbol of the science of music (see Chap. 8).

PSYCHOLOGY OF MUSIC

by

CARL E. SEASHORE,

PH.D., LL.D., SC.D., D.LITT.

DOVER PUBLICATIONS, INC.
NEW YORK

This Dover edition, first published in 1967, is an unabridged and unaltered republication of the work originally published by McGraw-Hill Book Company, Inc., in 1938.

International Standard Book Number

ISBN-13: 978-0-486-21851-9
ISBN-10: 0-486-21851-1

Library of Congress Catalog Card Number: 67-27877

Manufactured in the United States by LSC Communications
21851125 2018
www.doverpublications.com

To my comrades in research
for the last forty years
this volume is affectionately
dedicated.

PREFACE

THIS volume is dedicated to my comrades in research, professors and students, for the last forty years. I am writing as a spokesman for them all, attempting to present in high lights the new approaches developed during this period. This involves the right to draw freely from more than one hundred publications emanating from the group. Wherever possible I have named the person primarily responsible for the contribution; but the text embodies facts which in large part are common stock in the laboratory.

In doing the overhead work for all these years, it has been difficult to separate my own ideas from the ideas of collaborators because our policy has been to share ideas with the utmost generosity. In the interest of condensation and clarity, I have interpreted and classified as much as is consistent with the purpose and, therefore, have not used quotation marks extensively.

It is difficult to give proper acknowledgment to all the persons and sources represented. All authors of publications from which substantial units are drawn are mentioned in the text with a superscript number which refers to the corresponding number in the bibliography. The sources of illustrations are indicated in the text. Acknowledgment to authors and publishers for permission to use material is herewith gratefully extended.*

Owing to the nature of the situation, I have counted upon many of my collaborators to read and criticize the manuscript in whole or in part both from the point of view of science and from the point of view of music.

---

* The following note from the *Music Educators Journal*, September, 1937, is self-explanatory:

"In a series of reports from the laboratory-studio for the Psychology of Music, Carl E. Seashore has presented to *Journal* readers specimens of scientific findings dealing with various phases of the psychology of music. Appearing in the October issue of the *Journal* will be the tenth in a series, which will deal with the problem of the tempered scale as

The *Psychology of Musical Talent*,[137] published by Silver, Burdett & Company, in 1919, is a monograph which marks a new vantage ground in the psychology of music. It covers a restricted field in which it has permanent value and should, therefore, not be revised, but supplemented. In the present volume, I have aimed to avoid duplication of that work to which this is a logical sequel.

Concentration in this field of work has been favored by a generous attitude on the part of the University of Iowa toward this project and through a series of generous fellowships provided by Mr. George Eastman, the National Research Council, the Guggenheim Foundation, and the Carnegie Foundation. Through a special interest in this subject and such generous financial support, it has been possible to maintain a continuous project through trained investigators, working on a unified program for a generation.

The purpose of this book is to stimulate and guide the student of music in scientific observation and reasoning about his art. It is, therefore, not a summary of all the known facts on any subject, but rather a series of flashes illustrating the scientific approach from as many angles as space and material permit in an elementary textbook. Since the book is written for beginners, no technical description of apparatus or method is given except in most elementary general principles. Material for the student to work upon is, however, furnished abundantly. My attitude throughout may be expressed in the invitation, "Come with me into the laboratory-studio for the psychology of music and see how the study of science of the art of music works." As in my other textbooks the motto has been

Not psychology but to psychologize.

This book has been many years in the making. Certain chapters have been revised periodically as knowledge in the field has advanced. The present edition may, therefore, be regarded as a report of progress subject to revision in the near future; yet an effort has been made to deal only with firmly established facts,

---

opposed to the natural scale and others. Beginning in March, 1936, successive issues of the *Journal* have carried articles on the following subjects: (1) Pitch Intonation in Singing; (2) Approaches to the Experimental Psychology of Music; (3) Quality of Tone: Timbre; (4) Quality of Tone: Sonance; (5) Measurement of Musical Talent: The Eastman Experiment; (6) The Vibrato: What Is It?; (7) The Vibrato: What Makes It Good or Bad?; (8) The Vibrato: How Can We Approach an Ideal Vibrato?; (9) A Performance Score with Phrasing Score for the Violin."

even though fragmentary. Diversity in the style of figures is justified on the policy of retaining the form given each figure by its original author.

Upon invitation from my Alma Mater to give the so-called academic address at an anniversary celebration last year, I chose as my subject *The Power of Music.* This had been the subject of my class oration when graduating from the academy fifty-one years before. Half a century ago the adolescent lover of music began his oration as follows:

> Music is the medium through which we express our feelings of joy and sorrow, love and patriotism, penitence and praise. It is the charm of the soul, the instrument that lifts mind to higher regions, the gateway into the realms of imagination. It makes the eye to sparkle, the pulse to beat more quickly. It causes emotions to pass over our being like waves over the far-reaching sea.

That was what the music I lived in meant to me half a century ago. It was the expression of the genuine thrill of young enthusiasm. Considering what music meant to me then and what it means to me now after a life career in the science of music, there comes to me an analogy from astronomy. Then I was a stargazer; now I am an astronomer. Then the youth felt the power of music and gave expression to this feeling in the way he loved and wondered at the stars before he had studied astronomy. Now the old man feels the same "power of music," but thinks of it in the manner that the astronomer thinks of the starry heavens. Astronomy has revealed a macrocosm, the order of the universe in the large; the science of music has revealed a microcosm, the operation of law and order in the structure and operation of the musical mind. It is a wonderful thing that science makes it possible to discover, measure, and explain the operations of the musical mind in the same attitude that the astronomer explains the operation of the stars.

It is not easy to pass from stargazing to technical astronomy. It is not easy to pass from mere love and practice of music to an intelligent conception of it. To help the lover of music bridge this gap is the purpose of this volume.

CARL E. SEASHORE.

THE STATE UNIVERSITY OF IOWA,
June, 1938.

CONTENTS

LIST OF ILLUSTRATIONS

PSYCHOLOGY OF MUSIC

THE MUSICAL MIND*

THE late Horatio Parker once said in the way of a witticism, "There are no musicians in this country," and to my intimation that there must be some near-musicians he said, after some deliberation, "Well, there is one." On inquiry as to what his particular merits were, it came out that he was a composer. "But," I asked, "how about our great singers and instrumental performers?" "Ah, they are technicians." Ranging from such a conception of the musical mind to that of the mind of Blind Tom or, in a more extreme case, the musicial prodigies which we frequently find in the institutions for the feeble-minded, it is possible to recognize countless varieties of musical minds.

Avoiding as much as possible the account of technical methods of approach, analysis, and measurement, I shall aim to set up in this introductory chapter a skeletal structure in terms of which musical minds may be described and interpreted.

The point of view here presented as a result of laboratory experience is based upon the analysis of the musical medium—the physical sound. This rests upon the assumption that a musical mind must be capable of sensing sounds, of imaging these sounds in reproductive and creative imagination, of being aroused by them emotionally, of being capable of sustained thinking in terms of these experiences, and ordinarily, though not necessarily, of giving some form of expression of them in musical performance or in creative music.

In this objective approach, we must keep in the foreground the fundamental fact that the musical mind does not consist of its

---

* Reprinted by permission from the *Atlantic Monthly*.[130]

dissected parts, but in an integrated personality. In its evaluation we must always have regard for the total personality as functioning in a total situation.

Musical talent is not one, but a hierarchy of talents, branching out along certain trunk lines into the rich arborization, foliage, and fruitage of the tree, which we call the "musical mind." The normal musical mind is first of all a normal mind. What makes it musical is the possession, in a serviceable degree, of those capacities which are essential for the hearing, the feeling, the understanding, and, ordinarily, for some form of expression of music, with a resulting drive or urge toward music.

THE SENSORY CAPACITIES

The psychological attributes of sound, namely, pitch, loudness, time, and timbre, depend upon the physical characteristics of the sound wave: frequency, amplitude, duration, and form. In terms of these we can account for every conceivable sound in nature and art—vocal or instrumental, musical or nonmusical. We therefore recognize that the musical mind must be capable of apprehending these four attributes of sound.

But in this apprehending we find an inner screen which is more significant musically, being composed of the four fundamental sensory capacities in complex forms, namely, the sense of tone quality, the sense of consonance, the sense of volume, and the sense of rhythm. These four complex forms of capacity must be evaluated by themselves and not in terms of their elemental components. For example, rhythm depends upon the sense of time and the sense of intensity, as hydrogen and oxygen combine into water; yet water and rhythm are practical entities in themselves.

This classification of sensory capacities is probably complete, because it is based upon the known attributes of the sound wave. It must be borne in mind that the sound wave is the only medium through which music as such is conveyed from the performer to the listener; everything that is rendered as music or heard as music may be expressed in terms of the concepts of the sound wave. As in good reading we are not aware of letters or phonetic elements as such, but read for meaning, so in music we are, as a rule, not conscious of specific tonal elements or sound waves as such, but rather of musical design or impression as a whole. The lover of flowers may derive deep pleasure from flowers through his senses without knowledge or thought of the physics or chemistry of their structure. So it is possible to enjoy and perform music without insight or knowledge of its true nature; but the musician who knows his medium and thinks intelligently about it has a vastly greater satisfaction than the one who does not.

On the basis of our experiments in measuring these sensory capacities, we find that the basic capacities, the sense of pitch, the sense of time, the sense of loudness, and the sense of timbre are elemental, by which we mean that they are largely inborn and function from early childhood. After a comparatively early age they do not vary with intelligence, with training, or with increasing age, except as the exhibition of these capacities is limited by the child's ability to understand or apply himself to the task. This fact is of the utmost importance in that it makes diagnosis of talent possible before training is begun and points to certain very definite principles of musical education. We can measure these capacities reliably by the age of ten in the normal child; and this measure is likely to stand, except for the numerous vicissitudes of life which may cause deterioration. To take an example, the sense of pitch depends upon the structure of the ear, just as acuity of vision depends upon the structure of the eye. As no amount of training or maturing tends to increase the acuity of the eye, so no amount of training or maturing can improve the pitch acuity of the ear. However, training and maturing in both cases can greatly increase the functional scope of these capacities. The ear, like the eye, is an instrument, and mental development in music consists in the acquisition of skills and the enrichment of experience through this channel. This is analogous to the fact that touch and acuity of hearing are really on the whole as keen in seeing persons as in the blind who show apparently marvelous power of orientation through these senses.

The apparently complex forms of sensory capacities also tend to be elemental to a considerable degree; that is, the young child has the sense of tone quality, of volume, of rhythm, and the sense of consonance long before he begins to sing or know anything about music. It is the meaning, and not the capacity, of these forms of impression which we train and which matures with age in proportion to the degree of intelligence and emotional drive.

There seem to be four large trunks in the family tree of musicality, each of which may develop and ramify to a large extent independently of, or out of proportion to, the others. These four are the tonal, the dynamic, the temporal, and the qualitative. Each is the main trunk of a musical type. Those of the tonal type are peculiarly sensitive to pitch and timbre and dwell upon music in all its tonal forms—melody, harmony, and all forms of pitch variants and compounds; the dynamic have a fine acuity of hearing and sense of loudness and dwell by preference upon stress, or the dynamic aspect of music, in all forms and modifications of loudness; the temporal are peculiarly sensitive to time, tempo, and rhythm, and by preference dwell upon the rhythmic patterns and other media for the temporal aspect of music; the qualitative are peculiarly sensitive to timbre and are capable of its control, dwelling preferentially upon the harmonic constitution of the tone.

Of course, a great musician, or a balanced musician of any degree of greatness, tends to have these four trunks of capacity branching out in balanced and symmetrical form, but such cases are comparatively rare. Many distinguished musicians are dominantly of one of these types; their performance and appreciation and their musical creations all give evidence favoring dominance of one of the trunk lines, although within these trunk lines large and distinctive subbranchings may be recognized. Furthermore, great capacity in each of these types is not essential to marked distinction in musical achievement; very extreme sensitivity in one or more of them may even be a drawback to balanced musical development.

Let me give a very striking illustration on this last point. In measuring certain phases of musical talent in all of the available living members of six of the foremost musical families in the United States, Dr. Stanton found that the brother of one of the protagons of these musical families said that he had no musical talent whatever, and this seemed to be the opinion of the family. But the experimenter found that in the five basic capacities measured, this man was extraordinarily keen, indeed, conspicuously keener than his brother, the famous musician. The interesting confession came out that the reason he was not musical was that practically all the music that he heard seemed to him so bad that it jarred upon him and was intolerable. That was the reason that he was not musical in the conventional sense of the word; he was so keen that the ordinary humdrum of music, even in a musical family, continually jarred him. Is he in reality musical or is he not? The psychologist would say, "In terms of all the evidence at hand, he has extraordinary musical capacities." Yet in his family he was the one who had not "amounted to anything" in music.

Generalizing on the basis of all types of record available we may say that, so far as the sensory capacities are concerned, a balanced and distinctly gifted musical mind will in these capacities measure in the highest 10 per cent of the normal community. But great musical achievement may be attained by persons who may have as low as average sensory capacity in one of these four main lines.

But here it must be pointed out, of course, that success depends upon following the lead of natural capacity. For example, a person who has only an average sense of pitch can never become a good violinist or a great singer; but, with the other three skills well developed, he may become a pianist or a composer of great distinction. A person relatively lacking in dynamic capacities cannot become a great pianist, but might well find success with voice or wind instruments. It is not that the musician always engages in fine distinctions; it is rather that his possession of a fine sensitivity makes him live dominantly in that musical atmosphere to which he is most sensitive and responsive, even when he employs the most dissonant, rough, or unrhythmic characteristics of sound.

MUSICAL IMAGERY, IMAGINATION, AND MEMORY

Granting the presence of sensory capacities in adequate degree, success or failure in music depends upon the capacity for living in a tonal world through productive and reproductive imagination. The musician lives in a world of images, realistic sometimes even to the point of a normal illusion. This does not mean that he is aware of the image as such any more than he needs to be aware of sensation in seeing an object. But he is able to "hear over" a musical program which he has heard in the past as if it were rendered in the present. He creates music by "hearing it out," not by picking it out on the piano or by mere seeing of the score or by abstract theories, but by hearing it out in his creative imagination through his "mind's ear." That is, his memory and imagination are rich and strong in power of concrete, faithful, and vivid tonal imagery; this imagery is so fully at his command that he can build the most complex musical structures and hear and feel all the effects of every detailed element before he has written down a note or sounded it out by voice or instrument. This capacity, I should say, is the outstanding mark of a musical mind at the representation level—the capacity of living in a representative tonal world. This capacity brings the tonal material into the present; it colors and greatly enriches the actual hearing of musical sounds; it largely determines the character and realism of the emotional experience; it is familiarity with these images which makes the cognitive memory for music realistic. Thus, tonal imagery is a condition for learning, for retention, for recall, for recognition, and for the anticipation of musical facts. Take out the image from the musical mind and you take out its very essence.

No one maintains at the present time that a person can be of a single imaginal type; but, in natural musicians with a rich feeling for music, the auditory type dominates, and perhaps largely because realistic imagery is always intimately associated with organic responsiveness. The motor imaginal type is ordinarily also well developed. It is not necessary for us to quarrel about the relation of kinesthetic imagery to kinesthetic sensation, but we can agree upon this: that the motor tendency to image the tone or execute it in inceptive movements is highly developed in the musical mind. The auditory and the motor images are normal stimuli for organic reaction in musical emotion.

The necessity of living in a world of representation tends to bring out vivid visual imagery as well as imagery in the other senses, because there is a general tendency to reinstate, in the representation of a sensory experience, the whole of the original setting. Thus a musician not only hears the music but often lives it out so realistically in his imagination and memory that he sees and feels a response to the persons, instruments, or total situation in the rendition represented. Without this warmth of experience, music would lose its essential esthetic nature. It is a well-known fact that many persons who ply the art or business of music report having no developed imaginal life or concrete imagination. And it has been very interesting to observe in many such cases that, although they are engaged in the practice of music, their musical life is quite devoid of the genuine musical experience. They are often mere pedagogues or musical managers.

The power of mental imagery may be developed to a marked degree with training. There is also good evidence to show that the power of vivid imagery deteriorates with nonuse. A comparison of musicians and psychologists shows that the musicians stand very high in auditory imagery and the psychologists as a class comparatively low. This marked difference is probably due partly to selection and partly to training. There seems to be no doubt but that there are very great differences in the original nature of children in this respect.

Mere strength and fidelity of imagery is, however, of little value except insofar as it is the medium for imagination. Music is an art, and he who plies it successfully has the power of creative imagination. This may be of the sensuous type which is characterized by luxuriant and realistic imagery without much reflection; it may be of the intellectual type in which creation takes the form of purpose, theories, or postulates as to the material of musical content; it may be of the sentimental type in which the flow of imagery is under the sway of the higher sentiments which are often nursed into esthetic attitudes, sometimes called "musical temperament"; it may be of the impulsive type in which the drive or urge of emotion flares up but is not long sustained; it may be of the motor type, sometimes called "architechtonic," which takes the form of a realistic experience of action or of mere performance. According as a person is dominantly of any one or of a combination of these types, his personality as a whole may in large part be designated by such a pattern. Thus, among others, we may recognize as types the sensorimotor, sentimental, impulsive, reflective, motile, and the balanced musician.

While retentive and serviceable memory is a very great asset to a musical person, it is not at all an essential condition for musical-mindedness. A person may have naturally very poor memory of all kinds and get along well in music, just as an absent-minded philosopher may get along very well in his field. Furthermore, the possibility for the development of memory is so very great that with careful training a person with very poor memory may improve this manyfold to the point of serviceability. The musical mind that can reproduce many repertoires with precision is, however, a different mind from one which has neither large scope nor fidelity in retention or reproduction. But both may be musical. The personal traits in memory and imagination color and condition the musical life and often set limits to achievement in music.

MUSICAL INTELLIGENCE

Insofar as the power of reflective thinking is concerned, musical intelligence is like philosophical, mathematical, or scientific intelligence. Intelligence is musical when its background is a storehouse of musical knowledge, a dynamo of musical interests, an outlet in musical tasks, and a warmth of musical experiences and responses. Here, as in the case of imagination, the type and the degree of intelligence may characterize or set limits for the musical achievement. The great composer, the great conductor, the great interpreter live in large intellectual movements. They have the power of sustained thought, a great store of organized information, and the ability to elaborate and control their creative work at a high intellectual level. At the other extreme are the various kinds of small musicianship in which reflective thinking does not function; the experience and the performance are on a sensorimotor level. Such music is to real music as fantasy is to creative imagination. Between these extremes we may sort musicianships into markedly different qualities and levels in terms of some sort of intelligence quotient—a hypothetical musical intelligence quotient—which we might designate as M.I.Q. Thought is, however, not limited to the difficult and ponderous in music, for, as in all other realms of reflection, the highest and most beautiful achievements of thought often have the charm of simplicity.

We should not infer from this that a great mathematician or philosopher, who plays the violin or sings beautifully, does so as a great thinker. The violin and the voice are often a relief to him from the strain of sustained cogitation. He may not create music at all; he may not even interpret at the level at which he philosophizes; yet his sensuous and his imaginative experiences are chastened, mellowed, and balanced by the fact that he is a contemplative man.

Again the great intellect in music may dwell so exclusively upon the musical forms and upon conceptions of new musical structures as to become calloused to the more spontaneous appreciation and expression of music. He becomes hypercritical and may even lose the ability to enjoy music. The penetrating critic often derives more pain than pleasure out of music as it is.

My main point, however, is: as is the intelligence of a man, so is his music. If he is in a school for feeble-minded, his music may be spontaneous and appealing to a high degree; but it will, nevertheless, be feeble-minded. If it is the expression of the philosophical and highly trained composer or conductor, it will be a thought creation whether or not it has the more elemental musical appeals which reach the masses.

MUSICAL FEELING

Music is essentially a play upon feeling with feeling. It is appreciated only insofar as it arouses feeling and can be expressed only by active feeling. On the basis of the degree and the kind of feeling, we may again classify persons into characteristic types in terms of affective responsiveness.

As a fundamental proposition we may say that the artistic expression of feeling in music consists in esthetic deviation from the regular—from pure tone, true pitch, even dynamics, metronomic time, rigid rhythms, etc. All of these deviations can be measured so that we can now compare singers quantitatively in terms of their use of a particular one of the countless devices for deviating from the regular or rigid, including also adherence to the regular as a means of expressing emotion in music. The emotional medium at one moment may be primarily fine modulation in tonal timbre, at another in rhythm, at another in stress, and each of these in countless forms of sublimation or hierarchies. In the ensemble of such deviation from the regular lies the beauty, the charm, the grandeur of music. When Tetrazzini catalogues among the chief faults of singing "faulty intonation, faulty phrasing, imperfect attack, scooping up to notes, digging or arriving at a note from a semitone beneath" she, of course, is right but may fail to realize that in just such variables lie the resources for beauty and power of music.

In other words, our concept of feeling as expressed in music may become concretely scientific, so that, if the music critic praises or blames a singer for a certain emotional quality, it need no longer remain a question of dispute or opinion; but, just as we could snap the profile of the singer with the camera, we can get the profile of the sound wave and settle the dispute about the musical quality. The music critics, of course, have not yet adopted this technique, but the next generation will make a beginning. The expression of feeling in music, that mysterious and enchanting retreat for all things musical, is being explored; trails are being blazed, and the music critic will soon talk about musical expression of feeling in terms of precise and scientific concepts.

When Grace Moore sings in New York and the critics opine about the technique of quavers in her voice, we may have at the footlights a recording instrument which photographs every sound wave and enables us to preserve for all time the form of her expression of emotion. We are, of course, not thinking here about that mystic inner something which is spoken of as feeling, as such, but of the *expression* of feeling. In modern psychology, to feel is always to do, to express something—action of the organism. The expression does not take ethereal, magical, or even mystic form but comes to us through the media to which our senses are open.

There are two other aspects of feeling in music. One is the nature of esthetic experience, and the other is what we may call the "creative feeling" as it operates in the composer. It is evident that both of these will stand out in an entirely new light the moment the conception of the concreteness, describability, and tangibleness of the expression of emotion in music is recognized.

MUSICAL PERFORMANCE

Musical performance, like all other acts of skill involving unusually high capacity, is limited by certain inherent and inherited motor capacities. For example, a child may be slow and sure or quick and erratic in certain specific activities, or he may be found in any other combinations of the two series from the extremely slow to the extremely quick, and extremely precise to the extremely erratic. And, as a child is found, so will be the youth and the man. Such a "personal equation" is a personal trait, like stature or color of hair. Singing involves the possession of a favorable structure of the vocal organs and motor control. Playing various kinds of instruments calls for a high order of natural capacity, for speed and accuracy in control. Such motor capacities can be measured before musical training is begun. Musical action is, of course, also limited by limitations in each and all of the talents heretofore discussed; for example, a person who is low in sense of rhythm will of necessity be low in rhythmic performance. In the next generation, the music student and the music teacher and theorist will rate progress and quality in musical performance in relation to capacity, just as at the present time we are beginning to consider it reasonable not to expect as much from a moron as we do from a philosopher.

It is quite possible to recognize fundamental types of motor resourcefulness in musical performance, but for the present purpose the main thing to be stressed is that there is nothing indescribable about it and that individual motor fortes or faults of a basic character often determine the character of the musician.

The musician, in passing judgment upon a prospective musician, rightly says, "Give me the child with the musical instinct." By that he does not mean any one of the specific capacities we have discussed, but rather a fundamental urge, drive, or emotional dominance, craving expression in music from early childhood. This general trait is often feigned, fragmentary, or imaginary, but when genuine it constitutes the most certain indication of the presence of the musical mind that we have. When submitted to analysis, it is found to represent an effective grouping, dominance, or balance of fundamental sensory and motor capacities and therefore yields to measurement and scientific description and evaluation.

THE MEANING OF THIS ANALYSIS

This, in brief, is the skeletal structure I promised. In many respects it is but dangling and rattling dry bones. "Atomistic!" some of my confreres will say. Now, atoms are not roses, resplendent in bloom, fragrance, and configuration—living roses! The esthete, whiffing and raving about the beauty of the rose, can ignore the atom, but the botanist cannot. It is to the botanist that we look for a true revelation of the origin, the growth, the nature, and the role of roses in the economy of nature. It is the botanist who can make verifiable and permanent distinctions among roses.

Fifty years ago, Wundt was asked, "What have you learned from the reaction experiment?" to which his whole laboratory force had devoted its first three years. His reply was, "It has given me a new conception of the human mind." Speaking for those who take the scientific point of view in the psychology of music, I may say that experiment has given us a new conception of the musical personality as a whole—its infinite capacities and the intimate relationships among them, the marvelous range for possible training, growth, and substitution, the sublimation of musical interests in daily life, the necessity of viewing the personality as a dynamic whole.

Does this point of view oversimplify the musical mind? The argument I have made is that it can and should vastly enrich and deepen the concept; if you ask one question of nature in the laboratory, nature asks you ten, and each of these when pursued in turn multiplies into tens of tens of tens. For laboratory procedure is but the setting of conditions for more and more precise observations of specific, concrete, verifiable facts or features. What I have stated is, after all, merely a point of view. The details remain to be worked out, filled in, modified as science progresses. The whole appeal is to and for verifiable facts.

What shall it profit? Perhaps I may bring together in a constructive way some of the features which seem to me to be involved in the acceptance of scientific procedure in the interpretation, evaluation, and education of the musical mind.

It gives us a psychology of music in that it furnishes describable and verifiable facts as a basis for classification. The particular data I have presented are just plain psychology; not any particular brand, but rather an attempt to select and consolidate what is usable in the various modern points of view.

It furnishes us a technique for the development of musical esthetics. The armchair deductions about the nature of beauty in music give way to experiment, and conclusions must be limited to factors under control. Musical esthetics will soon loom up as one of the applied and normative sciences.

It forms a basis for the analysis and evaluation of musical talent and will furnish helpful data for vocational and avocational guidance in music.

It develops an intimate relationship between music and speech. Speech, especially dramatic art, is gaining recognition in esthetics because of its close relationship to music.

It lays the foundations for musical criticism, musical biography and autobiography, and musical theory in general, even for intelligent parlor conversation about musical thrills.

It furnishes the foundation for the essential facts for the construction of the curriculum, for the selection and motivation of the musically educable, for the evaluation of progress in training, and for countless improvements in the technique and economy of teaching. If a committee of scientifically trained musicians should make a survey of the economies or wastes involved in current methods of teaching music and should be free to set forth the pedagogical consequence of facing the new scientifically known facts about the musical mind, very radical changes would follow.

It helps to give music its true place and influence by enhancing the musical life for the musically gifted and thereby furnishing a natural drive for the effective functioning of music in the life of the people.

2

THE MUSICAL MEDIUM

THE medium with which the musician works is the sound wave; his works of art take the form of artistically built sound structures. The painter creates his work of art through the medium of physical paints; the sculptor models his creation in clay, or chisels, hews, and molds in metals or stone. The musician has but one medium, the physical sound.

MUSICIAN, MUSIC, LISTENER

The psychology of music may be divided into three large fields dealing with the musician, the music, and the listener, respectively. It is concerned with the description and explanation of the operations of the musical mind, the music as a thing in itself, and the musical activities of the listener. Naturally, it deals primarily with the music as a work of art in sound and from that works back to the producer of music and forward to the listener who hears it musically.

Psychology proceeds systematically by analyzing situations and reducing them progressively to their simplest terms. The first great step in approaching the psychology of music is to recognize that everything that the singer or player conveys to the listener is conveyed through sound waves or in terms of these. This conception simplifies our approach immensely in that it frees us from confusion with unnecessary accessories, furnishes us with a basis for classification and terminology, and paves a way for preservation of findings, measurement, and scientific explanation.

But, the reader may say, music is more than sound. It must have atmosphere; it ordinarily involves some degree of dramatic action; it is modified by the character of the audience, the personal appearance, manners and mannerisms of the performer, the total situation of which the performance is a part. In other words, music is essentially tied up with a larger setting in which it plays a leading role. This must be taken for granted, and we may recognize that there is a very interesting psychology of each of these accessories, such as the picture hat, the smile, the anticipated applause, the sentiment connected with the national anthem, or the mood of the listener. These contribute to the atmosphere and should be cultivated with care, but they are not the music. They present very interesting psychological problems; but it is to the advantage of the psychology of music to separate clearly the music in itself from its accessories.

It also is admitted that the music is in the first and last instances, in the mind of the composer and in the mind of the listener, not actual sounds but images, ideas, ideals, thoughts, and emotions. We shall find, however, that these are always in terms of the physical sound to which they refer. In this respect, the creations of the musician are analogous to the creations of the painter and the sculptor; they are purely objective.

The musical instrument or voice or any other sound-producing body sends out puffs or waves of air which radiate in all directions from the source. When segments of these waves strike the ear, they set up vibrations in the tympanic membrane. These in turn are transmitted through the middle ear as vibrations of three bones. They are taken up by the oval membrane, which in turn transmits them to the liquid of the inner ear. The vibrations in this liquid are transferred to the receiving mechanism of the nerve cells, the end organs of hearing in the inner ear. For each vibration, the mechanical shaking of the end organs of the auditory nerve sets up a nerve impulse. These nerve impulses are transmitted to the brain and give rise to the tone that is heard.

Thus, in terms of waves, we may trace the physical medium of sound from the vibration of the sounding body, such as a reed or the vocal cords, through the air as air waves and through the tympanic membrane, the bony system, the oval membrane, the liquid of the inner ear, and the receiving mechanism of the nerve cells, as physical vibrations of material bodies. Then follow the physiological stages consisting of the arousing of the nerve impulse in the end organ, its transmission over the auditory nerve, and the action set up in the various brain centers reached. It is this nerve impulse that primarily determines the tone which we hear.

In this way nature has provided a means of transforming the musical medium from one form of energy to another; and in this process the waves are adapted progressively to each medium, finally resulting in brain activity associated with the musical experience. The experience is not that of a wave, but of a tone having pitch, duration, loudness, and timbre. The following statement in *The Psychology of Musical Talent*[137] is apposite:

> Thinking of musical experience in terms of this physical medium, we are confronted with one of the greatest marvels of nature, the wondrous "transformation from matter to mind": out of mere vibration is built a world of musical tones which do not in themselves suggest vibration at all. So it is in all the senses. The vibrations of light reflected from the landscape give us the mental experience of color and form, and our minds are so endowed that we can experience beauty and see meaning in this display. It is the physical flower that we love and admire and seek to understand. No one doubts the existence of this physical flower; no one doubts the experience of its beauty. The love and understanding of things seen in nature and art take for granted this physical-physiological-mental series as an integrated unit. The artist and the common man who experience it need not think in terms of light vibrations, but the scientist who is to explain the experience must think in terms of physical, physiological, and mental processes as units—in terms of light waves, nerve impulses, and mental process.
>
> So it is with music. Musical art and the everyday experience of sound may proceed without any knowledge of physics, physiology, or psychology; but when the scientist attempts to explain these experiences he must deal with the series as a whole, the sound wave, the nerve impulse, and the experience of sound. The object of our study is music from the psychological point of view. Music is the center and core of our interest, the goal toward which we are working.

It is possible to intercept the sound wave by measuring instruments at any of these stages: in the condensation and rarification of the air, in the physical vibration of the various parts of the ear, or in the physiological pulsations of the nerve impulse in the end organ, the nerve, or the brain center.

The most serviceable approach is that of phonophotography, by which the air waves are intercepted and recorded faithfully with cameras suitable for the purpose. Our descriptions of the musical medium will, therefore, be given largely in terms of these phonophotograms which reveal all the characteristics of the sound wave in measurable form.

CHARACTERISTICS OF THE SOUND WAVE

As we have seen, sound waves have four, and only four, characteristics; namely, frequency, amplitude, duration, and form. Sounds of every conceivable sort, from pure tone to the roughest noise, can be recorded and described in terms of these four. The same four characteristics may be traced in the nerve impulse which results from the physical vibration; corresponding to these four

FIG 1.—Oscillogram of a pure and steady tone.

characteristics of physical wave and nerve impulse, we have the four characteristics of musical tones. The full and serious recognition of this parallelism vastly simplifies our problem and furnishes us a key to the understanding, the recording, the production, the description of musical phenomena; it enables us to know that we are taking all factors into account, since these four are all-inclusive; it furnishes us a terminology which is simple, consistent, and verifiable; it facilitates the adoption of units of measurement; it does away with the notion that tones may vary in an "infinite and unknowable variety of ways"; it furnishes a cornerstone for the psychology of music and musical esthetics.

Figure 1 is a phonophotogram of a pure tone, lasting 0.1 sec. In this picture there are 5 waves in this tenth of a second. Therefore, the number of waves in 1 second is 50, the *frequency* of the tone. The pressure or energy of the sound wave, which determines the *intensity* of the physical tone and loudness of the tone as heard, is expressed in terms of the amplitude or height of the wave from crest to trough. The *duration** is, of course, expressed in terms

* In physics, duration is not spoken of as a characteristic of the wave except insofar as it refers to wave length, which is the reciprocal of frequency. For psychological reasons,

of time length of the tone, that is, the continuation of the sound waves as recorded over the time line. The *form* of the wave determines its harmonic constitution, which gives us the experience of timbre. In this case, the smooth sine curve is an indication of the pure tone.*

Before proceeding to describe the sounds which we hear in terms of these four characteristics, it should be made clear that in reality the hearing of tones is rarely an exact copy of these physical characteristics of the sound, because hearing is seldom complete and many principles of distortion operate. We are subject to a great variety of faults and errors in hearing. These are due primarily to five sources: the physical limit of the sense organ, the physiological limitations, inaccurate or inadequate perception, principles of economy in hearing, and principles of artistic hearing. These deviations from direct correspondence to the actual physical sound we call "normal illusions." It is significant that they are not mere errors but may serve in the interests of economy, efficiency, and the feeling of beauty in mental life. And it is particularly significant for us at this stage that all these illusions may themselves be measured in terms of these same four attributes of the sound wave.

This principle is true in all our perception. When we see the color and form of the Japanese cherry tree in blossom, we rarely see the exact color or the exact detail or shape of the parts of the tree, yet we assert that we see the tree and recognize that it is the actual thing which really exists and which we ought to see. But we know numerous laws of illusion of color and form and the limits of sensation, all of which tend to modify the thing that we see. So, in musical hearing, we are fully justified in speaking in quantitative terms of the physical sound wave as the true description of the physical tone. But a large and very interesting part of the psychology of musical hearing consists of principles of deviation from the actual physical tone.

FREQUENCY: PITCH

The terms "frequency," "double vibrations" (d.v.), "number of vibrations per second," "cycles," and "waves" are synonymous

duration of the recurrence of waves is here spoken of as a wave characteristic; that is, something that can be measured in terms of waves.

* For latest definitions of terms in hearing see *Report of Committee on Acoustical Standardization.*[a]

and may be used interchangeably to designate frequency and pitch. It is now customary to use the sign $\sim$ to designate these. Historically, the term "pitch" has been used appropriately in two meanings: first, in the narrow sense, to denote an attribute of the sound as heard, that is, the mental experience; second, in a broader sense, to denote the total process, physical, physiological, and psychological. Current practice attempts to use "pitch" to designate the psychological experience and "frequency" to designate the physical vibration. However, in the science of music and speech we constantly have occasion to mean the whole situation—mental, physiological, physical; and then we employ the term "pitch" in the broader sense. The context generally indicates which of these connotations is intended.

In determining frequency, we count the number of waves per second or we measure the length of successive waves, counting from characteristic points such as from crest of one wave to the corresponding point in the next.

In musical hearing and performance, we demand answers to questions like these: What is the actual pitch of the tone? How faithful is it? How does it vary artistically? In what respects is it faulty? What license has the performer taken? How is pitch rendered in the attack, the release, or the portamento? What unusual characteristics of intonation, if any, are there? We may picture problems of this kind in terms of the following skeletal outline:

Musical aspects of pitch intonation

Actual pitch in terms of frequency
Faults of intonation

Ex. Level flatting or sharping; progressive flatting or sharping; erratic fluctuations

Musical ornaments

Ex. Trills and grace notes indicated in the score; vibrato and other periodic inflections not indicated in the score

Other varied inflections involving art principles
Unconventional artistic license

Ex. Pitch swoops in primitive music or semispeech intonation for dramatic effect

Glides in attack, release, or portamento
Intervals: melody, harmony

INTENSITY: LOUDNESS

For psychological purposes, the intensity of tone is expressed in terms of decibels (db). The decibel is a new term devised by electrical engineers for the measurement of sound in radio, talking pictures, sound abatement, and architecture; but it is destined to take its place among the common units of measurements, such as a degree of temperature. Like pitch and loudness, the decibel is a psychological unit representing the degree of loudness. Its physical counterpart, intensity, is expressed in terms of units of electrical energy. On the physical side, we speak of dynamic value in terms of intensity and on the mental side in terms of loudness.

However, intensity is frequently used to designate either the mental or the physical, or both, for the reason that it is the recognized term expressing an attribute of sensation in psychology, and, in a great variety of situations, the object is not to distinguish between the physical and the mental but to represent the total situation. Likewise, the decibel is used to designate both the physical and the mental. Types of questions which may be answered in terms of decibels are indicated in the following skeletal outline:

Musical aspects of loudness

Degree of loudness, or absolute intensity
Dynamic modulation

> Ex. Periodic variations in intensity as in the vibrato; progressive variations in intensity as in crescendo, diminuendo, swell, circumflex; dynamic license, as in acute swells and dips characteristic of primitive music and certain rare artistic modulations for the dramatic effect; and attack, release, and portamento

Dynamic rhythm (see Chap. 12)
Volume (see Chap. 11)

> Ex. Dynamic changes in relation to pitch, time, intensity, and timbre

Erratic changes in intensity

DURATION: TIME

Pitch and intensity are always recorded against time, expressing the duration of notes, pauses, or any specific feature of these. We may, therefore, take our time values from either the pitch record or the intensity record. Some of the musically significant time values are shown in the following skeletal outline:

Musical aspects of time

Actual duration of tones, pauses, or any specific aspect of these
Time and tempo
Temporal rhythm
  Ex. Measure rhythm, phrase rhythm, or sentence rhythm

Time of attack and release

  Ex. Asynchronization of chords or overlapping of notes through pedal action and syncopation

Artistic variations

  Ex. Accelerando, retardando, holds, legato, staccato, vibrato

Erratic and faulty variations in time

WAVE FORM: TIMBRE

Timbre is described in terms of the form of the sound wave. It ranges from the pure tone through an infinite number of changes in complexity up to the pitchless sound we call "noise." As we shall see later, timbre is determined primarily by the number, the order, and the relative intensity of the fundamental and its overtones as expressed in the wave form. It also is modified by the absolute pitch and total intensity of the tone as a whole. The physical structure of the complex sound is called its "harmonic composition." Psychologically it may be spoken of as the overtone structure. This is fully illustrated in Chaps. 8, 9, and 17.

In actual music, it is possible to have as many as 30 or 40 partials in combination, constituting a rich tone. As we shall see in the chapter on timbre, the wave form may be analyzed so as to show how many partials are present, the form of their distribution, and the relative amount of energy that each contributes. In terms of such facts, we can represent the harmonic constitution and, therefore, the timbre of the tone by a graph called a "tone spectrum."

An unscientific person listening to all the sounds in art and nature is tempted to pronounce the variety of differences indescribable; but, from the physicist's point of view, every physical tone is describable in terms of its partials which, from the point of view of hearing, we call "overtones," as expressed in timbre. In other words, the sound wave is capable of as many types of form as nature and art may be capable of sounding as variations in tone quality. We should here recognize that timbre as a fourth attribute of tone is by far the most important aspect of tone and introduces the largest number of problems and variables. Some of these may be indicated in the following skeletal outline:

Musical aspects of tonal timbre

The actual description of the quality of any tone

Ex. The exact and objective description of any voice, any instrument, any vowel

Variation in tone quality

Ex. Variation of timbre with register, loudness, duration, location of tone, nasality, placement, breathing

Norms

Ex. The determination of norms of beauty in tones, either actual or ideal: the relation of timbre to art forms

Ex. The expression of love, grief, fear, rage: musical mood

Any musician could extend this list in terms of questions about tone quality which he would like to have measured. Many of these questions arise alike in both music and speech, and the findings in one transfer to the other.

In this very brief outline, we have become aware of the elements which function in the musical medium, which are measurable in terms of the sound wave and which have distinct psychological and musical meaning. For full illustrations and discussion, we must pursue in turn Chaps. 5, 6, 7, and 8.

THE MUSICAL PERFORMANCE SCORE

If we bear in mind that all of these aspects of music which have been mentioned are measurable and capable of description and statement in exact scientific form, the question of scientific musical notation becomes urgent. Without such notation, the psychology of music would be in a position of mathematics without mathematical symbols. As has been outlined, every aspect of the musical medium can be measured, analyzed in great detail, recorded, described, and explained. We should soon be swamped with the mass of that type of information unless we had some standardized, very simple, scientifically accurate, and musically significant graphical language or symbols in which the facts could be preserved and made readily available in music.

Such language has been devised in the form of what has been called the musical performance score. Instead of taking space to illustrate and explain such scores at this stage, we may ask the reader to turn to Figs. 1 and 2 in Chap. 4, Fig. 1 in Chap. 18, Fig. 3 in Chap. 19, and Fig. 3 in Chap. 20, where we have full illustrations of its nature and use. It will be observed that these performance scores record three factors: namely, pitch, time, and intensity. Timbre is of such a complex nature that it must be reported in individual tone spectra as seen and explained in Chaps. 8, 9, 17, 18, and 20.

3

THE SCIENCE OF MUSIC

THE preceding chapter was an attempt to introduce the reader to the psychology of music by showing how this science describes and explains musical phenomena in terms of the musical medium. Let us now seek further insight into this new field of applied science and art, and obtain a bird's-eye view of the ground which lies before us. A full science of music cannot be written in one or in a small number of volumes. It therefore is necessary to select a specific point of view and recognize important limitations of the subject treated in this volume.

SCOPE OF THE SUBJECT

1. The subject is limited to a scientific approach. Description and explanation in music draw upon several sciences: primarily, physics, mathematics, physiology, anatomy, anthropology, and psychology, as well as the history and theory of musical practice. But it has come to be a function of the psychologist, as a student of human experience and behavior, to integrate these under the general concept of the "psychology of music." Although there may be much practical wisdom in popular psychology, resting on loose theory not suitable for verification by scientific method, such topics are excluded, and so is also the legitimate subject of philosophy of music.

2. It is limited to those topics which are peculiarly amenable to treatment in the psychological laboratory, thus excluding problems specific to other sciences, such as physics, physiology, and mathematics, except as accessories.

3. It is further limited to the treatment of topics on which the author has firsthand experience, emanating directly or indirectly

from the psychological laboratory. It therefore is necessarily selective, skeletal, and illustrative rather than systematic. It constitutes only a series of fair samples of problems, procedures, facts, and principles, both theoretical and applied.

Psychology of music, even in a narrow sense, is unlimited, because music involves countless varieties of musical performance, countless varieties of moods, emotions, and ideas to be expressed, and countless attitudes, capacities, urges, and interests of the listener. In a way it involves all psychology; because the understanding, description, and explanation of musical experience and behavior implies understanding, description, and explanation of fundamental experience and behavior in general. We must therefore seek to confine ourselves to the most essential situations exhibited in music and, among these, to those immediately essential for the understanding, appreciation, and expression of music.

Yet the treatment is not restricted to music. It carries many implications and interpretations which have a bearing on the science of fine arts in general. Because of the common elements involved, the analysis of the situation in the psychology of music has its analogies in other fine arts and interests, such as graphic and plastic art, dramatic art, and poetry. In other words, the science of music transfers in various degrees to each of these fields, in both their pure and their applied aspects. Furthermore, any contribution to the psychology of music becomes also a contribution to general psychology. Therefore, while music is our specific objective, a study of this kind throws much light upon the interrelations of the fine arts and their common problems, particularly with reference to vocational and educational guidance and training for skills.

THE PERFORMER, THE MUSIC, THE LISTENER

The musical performer. We must consider here the performer, either vocal or instrumental, his instrument, his physical organism and physiological condition on the physical side, and on the mental side, the cognitive, affective, and motor aspects of his performance.

On the physical side, we are concerned with the instrument, which may be the human voice or any other sound-producing mechanism that may have musical significance. The self-expression of the musician is naturally related to, and characterized by, the physical instrument which serves as his tool.

With reference to this aspect, we must take into account not only natural capacity for voice, as in singing, but also a number of other physical and neural mechanisms which favor or interfere with successful performance, in either voice or instrument. The character of the performance and the limits of achievement often are set by the physique of the performer, his physiological condition, such as the state of health, fatigue, adaptation, and other chronic or temporary physiological factors which affect sensitivity, mental alertness, muscular tonus, and general attitudes and impulses of the performer.

Given favorable physical and physiological conditions, we still find the largest variables in the psychological and educational aspect of the performer. Among these are the character of his knowledge and training, the development of his temperamental and emotional life, and the motor and interpretative skills which are the media of his musical expression. Each of these may be regarded from the point of view of natural ability, including his inheritance and environmental influences. On the other hand, each may be regarded from the point of view of mental development, maturation, musical tastes and leanings, and acquired skills. Thus the psychology of the performer involves the psychology of his instrument, his neuromuscular equipment, and all the factors which are determined by knowledge, feeling, action, and will power, both from the view of the natural capacity and as a result of nurture in his environment and of training.

The music. The central problem in the psychology of music is the description and explanation of the musical creation—the actual music—regarded on the one hand as the expression of musical feeling and on the other as the stimulus for arousing musical feeling. The psychology of music on the whole begins with and centers around the performance. The first step is to record it adequately, measure it, and analyze it as a work of art. As has been pointed out, the four characteristics of the sound wave may be recorded, measured, and classified in a relatively complete system and to a degree which far exceeds the limits of musical hearing. They may be reported in scientific terminology which is complete and adequate for the description of every possible element or variant in the song or instrumental performance as an art object. Therefore, the psychology of musical performance implies an adequate knowledge of the physical characteristics of sound, the mode of its transmission, and the countless physical and physiological conditions which determine its functioning.

The psychological problem here is to convert the objective record of the physical aspects of music as performed into terms of psychological experiences and responses which have musical meaning. Thus, instead of being concerned with frequency, intensity, duration, and form of sound waves, we shall speak and think in terms of pitch, loudness, time, and timbre, and all their derivatives and variants, giving a scientific account of the performance in terms of musical terminology. Here we must deal with a vast array of principles, such as the psychophysics of hearing, musical evolution, musical knowledge and training, the limits of the organism, individual differences, health, musical environment, musical guidance, practical norms, and esthetic principles, and shall aim in general to give an interpretative account of that which is transmitted from the performer to the listener as music.

Central to the interpretation of performance as musical art are a number of facts which are strictly musical; such as musical form and all its variants, musical theory involving all its aspects of composition, setting of words and themes, racial and historical aspects, and many other matters of musical esthetics.

The listener. Having considered the psychology of the performer and the performance, there remains the very important stage of the psychology of the listener. What is characteristic of the musical message as it is received? What are the factors, physiological, physical, psychological, and esthetic, which determine this response in hearing, interpretation, and enjoyment of music? Evidently the problems in the psychology of the listener are, in general, the same as the psychology of the performer, which we need not here repeat. Central among these, however, are the psychology of musical appreciation, the limits of the capacity for hearing, for interpreting and reliving the musical emotion which the artist has attempted to convey.

From these considerations it is evident that our subject is enormously involved and that therefore a single coherent treatment will of necessity be fragmentary and restricted. With this in mind, the present volume presents an outline in high lights for the purpose of stimulating and guiding the student in dealing with observation, reading, and thinking on the subject. Our aim is primarily to present the psychology of the subject in such a way as to lead the reader to psychologize about music himself.

GENERAL PRINCIPLES OF SCIENCE

Most of our knowledge is of the common-sense variety gained in uncontrolled observation. Very little is based upon experiment; yet, where there is no experiment, there can be no science. Furthermore, in a new applied science like this, there is a vast amount of so-called "experimentation" that is neither scientific nor valid. In planning an experiment or in evaluating the results of an experiment in the psychology of music, we should check the procedure against such criteria as the following six. Let us consider, for example, an experiment to determine the carrying power of voice or instrument.

1. The factor under consideration must be isolated in order that we may know exactly what it is that we are measuring. For example, we must take one factor, such as pitch, intensity, timbre, tempo, size of the room, or the acoustical treatment of the walls and isolate and define it adequately.
2. All other factors must be kept constant while the selected factor is varied under control. For example, if intensity is a selected factor, we must vary that factor in graded steps while all other factors in the tone and in the total environment are kept constant.
3. The observed facts must be recordable. For example, the intensity may be recorded in terms of the energy or power of the tone.
4. The situation must be repeatable for verification. It should be possible for any scientist with proper equipment to repeat the experiment under identical conditions.
5. The conclusion must be validated in relation to the total personality and in the total musical situation.
6. The conclusion must be limited to the factor under control. For example, we can only say that the most favorable intensity here found holds for the conditions here controlled and that it must therefore be integrated with other factors in a series of experiments in which each of these is taken in turn.

If the plan for an experiment fails on any one of these points, this may invalidate the conclusion to be drawn. If we wish to weigh the reliability of evidence from experiment, here is a fair scale. We should not maintain that every serious study in psychology should be scientific. There is nothing sacred about science. Science simply strives for accuracy and logical coherence of facts. In the interest of progress and practice, we must put up with a great many make-shifts, often of no scientific value but very useful in the process of trial and error at our present state of limited knowledge. The scientist makes the supreme sacrifice of being willing to devote time and energy to the study of one specific isolated factor at a time, regardless of how small a part it may be of the whole; but the reward for this sacrifice is adequate—the discovery of verifiable truth. The musician as a practical man must draw upon currently accepted truths through tradition, common-sense observation, and general knowledge, and do the best he can in the practical situation; but as science progresses, he will be more and more open-minded and eager for the fragments of scientific facts that dribble in or that he may discover by his own experiments.

The criteria here set up represent the bedrock requirements of science. A survey of the experimental literature in psychology shows that experiments generally accepted as more or less scientific range from those which conform rigidly to these requirements to those which can scarcely be said to follow any of them. In this situation formative science can be tolerated on the ground that "doing the best we can" from time to time is often a preliminary stage to mastery. In all sciences we find such regions of exploratory effort. Therefore, while we should not flaunt the criteria for simon-pure experiment in a censorious way, we should always hold before ourselves a goal which must be approached in a stabilized science and temper and evaluate our conclusions by the limitations thus set up in relation to this goal.

BASIC PRINCIPLES IN THE PSYCHOLOGY OF MUSIC

Laboratory experiments in the psychology of music have revealed progressively a number of principles which seem to facilitate experiment, introduce important elements of economy, insure exhaustive treatment, furnish criteria of validity, and form bases for the foundation of esthetic theories.

Some principles have emerged incidentally throughout the foregoing chapters. A selected number of these are here thrown into high relief in the interest of a combined review and forecast. It has been suggested that we call these a duo-decalogue for the psychology of music.

1. All that is conveyed from the musician to the listener as music is conveyed on sound waves. As was pointed out in Chap. 2, countless other factors—dramatic action, gesture, grimaces, smiles and frowns, picture hats and jewelry, personal charm, environment, and audience—all contribute to the pleasure or displeasure in the musical situation, but they are not music. Recognition of this fact simplifies our problem.*

2. The sound waves are measurable, and there are only four variables which have musical significance: frequency, intensity, duration, and form. Recognition of this is a great forward leap in that it brings order and simplicity out of chaos and despair; physically, the infinite variety of musical sounds can be reduced to these four variables and measured in terms of them.

3. The psychological equivalents or correlates of these characteristics of sound are pitch, loudness, time, and timbre. Rhythm, harmony, volume, and tone quality are compounds of these; thought, feeling, action, memory, and imagination are in terms of these. We thus obtain a basic classification of all musical phenomena and give each its place in the family tree with its four large branches: the tonal, the dynamic, the temporal, and the qualitative.

4. The correspondence between the physical fact and the mental fact is not entirely direct or constant; there are many illusions of hearing. While we describe, for example, the pitch of A conventionally and practically as having a frequency of 440 cycles per second (abbreviated 440 ~), which is an invariable factor, the experience of that pitch may vary under a large variety of conditions resulting in illusions of pitch, many of which are very interesting and of practical significance in actual music. It is a triumph of science, however, that we can identify, measure, and explain each of these illusions. Thank God for illusions! Without illusions there could be no musical art.

5. The medium of musical art lies primarily in artistic deviation from the fixed and regular: from rigid pitch, uniform intensity, fixed rhythm, pure tone, and perfect harmony. Therefore the

* The reader will do the author the kindness to assume that qualifying phrases could be added for this and other direct and categorical statements which lack of space compels us to make without qualifications. Such phrases as "other things being equal," "as a general principle," "subject to exceptions in minor detail," "in our present state of knowledge," etc., should be understood throughout.

quantitative measurement of performance may be expressed in terms of adherence to the fixed and so-called "true," or deviation from it in each of the four groups of musical attributes.

6. In each of the four categories, we have a zero point for a scale of measures. Thus, for pitch we may start from a standard tone; for intensity, from silence; for duration, from zero duration; and for timbre, from the pure tone.

7. On the basis of the above considerations, we may develop a definable, consistent, and verifiable musical terminology. For example, we shall be able to say exactly what timbre is and adopt adequate terminology for its variants. In the same way we shall be asked to scrap the hundreds of loose and synonymous terms used to designate timbre and be enabled to use the selected term correctly in the light of its new definition.

8. All measurements may be represented graphically in what we have called the musical pattern score or performance score, which symbolizes the language of scientific measurement in a graph that has musical meaning. This score carries the three factors, pitch, intensity, and time. Timbre must be represented in a series by itself in the form of tonal spectra.

9. Norms of artistic performance may be set up in terms of objective measurement and analysis of superior performance for the purpose of evaluating achievement and indicating goals of attainment.

10. The best performance of today can be improved upon. We must therefore look forward to experimental procedures to determine ideal norms which will set up new standards of attainment, vastly increased resources, power and beauty in music.

11. In the future, musical esthetics will be built upon the bases of scientific measurement and experimental analysis. With modern means of measurement, any advocated theories may be put to the acid test.

12. Where there is no experiment, direct or indirect, there is no science. Science, by virtue of its adherence to minute detail, is always fragmentary and incomplete. Its findings must always be supplemented by practical intuition, common sense, and sound philosophical theories of the art. Science deals with selected topics. The musician must deal with the situation as a whole with the means at his command.

There is an important scientific approach in the clinical field; for music may have marked therapeutic value. Clinical psychology of music will draw upon psychiatry, sociology, criminology, and education for scientific principles. But the field is yet quite unworked. *Van de Wall's Music in Institutions*[205] furnishes a good introduction to this subject and contains a full bibliography.

13. Musical talent may be measured and analyzed in terms of a hierarchy of talents as related to the total personality, the musical medium, the extent of proposed training, and the object to be served in the musical pursuit.

14. For musical guidance on the basis of scientific measurement, the application must be restricted to the factors measured; but it should be supplemented by an adequate audition, case history, and consideration of personality traits and avenues for achievement. All musical guidance should be tempered by the recognition of the extraordinary resourcefulness of the human organism and the vast variety of the possible musical outlets for self-expression.

15. Successful performance rests upon the mastery of fundamental skills which may be isolated and acquired as specific habits; but in artistic performance, these skills should be integrated so that in the musical mood there is no consciousness of habits, skills, or techniques as such.

16. To facilitate the acquisition of musical skills, objective instrumental aids may be used to great advantage, for both economy of time and precision of achievement. Among such aids are visual projection or quantitative indication of pitch, intensity, time, and timbre at the moment the tone is produced.

17. In the coming electrical organs, pianos, and other instruments, and in the criticism which all instruments will be subjected to as a result of the possibility of measurement, future progress will depend upon the adoption of the scientific point of view and the utilization of measurement. We are on the frontier of a new music. With the application of science, the composer will be set new tasks and given new opportunities; the performer will constantly be facing new problems; the listener will always be expecting something new.

18. If the pedagogy of music in the public schools is to keep pace with the pedagogy of all the other subjects, it must frankly face and adopt the scientific point of view. Music will have its first scientific approaches in the public schools rather than in the private studios or conservatories.

19. The psychology of music is ultimately not a thing in itself. In employing a technique peculiar to that field, one must fall back upon a general grounding in psychology. After all, the laws of sensation, perception, learning, thinking, feeling, and action in general need only be specifically adapted to the demands of the musical situation.

20. While the cold details of musical facts can be recorded and organized by a mere psychologist, validity and interpretation depend upon an intimate knowledge of music and feeling for it. The applied science will progress at its best when the musician can set the problem in compliance with the criteria enumerated above for scientific experiment.

A MUSICAL ORNAMENT, THE VIBRATO

THE vibrato is the most important of all musical ornaments, both in voice and in instrument.* It is the most important because it occurs in practically all the tones of artistic singing and in sustained tones of various instruments; because, of all ornaments, it produces the most significant changes in tone quality; and because it is the factor on which artistic singing and playing are most frequently judged, whether the factor is consciously recognized as vibrato or not.

NATURE OF THE VIBRATO

Definition. A good vibrato is a pulsation of pitch, usually accompanied with synchronous pulsations of loudness and timbre, of such extent and rate as to give a pleasing flexibility, tenderness, and richness to the tone.

* The purpose of this chapter is to give a single sustained illustration of the sort of facts which can be ascertained about any musical phenomenon taken into the psychological laboratory-studio for experiment. It is based upon the author's *Psychology of the Vibrato in Voice and Instrument.*[140] The mass of statements represents the principal conclusions reached in that book and the volume of studies, *The Vibrato,*[119] on which it was based. This chapter will make heavy reading because all of the detailed descriptions and illustrations in the original are omitted. The interested student will turn to the original for deeper satisfaction.

Fifteen years ago, practically none of the facts here cited was known. The vibrato was a bone of contention, grossly misunderstood and misinterpreted. The reader may judge for himself whether or not the present presentation of findings constitutes a fair sample of the science of a musical phenomenon. While every item in this chapter is based upon experiment and is verifiable, the condensation and abbreviation of findings necessarily calls for limitations, qualifications, and explanations which can only be given in a fuller treatment. The chapter should not be read as a story, but item for item, with time for reflection.

In general, we may say that a bad vibrato is any periodic pulsation of pitch, loudness, or timbre which, singly or in combination, fails to produce pleasing flexibility, tenderness, and richness of tone. Likewise, if we desire a generic definition of all vibratos, we might say that the vibrato in music is a periodic pulsation of pitch, loudness, or timbre, singly or in combination. In quantitative terms of these factors, any particular vibrato may be discussed adequately.

An experiment. To prepare for an actual and effective appreciation of the magnitude, the universality, and the complication of the vibrato in good music, let the reader perform the following experiment at this stage: Select the most beautiful song you have available on a phonograph record and play it once, listening critically for the vibrato. Then slow down the phonograph turntable to about 30 or 40 revolutions per minute and observe that: (1) these pulsations become shockingly bold; (2) they are present in every note; (3) there is a confusion of pitch, loudness, and timbre; (4) the slow rate makes the vibrato very ugly.

AN EXAMPLE OF THE VOCAL VIBRATO

Figure 1, from Harold Seashore,[155] is an example of the musical performance score. It is explained as follows: The pitch frequency of each note is designated by a graph. The wave in that graph on each note represents the pitch vibrato based on very precise measurement. Each vertical space for the pitch graph represents a half-tone step. Thus it will be seen that, while the extent of the pitch pulsation varies from note to note, the average for the whole song is about a semitone. In order to identify the graph, each note from the conventional musical staff is interpolated at the point at which the tone begins. The duration of the tone is indicated by the vertical bars which mark off seconds and by the dots and dashes which mark tenths of a second.

The loudness or intensity changes are indicated in terms of decibels. In this staff, one vertical space designates 4 db of intensity; zero is taken as the softest tone which is heard in the song. Thus, the first note comes in very softly and rises to 16 db during the first second, remains around 16 db in the second second, then goes up to 20 db in the third, and 22 db in the fourth. The main thing to bear in mind is that, as the curve rises, the intensity increases. Pauses are indicated by the drop in the intensity curve.

This score contains a vast amount of information about the character of the rendition of this song, but let us here consider only what it shows about the vibrato. To aid the reader, a series of

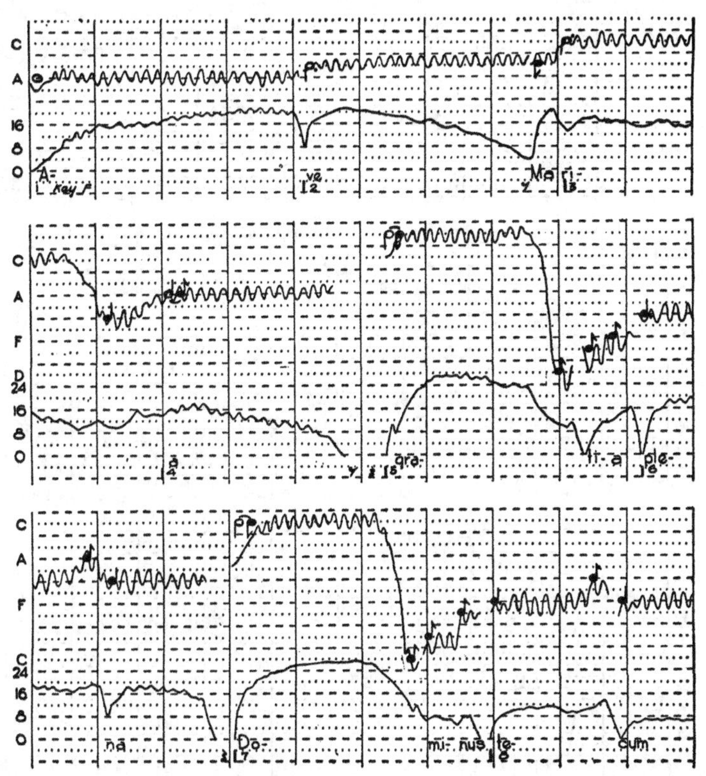

FIG. 1.—The Bach-Gounod *Ave Maria* as sung by Herald Stark. (*From H. Seashore.*[155]) Frequency (pitch) is represented by a graph for each note on a semitone staff; intensity, by the lower parallel graph in a decibel scale; and duration by dots in tenths of a second. Measures are numbered at the bottom of the staff for ready reference.

statements are made with the suggestion that for each one he *turn to the score and verify the statement.*

1. The pitch vibrato is present in every tone throughout the song, whether the tone is long or short, high or low, weak or strong.

2. It is present in the portamentos of the legato rendition and in the attacks and releases of the tones.

3. The pitch extent, that is, the width of the pulsation of pitch, averages about a semitone.

4. The rate of the vibrato cycles averages about 6.5 pulsations per second.

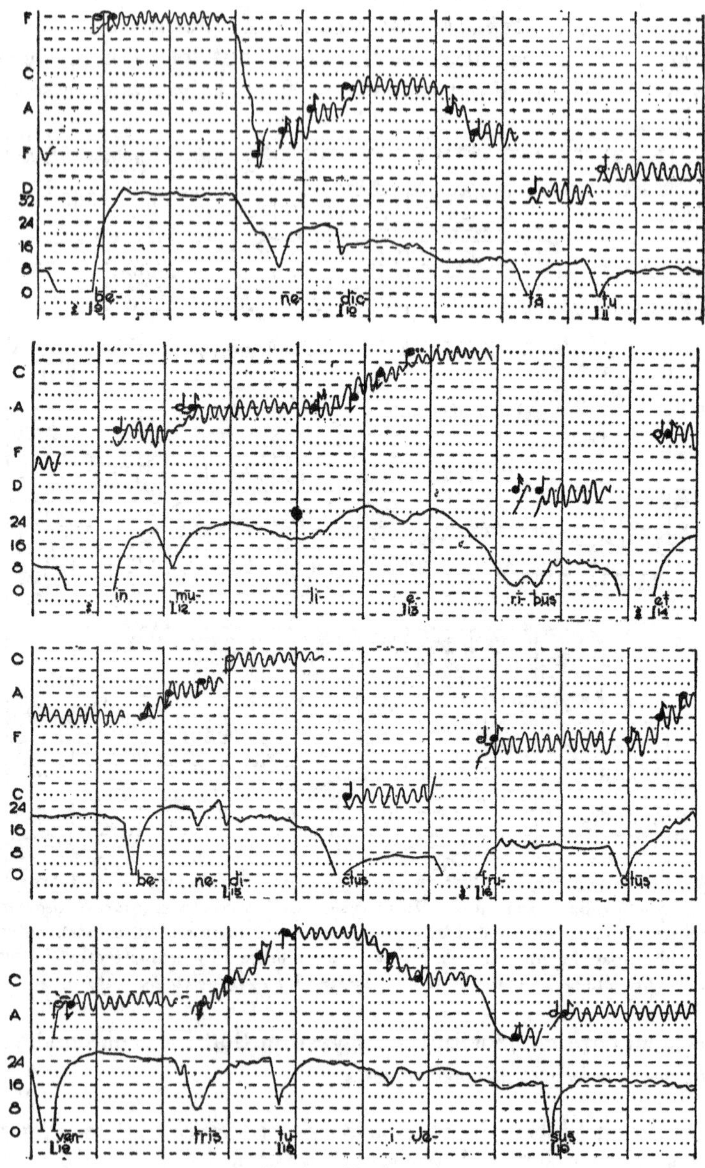

FIG. 1.—(*Continued*).

5. The form of the pitch pulsation is fairly smooth and constant, approximately that of a sine curve.

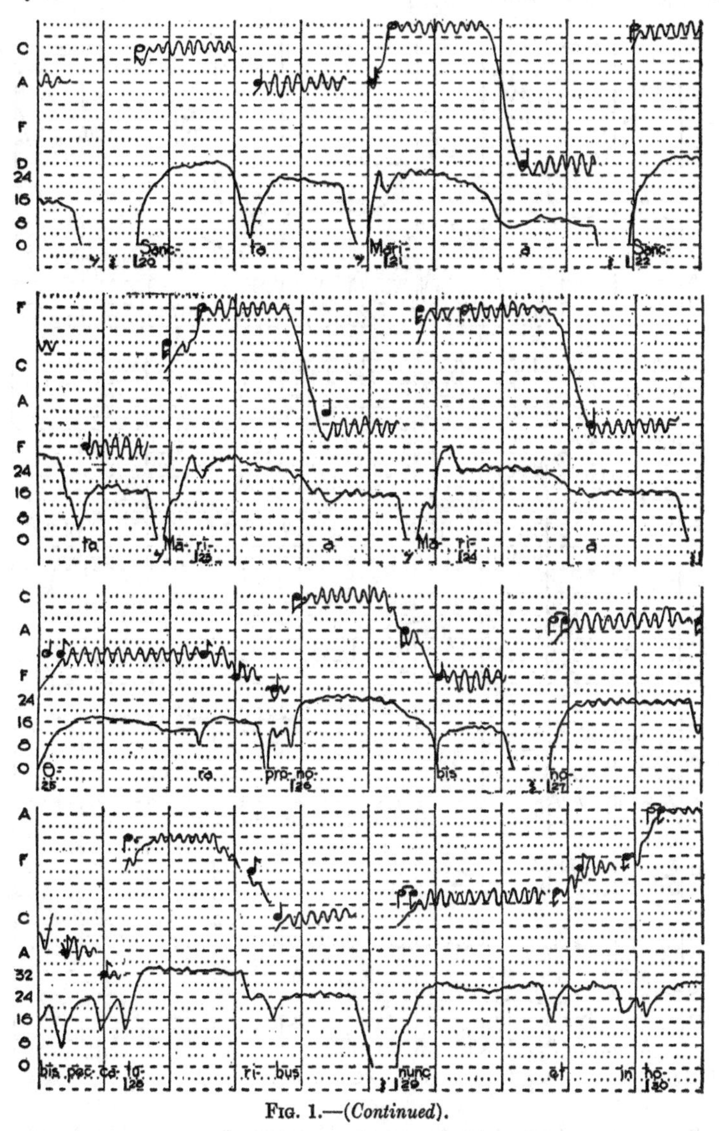

FIG. 1.—(*Continued*).

6. The extent of the pulsation of pitch is fairly constant and regular.

7. The rate of pulsation in pitch is fairly constant.

8. An intensity vibrato, though very small and often insignificant, is observable about one-third of the time.

9. The intensity vibrato is weak and quite irregular, seldom present at the beginning of a tone or in transitions.

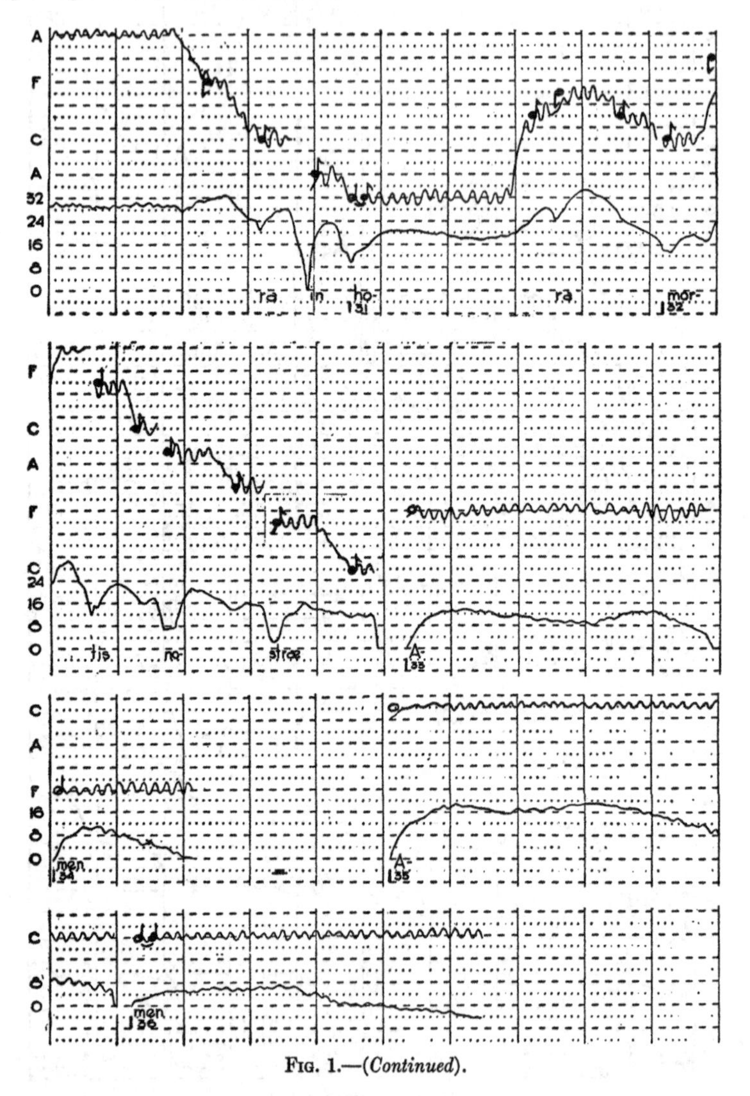

FIG. 1.—(*Continued*).

10. In view of the relative weakness and infrequent occurrence of the intensity vibrato, it must be regarded as incidental and subordinate to the pitch vibrato, which is dominant.

11. The rate of the intensity vibrato when present is about the same as for the pitch vibrato.

12. The crest of a pitch wave tends to coincide with the crest of the intensity wave, that is, as the pitch goes up in a vibrato cycle the intensity increases, but this relationship is neither uniform nor regular.

13. The mean pitch, that is, the mean between the crest and the trough of the vibrato cycles, coincides fairly with the true pitch.

14. The singer did not hold any note on even or true pitch.

15. If there is beauty in this pitch intonation it must lie in the artistic deviation from true pitch.

Here we have a very important array of scientific facts observable in a single song. Many of these facts are common to all singing. Many other specific details about vibrato are to be seen in this score; such as, the variation with length of tone, register, loudness, and vowel.

The timbre vibrato is not shown in the score but may be deduced in many respects from the pitch score. By an adequate selection of samples of songs and a fair sampling of singers, we can build up the science of the vibrato in vocal art.

Now turn to Fig. 3, and check to see to what extent the above facts apply to the singing of Lawrence Tibbett.

AN EXAMPLE OF INSTRUMENTAL VIBRATO

A perusal of Fig. 2 will reveal the following facts about the violin vibrato as summarized by *Small:*[166]

Pitch. 1. The vibrato is present in practically all tones produced by completely stopping the string, except in a trill. Ordinarily there is no pitch vibrato present when the open string is employed.

2. The vibrato is present throughout the entire duration of the tone in which it is employed.

3. As a rule, it is not present in the portamentos, although there are numerous exceptions.

4. The form of the pitch pulsation is fairly smooth and regular, approximating a sine curve.

5. The rate of pitch pulsation is relatively constant—about six pulsations per second.

6. The extent of the pitch vibrato is about a quarter tone and is fairly constant and regular.

7. The mean pitch of the tones tends to coincide with the pitch indicated in the printed score.*

* Exception to this rule is found in what may be called "tendency notes," for which there are recognized reasons for augmenting or diminishing the interval. Samples of tendency notes are C# to G in the third measure, and B to F in the fourth measure. The first represents both a natural tendency upward of a leading tone C# and the tendency of a diminished interval (here the diminished fifth) to contract. The second represents likewise the tendency of contraction in a diminished fifth, as well as the natural tendency of the fourth or subdominant step of a scale downward toward the mediant.

8. The movement responsible for the pitch vibrato is initiated most frequently with the movement toward the bridge, and the final vibrato movement is most frequently toward the scroll.

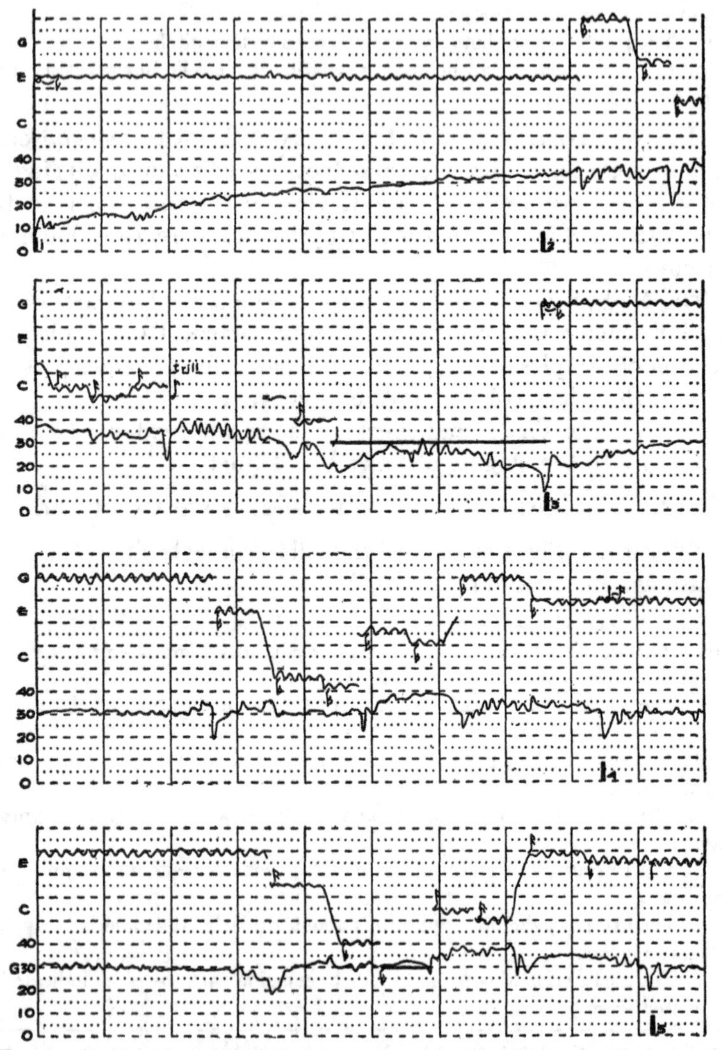

FIG. 2.—Bach's *Air for the G String*, as played by Arnold Small. (*From Small.*[166]) Frequency (pitch) is represented by a graph for each note on a semitone staff; intensity, by the lower parallel graph in a decibel scale; and duration by dots in tenths of a second. Measures are numbered at the bottom of the staff for ready reference.

9. Change of bow does not interrupt the vibrato-producing movement. Likewise, change of finger within a single position does not interrupt the vibrato-producing movement.

10. Tones devoid of vibrato occur infrequently.

11. The extent and possibly the rate tend to diminish toward the end of a tone which just precedes the use of the open string.

12. The extent of the vibrato increases with the increase of intensity of the tone over a large range in an extended crescendo.

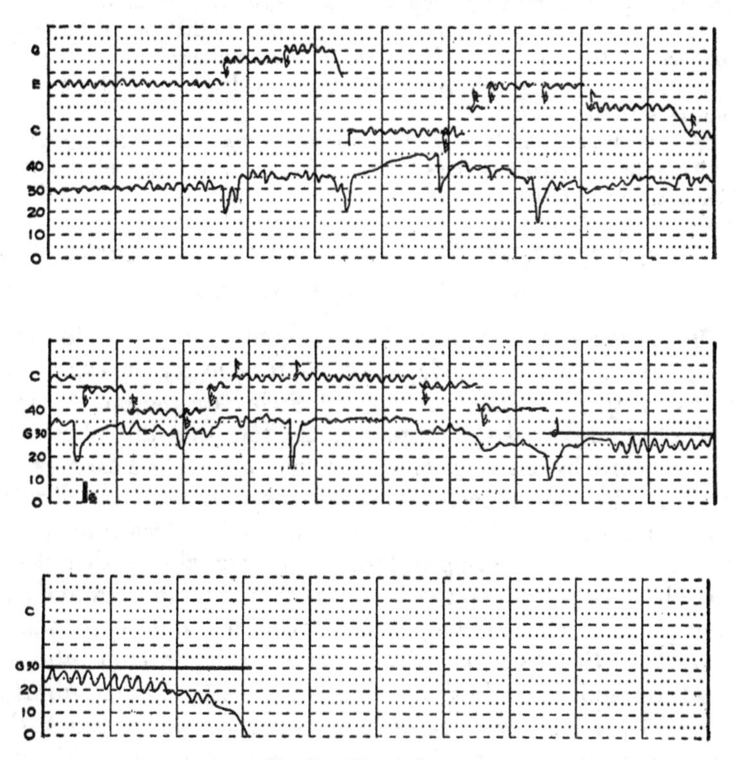

FIG. 2.—(*Continued*).

The trill. 1. The trill in measure 2 resembles the vibrato, but is faster (7.3 per second). As here employed, it begins slowly at the rate of 5 per second and increases in speed up to the third trill, from whence it is quite constant.

2. The interval between the main note and the accessory note remains quite constant from trill to trill.

Intensity. 1. The sustained intensity vibrato is present less than half as frequently as the pitch vibrato.

2. It is present on the open string as a result of the sympathetic vibrato produced intentionally by appropriate fingering.

3. It is seldom present throughout the entire duration of a tone.

4. The rate of pulsation tends to coincide with the rate for pitch, the average rate for intensity being 6.27 as compared with 6.10 pulsations per second for pitch.

5. The average extent of pulsation is 3.3 db and is quite irregular.

6. The phase relationship between the intensity pulsation and the pitch pulsation is not uniform or regular.

7. The intensity vibrato is of secondary importance in comparison with the pitch vibrato.

8. The extent of intensity pulsations due to sympathetic vibrations depends upon the resonance characteristics of the instrument in that they determine the prominence of the partials involved in the intensity pulsations.

9. These same pulsations may be eliminated by damping the string which is vibrating sympathetically.

The sympathetic vibrato. 1. The sympathetic vibrato is an intensity vibrato.

2. It exhibits practically the same rate as all other intensity vibratos, but is wider in extent (5.1 db).

FREQUENCY OF OCCURRENCE, EXTENT AND RATE OF VIBRATOS

The presence of the vibrato. How frequently does the vibrato occur in the best music of today? Among reasons for the existence of confusion upon this issue in musical circles are the following: the failure to know what the vibrato is; the fact that the vibrato cannot be heard by many people; the fact that it is heard as very much smaller than it really is; the assumption that the vibrato is eliminated when only the grosser and uglier forms have been omitted; habits of hearing in terms of tone quality rather than in recognition of periodic pulsations; the fact that an even and satisfying pitch, corresponding to the "true" pitch, is heard; musical versus analytical listening; absence of recording instruments.

All recognized professional singers sing with a pitch vibrato in about 95 per cent or more of their tones. Sustained tones, short tones, portamentos, attacks, releases, and other forms of transitions in pitch carry the vibrato. Successful voice students and well-trained amateurs exhibit the vibrato about as do recognized artists. Primitive peoples, such as the uneducated Negro or the Indian, exhibit the vibrato in acceptable form when singing with genuine feeling. The vibrato may appear early in childhood, as soon as the child begins to sing naturally and with genuine feeling. Great singers, teachers of voice, and voice students who are opposed to the vibrato and profess not to use it, do exhibit it in their best singing. A talented student who has no vibrato may develop it to a very satisfactory degree in just a few lessons. Well-trained singers may find it difficult to produce a song or even an isolated tone without the use of the vibrato. Crooners and jazz performers in general employ the excessive vibrato *ad nauseam*. The vibrato frequently appears in emotional speech. The tendency today is for

TABLE I. THE AVERAGE EXTENT AND RATE OF PITCH VIBRATO FOR 29 SINGERS

	Average rate per second	*Average extent of a step*
All artists	6.6	0.48
de Gogorza	7.8	0.46
Schumann-Heink	7.6	0.38
Galli-Curci	7.3	0.44
Macbeth	7.2	0.31
Caruso	7.1	0.47
Rethberg	7.0	0.49
Martinelli	6.9	0.44
Ponselle	6.9	0.48
Chaliapin	6.8	0.54
Jeritza	6.8	0.53
Lashanska	6.8	0.43
de Luca	6.8	0.58
Tetrazzini	6.8	0.37
Talley	6.7	0.54
Braslau	6.6	0.36
Marsh	6.6	0.52
Tibbett	6.6	0.55
Crooks	6.5	0.47
Gigli	6.5	0.57
Rimini	6.5	0.98
Stark	6.5	0.48
Onegin	6.4	0.41
Dadmun	6.3	0.46
Seashore	6.3	0.44
Baker	6.2	0.45
Hackett	5.9	0.47
Homer	5.9	0.51
Kraft	5.9	0.59
Thompson	5.9	0.53

In this table from *H. Seashore*,[155] data from *Metfessel*[89] are included with those of *Tiffin*[201] and *H. Seashore*.[155]

players on the violin, viola, and cello to use the vibrato on all sustained tones. The vibrato may be used in any of the band or orchestral instruments, but artists generally discourage it for woodwind or brass instruments, except for isolated and specific effects. It is probable that the vibrato was present in the feelingful self-expression of even the most primitive speech and song. The canary bird which is taught to sing songs can sing with a good vibrato. It is the main appeal in the cooing of the dove. The vibrato is present in the hearty laughter of the adult and in the vigorous crying of the infant.

In general, we may say that a pulsating quality of tone in the form of periodic rise and fall in pitch is almost universal in good singing, is freely imitated by instruments, notably by the string instruments, and frequently is present in emotional speech.

The extent and rate of the vocal pitch vibrato. The average extent and rate of the pitch oscillation varies to some degree with the character of the song and the singer, but the figures in Table I represent averages for fair samples of the singers listed. The reader must refer to the original articles for names of selections, size of samples, distribution of extent and rate, and other data for each singer.

The average extent of the pitch pulsation for good singers is 0.5 of a tone. This may vary among different singers from 0.3 to 1.0, or more, with a normal distribution. For about three-fourths of the singers, the extent is between 0.45 and 0.55. Each singer tends to have a characteristic average, but may vary from this from selection to selection and from tone to tone. The variation of individual vibrato cycles from this average in acceptable vibrato may be from 0.1 to 1.5 of a tone in a given singer. There are no marked and consistent variations with the sex of the singer, the vowel quality, the musical mode, the pitch level, or the loudness of the tone. For short tones, it is slightly wider than for long tones. The extent of the vibrato does not differentiate emotions expressed.

The intensity vibrato. The intensity vibrato, both vocal and instrumental, is seen in the performance scores, Figs. 1, 2, and 3. In general, we find for singers that the intensity vibrato is present about one-third of the time. Ordinarily it is less conspicuous than the pitch vibrato, but, like the pitch vibrato, it is underestimated in hearing.

In general, we may say that the intensity vibrato is less frequent, less regular, and less prominent perceptually than pitch vibrato. It is probably secondary to it, and is modified by room resonance. The phase relationship between the two varies widely.

The timbre vibrato. The timbre vibrato is a periodic pulsation in the harmonic structure of a complex tone (see Chap. 9). Every periodic change of pitch of a complex tone causes a parallel periodic change in each of its partials. Each partial may have its own intensity vibrato depending in part upon the permanent resonance regions of the vocal cavities, and the resonance characteristics of the instrument or the room. The timbre vibrato is ordinarily of such magnitude as to make it distinctly audible to the critical ear.

Stringed instruments. All violin artists of today employ the pitch vibrato on practically all stopped notes of sufficient duration to permit its execution. An intensity vibrato frequently occurs as a result of sympathetic vibration, produced either intentionally by fingering an unbowed string or as a result of coincidence of intervals. Each artist tends to have a characteristic rate which varies but little with emotional moods but increases with proficiency. The average rate is about 7, the extremes ranging from 5 to 10. The average pitch extent is about a quarter tone and does not vary significantly with emotional moods. The mean pitch of the vibrato cycles coincides with the true pitch except in the case of tendency tones, in which deviation from true pitch would be made in the absence of the vibrato. The rate and extent are approximately the same for the violin, the viola, and the cello.

Wind instruments. The vibrato occurs in all wind instruments but is comparatively rare, intermittent, and irregular, probably owing to the difficulty of its production. In solo parts, flutists, clarinetists, and trumpeters often exhibit a beautiful and well-sustained vibrato. The intensity vibrato of the organ is used excessively and with monotonous uniformity, probably on account of the simplicity of its mechanical control by a stop.

NORMAL ILLUSIONS WHICH MAKE FOR BEAUTY OF VIBRATO

1. The vibrato is always heard as of very much smaller extent than it is in the physical tone. For example, a pulsation of a semitone is ordinarily heard as less than 0.2 of a tone. It is this illusion which makes the vibrato tolerable.

The larger the pitch and intensity extent, the more it will be underestimated.

The faster the rate, within limits, the more the extent will be underestimated.

The richer the tone, the more the extent will be underestimated.

For good singing, pitch extent and intensity extent are heard as a small fraction of their true extent.

Instead of the full extent of the pulsation, we tend to hear only the extent of deviation from the main pitch or intensity.

The end result in hearing may be higher or lower than this, depending upon the presence or absence of other motives for illusion.

These reductions in the extent of hearing of pulsations tend to make the actual vibrato tolerable.

2. Much of the most beautiful vibrato is below the threshold for vibrato hearing and is perceived merely as tone quality. Individual differences in the capacity for hearing the vibrato are very large. In a normal population, one individual may be 50 or 100 times as keen as another in this hearing. Talent for hearing of the vibrato may be measured in two separate tests: (*a*) the capacity for hearing the presence of the vibrato and (*b*) the capacity for recognizing differences in vibratos. The most important factors which determine capacity for hearing of the vibrato are the structure and function of the ear and the brain, knowledge of the existence of the vibrato and of its nature, the attitude of the listener, and favorable forms of the vibrato.

In view of these large and often relatively fixed individual differences each individual has his own illusion, and his individual sense of the vibrato determines what shall be good or bad for him. This introduces a most serious obstacle to the efforts toward establishing norms for a vibrato which shall be pleasant to all listeners.

3. Regardless of the extent of pitch, intensity, or timbre pulsation, we always hear an even mean pitch corresponding to the true pitch, an even intensity and continuous timbre.

4. In addition to the mean pitch, a trained observer may hear an even pitch somewhat below the crest and another somewhat above the trough, so that he can hear in all four distinct pitches, namely, a pulsating pitch, a mean pitch, the upper limit pitch, and the lower limit pitch, by directing attention to them in turn.

5. The blending of pitch, intensity, and timbre vibratos.

6. Sonance (to be explained in Chap. 9), the vibrato as an aspect of tone quality.

THE NATURE OF BEAUTY IN THE VIBRATO

Beauty in the vibrato is found in artistic deviation from the precise and uniform in all the attributes of tone.

The vibrato is the most systematic, natural, and essential of musical ornaments.

Its beauty lies in a richness of tone, flexibility of tone, and expression of emotional instability.

It represents the periodic changes of pitch, intensity, and timbre in sonance.

Richness of tone results from successive fusion of changes of tone.

Flexibility of tone results from indefiniteness of outline.

Tenderness of tone results from awareness of organic trembling.

The genuine vibrato is automatic and expresses the truth like the smile and the frown.

To cultivate the vibrato, do not cultivate a sign of feeling which is not present, but cultivate the power to feel music genuinely.

The expression of feeling. Does the vibrato differentiate the emotions? Our answer to this question is "No." We cannot distinguish feelings of love from hatred, attraction from repulsion, excitement from tranquillity, by the vibrato. The expression of all kinds of feeling, even the most divergent, tends to take the same general character of the vibrato. It reveals feeling but does not differentiate in kind. This finding came to us as a great surprise in the laboratory.

We are therefore forced to the conclusion that, while the vibrato in both voice and instrument is a means for the expression of musical feeling of the first order, and is even essential to the expression of feeling, it does not differentiate among the feelings. Indeed, it is like an organ stop. So long as the stop is out, all tones have the quality represented by that stop. The vibrato merely indicates that we feel genuinely; it does not reveal the degree of feeling or the kind of feeling.

The desirability of the vibrato. The desirability of the vibrato is attested by the universality of its use, its automatic nature, its use in instruments, its survival in conflict with precision, and its place in tone quality.

EAR TRAINING FOR THE VIBRATO

Directions are given for training the ear with the eye by listening to a phonograph record and following the pattern score as in Fig. 3. This score is designed to show only the pitch vibrato. For each note, the upper number denotes the average extent of the pitch vibrato and the lower number the number of pulsations per second.

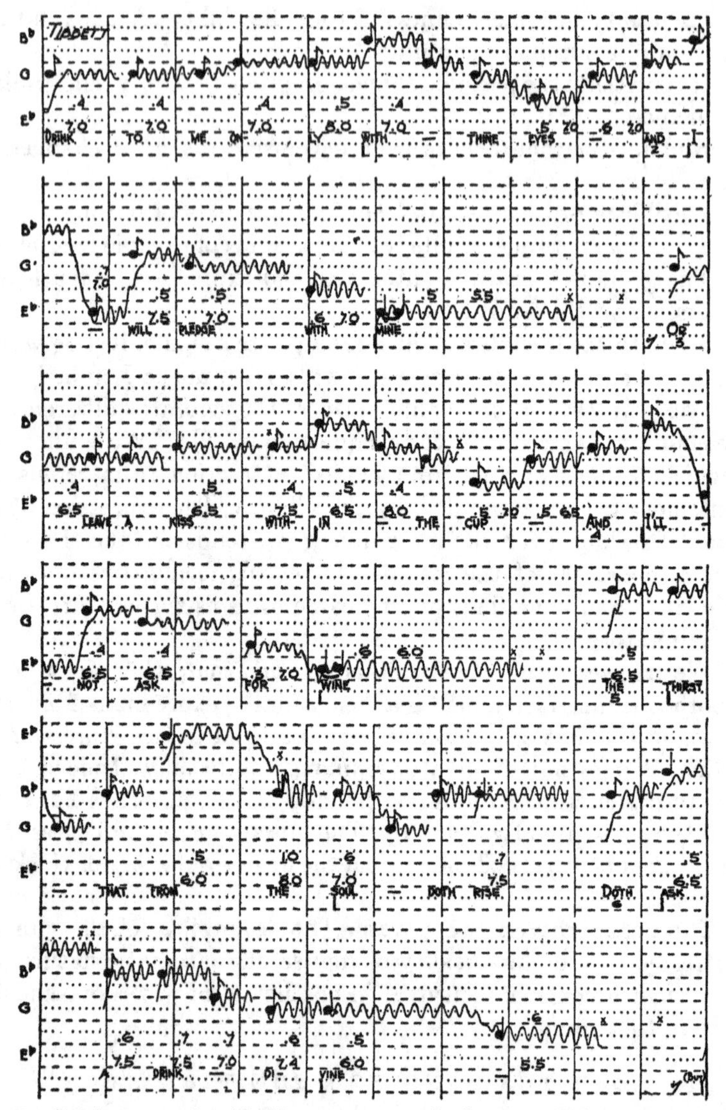

Fig. 3.—*Drink to me only with thine eyes*, as sung by Lawrence Tibbett. (*Victor Record* 1238.) (*H. Seashore.*[155]) For explanation of this figure, please see legend for Fig. 1.

Directions for training in the recognition of the rate of the vibrato in the singing of artists. First, play the phonograph record for Fig. 3 one or more times, and coordinate what you hear with the details of what you see in the performance score (Fig. 3) as to the rate of the pulsation. Then drill extensively on the calling out of the number which designates the rate the moment each tone has been heard, and have someone check for each whether you are right or wrong.

Directions for training in the recognition of the vibrato in one's own voice. First, sing a song with a playing record in the effort to

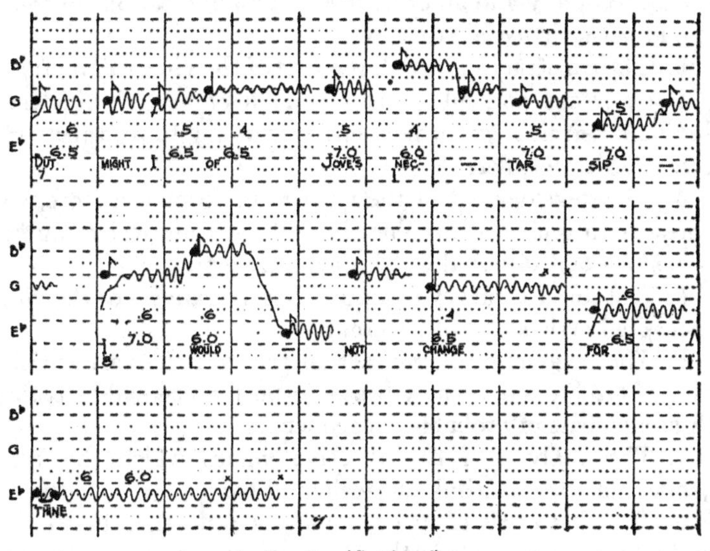

FIG. 3.—(*Continued*).

determine whether or not your vibrato is larger or smaller in pitch extent than that of the artist. Select only sustained tones. Then proceed in the same manner with the same song in determining whether or not your rate is faster or slower than that of the artist. The same procedure may be applied to the study of the extent of the pulsation.

There are three stages in the development of good vibrato through training. The first is the acquisition of scientific information and critical artistic appreciation of the true nature of the vibrato. The second is the training of the ear to acquire skills in critical hearing and judgment of performance. The third is the development of corrective adjustment.

USE AND ABUSE OF THE VIBRATO

As aids to the hearing, the evaluation and execution of a good vibrato, and the eradication of bad vibratos, the following contributions have been made:

1. Definition, description, and explanation of the true nature of the vibrato as an aspect of tone quality.

2. The invention of instruments of precision and technique for the adequate qualitative as well as quantitative measurement of the vibrato in any and all of its possible manifestations in the normal and actual musical situation.

3. The construction of a "language of the vibrato" by furnishing a consistent and adequate terminology and eliminating all redundant terminology which has grown up topsy-turvy in an unscientific atmosphere.

4. The development of the musical performance score, which enables us to represent graphically and with musical meaning all findings of exact observation and measurement.

5. A statistical survey of actual uses and abuses of the vibrato by accepted artists and other groups.

6. The beginnings of the factual array of the vast variety of modes of production of the vibrato, in both voice and instrument, with assignment of probable consequences.

7. The analysis of the affective values which the vibrato engenders in the beautiful and feelingful tone.

8. The discovery of the astounding difference between the actual vibrato as it exists in the physical tone and the vibrato as it is heard in the musical situation.

9. The explanation of some of the vast number of illusions which contribute toward the tolerance, beauty, or ugliness of the tone.

10. The determination of the limits of tolerance and the range of variability of rate and extent of the vibrato.

11. The isolation of the roles of pitch, intensity, and timbre as the media of pulsation, singly or in combination.

12. The exposure of the vibrato as militant against correct intonation, interval, melody, harmony, rhythm, and pure tone.

13. The explanation of the hearing of an even pitch, intensity, and timbre in the fact of the flagrant absence of these in the physical tone.

14. The tracing of the origin of the vibrato and its genetic development as a biological fact.

15. The provision of training devices for the effective hearing, rating, and evaluation of vibrato in one's own performance or the performance of another.

16. Suggestions for training and adjustment in its control.

17. The invention of tone integrators and other instruments by which any conceivable form of vibrato may be produced synthetically for experimental purposes.

18. Suggestions and procedure in the experimental musical esthetics for the purpose of determining ideals of vibrato in definable situations.

19. Demonstration of the fact that the vibrato does not differentiate particular feelings such as love and rage, quiescence or excitement.

20. The establishment of the probability that we are here dealing with a physiological rhythm, present not only in man but also in the higher animals whenever paired muscles are innervated under emotional tension.

These scientifically established facts are in contrast with expressed opinions of musical authorities.

THE VIBRATO, GOOD, BAD, INDIFFERENT, AND IDEAL

The most desirable average extent of pitch, intensity, and timbre, singly or in combination, is that which produces flexibility, tenderness, and richness of tone, without giving prominence to the pulsating quality as such.

Freedom from irregularity in extent is essential to a good vibrato.

An extent of the pulsation smaller than that first defined fails, in proportion to its smallness, to contribute toward the betterment of tone quality.

The most desirable average rate is that which causes the best fusion of tone quality in sonance, without producing a chattering through excessive rate.

In vocal vibrato the pulsations in pitch should be primary and dominant.

The combination of synchronous pulsations in the three media ordinarily makes a larger contribution toward tone quality than its occurrence in one or two.

In instrumental music relatively pure intensity pulsation is permissible, as in organ stops and in the use of beats within a region of tolerance for rate.

Artistic performance demands variation in extent and rate throughout a performance.

In solo parts, both vocal and instrumental, the artist has larger latitude for giving prominence to the vibrato than he has in ensemble.

The more nearly alike the timbres of the instruments within an orchestral choir, the greater may be the demand for the vibrato in that choir.

However, an ideal vibrato which can be gradually developed through musical criticism and musical education will probably be smooth in variations of rate and extent, will have a cycle which approaches the perfect sine curve, will probably be one cycle per second faster than the present, will have a higher artistic variability, will be adapted to solo and ensemble performances, will have a pitch extent of approximately one-half of the present average for voice, and will probably be present in all tones and transitions except where the nonvibrato is used for specific effects.

If this should come true, largely as the result of scientific investigations, one might well ask, "What is it worth?" And this question we can answer only by asking other questions: How would it affect musical theory? How would it facilitate musical training? How would it affect musical criticism? How much sweeter would music be to the listener?

5

PITCH: FREQUENCY

THE NATURE OF PITCH

PITCH is that qualitative attribute of auditory sensation which denotes highness or lowness in the musical scale and is conditioned primarily on the frequency of sound waves.

We note in this definition (1) that pitch is one of the four attributes of tonal sensation, and that it is qualitative in that it designates the kind of sensation, thus distinguishing sensations of tone from the other sensory modalities, such as color, odor, and taste; (2) that it denotes highness or lowness in the tonal continuum along which we locate the musical scale; and (3) that it is the mental and musical correlate of the frequency of the vibrations which constitute the physical tone.

While all music is objectively due to physical sound waves, we must bear in mind that we can never be directly aware of the rate of vibration as such, for we hear it as musical pitch. This is one of the wondrous transformations "from matter to mind." Out of mere vibration is built a world of musical tones which do not in themselves suggest vibration at all. Yet the human ear may be so keen as to detect in nature a difference of a fraction of a vibration in frequency. It is fortunate that we can live in a world of music without thinking at all of the physical counterpart; still, for the science of music and for the study of musical talent, such reference is necessary.

The ear is a most wonderful mechanism with its membranes, levers, and liquid conductors carrying the vibration to the harp structure, its means of analysis of all pitches in that structure, and its means of transmission of each pitch over its particular line to the brain. We cannot here undertake to discuss the structure of the ear, its physiology, and the numerous technical problems or theories of hearing. The reader who is interested in this phase of the subject must turn to books on the anatomy and physiology of the ear. But, for psychological purposes, it is necessary to make certain assumptions, of which the essential one is that there is a pitch-differentiating mechanism in the ear, capable of serving as a physical basis for the sensory phenomena with which we deal in the psychology of hearing; namely, pitch, loudness, timbre, volume, fusion, and consonance, and their derivatives or variants. For pitch, the harp theory furnishes at least a good analogy. *Seashore.*[131]

LIMITS OF AUDIBLE PITCH

Lower limit. The lower limit of pitch is that frequency which gives us the lowest sensation of tone. The lowest audible tone is usually said to be about 16 ~, but it varies with a large number of factors. There are two primary factors that determine the lower limit, the strength or intensity of the sound wave, and its form. If low tones are to be heard at all they must be relatively very strong. Therefore, the lower limit will vary with the intensity of the tone within a very wide range. The most favorable form of the wave is that smooth curve which gives us a pure tone. Under most favorable conditions, a good listener can get tonal fusion as low as 12~, whereas if the wave comes in the form of more and more acute puffs, as, in an extreme case, the sound waves coming from electrical sparks, the lower limit of tonality may be as high as 100~.

Upper limit. The average upper limit for an unselected group under the age of forty is probably about 16,000~, but this limit varies greatly with a number of important conditions, such as advanced age, and various types of defects and diseases of the inner ear. Even in the so-called "normal" ear, there are very large individual differences in the upper limit. These differences may have far-reaching significance for the character of what one hears. Reliable measurements still are not available for determination of the upper limit under the most favorable conditions and in sufficient detail for classification of types. It seems possible that the upper limit for human hearing in youth may rise to the height of 25,000~ in the most sensitive ear under the most favorable conditions. Yet, many people with apparently normal hearing cannot hear above 5,000~. In an unselected population, there is probably a large percentage of persons who cannot hear tones above 10,000~.

The average frequency in the chirp of a cricket is about 8,000~, but cricket tones as high as 32,000~ have been recorded. Certain birds are also known to produce tones higher than those produced by voice or musical instruments. It is probable that such animals, capable of producing high tones, can hear tones at least as high as those they produce.

Sounds in nature as high as 40,000~ have been recorded and artificially produced. Supersonic frequencies have been recorded as high as 2,000,000~. In brief, we are living in a world in which physical tones may exist within a very wide range, but each human being or animal can hear only a short section of these frequencies because the limits of audible tones for man or animal are set by the character of the receiving instrument, the ear. This normal limitation of the pitch range is a great blessing, in that it saves us from bombardment by the masses of higher frequency in nature which would serve but little purpose in auditory orientation.

Decline of the upper limit with age and disease. When Madam Gadski and her daughter were visiting the psychological laboratory, we tested them for upper limit of hearing and found that the famous prima donna could not hear any tone or overtone above 12,000~, whereas the young daughter could hear up to about 20,000~. This was a shocking discovery for the mother, but certainly no discredit to her as a musician. The simple explanation was that the mother was older. The upper limit of hearing suffers a normal and predictable drop owing to the fact that, as age comes on, the highest pitch mechanisms in the ear progressively become nonfunctional. Since this loss is a function of the intensity of the sound, further consideration of this matter will occur under that head.

PITCH DISCRIMINATION

The ability to hear small differences in pitch is called "pitch discrimination" and determines what is generally called the "sense of pitch." It is a measure of the capacity for using pitch in musical hearing and tone production. We shall use interchangeably the terms "pitch discrimination" and "sense of pitch."*

* The sense of pitch, pitch discrimination, sensory discrimination for pitch, threshold of pitch discrimination, differential pitch hearing are all more or less synonymous terms. It is usually abbreviated as Δf.

Measurement. Pitch discrimination is measured by sounding two pure tones in quick succession and gradually reducing the difference in frequency until the observer is unable to tell which of the two tones is the higher. The steps usually employed in such a series are 30, 23, 17, 12, 8, 5, 3, 2, 1, 0.5~, at the level of international A, 435~. The standard procedure has been to use tuning forks with resonators, but various forms of electrical oscillators are now available and more convenient.*

For group measurements, the test material from the best available instruments is recorded on a phonograph record which is economical, standard, durable, and relatively foolproof in use.

There are two fundamental methods of procedure. One is to begin with the smallest differential and take about 100 trials on each step up to the step in which 80 per cent of the answers are right. This step is regarded as the threshold of pitch discrimination, which is a measure of the sense of pitch. This is the best method to use in individual testing. The other method, better adapted for group testing, is to take a block of the 10 steps named above, making 10 trials for each step, and, using the 10 units as a single block, determining what per cent of right judgments can be made in all of these 100 trials as a block. This is the method used in the phonograph record.[125]

Norms. On the basis of thousands of trials by the above method, norms have been established in terms of centile rank. This method is convenient in that the same scale can be used for all kinds of measurements that are made and for which sufficient data are available to determine norms. According to the scale, rank 50 means average, rank 1, the lowest or poorest 1 per cent found, and rank 100, the highest 1 per cent found, intervening ranks being proportional to the numbers.

The average threshold for an unselected group of adults is about 3~ at the level of international pitch, 435~. This is 1/17 of a tone, but a very sensitive ear can hear as small a difference as 0.5~ or less, which, at this level, is less than 0.01 of a tone. Some persons who pass in a community as having normal hearing may not

---

* These tuning forks with resonators may be obtained from the C. H. Stoelting Company, Chicago, but anyone desiring to do so can take forks of 435~ or 440~ and tune them by filing near the tip of the prongs and counting beats. Resonators may also be improvised by partly filling a half-pint cream bottle with water until it "speaks" to the fork. For a full account of the standardization of this measurement see *Seashore*.[127]

be able to hear a half-tone or even a whole-tone difference. In extreme cases we may have pitch deafness.

Stucker[188] examined the discrimination of 16 professional musicians in the Royal Opera in Vienna and found that for A_3 in international pitch, they had the following thresholds in terms of vibrations: 0.1, 0.2, 0.2, 0.2, 0.3, 0.3, 0.4, 0.5, 0.5, 0.6, 0.8, 0.8, 0.9, 0.9, 1.1, 1.1. At this level one whole-tone step represents 54~. Therefore, the keenest of these musicians could hear $1/540$ of a tone, and the poorest $1/49$ of a tone. These exceptionally fine records are not to be attributed significantly to training. They are probably due primarily to the principle of selection, in that persons with unusually fine ears have sought and received this high order of training and recognition.

Physiological limit. The physiological limit of any sense organ is that limit for sensation and perception which is set by the structure of the sense organ and the brain. In measurements of this kind we do not always reach this limit but attain what is called a cognitive limit of discrimination. A good test in the hands of an expert may properly establish the physiological limit of pitch discrimination in the first trial for a majority of the subjects in a group test, whereas in an individual test the physiological limit may be determined with a high degree of certainty for practically all. The difference between these two limits, the physiological and the cognitive, is an indication of the uncertainty and the unreliability of a test. It usually is due to a lack of understanding of the test requirements, or a lack of mental development, or of good will, or of general power of application on the part of the subject tested. This margin may be reduced or eliminated by a repetition and by individual testing by an expert.

Relation to intelligence. The physiological limit for the sense of pitch does not vary significantly with intelligence. The moron may have as keen a sense of pitch as the philosopher. Measurements on children and adults in which pitch discrimination is compared with intelligence show no significant correlation. The slight correlation that is found is due primarily to lack of the capacity for understanding the test conditions and not to the capacity for pitch hearing as such.

There are three significant issues with which we must not confuse this negative finding about intelligence: (1) It has no bearing upon the opprobrious question often heard, "Are musicians dumb?" We have no evidence to show that the distribution of intelligence among musicians differs from the distribution in an unselected population. Our best guess is that the distribution is approximately the same. The common observation that musicians live more in the realm of feeling proves nothing in regard to the distribution of the capacity for intelligence. There also may be such a thing as a feelingful intelligence. (2) It does not imply that intelligence is not essential to a high degree of musicianship. Music is a learned occupation. Like lawyers and physicians, the musician must show a high order of intelligence in order to gain professional distinction. (3) It does not depreciate the necessity for employing intelligence in the use of pitch in all phases of musical performance.

Relation to age. In the absence of disease, the physiological limit for the sense of pitch does not vary with age. A standard group test can be made on children as low as the fifth grade. The average achievement of children in the grades is not so high as for adults. As we have seen, there are different age norms. The reason for this lies, of course, in the relative cognitive immaturity and not in the capacity of the sense organ. However, an expert working with intelligent children may reach this limit in individual tests as early as at the age of five.

It seems probable that just as the physical eye of the child at the age of three is as keen as it ever will be, so the pitch sensitiveness in the ear probably reaches its maximum very early. Development in the use of the sense of pitch with maturation consists in acquiring habits and meanings, interests, desires, and musical knowledge, rather than in the improvement of the sense organ.

Relation to training. The physiological limit for hearing pitch does not improve with training. Training, like maturation, results in the conscious recognition of the nature of pitch, its meaning, and the development of habits of use in musical operations. Training probably does not modify the capacity of the sense organ any more than the playing of the good violin may improve the quality of its tone.

Fortunes have been spent and thousands of young lives have been made wretched by application of the theory that the sense of pitch can be improved with training. It is the cause of the outstanding tragedy in musical education. On the other hand, ear training is one of the most neglected elements of musical education. However good the sense of pitch may be, it demands training in proportion to the natural capacity in this sense. The training is significant not only for the appreciation of "pitch play" in music, but even more significant for the control of performance. The trouble with flatting, slovenly intonation, inability to sing intervals, poor timbre control of voice or instrument by a person with a good sense of pitch, may be a slovenly ear, an uncritical ear, or an untrained ear, not motor or muscular trouble.

Limit elemental. The physiological limit is elemental in the sense that it indicates a specific capacity in one sense attribute which is relatively independent of intelligence, age, and training. It is a moot question whether any psychophysical capacity can be elemental, in view of the fact that a certain amount of knowledge and experience is necessary in order to make the test. It is probable that in this particular measurement of pitch discrimination we come as near to securing an elemental measure as can be found in any of the senses. However, we must always bear in mind the possibility and probability that we may be dealing with the cognitive limit instead of the physiological one. Nevertheless the concept is a useful one. We should not think of the physiological limit as fixed, because within a small range it in itself can vary with factors which either raise or lower the functions of the nervous system, such as fatigue, rest, the action of either depressive or stimulative drugs, or disease.

Inheritance. There is good evidence to show that a musical ear, by which we mean primarily an ear with good sense of pitch, is inherited to considerable extent and that with this inheritance follows variability in the tonal capacities which depend upon pitch discrimination, such as tonal memory, the sense of timbre, the sense of consonance, and auditory imagery. This topic will be discussed in a later chapter.

Frequency level and sensation level. Pitch discrimination varies in a systematic manner with the frequency within the tonal range and with the intensity of the tone. This is shown graphically in Fig. 1. In brief, the figure shows that (1) pitch discrimination is poorest for low tones and best above 1,000~; (2) this variation with frequency holds for all sensation levels from 5 to 60 db; and (3) it is keener for strong tones than for weak.

Figure 1 is based upon measurements with pure tones. It is well known that discrimination is finer for rich tones. It varies with both degree and kind of richness.

Number of just-noticeable differences. How many differences in pitch can the average person hear? This is determined by starting with the lowest audible pitch and proceeding step by step in terms of just-noticeable differences (j.n.d.). Figure 2 is a typical record. It has been found that the average ear can hear approxi-

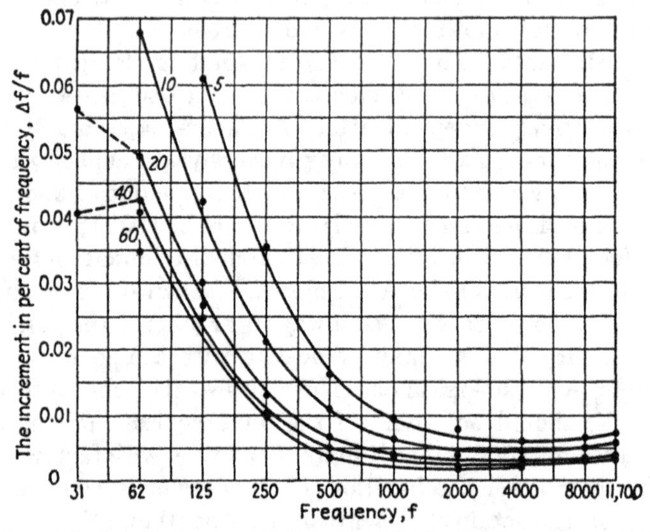

FIG. 1.—Variation with frequency level and sensation level. The numbers at the bottom denote frequency; at the side, the increment in per cent of frequency. The numbers within the figure denote sensation level, that is, number of db above the threshold of audibility. For example, for the frequency of 125~, the increment must be 6 per cent for a 5 db tone, 4 per cent for a 10 db tone, and between 2 and 3 per cent for 20, 40, and 60 db tones, respectively. (*Shower and Biddulph.*[161])

In music it is helpful to think of the data in Fig. 1 in terms of fractions of a tone rather than in terms of per cent of the fundamental frequency. Since a whole-tone step is 9/8 of the fundamental frequency $\left(\frac{\Delta b}{f}\right)$, we may convert the figures at the left of the table into hundredths of a whole-tone step by multiplying each by 8. These numbers would then read, from top downward: 0.56, 0.48, 0.40, 0.32, 0.24, 0.16, and 0.80.

mately 1,400 steps of difference in pitch of a medium-loud pure tone. However, it must be remembered that this is an average figure and that this number varies with several factors, among which four are outstanding: (1) individual differences—one person may hear more than a hundred times as many pitch differences as another; (2) intensity—more steps in pitch can be heard in strong tones than in weak tones; (3) duration—the most favorable discrimination occurs when there is an abrupt transition from one pitch to the next within a tone; (4) timbre—more steps in pitch can be heard for rich tones than for pure tones. This concept of the number of perceptible steps in pitch is a very important one because it is an index of the extent to which hearing differences function in daily life.

Binaural versus monaural discrimination. Binaural is finer than monaural discrimination by about 10 per cent for most musical tones. The difference decreases gradually to about 2 per cent for tones at or above 500∼.

Duration. There are three types of musical situations which may be recognized in the measurement of pitch discrimination: (1) going

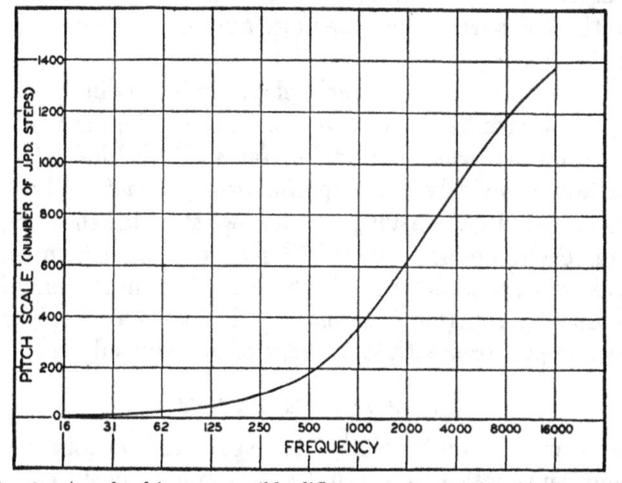

FIG. 2.—A scale of just perceptibly different pitch steps (j.n.d.). (*Lewis.*[77])

from one note to another with a complete break between them, as in the standard test where we sound two notes, each of which is one second in duration but differing in pitch and separated by a very short interval of time; (2) legato rise or fall in pitch or pitch vibrato; and (3) sudden shift in a single note without break in tone, as in erratic intonation.

The discrimination is different for each of these three, the necessary increment being about twice as large for the first type as the third, and the second falling between these two. These differences are related to the differences in total duration of each tone.

The minimum duration necessary in order to identify the pitch of a tone clearly varies with the frequency and to some extent with the loudness. It has been found that in order to be heard clearly as of definite pitch, a tone at 128~ must have a duration of 0.09 second; for 256~, about 0.07 second; for 384~, about 0.04 second; and for 512~, about the same.

Masking. The damping of one tone by another is called "masking." This is due to interference of vibrations in the basilar membrane of the inner ear. A low pure tone tends to "drown out" a higher tone of any frequency, but a high tone has but little effect upon a lower tone. It is much easier to talk or sing against high noises than against noises of low frequency. The low partials in a rich tone tend to dampen the higher partials. Therefore, as a piano tone is made stronger and stronger, the timbre of the tone changes because the low partials become more and more effective in drowning out the higher partials.

This is a phenomenon which plays an exceedingly important role in the determination of tone quality. In the past the artistic composer and performer have taken facts of this kind into account more or less intuitively, but experiments by *Fletcher*[27] have established definite laws of masking which now can guide the composer in producing certain effects. *Stewart*[185] gives a good account for musicians. Likewise, these laws guide the performer in the modifying of tone quality by control of intensity and in the balancing of chords for the same purpose, with knowledge of masking effects.

ABSOLUTE PITCH

The term "absolute pitch" is used with various meanings. It is common practice to say that a person has absolute pitch if he can name instantly any key that is struck on the piano. This capacity is rather common. The term probably should be restricted to possession of the ability to identify tones by much smaller steps than those of the musical scale, for example, from 0.01 to 0.1 of a tone. If the violinist is right when he says, for example, that a given violin is tuned 0.05 of a tone above international pitch, or any other recognized standard, without having had any chance for comparing the tone to any audible standard of reference, then he has absolute pitch. Such capacity is very rare. The possession of absolute pitch to any degree is a safe guarantee of a good sense of pitch and of ear-mindedness.

To measure absolute pitch, it is necessary to make only one trial at a time and to make that just after waking up and before any comparison of tone has been heard. The measurement can be made by a series of tuning forks differing in small steps as in the discrimination test. It is generally believed that the musical ear acquires a standard reference tone, perhaps C_3 or A_3, and that any tone that is sounded in the musical continuum is placed with reference to that in the musical scale. That answers the question as to how it is possible to identify all the audible tones. A more important question pertains to the basis of the reference tone. It is quite generally agreed that the identification is not only in terms of pitch, but also in part in terms of timbre or tone quality, particularly in relation to a similar instrument.

THE SIGNIFICANCE OF INDIVIDUAL DIFFERENCES

Since pitch is the fundamental character of a tone, and pitch discrimination is a measure of the capacity of this sense, it ordinarily may be regarded as the most basic measure of musical capacity that we have. It determines not only what we shall hear, but fundamentally what we shall remember, imagine, and think, and, most important of all, it determines in large part what emotional reaction we shall have for the tone. These differences, often enormously large, must therefore be taken into account in selection and guidance for musical education, in musical criticism, in choice of instruments, and in judgment concerning extraordinary capacity or incapacity, for musical purposes.

NORMAL ILLUSIONS OF PITCH

"Things are not what they seem." As was pointed out in Chap. 2, the ratio of 1:1 between the physical fact, such as frequency, and the mental fact, pitch, is not always exact. Thus 440~ does not mean always the same pitch. The pitch would vary in predictable ways with differences in intensity, duration, and harmonic constitution of the tone, that is, with amplitude, duration, and form of the sound wave. In a predictable way, we speak of the deviation as a normal illusion. An illusion is said to be normal when all persons under similar circumstances tend to get the same result. It is called illusion because the perception does not correspond to the physical object to which it refers. The illusory perception is always positive; that is, it represents a genuine perception and may be just as strong and clear as the perception in which no illusions are involved. The normal illusions often represent short cuts to meaning and an economy in our response to nature and art. A single illusion may be due to half a dozen causes or motives, some cooperative and some inhibiting. Since illusions are measurable and play a very important role in our hearing and rendition of music, the future psychology of music will be expected to state the fundamental laws of illusion of pitch as well as other sensory characteristics.

A beautiful example of the measurement of illusion of pitch due to the varying of the intensity of the tone has been made recently by *Fletcher*.[24] Indeed, his measurements reveal several normal illusions of pitch governing the relation of pitch to intensity. The reader who is interested in good examples of law in illusion of tone should consult this authority.

In general it has been found that tones having frequencies below 2,000~ become lower in pitch while those having frequencies above this level become higher when the intensity of a pure tone is increased.

Three general problems were suggested by his experiment. (1) Would the same be true of rich tones? It was found that for rich tones, such as violin tones, the illusion is only one-fifth as large as for pure tones. (2) Will two such tones of different intensity sound discordant when produced together? It was found that they will not. (3) Does the violinist make correction for these illusions in his playing of intervals? *Lewis* and *Cowan*[79] conducted a series of experiments on this and found that he does not. Knowledge of this illusion, is, of course, of very great interest and significance to the musician, and it explains many of the well-known inconsistencies between pitch and frequency.

Six illusions were illustrated in Chap. 4. The entire field of "subjective tones" falls largely within the realm of normal illusion.

SUBJECTIVE TONES*

A very large number of the tones which play leading roles in music are purely subjective; that is, the frequencies represented are not present in the physical tone but are supplied by the individual in hearing. When two or more tones are sounded together, the trained listener can hear not only these two generators but a con-

* The content of the remainder of this chapter overlaps with Chap. 8. Therefore, those readers to whom this material is new will do well to coordinate the reading of this section with that chapter.

siderable number of subjective tones which may be quite conspicuous and always play a very important role in music. In order to illustrate the character of subjective tones, we shall draw upon the following experiment.

A subjective-tone experiment. *Wegel* and *Lane*[211] devised a very fine illustration of the existence of four kinds of subjective tones. They used two strong pure generating tones. To detect the presence of subjective tones, they employed an "exploring tone" which could be varied through a large range of frequencies. This could be set so as to differ 1 or 2~ from a theoretical subjective tone. If

TABLE I. SUBJECTIVE TONES DETECTED IN A TWO-CLANG TONE COMPOSED OF 700~ (A) AND 1,200~ (B) PURE TONES AT 80 DB SENSATION LEVEL

(Adapted from *Wegel* and *Lane*[211])

1. **500** $(B - A)$
2. **200** $(2A - B)$; **900** $(3A - B)$; **1,700** $(2B - A)$; **1,000** $(2B - 2A)$; **2,900** $(3B - A)$
3. **1,900** $(A + B)$
4. **2,600** $(2A + B)$; **3,800** $(2A + 2B)$; **3,100** $(A + 2B)$; **4,300** $(A + 3B)$; **3,300** $(3A + B)$
5. **1,400** $(2A)$; **2,100** $(3A)$; **2,800** $(4A)$
6. **2,400** $(2B)$; **3,600** $(3B)$

1. First difference tone
2. Other difference tones
3. First summation tone
4. Other summation tones
5. Harmonics of the lower generating tone
6. Harmonics of the higher generating tone

the subjective tone was sufficiently loud, it would beat with the exploring tone.

This was a very simple and strategic device for the securing of objective evidence for the existence and location of subjective tones. Naturally many of the weaker subjective tones would be too faint to cause a perceptible beat, but a sufficient number of them were strong enough to present a most formidable array of the subjective tones that can occur in such a simple situation.

They used two pure tones, 700 and 1,200~, each 80 db above a standard, as generators. Let us call the first A and the second B. These tones were sounded together and a search was made throughout the audible range for subjective tones which would beat with the exploring tone. The location of these was, of course, predictable according to theory. By this method they were able to demonstrate that, in this two-clang combination, 17 subjective tones were present and sufficiently loud to cause beats. The results are expressed in Table I, which is very illuminating and helpful in the classification of these phenomena. The black-faced numbers denote the pitch of each of the 17 subjective tones recorded. The structure of each tone may be seen at a glance in the formula given in parentheses where A denotes 700~ and B 1,200~.

This table is a revelation to the student of music, showing that in this very simple situation 17 distinct subjective tones could be heard clearly enough to have their pitch measured with precision. Incidentally, it may be said that they also were strong enough so that their actual loudness could be measured. Theoretically, more are predictable and may be identified with further refinement of measuring technique.

But it is even more baffling to realize that the complexity of the situation increases in geometric ratio with the addition of one or more tones to the chord or discord and that again it increases vastly with the utilization of rich generating tones, such as those of stringed instruments which have prominent harmonics, since each harmonic may act as an independent generator.

Fortunately, in musical hearing we do not ordinarily hear these subjective tones individually. Like overtones, they fuse into the complex tone which we hear and are, in large part, recognized as the determinants of timbre and tone quality. But by numerous forms of experiment, they may be classified, isolated, and studied one by one. Let us here give some consideration to each of the three main groups.

THE FIRST DIFFERENCE TONE

The most conspicuous and best known of the subjective tones is ordinarily the first difference tone ($B - A$) in the first line of the table. If we use two pure tones, keeping one constant and varying the other, we may produce as many difference tones of this order as there are differences in the frequencies ranging from the lowest audible up to the highest audible tones. For example, the first difference tone for the clang 200 and 300~ is 100~; for 200 and 800~ it is 600~; for 200 and 1,000~ it is 800~.

The identification of these difference tones throughout the audible range furnishes a most excellent exercise in ear training. The best technique is to use vacuum tubes for producing pure tones. The old method was to use glass whistles, called Quinke's tubes, which produced relatively pure tones. These Quinke's tubes can easily be made by the student himself from the description in some textbook of physics.

OTHER DIFFERENCE TONES

As is shown in the second item of Table I, other difference tones are present, at the frequencies of 200, 900, 1,000, 1,700, and 2,900~, respectively. These are all equivalent to a number of pure tones added to enrich the clang. None of them belong in the harmonic series, and they contribute by the introduction of more or less discordant elements in the quality of the clang.

SUMMATION TONES

Items 3 and 4 in Table I give examples of summation tones, each represented by the sum of the frequencies of the two generators or the sum of some multiple of the two fundamentals. The most conspicuous of these is perhaps the first summation tone, $A + B$. None of these falls in the harmonic series and, therefore, their function, like that of the second group of difference tones, is to increase the complexity of the clang by more or less discordant elements.

SUBJECTIVE HARMONICS

The reader who is not familiar with the harmonic structure of musical tones will do well to cast a preliminary glance at Chap. 8, which is devoted to that subject. In accordance with harmonic theory, a good rich musical tone is composed of a fundamental and a series of partials, each being a multiple of the fundamental. In the experiment reported, pure tones were used. That means that no physical partials were present. If the tone from a stringed instrument had been used, the partials for the lower generator could have been 700, 2,100, 2,800, 5,600~, etc., each a multiple of the fundamental, and for the higher tone they would be 1,200, 2,400, 3,600, 7,200~, etc., depending upon the richness of the tone. Theoretically, in this experiment, if the tone had been weaker, no physical partials should have been present, but 80 db is a very strong tone, and the effect of such intensity upon the inner ear is to produce subjective partials; that is, partials which have a distinct pitch, loudness, and harmonic relation to the fundamental but have no corresponding physical frequency. For the lower generating tone, Line 5, Table I, the second, third, and fourth partials were observed in spite of the fact that they came from a tone which generated no physical partials. Likewise, for the second generator, the second and third partials were present under the same circumstances. Here we have a third type of contribution to the character of the clang as heard, namely, the presence of five partials, each of which contributed to the richness of the tone of each generator in spite of its physical purity. It should be noted, however, that these subjective harmonic partials are produced only for extremely loud tones, such as do not ordinarily function in musical performance. To what extent they are present in ordinary musical tones in a lower degree of loudness than that here measured remains to be shown by experiment.

In the interest of clarity, the illustrations here given have been carried in the simplest terms, namely, a clang composed of two pure tones. It is easy to see that if we add one or more pure generating tones to the musical chord, we shall increase the complexity of the situation in geometric ratio but all in accordance with the principles here laid down for two generators. Again, if instead of pure tone generators in the chord, we use rich tones, such as those of orchestral instruments, we shall again increase the complexities of the situation to a most baffling degree, and yet one not defying analysis and experimental illustration.

THE DIFFERENCE TONE A SUBSTITUTE FOR A LOW FUNDAMENTAL

A rich tone from a musical instrument may be modified by introducing a filter, either mechanical or electrical. A filter is a means for eliminating completely the frequencies of any desired partial or group of partials in the musical tone. Suppose now that we have a tone of 200~ played on the G string of a violin, and we eliminate the fundamental frequency by filtering, without interfering at all with the partials above the fundamental. The musical listener may fail to notice any difference between this tone and the tone in which the fundamental is present and is absolutely certain to hear the pitch of the missing fundamental, namely, 200~. If, again, we eliminate the fundamental and the second and third partials, we still hear the tone definitely as of a pitch of 200~, although there is no physical frequency present lower than 800~. Furthermore, as we shall see in Chap. 17, there is comparatively little energy in the fundamental of low tones in voices and instruments. But the fundamental not only gives the pitch to the tone as a whole, but often stands out as dominant, owing to reinforcement by the subjective tone.

The reason for these phenomena is that successive partials are always multiples of the fundamental; in this case 200~ (first partial or fundamental) has 400, 600, 800, 1,000~ etc., as multiples of itself. The difference between the fundamental and the first overtone is, therefore, 200, and the difference of any two adjacent higher partials is always the same—200~, which is the pitch of the

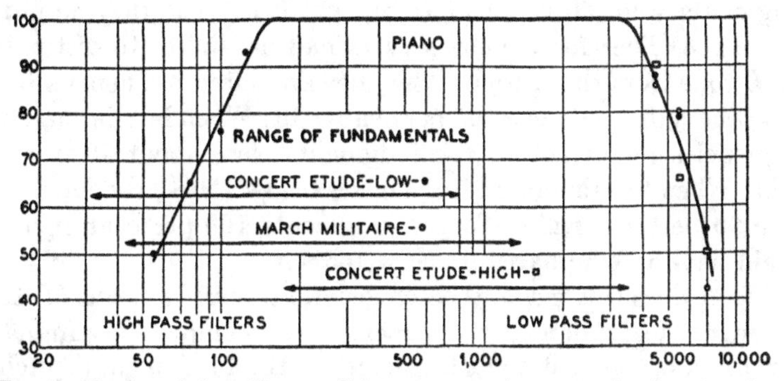

FIG. 3.—Number of times filter condition was correctly preserved as function of cutoff frequency for the piano. Figures at the bottom denote frequencies; figures at the left, per cent of correct judgments. The instrument was the piano. The range of the fundamentals for each selection is shown by the arrowed lines under the name of the selection. "High-pass filters" means that low frequencies were eliminated; "low-pass filters" means that high frequencies were eliminated. Thus in the *Concert Etude*, symbolized by a dot, the range was from 32 to 800~. For the *Marche Militaire*, symbolized by a circle, from 42 to 1,300~; and for the *Concert Etude*, symbolized by a square, from 192 to 2,500~. (*Snow*.[170])

fundamental. The result is that we get a difference tone of the pitch of the fundamental for each successive pair of partials; and, since this is always the same, the effect becomes cumulative and adds to the loudness of the subjective fundamental. This is equivalent to the sounding together of a number of pure tones of 200~.

The limits of effective frequency in the piano. *Snow*[170] performed a very interesting series of experiments to determine to what extent the highest and the lowest frequencies of the musical tone are negligible. He used trained observers under most favorable conditions in observing low and high tones in the three musical selections. His findings are summarized in Fig. 3 for the piano. Let us consider first only the low tones.

His method was to compare the regular nonfiltered tone of the piano, which we shall call *N*, with the same tone, *F*, which had various lower frequencies eliminated by filtering. He eliminated, in turn, all frequencies below 70, 80, 90 and 100~ to determine whether or not the fundamental below these limits would be heard, and whether or not the *F* tone could be distinguished from the *N* tone. His records were kept in terms of the percentage of right judgments on whether or not the two tones sounded alike. The result may be seen at the left side of Fig. 3.

We see that when all notes below 55~ were eliminated, the judgments were 50 per cent right, which is what they would be by chance. Therefore, the observers had no ability to distinguish the *B* tone from the *A* tone. When he eliminated frequencies below 65~, the judgments were 65 per cent right. When he eliminated all frequencies under 100~, the judgments were about 78 per cent right. When he eliminated frequencies below 130~, the judgments were 90 per cent right. To get judgments 100 per cent right, he would have to eliminate all below 165~.

What does this mean, then, in general terms? It means (1) that, although the fundamental frequency was completely eliminated in these low tones, it was still heard as the fundamental pitch of the tone; and (2) that a considerable amount of filtering could take place in tone *B* without altering the perceived character of the tone. This is a very impressive illustration of the role of subjective tones in the everyday hearing of piano music.

On the other side of the chart, we see what happens if we compare *N* and *F* tones when the *F* tone has certain higher partials eliminated. The conclusion from this is that, above the region of 5,000~, the high overtones gradually cease to be heard either as pure tones in themselves or as modifying the character of the tone perceptibly.

Audible frequency range for music, speech, and noise. Following the same method of experimentation, *Snow*[170] investigated the principal types of instruments and voices, with the result shown in Fig. 4. The whole solid line shows the normal frequency range of the instrument; the circle on a line shows the limit below which lower frequencies could be eliminated before the observers could make 80 per cent right judgments in distinguishing the *F* tone from the *N* tone. The same principle applies to the upper limit. The regions indicated by short bars at the right are the regions of accessory noises for each type of tone. *Snow*[170] summarizes his findings as follows:

1. The piano was alone in producing tones with inaudible fundamentals.

2. Audible frequencies down to 40 cycles were produced by the musical instruments, but reproduction only to 60 cycles was considered almost as satisfactory.

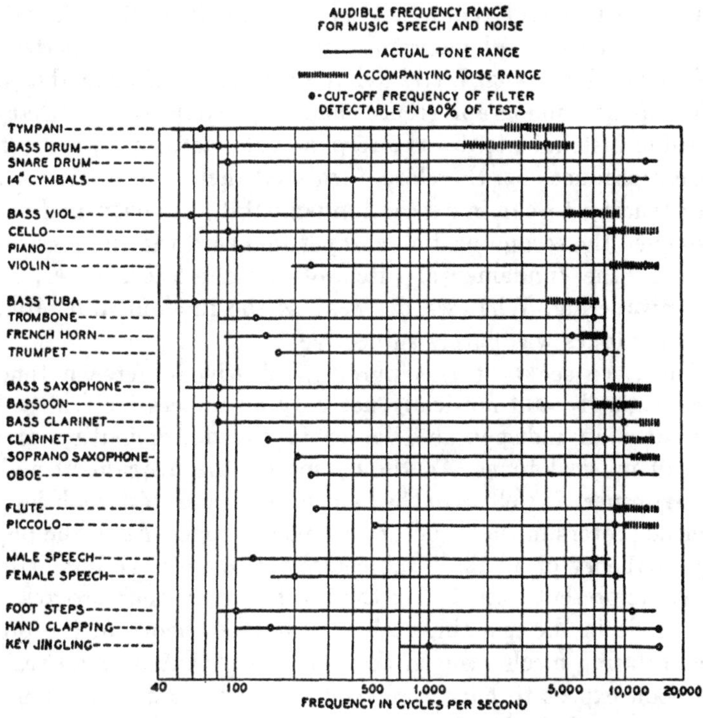

FIG. 4.—Audible frequency range for music, speech, and noise. (*Snow.*[170])

3. It was found that transmission of the highest audible frequencies was needed for perfect reproduction of musical instruments, mainly because of the noises accompanying the musical tones. A 10,000 cycle upper cut-off had slight effect upon the tone quality of most instruments, but a 5,000 cycle cut-off had an appreciable effect upon all except the large drums.

4. The quality of reproduction of orchestral music continued to improve materially as the lower cut-off was extended to about

80 cycles and the upper cut-off to about 8,000 cycles. Reproduction of the full audible range was preferred to any limitation of band width.

5. Noises required reproduction of the highest audible frequencies. A 10,000 cycle cut-off caused appreciable reduction of naturalness on common noises. It was felt that this cut-off probably would never preclude recognition of a noise.

Phonograph and radio. Let us take an illustration from the situation with the phonograph and radio before the perfection of electrical recording. Little did the listeners realize in the early period of the phonograph records and radio transmissions that the recording instruments did not respond satisfactorily to low tones. These reproductions, therefore, furnished their own filters for low tones tending to eliminate the fundamental frequency and sometimes even the second partial, and yet we heard with unquestioned certainty the fundamental pitch of these musical tones, fixed and unwavering. What we did hear as the fundamental pitch in these low tones was purely subjective.

Thus, we see that this purely subjective difference tone is psychologically and musically not only an impressive reality but frequently an indispensable factor in the determination of the pitch of musical tones. To the composer, the instrument-maker, the performer, as well as to the listener, they are stern realities and essential factors in the structure of musical tones. As to the physiological theory of all these subjective tones, we have but little to say at the present time, but in the last five years such progress has been made in the experimental work on the theory of the pitch-differentiating mechanism in the human ear that we may reasonably soon expect to have a physiological explanation in terms of the function of the inner ear.

It should be noted that although we must deny the physical existence of frequencies corresponding to these tones, the oscillograph faithfully records wave patterns in terms of which many of the subjective tones may be identified. The theoretical existence may, of course, be predicted in purely mathematical terms, the only psychological problem being to determine to what extent they are audible.

Audible frequency range in voice and instrument. Each voice or instrument has its typical frequency range for acceptable tone

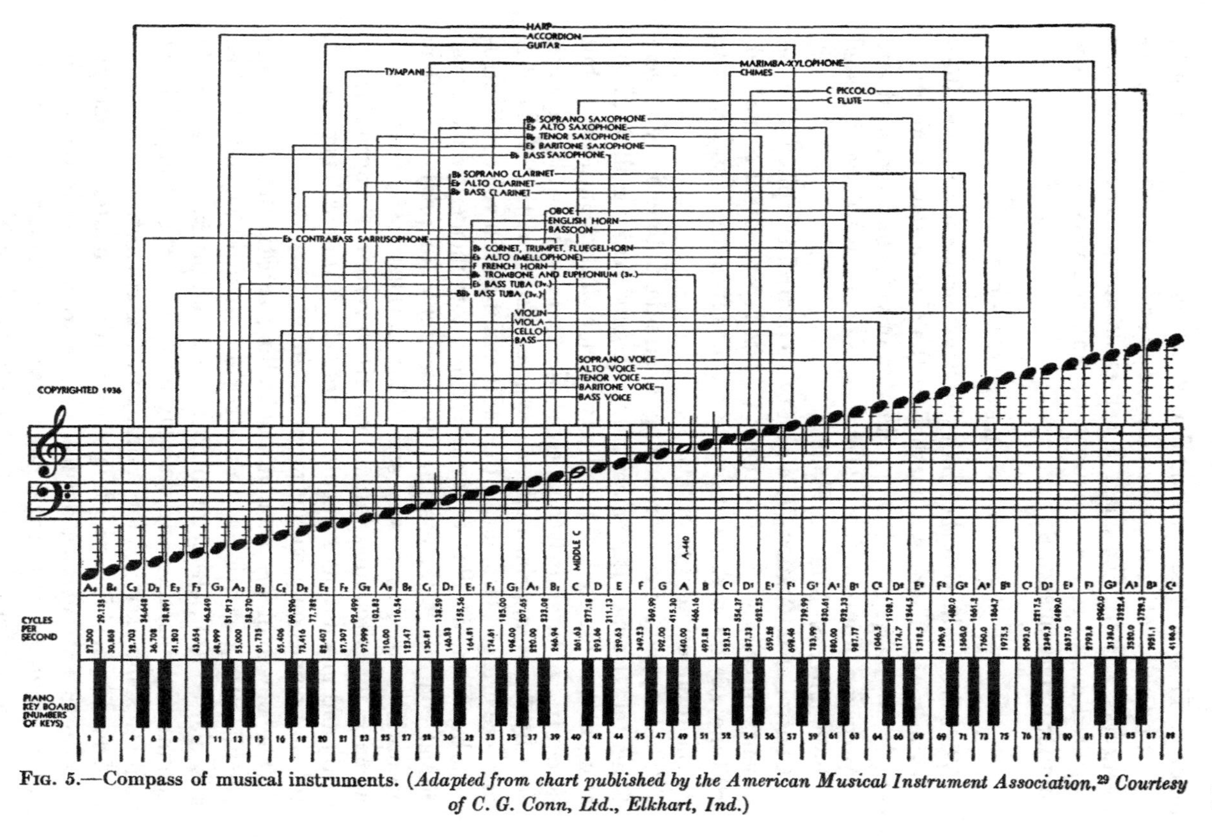

FIG. 5.—Compass of musical instruments. (*Adapted from chart published by the American Musical Instrument Association.*[29] *Courtesy of C. G. Conn, Ltd., Elkhart, Ind.*)

quality. This is illustrated in Fig. 5, which is a copy of a chart issued by the National Association of Musical Instrument Manufacturers,[101] 1927. The chart is self-explanatory. The limits here indicated are merely approximations and can vary under a large number of circumstances.

PITCH PERFORMANCE

We have dealt with the ability to hear tones and to hear differences in tones. There is a parallel on the side of tone production; namely, in the range of tone production of voice or instrument and the precision of intonation. Various aspects of this will be discussed in the chapter on Musical Skills.

Control of intonation. The ability to control the pitch of tones presents three types of situations: (1) the reproduction of a standard tone; (2) the making of fine deviations from the standard; and (3) the production of intervals.

The capacity for reproducing a standard tone is relatively elemental. It depends primarily upon a good sense of pitch. Naturally one cannot control pitch any finer than he can hear it; but the control of pitch is frequently subject to considerable improvement by training, principally the type of discipline that makes the ear more critical. Ordinarily the fault is not in the voice or instrument but in the fidelity of the ear and auditory imagery. To exercise critical control, it follows that the capacity for pitch control in intonation varies in a way somewhat parallel to a variation in capacity for pitch discrimination. However, in stringed instruments and in wind instruments, a large element of skill is required, and that comes only with rigorous training.

The power of precision in controlling artistic deviation from true pitch is again primarily a matter of a sensitive ear, rather than muscular control, although in both voice and instrument a certain amount of experience and training is necessary. In Chap. 27, we shall see some exercises for training in this respect.

The control of intervals hinges primarily upon interval concepts. Some of the intervals are natural; others are more or less arbitrary. But a certain amount of training is necessary in order to standardize the concept of interval. Historically speaking, there has been a variety of scales, and even at the present time in modern music there is considerable dispute about minor differences in intervals which constitute scales. But, given the concept of interval, precision in singing or playing intervals depends to a great degree upon precision in the reproduction of a tone and in the control of fine differences in pitch.

Interval. Melody and harmony are both built upon the conception of intervals, some aspects of which we shall discuss under the head of Consonance. There is a very extensive literature on this subject, particularly with reference to musical scales. Much of it awaits verification, criticism, and extension by means of laboratory experiments. As an example, we may mention the contest over the tempered scale and just intonation in violin playing.

6

LOUDNESS: INTENSITY

THE ROLE OF INTENSITY

We have seen that there are four fundamental aspects of all music: the tonal, the dynamic, the temporal, and the qualitative. The tonal aspects are primarily the outgrowth of pitch and timbre; the dynamic are usually reduced mainly to intensity; the temporal rest basically upon time but are greatly modified by intensity; the qualitative rest primarily upon timbre, but this is greatly modified by pitch, intensity, and time in sonance. We see, therefore, that intensity plays one of the four basic roles in all music.

We are perhaps less conscious of intensity than any of the other three attributes in music, for several reasons. In terms of pitch, we have musical scales, melody, and harmony with exact quantitative determinations for each. The musical score shows pitch and time with precision but shows only very crude indications of intensity. Therefore, owing to the relative absence of definite concepts, their conspicuous absence in the score and, until recently, the absence of units of measurement, little or nothing is said in musical literature about intensity or loudness, and yet this attribute of tone is comparatively conspicuous for musical hearing and musical expression.

In phrasing, for example, which is the very heart of musical interpretation for both the performer and the listener, the pianist can do comparatively little or nothing to modify pitch and comparatively little to modify timbre. The pianist's musical interpretation deals almost entirely with intensity and time. The singer expresses his musicianship primarily in two ways: in the control of the quality of tone and in phrasing. The quality of tone assumes a fairly fixed character at a given stage of training, but the musical phrasing is the most plastic unit in terms of which the singer or the violinist expresses personality and musical interpretation, and phrasing is largely a matter of time and intensity.

The builder of instruments, the musical critic, the teacher, and the scientist dealing with the art of music must develop a more conscious recognition of the role of intensity than that which now prevails in judging the beauty of music. The student must become aware, not only of principles of dynamics in music, but also of his own sensitivity and power of discrimination, and the countless devices which must be at his command in controlling, modifying, and utilizing loudness characteristics in tone production. Fundamentally, there are two goals, effectiveness and agreeableness. The former pertains to carrying power and intelligibility of the sound, the second to the art of dynamic modulation as an element of beauty in itself and as a medium for the control of tone quality.

There are two measures which are basic to all dynamic aspects of tone, sensitivity and discrimination. The first is the measure of the natural capacity of the ear for becoming aware of sounds; the second is a measure of the capacity of the ear for hearing differences and, therefore, the power to use the ear in a musically significant way dynamically, that is, to assign musical meaning to loudness characteristics. On the motor side, we are correspondingly concerned (1) with the ability to control the intensity in intonation, and (2) with the ability to produce artistic deviations in intensity.

SENSITIVITY OR HEARING ABILITY

Audiometry. The art of measuring the sensitivity, usually called hearing ability or acuity of hearing, is just coming into the medical profession and into activities which are affected by keenness of hearing or hearing loss, such as music, speech, and various industries. This is largely because it is only within the last few years that reliable measuring instruments and units of measurement have been available in the fields of psychology, physics, and engineering.

Sensitivity is best measured with an audiometer, which produces pure tones at different levels of pitch in the tonal register. The measurement consists in determining the weakest sound that can be heard. This measure, as we have seen, is expressed in decibels.

It usually is plotted in terms of the number of decibels of deviation from standards for normal hearing of persons not above forty years of age and is designated as "hearing loss." Thus, we say a person has so many decibels hearing loss for different levels of frequency.*

On the conventional hearing chart in Fig. 1, various types of hearing loss are represented. A word of comment in regard to each of these is in order.

Normal hearing. The straight line numbered 0 represents normal hearing for young adults and is taken as a base line from which hearing loss is measured. The ear is probably as sensitive to sound

---

* Very rapid progress is now being made in the design and marketing of audiometers. Dr. Scott Reger, specialist in matters pertaining to audiometry, lists instruments now available as follows:

A. Western Electric No. 2-A Audiometer. Battery operated: generates eight frequencies in octave intervals from 64 to 8,192 cycles.

B. Western Electric No. 6-A Audiometer. A.C.-D.C. operated: generates a continuously variable range of frequencies from 128 to 10,000 cycles.

C. Western Electric No. 4-A Audiometer. Designed to test the hearing for spoken speech reproduced from phonograph records of as many as 40 pupils simultaneously. This instrument is used principally for the group testing of school children.

D. Western Electric No. 5-A Audiometer. A.C. operated: generates a single complex "buzzer" tone.

E. Western Electric No. 3-A Audiometer. Battery operated version of the Western Electric No. 5-A Audiometer. The Western Electric No. 5-A and 3-A Audiometers were designed for use in various industries where a rapid approximation of hearing acuity is desired. The Western Electric Audiometers may be obtained from the Graybar Electric Co., Graybar Building, New York City.

F. Sonotone Jones-Knudsen Model 1 Audiometer. A.C.-D.C. operated: generates seven frequencies in octave intervals from 128 to 8192 cycles. Also provides a continuous sweep of frequencies from 2500 up to 16,000 cycles in two ranges: 2500 to 7500, and 8000 to 16,000 cycles. Sonotone Corporation, 19 West 44th Street, New York City.

G. Maico Model D-4 Audiometer. Generates frequencies from 32 to 12,288 cycles. (Complete detailed information on this instrument is lacking.) The Medical Acoustic Instrument Co., 730 Hennepin Ave., Minneapolis, Minn.

H. Auragraph Audiometer. A.C.-D.C. operated: continuously variable from 64 to 8192 cycles. The Marvel-Clark Co., Grand Rapids, Mich.

I. Brenco 34-C Audiometer. A.C. operated: generates eight frequencies in octave intervals from 64 to 8192 cycles, plus the additional three frequencies of 12,000, 16,000, and 20,000 cycles. Physicians Supply Co. of Philadelphia, 116 South 16th Street, Philadelphia, Pa.

Audiometers C, D, and E measure hearing acuity in terms of percentage loss; A, B, F, G, and I are so calibrated that the results are read in terms of decibels hearing loss; nothing is known about the intensity calibration of H. All of the above Audiometers except C, D, and E are equipped with both headphones and bone conduction vibrators for testing acuity for both air and bone conducted vibrations. Audiometers B and F are also equipped with microphones to enable conversation and the selection of hearing aids for the hard of hearing.

in the first year of childhood as it ever will be thereafter. The change that takes place with maturation and education consists of the development of the ability to assign meaning, develop habits of selection, and give accurate account of it. There is, of course, a considerable latitude of variation around this normal, up to 10 db or more above or 10 db or slightly more below at all frequencies.

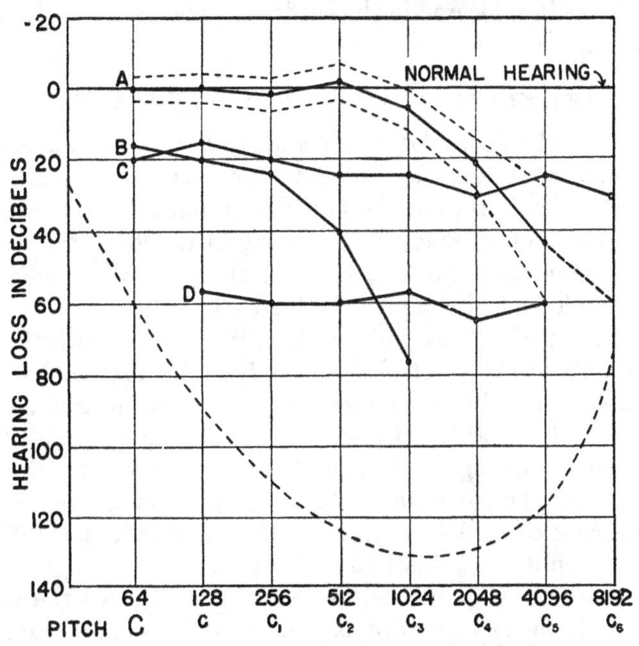

FIG. 1.—Audiograms showing types of hearing loss. Straight line at zero, normal hearing regarded as a base line; *A*, normal loss due to age; *B*, middle-ear lesion, advanced in impairment; *C*, acoustic neuritis, hearing loss approximately uniform; *D*, extreme form of acoustic neuritis. The dash lines show the average deviation from line *A* for persons above 60. (*Kelley*.[58,59])

There may also be ups and downs of a minor sort within this range of about 10 db on each side.

Acoustic neuritis. Line *B* shows a typical case of acoustic neuritis due to some form of pathology in the inner ear. This, as the curve shows, is rather severe and usually does not respond to treatment.

Middle-ear lesion. This is commonly due to disturbances in the bones or membranes of the middle ear. Line *C* shows a mild type, in which the subject clearly recognizes that he is hard of hearing but does not ordinarily need a hearing aid; whereas, Line *D* is of a severe type in which it becomes advantageous to wear some hearing aid. In certain types of middle-ear lesions, the patient may obtain better results from a bone-conduction hearing aid than from the ordinary sound-amplifying (air-conduction) instrument.

The threshold of pain. The dotted line at the bottom represents the limits at which sounds are loud enough to produce a feeling of pain. This pain is located in the eardrum and serves as a protection for the ear.

DETERIORATION WITH AGE: PRESBYCOUSIS

There is a tendency for aged people to have some degree of loss of hearing. Such loss of plasticity is observable in other sense organs as well as in the muscles and glands; but in hearing we have a peculiar situation in that, while hearing in the lower register may remain normal into old age, there is always a very radical and progressive loss of hearing for the higher tones.

Line *A* in Fig. 1 is from *Kelley's*[59] recent investigation. He selected only the cases of old persons between sixty and seventy-five years of age who had approximately normal hearing, at least up to 500~, in order to get cases which are unquestionably due to deterioration with age. This condition was certified by otological examination. The curve shows that, on the average, these people had a hearing loss of 8 db at 1,000~, 24 db at 2,000, 44 at 4,000, and probably would have about 60 at 8,000~.

The dash lines above and below the line *A* show the average deviation from this average in 70 cases. This close agreement with the average indicates that this type of decline follows a fairly fixed law. As we grow old, we may therefore have the comfort of companionship in this loss for high tones.

To verify this in actual music, he took a violin tone which had a rich spectrum of high tones and, by filtering, eliminated in different experiments those above 2,000, 4,000, and 8,000~. Careful re-measurements were made to see whether the aged person could tell the difference between the filtered tone and the full violin tone. What was predicted proved true: an aged person cannot hear any overtones above what is indicated by his hearing loss. Therefore, both music and speech are to him radically different from what they were in youth. These losses come on so gradually that the sound of the human voice or of a violin does not seem to be noticeably different from what it was in youth.

This state of partial deafness arising from senile changes in the ear is called "presbycousis." The term should be applied to that type of hearing loss which has been described in the preceding paragraph and should not be applied to the loss of hearing below the region of 1,000~ due to old age.

Kelley[59] investigated seventy cases of persons above sixty years of age and found that about 75 per cent had normal hearing, that is, not more than 10 db hearing loss at 64 to 500~, and only a slight hearing loss at 1,000~. This shows that loss of hearing in the lower register does not necessarily come from age or occur with age. In the 25 per cent of the cases in which there was a loss in this region it could be traced to such specific causes as may operate at any age. This is a comfort to those who have fatalistic fear of loss of hearing. It has been shown that where the tympanic membrane is destroyed, a person can employ stronger hearing aids than otherwise, because the sense organs of pain that protect the ear are located primarily in this membrane. *Lewis and Reger*[82] have shown also that the hearing of subjective tones is not dependent upon the presence of the tympanic membranes.

CHILDREN'S HEARING

The measuring of hearing ability of school children has been grossly neglected on account of the absence of measuring instruments and the lack of realization of the deep significance of hearing loss in children. Many children are regarded as dull and become problem cases simply because they do not hear. It is typical of both children and adults, as a rule, to pretend to hear and to develop defense reactions. They also develop skill in drawing inferences from situations, in guessing from partly heard sounds, and especially in the art of lip reading, which in extreme cases may become an actual substitute for hearing.

In the public schools of today, it is found that from 5 to 10 per cent of the school children have some significant hearing loss. Many of these defects are unknown to schoolteachers and parents. In fact, only one out of five can be detected by ordinary methods. The audiometer permits a survey test that discovers all hearing-deficient pupils. Loss of hearing may be due to a great variety of causes, and many forms may be treated successfully, especially in a growing child, but most important is the provision of preventive measures and precautions which save the child from developing deafness.

It is evident that loss of hearing ability becomes an impediment to the hearing, appreciation, and performance of music. The person so affected lives in a different sound world from the person who has normal hearing. Many peculiarities in musical interpretation, likes, and dislikes are due either to hypersensitivity or to loss of sensitivity to sound. Hypersensitivity is a very potent source of that type of

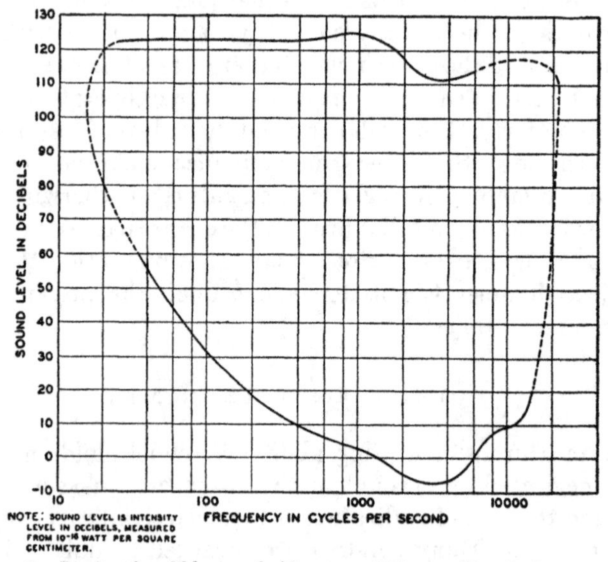

FIG. 2.—Limits of audible sound. (*Courtesy of Western Electric Company.*)

irritation which shows itself in eccentricities of the musical temperament.

The field of hearing. There is an upper and a lower limit of hearing. How strong a sound can the ear endure? The solid line at the top in Fig. 2 indicates that at this point the sound becomes so strong that it arouses pain and cannot be endured above that level. This is the upper limit, in the region of 125 db.

How strong must a sound be in order to be heard? That is, what is the lower threshold of hearing? In other words, what does "normal" hearing as represented by the base line (0) in Fig. 1 mean? The answer is given in the lower part of Fig. 2. This figure is only an approximation to the more recent measurements, but it shows the important fact that the ear is highly sensitive in the region of 500 to 4,000~, which is the region most significant for music and speech. Above and below this region of frequency, sound must be increasingly stronger in order to be heard. The broken parts of the curve indicate high and low regions for which the curve is more or less hypothetical.

There are very large individual differences in hearing ability from the supersensitive to the stone deaf, and this influences their activities in daily life to an extraordinary degree. The person who

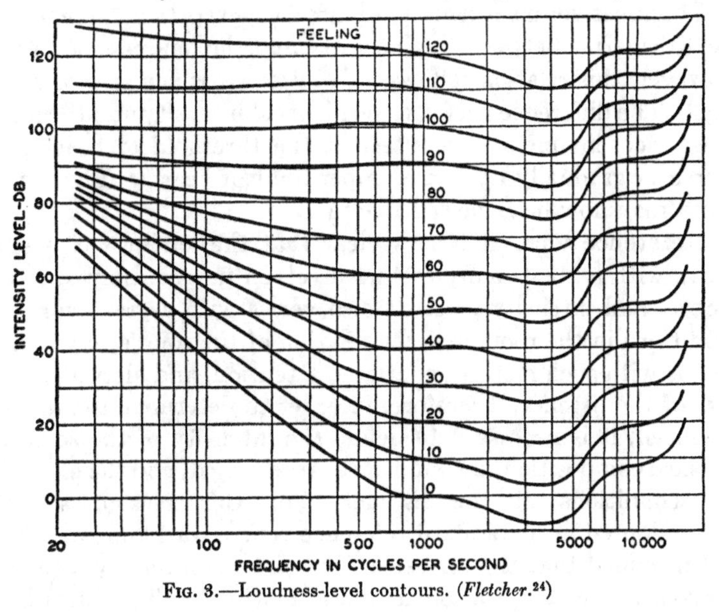

FIG. 3.—Loudness-level contours. (*Fletcher.*[24])

has an especially keen ear perceives and responds emotionally to countless sounds that his neighbors cannot hear. The person who is hard of hearing has the advantage of freedom from disturbing noises but also suffers a loss of power in his daily adjustments.

These limitations are, in a way, a great blessing because they save us from hearing a great mass of rumblings and roarings which occur in nature and also from the infinite variety of high tones which are ever present but are of little or no significance for music and speech. In other words, the ear is selective in that it is responsive to that region of sounds which is of greatest significance and use.

More significant than hypersensitivity in this respect is the mental set which centers consciousness upon sound rather than upon other stimuli. Keen hearing ability and vivid auditory imagery coupled with a dominating interest in sounds is what throws the musician under the spell of sounds. Harshness, discord, volume have meaning to him just as purity, harmony, and modulation have. It is therefore important to recognize that, although a musician may have just a normal hearing ability, he may be extraordinarily responsive to sounds which to the nonmusician pass unobserved.

Loudness versus intensity. Figure 2 suggests that there must be great disparity between the intensity and the loudness of a sound. However, this relation follows a definite law which is expressed in Fig. 3. The difference between the physical intensity and the mental experience, loudness, is greatest at the threshold of hearing and decreases gradually up to the upper limit of hearing. Figures 1, 2, and 3 may now be reviewed together.

Reference tone. It is now clear that the loudness of a sound varies with a great many factors involved in frequency, duration, timbre, and intensity level. It also varies with a great variety of conditions in the room and the relation of the source to the ear as well as with such factors as fatigue, attention, and alertness on the part of the listener. Therefore, in order to determine the loudness produced, it is necessary to define the intensity of the sound, its physical composition, the kind of ear receiving it, and the physiological conditions of the listener. For this reason, scientists have adopted as a standard reference tone a pure tone of 1,000$\sim$ and provided that the reference intensity for intensity-level comparisons all be 10^{-16} watts per square centimeter. This furnishes us a fixed base from which intensity and loudness measurements can be made under all sorts of conditions.

DISCRIMINATION: THE SENSE OF INTENSITY

Intensity discrimination is measured with a special type of audiometer by determining the smallest difference in loudness that can be heard. For practical reasons 1 db is usually considered the magnitude of the just noticeable difference. This, however, is an arbitrary standard because the j.n.d. varies a great deal with the pitch level, the absolute loudness, timbre, and duration of the tone. It also varies in a large range with the individual differences of the listeners.

Intensity discrimination measures the ability to hear differences in loudness and is therefore a measure of a person's capacity for using loudness differences in every dynamic aspect of music and in other hearing situations in daily life. For group measurement, the phonograph record, "The Sense of Intensity," No. 53003-D, from the Seashore *Measures of Musical Talent*, is satisfactory. The record by this method is given in terms of centile rank in the same manner as for the other measures, which makes such capacities readily comparable.

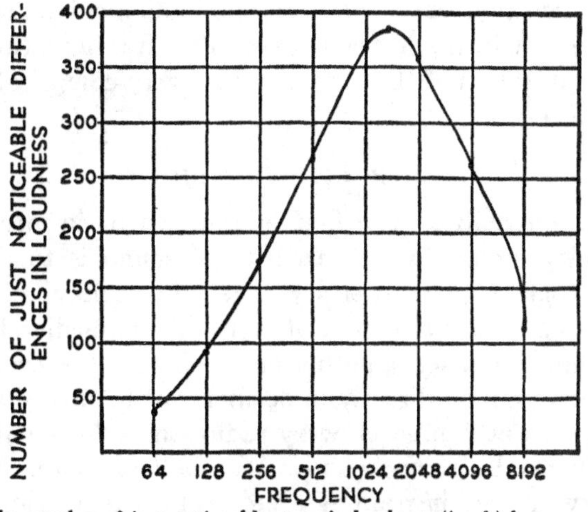

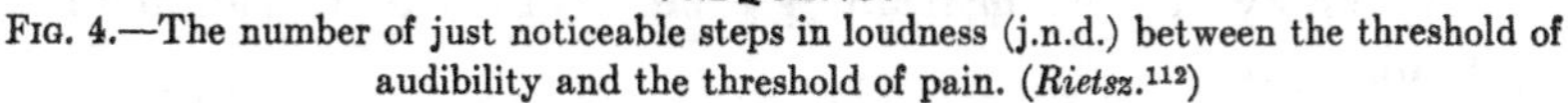
FIG. 4.—The number of just noticeable steps in loudness (j.n.d.) between the threshold of audibility and the threshold of pain. (*Rietsz.*[112])

There are very great individual differences in this capacity. When individual measurements are made with an audiometer, it is found that there is an approximately normal distribution of capacities, ranging from 0.2 to 20 db or more. These differences are fairly independent of age, intelligence, and training. They play a very important role in determining success or failure in ordinary intercourse and in vocations which involve discriminative hearing, particularly in music and speech.

NUMBER OF AUDIBLE DIFFERENCES IN LOUDNESS

How this capacity varies with pitch level is illustrated in Fig. 4, which shows that, at a pitch of 64~, the average ear can detect about 45 different steps in loudness, an octave above that, about 95 steps, and at C_3, about 175 steps, etc.; the finest discrimination is found in the third octave above C_3 at which the average ear can detect about 375 steps or differences of loudness.

But this curve is for an average ear. For a superior ear, it would rise much higher at all pitch levels, and for an inferior ear, it would fall far below the present curve.

Similar illustrations might be made to show that the capacity for intensity discrimination varies with absolute loudness, time, and timbre. In general, we may say that the ear is most discriminating for differences in loud tones and least discriminating for differences in soft tones, and that these differences for loud, medium, and weak tones are greatest in the lower octaves. The discrimination varies also with the duration of the tone and, in a very complicated way, with the timbre.

MOTOR CAPACITIES

Matching intensities. The first of the two basic measures of motor capacity for control of intensity of sound is to match or reproduce a tone of given intensity. The subject may be required to sing or play a tone of any intensity and then immediately repeat it with the same intensity, all other factors held constant. The two intensities may be read directly in decibels on the dial of a power-level meter, such as is used in every radio studio for regulation of the intensity of the radio sounds. We shall see later how this principle may be used in training exercises for the development of dynamic skill.

Differentiating intensities. This is measured in the same manner as above with voice or instrument. The capacity thus revealed is a measure of the ability to produce artistic deviation in loudness. It is the fundamental key to the art of interpretation, as in musical phrasing. While the loudness discrimination is a relatively elemental capacity, the motor skill involved in its artistic use is subject to marked refinement by training, and artistry consists largely in the development of fine and meaningful modulations of intensity.

Naturally the limits for matching intensities as well as for varying intensities are set mainly by the capacity for intensity discrimination. For two persons, one of whom can hear a difference of only 4 db under standard conditions and the other can hear 0.4 db difference, we should expect a corresponding difference in the ability to control the intensity. In general, however, a person cannot produce a given loudness so accurately as he can hear it, because there are various elements of motor skill involved. Measurements show that a fine pianist may be able to hear and reproduce differences as small as 0.1 db in the middle register. The pianist perhaps has the greatest responsibility for the mastery of intensity control since this is one of the two principal media under his control, and the instrument responds favorably to fine shadings in touch. Performance on wind and percussion instruments is far less accurate. This topic will be discussed further in the chapter on Musical Skills, Chap. 27.

INTENSITY CHARACTERISTICS OF MUSICAL TONES

Beats. One of the basic determinants of harmony is the phenomenon of beats, which consists of the periodic pulsation of intensity. Below 12 or 15 pulsations we do not hear tones but distinct beats. The number of beats per second indicates the number of vibrations in the difference of the frequencies of the two beating tones. Above the threshold of tonal fusion the tones are characterized as harsh or rough. The roughness decreases with the increase in number of beats up to certain levels. Thus, a minor third is rougher than a major third.

Beats are more conspicuous in pure tones than in rich tones. If two pure tones beat, they tend to cancel each other, so that for each beat there is a moment of silence; but the richer the tone is, the more complicated the situation becomes.

Resonance. If we suspend a violin string between two solid supports without any resonance box, the string must be bowed hard before the tone can be heard at all. The real tone which we hear from the violin is caused by the sympathetic vibration in the resonance of the box. That is, what we hear is not primarily the vibration of the string but the vibration of the various parts of the resonance mechanism. The same is true in principle for all forms of instruments and especially for the human voice, in which the oscillation of air caused by the vocal cords alone is significant in comparison with the oscillation which emanates through the mouth from the resonating cavities.

It is this differential modification in the loudness of partials which governs the timbre of tones.

Reverberation. Another factor which plays a large role in modifying the character of the tone by changes in intensity is that of reverberation. The ordinary music room or music hall is in effect a resonance box. Every sound we have goes out to the walls, the ceiling, the floor, the furniture, and the occupants, and is reflected back in a mass of sound waves of increasing complexity. Therefore, a violin tone may be radically different in one room from what it is in another, or different in one part of the room from what it is in any other part, because of these characteristics of reverberation. By taking basic measurements in the dead room, which eliminates the element of reverberation and transmission of sounds from the outside, we can determine the character of the instrument or the voice in itself, and then by taking corresponding measurements in any music room or any part of the music room we can determine exactly what it is that the room contributes. The adoption of scientific principles in the construction and sound treatment of auditoriums and music rooms is one of the most recent triumphs of architecture and is destined to contribute much to the refinement and mastery of musical performance.

AMPLIFICATION OF SOUND

The engineering development in the control of the dynamics of tone in recording, reproducing, and broadcasting is one of the most important contributions that has ever been made to the populariz-ing of music. In recording a sound film, for example, not only can the man at the instrument change instantly the loudness of the tone as a whole, but he can deal with any particular element of the tone selectively in such a way as to improve upon the perform-ance of the instrument or the voice. This is called building up the tone. As a result of this, we hear over the radio voices which are much better balanced through the radio rendition than in the actual delivery of the voice. One of our most famous baritones has a voice which is naturally weak in the lower registers and, therefore, im-presses one as thin and top-heavy. But in the radio rendition, and to some extent in the phonograph, this voice is rebuilt so that it approximates an ideal distribution of the loudness for each register and for each partial in the complex tone. This phenomenon can easily be observed when one has the opportunity of hearing the singer in person and hearing one of his latest recordings so that a comparison can be made between the record and the sound in the performance of the voice. This does not imply, necessarily, that in every respect the recording of the tone is better than the natural voice, but is emphasizing the fact that it is possible to make a voice sound better than it really is. We are familiar with the analogy to this in painting and photography.

A scale of musical dynamics. To most of the readers of this book the term "decibel" is new. As yet it has a very slight place in musical language; but it must be recognized that the appearance of this term, or its equivalent, was a condition for the scientific discussion of dynamic expression in music and for the application of exact terminology in musical composition, performance, and criticism. When Stokowski directs his orchestra over the radio control board, he has before himself an intensity meter which shows the loudness of the orchestral performance from moment to moment. He can, therefore, adopt and enforce specific standards.

It will not be long before there will be in music studios meters which will register loudness in decibel readings for any voice or instrument so that the terms will have a fixed value in the score and can assume specific and permanent values in the conception of the composer and the performance of the artist. It will require a great deal of experimenting to standardize such norms.

At the present time we can only make a rough estimate. *Dr. Scott Reger*, who is an expert in this field of measurement, suggests that tentatively we may adopt the following scale: For a 75-piece orchestra in decibel equivalence above the threshold, *ppp*, 20 db; *pp*, 40 db; *p*, 55 db; *mf*, 65 db; *f*, 75 db; *ff*, 85 db; *fff*, 95 db.

The intensity of an average whisper when the mouth of the speaker is 4 feet from the ear of the listener is about 20 db above the threshold. The loudest sounds of average conversational speech are about 60 db above the threshold under similar conditions. There is an intensity-level range of about 73 db in a crescendo from the average level of the softest violin playing to the peaks in the heaviest playing of a full orchestra. If the intensity of the softest violin were 20 db above the threshold, the heaviest playing of the orchestra would be about 95 db above the threshold.

Measurements of this kind will, of course, be of very great value in the determination of such features as carrying power of voice and instrument, the acoustic characteristics of each and every part of an auditorium, discussion of the volume of voice or instrument, and scientific statements of principles of dynamic expression.

7

DURATION: TIME

NATURE OF THE PERCEPTION OF TIME

THERE are two aspects of the sense of time; namely, that concerned with fine distinctions of short intervals of time and that concerned with the judging of the flow of time in longer periods, such as seconds, minutes, or days. Individuals differ extraordinarily in their abilities and habits for judging sustained intervals of time. The judgment depends largely upon an appraisal of the net result of the flow of events which occur within a time period, such as the speaking of a sentence, the delivery of a speech, or the work of the day. Every moment of time is filled in some way, and an infinite variety of clues are used in judging the progression. For example, an undesired visitor may engage in small talk for an hour without noticing the flight of time, whereas the host may be very restive and overestimate the duration. In other cases, the estimate may be based upon observed events which take a fairly even, customary course. For example, a man can get some idea about what time he has arisen in the morning by observing the length of his beard in shaving. There are definite, established principles of overestimation and underestimation of time, for example, an inexperienced after-dinner speaker always underestimates the time that he has talked. But we need not say anything more about the judgment of the flight of time, because that plays only a secondary role in music. Everyone will, however, think of how differently the time passes in a boring musical program from the way in which the time passes in which the listener is on the verge of ecstasy in the appreciation of music.

Sensitivity to time differs from sensitivity to pitch, intensity, and timbre in that there is no evidence to show that it depends upon the structure of the ear under normal conditions. There are very great individual differences in the capacity for hearing time, but these differences are due to a large number of factors, such as the capacity for differential attention, or, ear-mindedness, that is, the tendency to live in a tonal world in which significance is attached to the temporal aspects of sounds. This is characterized as perhaps the most important factor in the capacity for imaging the time value of tones and for remembering the time value of sounds. We, therefore, attach no great significance to the measurement of sensitivity to time but make large use of the discrimination for time which we usually call the sense of time.

DISCRIMINATION: THE SENSE OF TIME

"The Sense of Time" record, in the Seashore *Measures of Musical Talent,* illustrates a method and furnishes the means of measuring this capacity. A series of time intervals are marked off by clicks in which the differences of two compared intervals vary from 0.02 to 0.20 second, and the subject is asked to say which of the two intervals is the longer. From the percentage of right answers the centile rank is established, showing norms for adults and for fifth- and eighth-grade children.

A common method in the laboratory is to vary the difference in time intervals by increasing the magnitude and determining the length of interval for which about 85 per cent of the answers are right. This is spoken of as the threshold, or the limit for time discrimination. It is found that a very fine musical ear may detect a difference in the length of two notes as small as 0.01 second, whereas another ear may require as much as 0.10 or 0.20 in order to hear the difference. It is perfectly evident to anyone that these differences in the sense of time are very important determinants of what a person can hear in music and the accuracy with which he can perform. *Tempo rubato* is one of the most important means that the artist has for interpretation of music, and this depends upon the ability to hear and the ability to produce fine shadings in time in order to produce the desired modulation.

It is evident that these individual differences in the capacity for hearing time are at the base of the capacity of feeling for time, which plays such an extraordinary role in the enjoyment and the production of music. A person with a fine sense of time tends to feel the musical value of fine shadings in time corresponding to his capacity for hearing them. The feeling aroused may be agreeable or disagreeable. It tends to give rise to attitudes of attraction or repulsion. In piano playing, for example, where time is one of the only two media that the artist has for interpretation, we may say roughly that half the feeling value for or against the musical rendition hinges upon the role played by fine distinctions of time, as, for example, in the asynchronization of chords, in the overlapping of notes, and in all forms of artistic deviation from rigid time or fixed tempo.

This is about all we need to say about time as a sensory capacity. Of course, this capacity functions throughout music in countless forms of perception, memory, imagination, feeling, and action. Tempo, synchronization, rhythm, and all other forms of precision or artistic deviation in terms of temporal aspects constitute at least a good fourth of the content of the musical medium.

NORMAL ILLUSIONS OF TIME

The perception of time in music is subject to a great variety of normal illusions. Aside from cases of mere incompetence and errors, these subjective variables tend to follow natural laws and are, therefore, predictable. In psychological measurement involving time, such factors must be controlled. Psychologists have measured scores of these illusions. But the significant thing for music is that a very large part of the artistry in music lies in the utilization of these principles. Without them, accent, rhythm, and phrasing would be hopelessly sterile.

MOTILITY

Temporal activity will be discussed under various heads, such as Rhythm, Tempo, and Time, which are analyzed in the actual musical situations; but the problem of motility, which involves various aspects of speed and accuracy in movement, underlies all these. A person may be quick and accurate, quick and inaccurate, slow and accurate, or slow and inaccurate in various degrees and combinations.

In instrumental music, there is a natural limit to the speed a musician can exhibit, and in this limit there are large individual differences. The real significance for music, however, does not lie in the upper limit for speed of action, but rather in the fineness of the control of time and action which is involved in musical interpretation. The problem for the musician is not so much, "How fast can I move my fingers?" but rather, "How accurately can I make fine time distinctions in the movement?"

Music is a form of "serial action"; that is, the time value of a note depends upon its integration in the melodic and harmonic progression. Therefore, measurement of skill and talent for time must be validated in relation to the types of function that actually occur in music. These may take countless forms. All our performance scores are measures of this sort. The record of an arpeggio at high speed is a good measure. The complete record of artistic deviation in time is by far the most significant. For specific purposes, record of capacity for performance in metronomic time may also have some value.

Motility represents one of the standard psychological measurements of capacity. The test has been standardized by *Ream*,[107] and he has evaluated the extensive literature on the subject critically. The standard form of measurement is to tap with a finger on a telegraph key which records the speed. A simpler way is merely to tap with a minimum movement with a pencil held in the most favorable position and count how many taps can be made in 5 seconds. But for practical purposes the test should be on a movement which is identical with, or analogous to, the movement that is to be predicted. Thus, for the prediction of speed of movement in piano playing, the motility test might well be made by recording the rate of tapping a piano key with one finger.

There is a slow improvement with practice. Ream found that, in 20 days of intensive practice in the act, the average for six normal adults on the first day was 8.5 taps per second, and that this rose gradually to 9.3 taps on the twentieth day. Men average one-half tap per second faster than women. The rate of tapping increases with age: age five, 3.8; age six, 4.4; age seven, 4.6; age eight, 5.5; age nine, 5.8; age ten, 6.3.

Numerous investigations have been made of the relation of motility to various forms of intelligence and efficiency in various acts of practical skills in art and in industry. It is found that a certain degree of prediction can be made if the measure of motility takes the age and learning curves into account and is made in a closely related form of movement; that is, for a particular type of motion each individual manifests a natural capacity for speed of action. In general, the correlation with intelligence in acts which involve some degree of discrimination, choice, or deliberation is fairly high; but for mere repetitive acts, such as tapping, it is low or negligible.

Motility is not a simple phenomenon but a complex of such factors as rapidity, steadiness, precision, endurance, and strength of movement. It has often been spoken of as a personal equation, meaning the characteristic way in which a given individual can act. It is obviously in evidence as a mark of temperament, physical welfare, motivation, and skill and deserves the most careful consideration in the selection and training of musical talent. The highest speed on reliable record for the simplest form of tapping is about 12 taps per second, although rates as high as 15 have been reported.

8

TIMBRE: WAVE FORM

THIS chapter and the next will deal with the broad subject of tone quality. In nature and in art, we find an almost infinite series of varieties of tone quality; and yet it is possible to discover in them a fundamental and relatively simple basis for their classification and description. Indeed, it is possible in the laboratory to produce a million variations in the quality of a tone, any one of which can be described in physical terms so accurately that it can be reproduced with precision by a tone generator.

Tone quality has two fundamental aspects, namely, (1) timbre, which is the simultaneous presence or fusion of the fundamental and its overtones at a given moment, and (2) sonance, the successive presence or fusion of changing timbre, pitch, and intensity in a tone as a whole. The first may be called simultaneous fusion; the second, successive. Each of these may be reduced to the constituent factors which are recordable and measurable and, from the physical point of view, represent the structure of the tone. The present chapter will be devoted to the study of timbre and the next to sonance. Chapter 17 is devoted entirely to illustrations of the timbre of band and orchestral instruments and should, therefore, be read in connection with the present chapter.

THE NATURE OF TIMBRE

Tones may occur in all degrees of complexity from a pure tone, sounded by a tuning fork, up to the chaotic sound mass which we call noise. In musical tones, there is a definite relationship among the various groups of vibrations which give richness to the tone. This relationship is well illustrated in the case of the violin string.

The open string vibrates as a whole. This represents the fundamental pitch of the tone. It also vibrates in a series of parts, each part representing an overtone. Thus, a string vibrates in halves, giving us the first overtone; it also vibrates in thirds, giving us the second overtone. Each string also vibrates in four equal segments, giving us the third overtone; and in five segments, giving us the fourth overtone.

In this series, we notice the simple order that the first overtone is twice the frequency of the fundamental; the second overtone is three times, the third overtone is four times, the fourth overtone is five times the frequency of the fundamental, etc. As we have seen in Chap. 2, in physics we speak of the same phenomenon in terms of partials. If the partials are in a harmonic series they may be spoken of as harmonics. Since the fundamental is called the first partial in physics, each partial is always one number higher than the corresponding overtone. The ordinal number of a partial always corresponds with the number of segments vibrating for a given frequency; whereas, the ordinal number of an overtone corresponds with the number of nodes in the string or other vibrating media.

A tone is rich according to the relative number and prominence of overtones. The beauty of the violin consists mainly in the richness and balance of its overtones. This may be illustrated with a series of tuning forks which are tuned in a harmonic series in which each fork represents a partial. We can vary the tone by varying the number of forks sounded and the degree of force applied to each fork. When we take an oscillogram of any such tone, analysis will tell us which forks were sounded and how loud each fork was in relation to the total tone.

Insofar as we are dealing with a musical tone, aside from its accessory noises or other disturbing elements, we have a simple system which enables us to speak quantitatively in terms of these components, employing exact and definable terminology. Be it the tone of the prima donna, the harp, the drum, the sighing of the wind, or the hum of the motor, it is described adequately by stating the components which may be derived by an analysis of the form of the sound wave.

In general, we may say that, aside from accessory noises and inharmonic elements, the timbre of a tone depends upon (1) the number of harmonic partials present, (2) the relative location or locations of these partials in the range from the lowest to the highest, and (3) the relative strength or dominance of each partial. We have, thus, not only a faithful photograph of the sound wave, immediately verifiable and identifiable, but also a quantitative analysis of its components and, therefore, a language which becomes the basis for musical terminology that is exact, verifiable, and uniform for all lands and times.

Putting all these facts together, we obtain a definition of timbre as follows: Timbre is that characteristic of a tone which depends upon its harmonic structure as modified by absolute pitch and total intensity. The harmonic structure is expressed in terms of the number, distribution, and relative intensity of its partials. Recent experiments show that we must also take phase relations into account. Physically the timbre of the tone is a cross section of the tone quality for the moment represented by the duration of one vibration in the sound.

This array of facts may seem appalling, but, if examined in detail, the scheme is found to be comparatively simple, convincing, and complete. Compare this scientific procedure with the conventional use of terms descriptive of tone quality, even in the most serious instruction or musical criticism! Our terminology must be lifted out of the chaos which now prevails in the direction of a more and more scientific terminology for the art.

HARMONIC ANALYSIS

As was intimated in Chap. 2, we can intercept any sound wave with a device called an "oscillograph" and by its use secure a faithful and detailed picture of the form of the wave. The harmonic structure, as just explained, is obtained by accurate measurements upon the form of such a wave. It is based upon a mathematical formula called Fourier's theorem.

It has long been known that the form of a sound wave can be analyzed into its harmonic components. This is a broad principle applying to the analysis of the waves of the ocean, periodicity in the movement of the heavenly bodies, and the hum of machinery. But we are here concerned with the musical tone. Those who are interested in the technicalities of this measurement must turn to treatises on that subject. Suffice it to say that modern science has devised mechanical instruments which make this analysis of the sound wave more or less automatically.

It is only in recent years that the oscillograph has been perfected so as to produce a faithful wave form, suitable for accurate

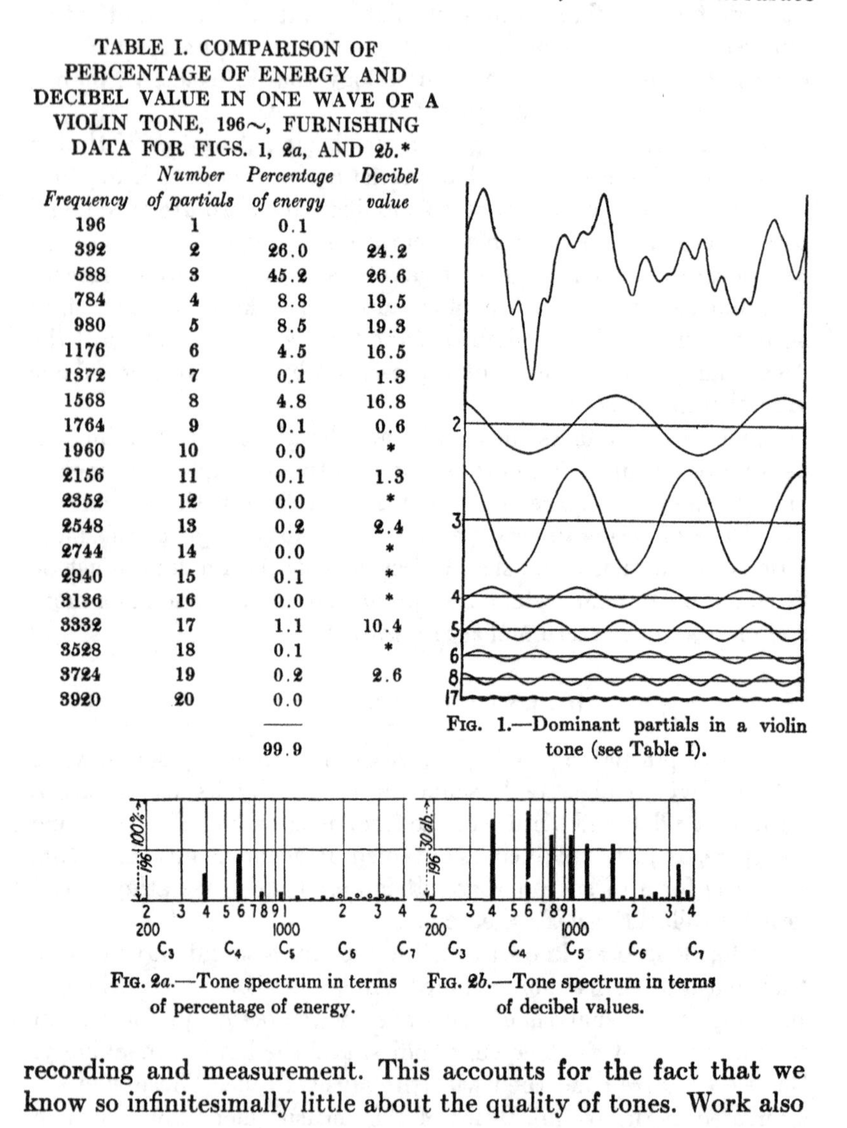

TABLE I. COMPARISON OF PERCENTAGE OF ENERGY AND DECIBEL VALUE IN ONE WAVE OF A VIOLIN TONE, 196~, FURNISHING DATA FOR FIGS. 1, 2a, AND 2b.*

Frequency	*Number of partials*	*Percentage of energy*	*Decibel value*
196	1	0.1	
392	2	26.0	24.2
588	3	45.2	26.6
784	4	8.8	19.5
980	5	8.5	19.3
1176	6	4.5	16.5
1372	7	0.1	1.3
1568	8	4.8	16.8
1764	9	0.1	0.6
1960	10	0.0	*
2156	11	0.1	1.3
2352	12	0.0	*
2548	13	0.2	2.4
2744	14	0.0	*
2940	15	0.1	*
3136	16	0.0	*
3332	17	1.1	10.4
3528	18	0.1	*
3724	19	0.2	2.6
3920	20	0.0	
		99.9	

FIG. 1.—Dominant partials in a violin tone (see Table I).

FIG. 2a.—Tone spectrum in terms of percentage of energy.

FIG. 2b.—Tone spectrum in terms of decibel values.

recording and measurement. This accounts for the fact that we know so infinitesimally little about the quality of tones. Work also

* The partials marked * in the table fall below the 30 db range. The short partials representing them, therefore, merely indicate the presence of relatively insignificant partials.

has been delayed because the analysis of a single wave in accordance with the mathematical theorem is extremely elaborate and time consuming.

There are now various forms of analyzers on the market. Of these the Henrici harmonic analyzer illustrated in the frontispiece is perhaps the best. In a nutshell, the process of harmonic analysis involves the following steps: Sound waves are recorded from a high-speed oscillograph on a moving-picture film. From this film a desired wave is selected and enlarged to the length of 40 centimeters by means of a projection apparatus. This enlarged wave form is laid on the platform in front of the analyzer and the experimenter moves a tracing point over the exact contour of the wave. As this is done, the machine accumulates on a series of dials a record of the presence of each partial in figures from which the exact amount of energy in each partial may be computed.

The principle of harmonic analysis may be illustrated in a concrete case represented in Fig. 1. The top wave is a tracing of a single wave in the oscillogram for a violin tone on the open G string played with medium intensity. The great irregularity in this wave is an indication of the prominence of its overtones. This wave was analyzed up to 20 partials.

The third column in Table I shows the percentage of energy in each partial. If we disregard those partials which carry only 1 per cent or less of the energy as relatively insignificant, there remain seven which are the components that in the main determine the timbre of the tone. Thus, even the first partial, the fundamental, is relatively insignificant and the body of the tone lies in seven partials. These seven are represented in the individual curves below the original wave. The number of each partial is indicated at the left, and the relative amount of energy is indicated by the relative amplitude of each wave. We may think of the total tone as being made up of so many partials sounded together as individual pure tones.

Figure 2*a* is a graphic representation of the data in the third column of Table I in the form of a tone spectrum in which each vertical bar indicates the percentage of energy in a given partial in terms of the height of the bar. Circles indicate the absence of a partial; frequencies are given at the bottom.

However, for the purpose of psychology of music and acoustics in general, the graphs become more significant if they are expressed in terms of decibels instead of percentage of energy, because the unit of decibels is on a logarithmic scale and indicates degree of perceptibility. The fourth column of Table I gives the decibel values corresponding to the data in column three. These are represented in the spectrum of *2b*. In this figure the plat of the spectrum is laid out for a scale of 30 db, in which the intensity of the partial is represented by the height of the bar above an arbitrary reference level, indicated by the base line. If there should be only one partial present, the height of that bar would present the magnitude of total intensity for the tone.

For practical purposes, all the reader needs to think of is that the significance of a partial is expressed in terms of the relative height of a bar.

Here, then, we have in the table and the three figures a fairly complete picture of the timbre of the tone under consideration. Figure 1 shows how the form of a sound wave is determined by the number, the distribution, the intensity, and the phase relationships of the component partials. The difference between spectra *2a* and *2b* is that the former represents percentage of physical energy of a partial, whereas the latter represents the degree of perceptibility of each partial. The two spectra differ very materially in the proportions of the partials. In *2b*, partial 17 is given considerable significance, and the thirteenth and the nineteenth partials gather a higher rating than in *2a*. It is evident that the degree of perceptibility in terms of decibels is more significant than in the percentage of energy. The decibel type of spectrum will be used in the following chapters.

In the early stages of our work in the psychology of music, we fully realized the importance of exact measurement of timbre but said for many years that we could pass that up for the next generation. In the last few years, however, the development of the oscillograph, with microphones that give a linear response, and the improvement of harmonic analyzers have opened up this field. It is the most fascinating of all fields in the psychology of music, for exact scientific work which has the most far-reaching significance in the understanding of music, musical education, the evaluation and construction of musical instruments, and musical criticism. It certainly is one of four cornerstones of the psychology of musical esthetics. But for the reason stated, this is all a virgin field, quite uncharted but certain to be explored and possessed by the musical world in the immediate future.

Fundamentally, all musical instruments, including the human voice, tend to produce tones composed of a series of partials whether the tone originates from a string, a reed, a column of air, or any other sound-producing movement. Ordinarily, however, the pure harmonic structure is supplemented by accessory noises and inharmonic elements which add to the quality of the tone. These, such as the accessory noises accompanying a piano tone or the rasping of the violin bow, may in turn be measured and added to our description of the timbre of the tone.

To be able to describe a tone in terms of such procedure represents a great achievement and triumph for the science of music, but even with the best of instruments it is a slow procedure. It is not necessary that the musician perform this experiment, or even that he should understand the mathematics and physics underlying the principle. What is essential for the musician is that he should acquire a clean-cut concept of the structure of the tone and that he should learn to think of a rich musical tone in terms of partials, that is, the number present, their distribution, and their relative intensities. When such terminology is once accepted, his trained ear may enable him to hear and name the dominant characteristics of a tone. To lay foundations for this type of understanding and terminology we shall consider a series of illustrations from instruments and voice in later chapters.

SYNTHETIC TONES

Harmonic tones of any timbre may be produced by the Iowa tone generator recently designed by *Larsen* and *Kurtz*.[68, 72] This is not the place for a technical account of the construction of a tone generator; but it may be pointed out that with this specific generator we can produce thousands of different tones and for each one we can say exactly what is the fundamental frequency, what partials are present, what percentage of energy is in each partial, what is the phase relationship of each wave. Such a generator may be thought of as producing one note in an electrical organ in which each key of the organ may have the resources that this generator has for a single tone. A series of stops have been designed to control for each key as many types of tonal timbre as may be desired.

TIMBRE DISCRIMINATION: THE SENSE OF TIMBRE

As a result of the developments just described, we now are able to produce and standardize measurements of talent for the hearing of timbre differences and natural capacity for rendering timbre musically.

The "Sense of Timbre" record in the new series of *Measures of Musical Talent* is designed for tests in schools and other groups to determine quickly what centile rank in the sense of timbre each person tested can gain. Preliminary tests indicate that there will be large individual differences, perhaps comparable to those in the sense of pitch, but the test may not be quite so elemental as the measurements for pitch and intensity.

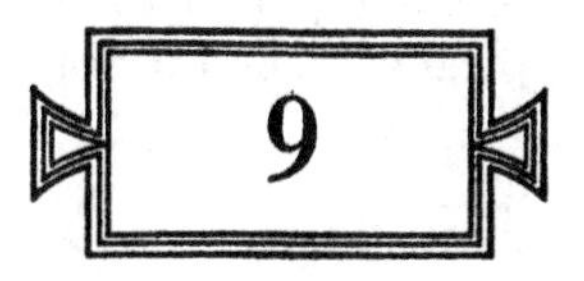

TONE QUALITY: SONANCE

THE term "sonance" was coined in our music laboratory in order to provide a specific name for the successive changes and fusions which take place within a tone from moment to moment. It was first used by *Metfessel*.[62] The need and significance of such a concept had not been fully realized before objective analysis of tones was undertaken.

ANALOGY IN MOVING PICTURES

We may illustrate the nature of sonance through an analogy. Suppose we throw on the screen a single picture at the rate of 20 or 30 exposures per second; the picture we see then will stand still and have every appearance of being a single continuous picture because the successive snapshots fuse. If, then, we project a series of pictures of objects in motion under the same conditions, the successive snapshots will again fuse; and the resulting picture will reproduce the actual motion of the object. At no moment do we see any single exposure.

The position, form, color, and even relief may be reproduced true to life as a result of the fusion of impressions in the eye.

The same principle of fusion appears in hearing. In tonal hearing, successive waves come so fast that they cannot be heard as individual waves; that is, we cannot separate the timbre or the pitch or the intensity in one wave from that in the next wave by hearing. The result is that they fuse and for a given period of time, the mean period for clear perception, we hear a resultant pitch, intensity, or timbre which tends to be an average for what is represented in the series of waves that can be grasped in one moment of perception. The timbre of a tone corresponds to the single instantaneous picture; sonance corresponds to the picture progression. Let us examine a few typical cases in order to learn the significance of this principle.

TYPES OF SONANCE

Sonance in the vibrato. In Chap. 4 we learned that no good singer ever sings in steady pitch. The most outstanding ornament is the vibrato. The tone shows a periodic oscillation in frequency covering, for example, a half tone in extent at the rate of 6 or 7 times per second; yet we hear in it a relatively even pitch. This pitch represents an approximate average between the extremes in the pulsation and is the result of the tendency of successive vibrato waves to fuse.

The same principle applies to the intensity pulsations and timbre pulsations in the same sound. We tend to hear a unified, single, fairly steady tone which is, however, the resultant of a very complicated series of pulsations. We hear a rich, musical, and fairly steady tone which, through the pulsation, acquires the three characteristic tone qualities of flexibility, richness, and tenderness.

Sonance in erratic fluctuations. In the typical performance scores shown in this volume the fluctuation of pitch and intensity is smoothed out so as to show approximately what we hear.

In very detailed recording an oscillogram shows large and irregular differences in the length (reciprocal of frequency) of successive sound waves, both for voice and for instrument. The more detailed, the more ragged the record will appear. Instead of bringing this out in performance scores, our recording instruments and the methods of reading are so adapted as to smooth out these wave-to-wave fluctuations and give us a graph which corresponds approximately to what is significant musically and what is heard as pitch. This roughness in frequency, however, contributes to sonance as the quality of a tone varies with the degree of roughness.

Sonance in progressive change. There is a third type of fusion which tends to blot out fast progressive changes in the pitch, intensity, or timbre of a tone which are not periodic. The fusion in this case is analogous to the fusion of the vibrato, except that we are not hearing a periodic change which has musical merit, but rather an erratic intonation or rough tone within a narrow range. The result is that we may credit a tone with being correct in each of the three elements while objective analysis will show that there is a great variety of minor changes from moment to moment in the tone.

Another aspect of the same principle is shown in the case of progressive change which we note, for example, in the songs here recorded. There may be a gradual simple or complex rise or fall in pitch or in intensity which is clearly heard as such. Although the objective record shows rough jags in both pitch and intensity curves, these are blotted out, and what we hear is the general rising or falling tendency in the mass of the tone as a whole.

The same principle applies to intensity: the intensity fluctuates from wave to wave in various degrees, but, in the recording and graphing of performance, we have retained only as much of this roughness as is significant for the hearing of the intensity of the tone. Yet the degree of roughness of this sort is a significant determinant of the tone quality of sonance. The same principle applies also to timbre irregularities.

SONANCE IN ATTACK, RELEASE, AND PORTAMENTO

Figure 1 shows a group of typical attacks of vocal tones in intonation. Here not only the vibrato and the wave-to-wave irregularity but a steep rising or falling of the body of the tone as a whole is a striking characteristic. All these changes tend to fuse, so that if the attack is short the tone is heard as if attacked on an even pitch or intensity; but if it is comparatively long, what we hear is a clear-cut rapid rise or fall of the mass of the tone as a whole.

The principles here illustrated for the attack apply also to the portamento, as has been shown by *Harold Seashore*[155] for voice and by *Small*[166] for violin. They apply also to the release that becomes a part of the portamento. But the free release of a tone tends to be relatively even, that is, free from a glide, although there is a tendency toward a downward glide.

A very interesting adaptation has taken place in the evolution of the attack. *Lewis* and *Cowan*[80] took phonograph records of attacks like those in Fig. 1, varying in length and duration of the glide, and reversed them so that the gliding attack became a release and the even release became an attack. The musically acceptable glide at the beginning of the tone became utterly intolerable when placed at the end of the tone. This experiment opens a very fertile field for the investigation of reasons for adaptive or habitual hearing.

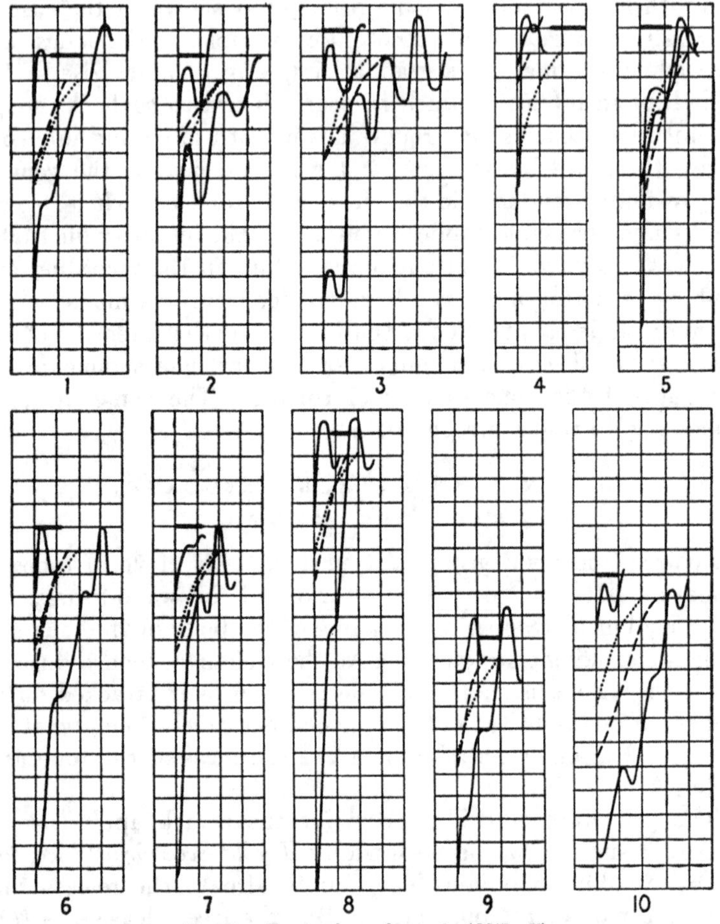

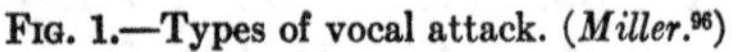

FIG. 1.—Types of vocal attack. (*Miller.*[96])

The dash line shows the form of the average gliding attack for each song; the dot line the average form for all these songs. The top curve represents the shortest sweep of attack; the lower, the longest sweep. The horizontal heavy dash line at the top represents the true pitch of the main body of the tone as approached by either the smallest or the largest glide. Horizontal spaces represent time in 0.1 second, and the vertical spaces represent pitch in 0.1 tone.

1, Alma Gluck; 2, Frances Alda; 3, Rosa Ponselle; 4 and 5, Galli-Curci; 6, 7, 8, and 9, Enrico Caruso; 10, Theodore de Lay.

Sonance in subjective tones. As we saw in Chap. 5, subjective tones play an important part in musical hearing. These shift in

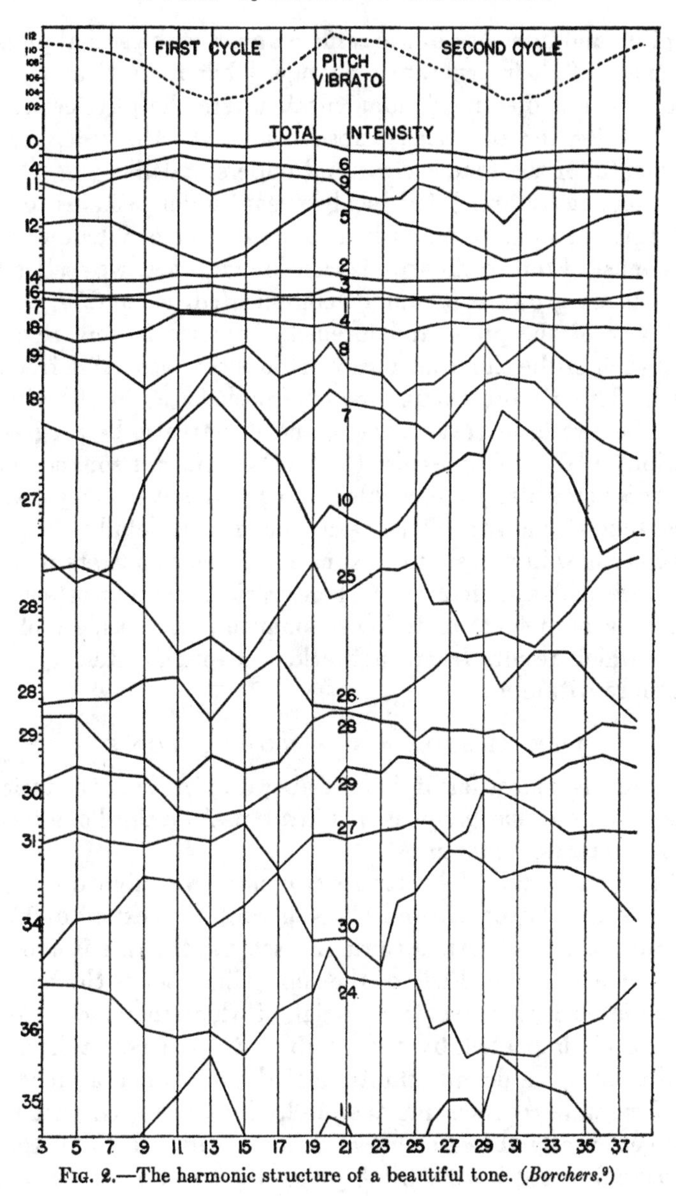

FIG. 2.—The harmonic structure of a beautiful tone. (*Borchers.*[9])

both pitch and intensity in the same manner as the actual physical frequencies of their generators change. That is particularly conspicuous in a subjective fundamental, where the physical fundamental is low or practically absent and yet the pitch of the fundamental of the tone is clear and understandable.

Sonance in timbre. What has been said so far pertains to pitch or intensity in a pure tone, or in a tone as a whole. When we recall that a musical tone ordinarily is rich in overtones, we realize that here sonance grows exceedingly complicated, as in Fig. 2. The complexity of the pitch and intensity sonance is here revealed, in that each of the simultaneous overtones behaves like a free tone in itself. This timbre change may be periodic as in the vibrato. It may be erratic in various ways, and it may also be progressive in various ways. This presents the most significant sonance musically. It is particularly noticeable in the progressive changes within a vocal tone which we shall now examine in some detail.

We are now in a position to sum up, in some concrete pictures, the nature and significance of these various aspects of sonance, which may be defined as follows: sonance is that aspect of tone quality which results from fluctuations in pitch, intensity, time, and timbre within a tone.

THE INSIDE OF A VOCAL TONE

Figure 2 is a most faithful and elaborate picture of the inside of a tone. It shows what happens within a tone for a third of a second. Let us enumerate its features.

The pitch vibrato. The tone represents two vibrato cycles in pitch moving between 103 and 112~, giving us an extent of 0.7 of a tone. Since this tone lasts a third of a second, the rate is about six pulsations per second. Each of the zigzag lines below the base line for total intensity represents a partial, of which there are 18 represented, each indicated by its number. Now, since a harmonic partial is always a definite multiple of the fundamental, it follows that, if we were representing the pitch vibrato in each partial, we would get exactly the same curve as for the fundamental; that is, each partial would have a pitch pulsation 0.7 of a tone in extent and at the rate of six pulsations per second.

The graph for each partial being exactly the same as that given at the top for the fundamental, which is the same as for the tone as a whole, it would have cluttered our figure to draw in all these identical graphs. The reader is, therefore, asked to imagine the complete system of pitch vibratos in these cycles by remembering that they are present in every partial. The situation is the same as if 18 individual pure tones were played simultaneously with the same vibrato. This gives us an enriched conception of the harmonious movements of every partial in the production of a pitch vibrato in a clear tone.

Relative dominance of partials. The tonal intensity of the tone is represented by the first line marked total intensity, that is, the loudness of the tone as a whole. In order to simplify the presentation, a tone was selected in which the total intensity is relatively even and in which there is no intensity vibrato.

The intensity level of each partial is inversely proportional to its distance away from the zero line, which represents total intensity; that is, the intensity of a partial is represented by the number of decibels by which it is less intense than the tone as a whole. The numbers at the left show for each partial the mean level of the intensity for that partial for the duration of a third of a second, as just stated in terms of how many db it is weaker than the tone as a whole. The up-and-down zigzag in each partial shows the fluctuation in intensity during this third of a second. Only the odd-numbered waves in the tone were analyzed. The numbers at the bottom represent the assigned numbers of these.

Let us notice first the relative dominance of the partials. The sixth partial is the strongest. Next to that is the ninth and next to that the fifth. These three dominate and give the general character to the tone. Then follow the second and third partials. The first partial, which is the fundamental of the tone, holds sixth place; that is, it is not prominent. Below these follow in order the weaker partials as numbered. The lower down below the mean intensity a partial is, the less it contributes toward this total intensity. Yet all are significantly present.

The intensity vibrato. As just stated, we selected a tone which had no intensity vibrato in the tone as a whole. Yet some of the curves for these partials show a distinct intensity vibrato. The tenth partial, for example, represents a marked rise and fall for each vibrato cycle. The twenty-fifth partial is the reverse, falling and rising for each vibrato cycle. The thirtieth partial parallels the tenth, and the twenty-fourth parallels the twenty-fifth; the fifth parallels the twenty-fifth, and the seventh parallels the tenth.

It is this pairing of the intensity vibratos in the partials that obliterates the effect of the intensity vibrato on the tone as a whole. It is clear, therefore, that while the tone as a whole is of even intensity some of its partials show very distinct intensity vibratos, and the even intensity of the tone as a whole is accounted for by the opposition among pairs of the partials. An intensity vibrato in a rich tone results when a number of the leading partials are in the same phase and, therefore, cooperate instead of counteract.

Changing spectra. To simplify the figure we analyzed only every other wave, the odd numbered. The spectrum for each of these waves, as numbered at the bottom, is seen by the intersection of the partial line with the vertical line above the number designating the wave. Bear in mind that the relative strength of each partial is designated by the number of db by which it is weaker than the total intensity of the tone. It is easy to imagine a bar spectrum in which the sixth partial is the longest, the ninth the next, and so on, down to the higher partials, which represent comparatively small amounts of energy. For each of these spectra we know the fundamental pitch, the pitch of each partial, and the relative amount of energy in each partial.

The meaning of sonance. To return to our analogy of moving pictures, each of these spectra represents an instantaneous picture defining the timbre of the tone at that point. The progressive change of spectra from wave to wave represents the character and the movement of all the elements which fuse, just as form and movement are expressed in a moving picture. Therefore, in order to give a complete description of the quality of a tone it is evident that we must know the spectrum of each wave at representative stages and the character of the change in spectra which takes place for the duration of the tone.

This is not all that our picture shows, but it is enough to indicate what sort of questions a musician may ask and answer in terms of this type of analysis. To repeat, our simplified scheme is this: in our experience of hearing and feeling of tone, the sonance depends upon the three factors of pitch, intensity, and timbre in the change from wave to wave and from vibrato cycle to vibrato cycle. In a secondary way, we might add to these factors the rate of change. The psychological result of a complex situation of this kind we may call a "tonal band," consisting of a certain range or massiveness of pitch, intensity, and timbre changes, with vanishing and irregular fringes of each. When, as in this case, 18 variable tones impinge upon the physical ear, we do not hear the details, but we hear tone quality. This tone quality may be either musically agreeable or disagreeable. If the changes are strong and irregular, we get the quality of roughness. If they are smooth and moderate, we may get the qualities of flexibility, tenderness, and richness of tone.

There are two outstanding aspects of this phenomenon of sonance, one of mental economy and the other esthetic. The fusion which we have described represents economy in perception. We have developed the power to preserve enough detail of irregularities in a tone to give it musical unity. Nature has been satisfied with this power, although it is quite conceivable that the human mind should have developed the power to hear in detail a very large portion of these irregularities in tone. The other aspect is that this phenomenon is necessary in order to give the tone its beauty as a musical meaning. The habitual perception of fine details would take the most desirable musical quality out of tone. Sonance is, therefore, in the process of evolution, a result of the principle of economy in perception and the adaptation of these economies to the demands of beauty and efficiency in music and speech.

WHAT IS IN A NAME?

It is recommended that musicians scrap a mass of the current synonyms for tone quality, because these words do not connote any demonstrable differences in content. The diversity of words simply adds to the confusion. "Tone quality" is a term which is adequate and clearly defined, and has the same meaning in music and all the sciences of tone. When we wish to distinguish between its two aspects, a cross section of the tone and the whole tone, we have the two adequately defined terms, "timbre" and "sonance"; but for most musical purposes in daily use, the generic term, "tone quality," should be used in the technical sense of sonance.

SONANCE IN SPEECH

Musicians would find very illuminating reading in the elaborate recordings of artistic speech by *Cowan*.[14] Figure 3 is a fair sample. In order to realize its significance, it is suggested that this speech be read aloud without any thought of, or reference to, the graph, and that each word and phrase be repeated for direct comparison between hearing and the speech performance score. This record is full of exceedingly interesting information, but at this point it is

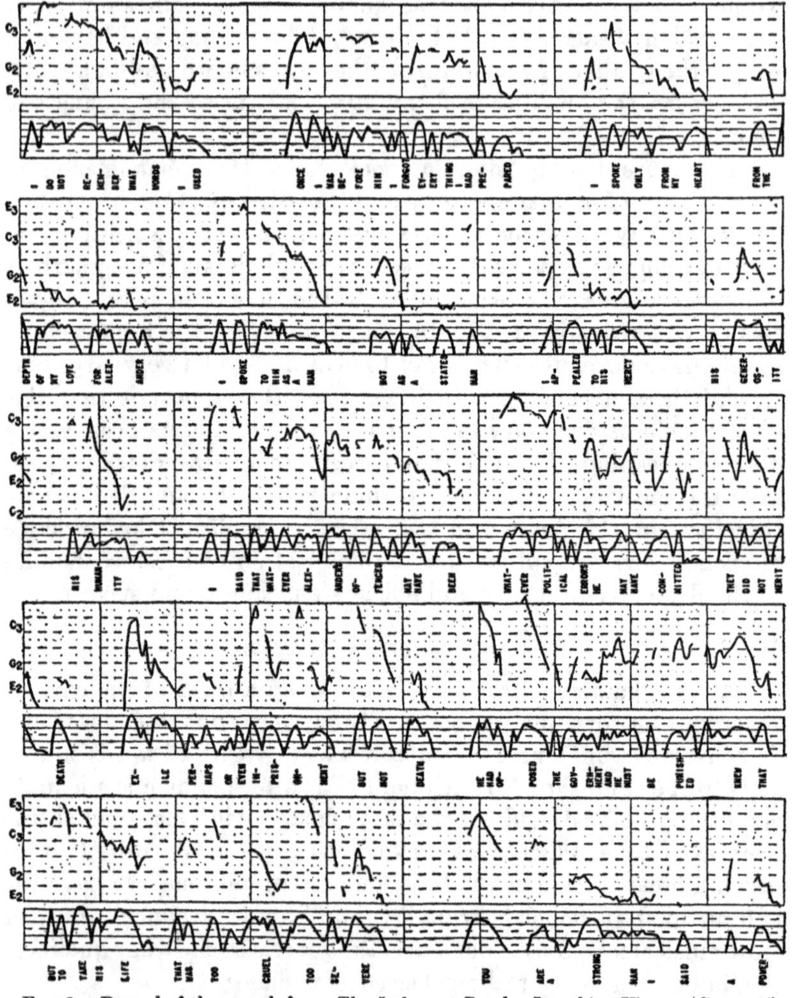

FIG. 3.—Record of the speech from *The Judgment Day* by Josephine Victor. (*Cowan.*[14])
The pitch, time, and intensity record in this graph is analogous to a performance score in music.

introduced only to show how sonance operates in beautiful speech. Aside from tone quality, beauty in speech consists in large part of fine pitch inflection and dynamic expression in rhythmic measure with effective pauses, all represented in the graph. The observation suggested will reveal that we do not hear the numerous fine pitch and intensity fluctuations represented in the graph. We hear a smooth inflection of pitch and smooth points of emphasis in intensity. Yet these graphs, like our music graphs, are already smoothed so as to eliminate the roughness represented by fluctuations from wave to wave.

From this dynamic record it is easy to see its analogy in song. In artistic qualities they are parallel and closely related; but the fusion which takes place is greater in speech than in music, because ordinarily speech is more rapid.

NATURE OF THE VOWEL IN MUSIC AND SPEECH

As was intimated in Chap. 2, music and speech involve fundamentally the same problems, with but minor adaptations. Measurements are made with the same instruments, by the same techniques, and in the same attitude toward science and art. Recognition of this fact has enabled us to effect many economies, to secure cooperative attitudes between departments, and to deepen our insight into the larger problem of the acoustic arts. Of this sort of participation, the study of the vowel is a good illustration.

The problem of the vowel is entirely a problem of tone quality. Whether it be in song or in speech, it is the vowel that furnishes the body of the quality of the sound. The vowel is, however, more sustained in music than in speech. In the remainder of this chapter we shall touch upon some of the fundamental aspects of the science of vowels.

Timbre and sonance in a vowel. *Black*[8] studied the pronunciation of the vowel "o" as pronounced in the word "top" in a conversational tone. In Fig. 4, we have the result of the effort of the same speaker to pronounce the vowel twice in the same way. This method of graphing was devised by *Tiffin*. In Fig. 5, we have comparative results of the pronunciation of the same vowel by two different speakers. In other words, we have here four pictures of the overtone structure, that is, the harmonic constitution of the same vowel under the conditions named.

Let us first consider the timbre. Each slanting line with its upright riders is a tone spectrum of the wave indicated by number at the bottom. The height of the vertical lines indicates the relative prominence of each of the respective partials represented in terms of decibels. In other respects the terminology in these figures is self-explanatory. In terms of these spectra we can see exactly what the structure of the vowel was from wave to wave.

The sonance is expressed in the progressive change in the timbre of these spectra in successive waves from the beginning of the vowel to the end. No two spectra are alike, yet there is an orderly progression from wave to wave.

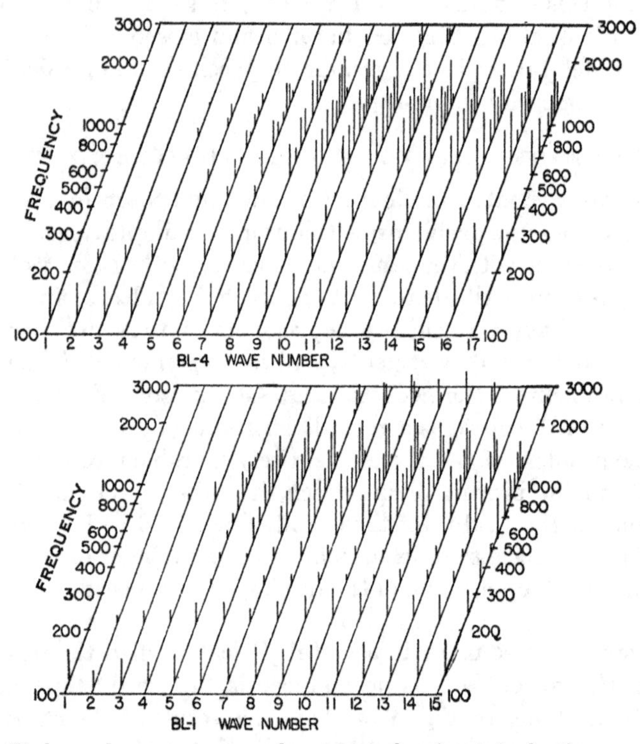

FIG. 4.—Timbre and sonance in a vowel; same vowel spoken twice by the same person. (*Black.*[8])

The principal lesson contained in these pictures is the fact that, in terms of the timbre spectrum of each wave and the progressive change from wave to wave in sonance, we have a complete description of this vowel in terms of which definitions may be formulated.

In an elementary way, these two figures show that probably no person can repeat the same vowel exactly the same way and no two persons can express the same vowel even after the best of efforts of standardization through phonetic definitions. Numerous other factors are illustrated in these graphs; but they must serve as merely samples of materials that may be treated statistically in analytical and qualitative terms. It will be very interesting to study graphs of this kind for each of the phonetic elements of each of the recognized variants of each vowel. Such studies will solve many of the profound mysteries about the vowel in music and speech and will have an immensely practical value in these arts.

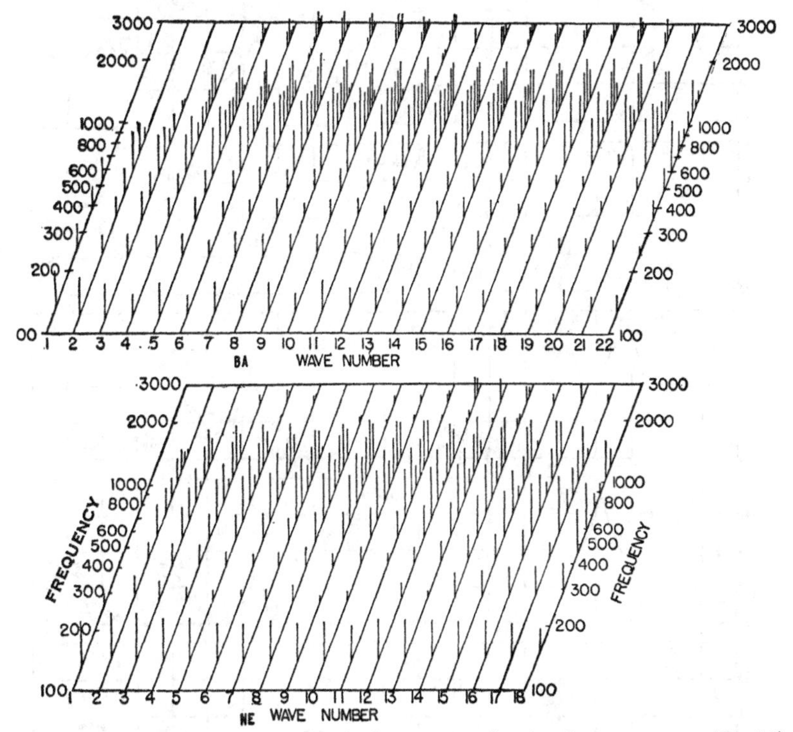

FIG. 5.—Timbre and sonance in a vowel; the same vowel spoken by two persons. (*Black.*[8])

THE PROBLEM OF FORMANT REGIONS

These pictures of the harmonic constitution of the vowel suggest that the distinction among all variants of each vowel is probably to be found in the number, location, and relative dominance of formants or formant regions, due consideration being given to fundamental pitch and total intensity and progressive change of the sound. There has been a long-standing controversy in regard to the nature and the stability of these formants in the vowels. In the older discussion, one party contended that each vowel has a fixed formant pattern which simply moves up or down with fundamental pitch. The other party contended that there are fixed formant regions due to resonance characteristics of the vocal cavities. The most recent investigations reveal a reasonable compromise

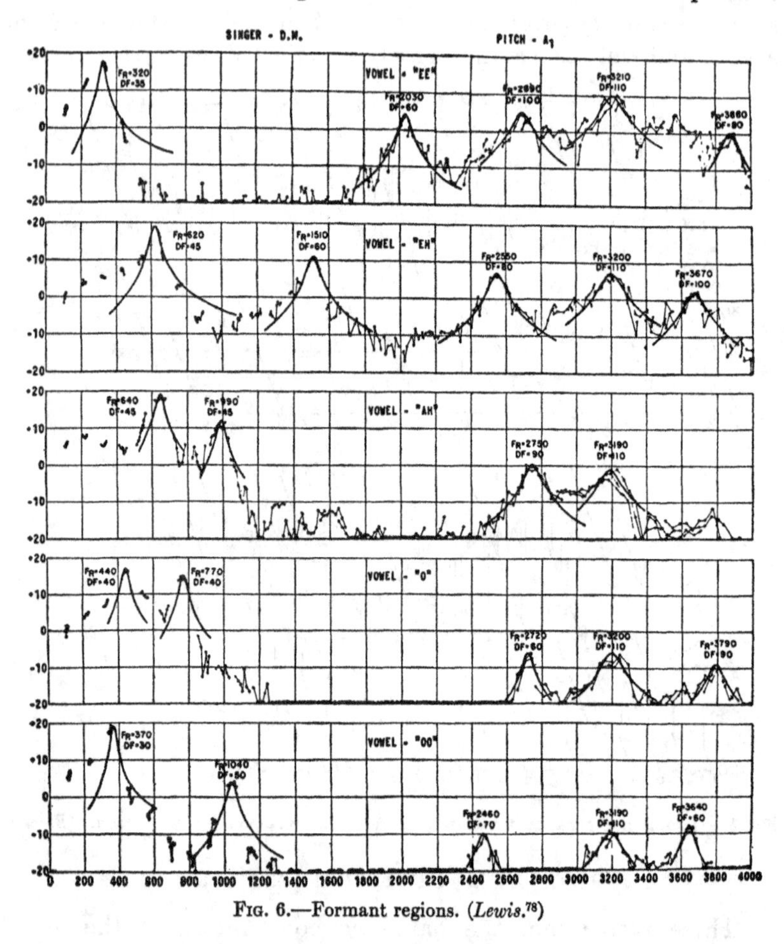

FIG. 6.—Formant regions. (*Lewis.*[78])

between the two contentions, the tendency being more in favor of the latter assumption. Some significance is also attached to the presence of inharmonic elements in the vowel. The current work of *Lewis*[78] may be taken to illustrate some elements and some findings in the problem. Figure 6 shows the record of a trained baritone singer intoning five different vowels at the frequency of A_1. The recording was done in the dead room and therefore is free from room resonance and outside sounds.

Frequency is given at the bottom and intensity at the side. Each dot represents one measurement. A smooth line is drawn through groups of these dots which seems to represent the peaks which we call resonant regions from the point of view of the resonators in the oral cavities, or formants from the point of view of the physical spectrum of the sound. The peak lines here used in attempting to get the best fit are, of course, merely "best approximations" by direct inspection to aid the eye in the identification of the peaks. The legend Fr 320∼, for example, indicates that the apex of this first formant in the first tone is at about 320∼. The DF is a technical measure which indicates the damping constant of the resonator. The zero for the decibel scale is an arbitrarily chosen mean intensity value from which decibels are indicated above and below.

With this orientation, we may see what this chart shows about the vowels. It so happens that each vowel has five formant regions, although there are two somewhat doubtful regions in the third vowel, namely, a third and a sixth. These regions are somewhat differently distributed for the different vowels. Only one formant, the fourth, at 3,200∼, is fairly fixed, as is indicated by the straight vertical column of these peaks. The first region varies from 320 in the first tone to 640 in the third tone, and the fifth region varies in about the same degree. The prominent second region in the first vowel and in the second vowel is absent in the other three vowels. In the last three vowels the second region is closer to the first. With possible theories in mind, the scientists will observe many other significant features in these records. The assumption underlying these figures is that the vocal cords generate the complex tone and that those groups of partials which fall within the natural resonance region of the oral cavity will be intensified. Variations of this sort would be expected even if we had a perfect series of resonators, but from this we should not conclude that the resonating regions in the vocal mechanism are fixed.

But the main thing that stands out in this illustration is the fact that the character of the vowel is determined primarily by the number, the position, the width, and the relative intensities of its formants.

This sample of a record illustrates the procedure which is being followed in trying to solve the problem of formant regions with all the intricate issues, theoretical and practical, involved therein. The problem of the vowel is simplified and brought under experimental control in this manner by our fundamental recognition of the fact that we have to deal with only the four attributes of the sound wave. The leading issues will hinge upon the roles of frequency, intensity, and time in the determination of formants which characterize each vowel. Let us see an example of what can be accomplished by varying the frequency and the intensity under control in an experiment.

DEPENDENCE OF HARMONIC STRUCTURE UPON FUNDAMENTAL PITCH AND TOTAL INTENSITY IN THE VOWEL

This problem was recently approached concurrently by *Laase*[71] and *Stout*,[187] one studying the spoken vowel and the other the sung vowel under analogous conditions. In order to make the results comparable, they proceeded by the same techniques of measurements and employed the same three vowels "AH," "EE," and "OO" recognized as the vowels placed at the corners of the vowel triangle by phoneticians. Trained speakers and musicians were employed as subjects. From *Laase's*[71] work we may take a sample illustration of the vowel "AH" pronounced like "o" in the word "top." Figure 7 is by this time self-explanatory.

Laase summarizes his harmonic analysis of 270 sound waves taken from 54 separate phonations representing 18 conditions of phonation for each of three subjects as follows:

1. Increases in intensity, pitch constant, are accompanied in every instance by increases in the percentage of energy in the higher partials.
2. Increases in pitch, intensity constant, with but three exceptions in 54 phonations, are accompanied by an increase in the amount of energy in the fundamental and a decrease in some of the higher partials.
3. There is a tendency for the number of energy regions to increase with a rise in intensity, pitch constant, and to decrease with a rise in pitch, intensity constant. This tendency may or may not be a function of these two variables.
4. The unsystematic action of the fundamental in successive waves seems to be related to the counteracting effects of increases in pitch and intensity.

5. The amount of energy in the fundamental seems to be more a function of the vowel than of either pitch or intensity. The fundamental is relatively less intense for the vowel "AH"

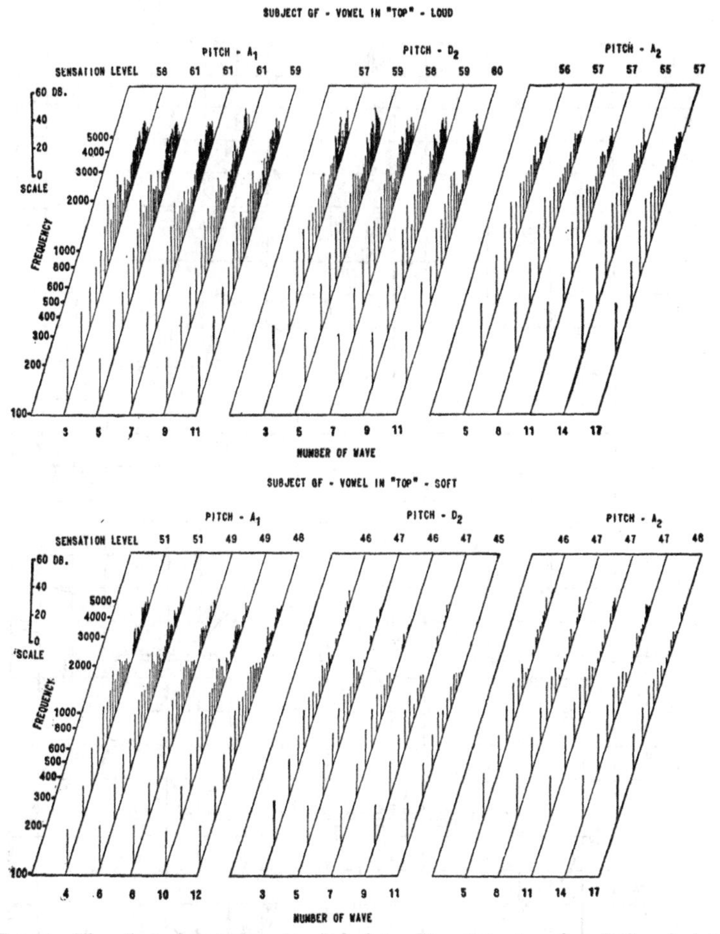

FIG. 7.—The effect of variations in pitch, intensity constant, and variations in intensity, pitch constant, on the harmonic composition of the vowel "AH" for subject GF. (*Laase.*[71])

than in the vowels "EE" and "OO" in which it is frequently the most intense partial in the wave.

6. No systematic variation was found in the direction of shift of the energy regions as a function of either pitch or intensity, indicating that the location of the energy regions is probably

more a function of the use of the resonators than of either pitch or intensity.

7. The characteristic energy regions found for the vowels in this study agree within limits with those reported by other

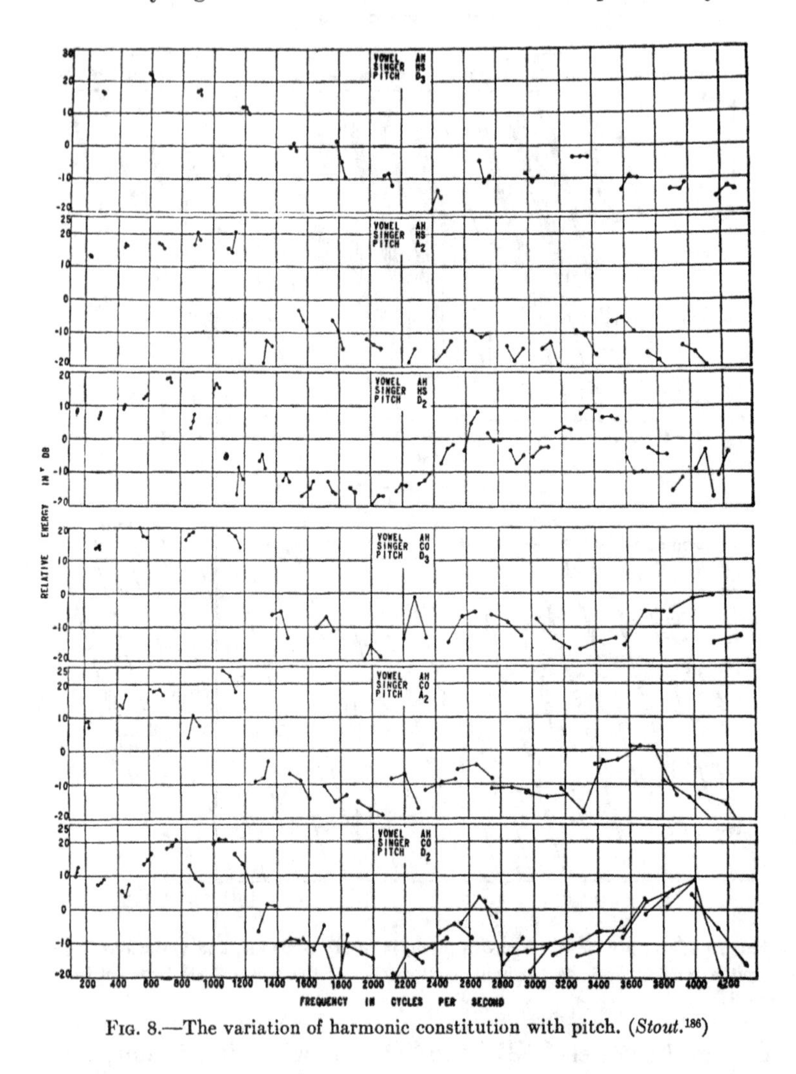

FIG. 8.—The variation of harmonic constitution with pitch. (*Stout.*[186])

investigators. The characteristic energy regions for "EE" and "OO" were very similar except for a difference in the amount of energy above 2,000∼.

8. As many as five energy regions were found in a number of the waves analyzed, suggesting the presence of five distinct vocal resonators which may influence the distribution of energy in any given phonation. There was no evidence to support the presence of fixed resonance regions from vowel to vowel.

9. The results tend to indicate that there can be considerable variation in the composition of the spoken vowel and the character of the vowel still be clearly recognizable.

Stout,[187] working under similar conditions with vocal tones which involved the vibrato, represented his results on the plan devised by *Lewis.*[78] Figure 8 is a sample of his record for the effect of varying pitch. Similar records were made for the effect of varying intensity. It is interesting to compare the findings on the sung vowel with the findings about the spoken vowel. We therefore quote *Stout's* summary as follows:

The results of the present study indicate (1) that the most important change in the harmonic structure of the vowels "AH," "OO" and "EE" which accompanies an increase in intensity, pitch remaining constant, is an enhancement of the relative importance of the partials lying above the frequency 1,800∼; (2) that this enhancement is greatest at the low pitch for the vowel "AH," greatest at the high pitch for vowel "EE" and about the same at all three pitches studied for vowel "OO"; (3) that the increase in total intensity is very slight for the vowel "AH," considerably more for the vowel "OO" and greatest for the vowel "EE." There were other changes which did not appear consistent enough to warrant any general statements.

The results of the study also indicate (1) that the most important change in the harmonic structure of the vowels "AH," "OO," and "EE" that occurs with a rise in pitch, intensity remaining constant, is a decrease in the relative intensity of the partials lying above the frequency 1,800∼; (2) that the contours outlining the intensity areas at frequencies 600 to 800∼ and 1,000 to 1,200∼ for the vowel "AH" appear to become less definitely two contours, the higher the pitch, until at the highest pitch they appear to have merged into one large contour; (3) that in the case of all three vowels, the fundamental appears to absorb a considerable part of the energy which has shifted from the high frequency regions to the low.

That there is no consistent change in frequency location of the major intensity areas with either an increase in total inten-

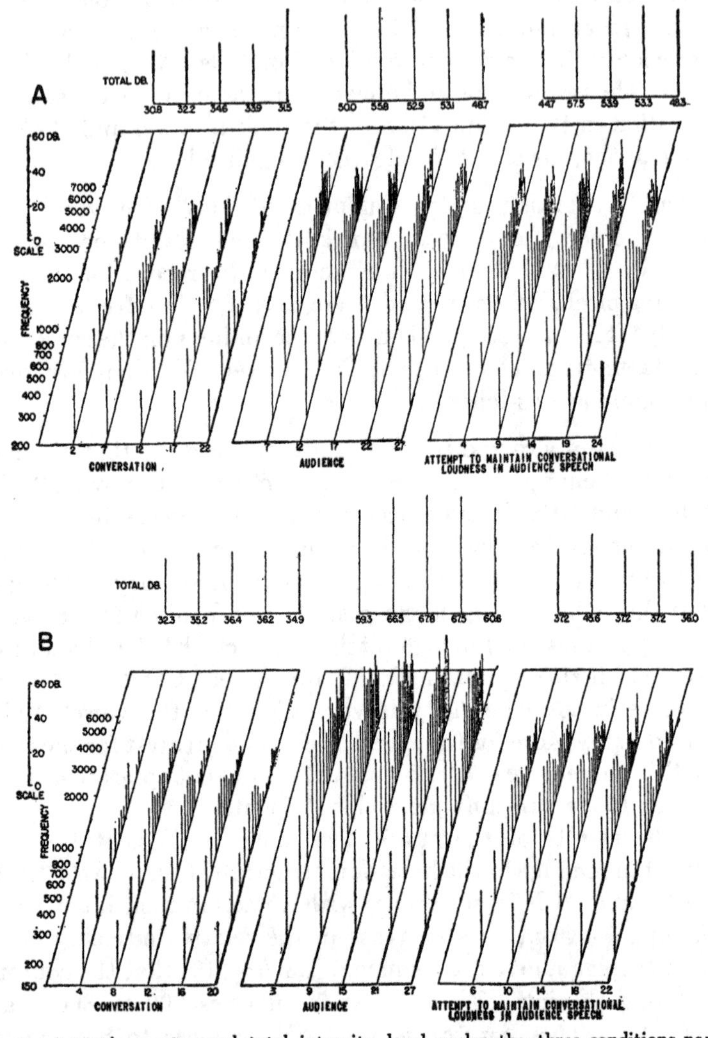

FIG. 9.—Acoustic spectra and total intensity level under the three conditions named. (*Talley.*[195])

sity or a rise in pitch is quite definitely indicated by the results of this study.

CONVERSATIONAL VERSUS AUDIENCE VOICE

Talley[195] has made a comprehensive study of the vowel structure in conversational speech as compared with speech before an audience. Figure 9 illustrates the principles of his comparisons. Working with the single vowel "AH" pronounced as in the word "top," he had trained speakers use this vowel in a sentence: (1) as in ordinary conversation, (2) as in addressing an audience of 2,000 people, and (3) in an effort to maintain conversational loudness before an audience. Typical findings are shown in Fig. 9. This opens a most important problem in speech; namely, the problem of carrying power in public address. *Talley* showed what characteristic changes the speakers made spontaneously. He summarizes his findings as follows:

1. There was no systematic variation in either intensity of the fundamental or duration of the vowel with the changes in conditions of recording the vowel.
2. There was a marked tendency to increase both pitch and intensity when a shift was made from conversation to audience speech.
3. There was a marked shift in relative intensity from the lower to the higher partials with the change from conversational to audience speech.
4. Attempts to speak as if to an audience, which were accompanied by only a small rise in total intensity, also evidenced a much less marked shift of energy into the higher partials.
5. Attempts to speak as if to an audience, which were accompanied by no rise in total intensity, showed no systematic variation in the harmonic composition of the vowel.
6. A loss of intensity during a vowel was accompanied by a greater loss of intensity in the upper partials than in the lower.

In general, when a speaker changed from conversational to the audience type of speech, three changes in the sound wave produced by his voice took place simultaneously, namely, heightened pitch, increased intensity, and a shift of energy from the lower to the higher partials. Although similar characteristic changes in sung tones have recently been observed, it does not seem possible at present to evaluate the relative importance of the three factors nor to state whether one element causally influences the other two.

The real problem raised by this investigation must be solved by an elaborate study of all the factors of the sound which we have now isolated and can control in order to determine the relative roles of each of these in determining the carrying power, sometimes called the projection of the sound. The singer of the future may look forward to acquaintance with a definite system of principles that should be followed in making the voice carry before an audience. This is not simply a problem of a performer but also of the composer and the writer of the words and for all is ultimately a problem of tone quality.

CONSONANCE

THE NATURE OF CONSONANCE

THE theories of melody and harmony represent by far the most highly developed fields in the history of musical literature. They have also attracted the serious attention of mathematicians, physicists, anthropologists, and psychologists in the scientific laboratories. The history of music is written largely in terms of scales or musical modes, showing the development of the concept of intervals from period to period. The most interesting aspect in the field of musical anthropology has centered around the problem of the evolution of scales and the attempt to explain why they have arisen, why they have survived in such great variety, and what their interrelations are in the family tree of musical modes.

Harmony as we now think of it is of comparatively recent origin. Its precursor and present companion piece is melody. The basic principles which now function in harmony were first developed in the theory and practice of melody. It would be extremely interesting if space could be devoted to a chapter on the origin and evolution of melody because in that we should see the foundations of harmony in the process of evolution. The underlying conception, common to both, is that of the interval. The title of this chapter might, therefore, well be The Interval; but in scientific procedure, where we always reduce the situation to its simplest elements, it is customary to speak of the problem in terms of kinds and degrees of consonance. The difference between harmony and consonance is that consonance deals with intervals in terms of two notes only; whereas harmony usually deals with more complex situations. The difference between consonance and melody is that consonance deals with simultaneous tones in a dichord; whereas, melody deals with sequence of tones.

Consonance depends fundamentally upon the degree of coincidence of sound waves. This led very early to the mathematical theories based on this physical fact. In the main this is correct and applies in large part to all scales; but there are very important exceptions, so that no such simple rule can be applied throughout to determine the degree of consonance or dissonance. Coming out of the vast network of modifications of this principle, modern Western music is built largely on the diatonic scale in major and minor modes. The ratios of successive notes to the tonic in the major mode are 9:8, 5:4, 4:3, 3:2, 5:3, 15:8, and 2:1. In the minor mode the corresponding ratios are 9:8, 6:5, 4:3, 3:2, 8:5, 9:5, and 2:1.

According to present conventions, this natural scale represents the most desirable intervals; but in the construction of keyed instruments, it was necessary to make a compromise on the 12 half-tone steps in order to make it possible to play in different keys on the same instrument, such as the piano. This modified scale is known as the "tempered scale." The relation of the natural scale to the tempered scale is shown in Table I.[1a]

THE PSYCHOLOGICAL APPROACH

We now recognize the following approaches to the problem: (1) The spontaneous outcropping of intervals among primitive peoples throughout the world and their gradual empirical development in various culture stages up to the present, all in the absence of theory. (2) The development of technical theory, since the time of ancients, on the part of musicians, largely as an empirical adjustment of the early-recognized mathematical ratios in terms of feeling values. This has resulted in principles of augmentation or contraction of intervals as represented in tendency tones away from the natural or the tempered scale. (3) The development and criticism of these theories in terms of the harmonic structure of the tone, the function of subjective tones, and the physiology of the mechanics of the ear by mathematicians, physicists, physiologists, and psychologists. (4) The psychological procedure of analyzing consonance into its component factors and the determination of degrees of consonance on the basis of judgments reached in an experimental situation in terms of these factors.

TABLE I. MUSICAL INTERVALS

		Interval					
						Milli octaves	
		Frequency ratio				Natural	Tempered
Interval name	*Note*	*Natural scale*		*Tempered scale*		*scale*	*scale*
Unison	C	1	1.000	1	1.000	0	0
Comma		81/80	1.013	1	1.000	17.92	0
Semitone or Diesis	C#	25/24	1.042	$2^{1/12}$	1.059	58.89	83.33
Limma		16/15	1.067	$2^{1/12}$	1.059	93.11	83.33
Minor second	D♭	27/25	1.080	$2^{1/12}$	1.059	111.0	83.33
Minor tone		10/9	1.111	$2^{2/12}$	1.122	152.0	166.6
Major second	D	9/8	1.125	$2^{2/12}$	1.122	169.9	166.6
Augmented second	D#	75/64	1.172	$2^{3/12}$	1.189	228.8	250.0
Minor third	E♭	6/5	1.200	$2^{3/12}$	1.189	263.0	250.0
Major third	E	5/4	1.250	$2^{4/12}$	1.260	321.9	333.3
Diminished fourth	F♭	32/25	1.280	$2^{4/12}$	1.260	356.1	333.3
Augmented third	E#	125/96	1.302	$2^{5/12}$	1.335	380.7	416.5
Perfect fourth	F	4/3	1.333	$2^{5/12}$	1.335	414.8	416.5
Augmented fourth	F#	25/18	1.389	$2^{6/12}$	1.414	473.9	500.0
Diminished fifth	G♭	36/25	1.440	$2^{6/12}$	1.414	526.1	500.0
Perfect fifth	G	3/2	1.500	$2^{7/12}$	1.498	585.0	583.3
Augmented fifth	G#	23/16	1.562	$2^{8/12}$	1.587	644.0	666.6
Minor sixth	A♭	8/5	1.600	$2^{8/12}$	1.587	678.1	666.6
Major sixth	A	5/3	1.667	$2^{9/12}$	1.682	737.0	750.0
Augmented sixth	A#	125/72	1.736	$2^{10/12}$	1.782	795.8	833.3
Minor seventh	B♭	9/5	1.800	$2^{10/12}$	1.782	848.0	833.3
Major seventh	B	15/8	1.875	$2^{11/12}$	1.883	906.9	916.6
Diminished octave	C♭	48/25	1.920	$2^{11/12}$	1.883	941.1	916.6
Augmented seventh	B#	125/64	1.953	2	2.000	965.7	1000.00
Octave	C′	2	2.000	2	2.000	1000.0	1000.00

SIX PSYCHOLOGICAL PROBLEMS

Among the problems which confront us in the study of consonance are the following six: (1) the determination of the exact size and number of the intervals in the building of scales; (2) the determination of desirability and reasons for admission of tendency tones under specific musical conditions; (3) the criteria of consonance-dissonance; (4) the establishment of rank order of intervals in the chromatic scale on different criteria; (5) a compromise best judgment about the order of rank, taking all criteria into account; and (6) the setting up of a measure of consonance as a member in the battery of measures of musical talent.

Number of steps in the octave and size of the interval. This problem has been solved progressively in the process of evolution on the principle of natural selection, the survival of the fittest. When we inquire why the present scale of 12 steps has survived, we find the answer in psychological experiments in the laboratory. It is found that, on the whole, our present half-tone step is as small a step as the average of an unselected population can hear with reasonable assurance, enjoy, and reproduce in the flow of melody and harmony in actual music.

However, anthropology has shown that in the process of evolution we can discover a variety of units which have become conventional in a certain culture, some of them larger and some of them smaller than a half tone. Instrumentalists unquestionably imitated the tendencies of the human voice in playing their intervals; and when, in comparatively recent times, keyed instruments were introduced, or a certain number of strings or other vibrating media were played together, the prevailing tendency was crystallized. Yet we have at the present time quarter-tone instruments. Music is being written in quarter-tone steps, and this mode of music reveals resources entirely beyond the possibilities of the half-tone steps. Nor should we ignore the fact that in many instruments and many types of musical performance, fixed intervals are relatively ignored and the melody flows like the soaring bird in abandon on its wings.

Two things are clear, then, on this point: (1) that artistically there is nothing rigidly mandatory for our present diatonic scale, and (2) that the tendency to support it is one of economy, of desire for cooperation, and of recognition of natural limits, particularly in the ear and the voice.

Scales and tendency tones. In the development of modern music we find a gradual crystallization of a number of tendencies or principles in the form of license in deviation from mathematically equal steps, or from any of the now current scales. These principles are never adequately treated in the musical literature. It is quite common for an artist to speak of "his" system. As we shall see in Chap. 21, good artists differ greatly in this respect, and probably should; for it involves freedom in the use of artistic principles of deviation from the regular. In current musicology this is becoming a central problem and is being discussed with great acumen and with marked signs of progress. To the musician it is a real problem which can be settled only in terms of artistic demand. But it will be the function of psychology to submit these demands to objective analysis for the purpose of collecting fair samples from performance scores and of seeking psychological explanations for their existence. This very intricate problem we are not prepared to report upon fully at present; but there is rich raw material to work upon in the performance scores of Chaps. 18 and 20.

The physical and psychological determinants of consonance and dissonance. This is a central problem which the psychology of music now faces and on which an inceptive attack has been made. Psychology must fractionate the problem and deal with one factor at a time. It must recognize that there are kinds as well as degrees of consonance. We cannot identify it with feeling, however conspicuous the feeling aspect may be, but must show how and why feelings are involved. Music employs not only consonances, but also semiconsonances and gross dissonances in creating power and beauty of tone. Dissonance is an essential for esthetic value in modern music, and consonance out of place may be decidedly disagreeable.

Preliminary experiments have revealed four factors which represent conditions determining consonance and their respective psychological effects in feeling value. These are smoothness, purity, blending, and fusion. It has been found possible to make a purely logical judgment, without involving any feeling about it, by observing, for example, that the minor third is smoother than the minor second and that the minor third is rougher than a perfect fourth. It is important to know that such a judgment may be purely logical and independent of affective value, the problem being merely to determine which is the smoother or the rougher tone. Whether we crave or abhor roughness or smoothness is another matter. Now roughness may be explained entirely on the basis of the operation of beats. It is the prominence of the beats that determines the roughness of the tone, and this principle operates until the interval becomes so large that the hearing of the beat effect tends to disappear. On this criterion alone, then, we can arrange dichords, at least from the minor second up to the fifth, with certainty in a graded series of consonance-dissonance.

Another factor is that of relative purity. It is possible to arrange intervals in the order of purity in a purity-richness series which corresponds largely to the order of consonance-dissonance. From unison to the minor second we observe an increasing order of richness as determined by harmonic analysis. But we must observe not only the degree but also the kind of richness. These two factors, smoothness and purity, are objective physical factors, measurable and definable. In a way they are complementary and on the whole tend to dovetail and agree as bases for classification.

A third factor is blending, the quality of seeming to belong together. The two notes in the major second do not seem to belong together; they do not blend. Likewise, the notes of the interval of the seventh do not seem to belong together, but for entirely different reasons from those in the minor second.

Here the issue is: do the two tones in this interval seem to belong together? It is not a question of liking or disliking, agreeableness or disagreeableness, but purely a logical judgment on the specific issue. The tones may not seem to belong together because they are too close, causing roughness, or do not seem to belong together because they are far separated. In other words, the psychological judgment on blending is one which ordinarily rests on the physical facts, smoothness and purity. There is only a difference in the point of view.

There is a further factor which we call "fusion." This was originally sponsored by *Stumpf*[190] and is to the effect that the difficulty of judging whether you hear one tone or two tones becomes a measure of the degree of consonance. This difficulty can be measured in terms of reaction-time, on the theory that the length of time that it takes to decide whether you hear one or two tones is a measure of the degree of fusion. This psychophysical principle undoubtedly operates in a number of intervals, notably the more consonant ones, and to that extent contributes to the explanation of consonance-dissonance. But, as we shall see, it leads to contradictory results.

The distinction between the logical and the affective judgment is of the utmost importance in scientific procedure. So long as we deal in terms of likes and dislikes we are dealing with intangibles, grossly fluctuating factors, quite indefinable. It is only when we define each factor and isolate it in the experiment that we can lay down verifiable principles as to the nature of our problem.

This analysis of consonance is analogous to our analysis of the vibrato, where we reduced the actual musical phenomenon to the operation of three types of pulsation, each of which could be defined and measured accurately, and where it became possible to name corresponding specific qualities of the tone generated by them.

ORDER OF MERIT IN EACH OF FOUR CRITERIA

Twenty years ago we performed an experiment in the Iowa laboratory to discover the relative merits of these four factors as determining consonance-dissonance. The procedure in the experiment conducted by *Malmberg*[84] was unique. It consisted of having a jury of musicians and psychologists who sat in sessions throughout the year under the strictest experimental conditions and with the demand that the sessions should continue until a unanimous verdict could be reached on all the issues involved. A paired comparison of all the intervals in the octave was made (1) with two pure tones

TABLE II. FINAL ORDER OF MERIT AGREED UPON ON THE BASIS OF *S* (SMOOTHNESS), *P* (PURITY), *B* (BLENDING), *F* (FUSION)

Interval	*S*	*P*	*B*	*F*
Octave	1	1	1	1
Minor second	12	12	12	2
Major second	11	11	11	3
Minor third	9	7	7	4
Major third	4	5	3+	5+
Perfect fourth	3	4	4	6
Diminished fifth	7	8	8	8
Perfect fifth	2	2	2	7
Minor sixth	6	4	6	9
Major sixth	5	3	5	10
Minor seventh	8	9	9	11
Major seventh	10	10	10	12

generated by tuning forks in front of the Koenig resonator in the natural scale; (2) by pipe-organ tones using the diapason stop; and (3) piano tones in the tempered scale, where the two strings for each tone were damped so as to allow the vibration of only one string for each note.

A separate series of experiments was run for each of the four factors: smoothness, purity, blending, and fusion; and for every presentation of a pair of clangs a secret ballot was taken on the question as to whether the second clang was, for example, in the smoothness series, smoother or rougher than the first. As soon as all agreed on a pair, that decision was regarded as final, and the experiment was repeated for all the intervals for which there was disagreement, a full discussion being held about the nature of the situation before each series of ballots was taken. This method was continued until unanimous verdicts had been reached on all the four factors. The result of this experiment is shown in Table II. The most outstanding finding in this table is that there is considerable agreement on the first three factors, but on the fourth there is very radical disagreement with the other three, as well as with the generally accepted order.

ORDER OF RANK ON THREE CRITERIA COMBINED

With the recognition that the classification on the basis of fusion did not correspond with accepted musical classification, this was eliminated, and the experiment was repeated with the tuning forks under the instructions that in each ballot the three

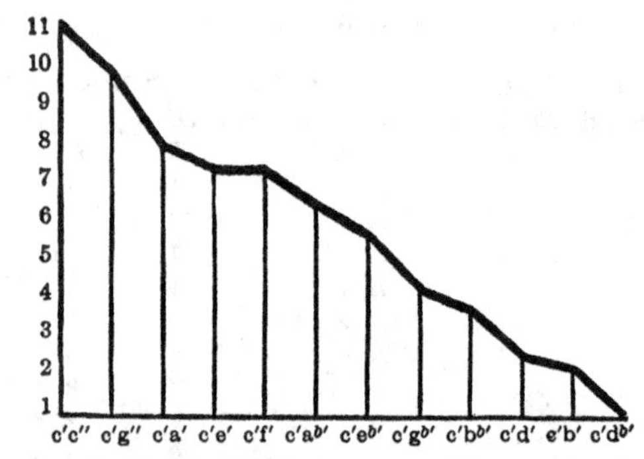

FIG. 1.—Order of merit of interval in the consonance-dissonance series. (*Malmberg.*[84])

remaining factors should be given consideration, so that we should obtain an order of merit on the basis of the recognition of the combined results of these three factors under experimental conditions. The result is shown in Fig. 1.

The significance of the above experiments lies not so much in the determination of consonance-dissonance as in showing what the contributing factors are. In general, we may say that consonance-dissonance depends primarily upon two factors; namely, roughness-smoothness and purity-richness. The factor of blending covers both of these and does not seem to add any new element, but merely represents a point of view in the judgment.

THE SENSE OF CONSONANCE

In the original series there was a measure of the sense of consonance. While this measure has been found very significant, in the diagnosis of talent it has certain defects which have been remedied in the forthcoming revision. These difficulties were that (1) the instructions, giving the directions for observation, were too involved, especially for children; (2) the judgments "Better" or "Worse" suggest agreeableness; and (3) there was a tendency to judge in terms of likes and dislikes.

Many other tests involving consonance would be desirable and are quite feasible, especially for measures of achievement. But for the purpose of forecast, and independent of musical education, a test of the present order seems essential.

VOLUME

VOLUME as a musical characteristic of tone is a complex experience resting upon the frequency, the intensity, the duration, and the harmonic constitution of the physical stimulus, and largely influenced by associational, affective, and motor factors in perception. The following analysis outlines the principal factors which function in the perception and control of volume.

SPATIAL FACTORS

Extensity. Extensity has often been considered a fifth attribute of sensation as experienced in each of the different senses. Literally it means bigness, and usually represents an association with the size of the sounding body. For this reason it corresponds exactly to wave length, which is the reciprocal of frequency. A low pitch comes from the vibration of a long string or a large cavity, whereas a high sound comes from a short string or a small cavity. Thus, as frequency varies with the size of the sounding body, we have come to associate bigness or littleness with the size of the sounding body. Extensity is, therefore, entirely parallel to pitch. A low tone is more massive than a high tone; it comes from a larger space; and we can arrange extensities in a single series in the same way as we arrange pitches. To secure volume, use relatively low tones.

Location. The spatial distribution of the individual tones in a complex sound also affects the volume. This is strikingly illustrated by the fact that the pipes or resonators of a very complicated organ might be distributed, as in a museum, in a large number of rooms on different floors, but all audible in the central aula. In this case, there is an interesting illusion of space. All the tones that come from the pipes of the same pitch, regardless of what floor or location on the floor, are found to come from the same source, which represents an accurate location determined by the loudness of each part and the distance and direction from the listener. Thus, two pipes of the same pitch and intensity, but located one at each end of a long hall, will give a single tone which is located very definitely at the midway distance. But if a third tone comes from a similar source in a side hall, the location of the tone will shift from its central position in the main hall into the side hall toward the source of the third tone. The result is that the music of the organ seems to come from all over the building and that the listener can clearly hear each note as coming from a specific location in distance and direction.

This may be observed on a small scale in listening to a pipe organ at close range. A most striking illustration can be found in the noises of nature in which similar sounds arise from within a large area of space.

QUANTITATIVE FACTORS

Intensity. Volume is often confused with loudness, which depends upon the intensity or power of the physical tone. Volume, however, is a much more comprehensive term in which intensity is only one of the leading elements. Yet, other things being equal, the more intense the tone, the more volume it has. Since we are, by this time, familiar with the role of intensity and loudness, no more need be said here.

Number of tones. The addition of one or more tones of the same intensity tends to increase the total intensity in the volume, but only to a slight degree. For example, if we have a piano tone of 50 db and we add to that another tone of the same intensity, the combined effect will be about 53 db. If we add a third tone, the total intensity is likely to be 55 db. Thus, the addition to the total intensity decreases with the number of units combined; and in every case the increase is small in comparison with the original intensity of one element. This increase in intensity results in a corresponding increase in volume.

Reverberation. Volume is increased quantitatively by resonance of the instrument, reverberation of the room and surrounding bodies in that these reverberations have the effect of multiplying the stimulation. Other things being equal, the more resonant the instrument and environment, the greater the volume will be.

QUALITATIVE FACTORS

Timbre. Volume varies with timbre in many respects. In general, the richer the tone, the greater the volume will be. The full tone seems larger than the pure tone in proportion to its richness. Volume varies also with the position of the dominant formants or resonance regions of the rich tone. In accordance with the principle of extensity, dominance of low partials makes the tone seem more voluminous; dominance of high partials makes it seem less voluminous.

Sonance. The tone quality as affected by change in the form of a sound wave from vibration to vibration, which we call sonance, also has a marked effect upon the apparent volume. This is illustrated in the case of the vibrato, in which periodic pulsations of pitch, intensity, and timbre give the effect of a tonal band or largeness of tone as compared with a straight tone. The same principle applies also to erratic changes in sonance.

TEMPORAL FACTORS

Duration. The duration of a tone modifies its volume. A sound lasting 1 second is more voluminous than a sound lasting 0.01 or 0.1 second. The reason for this lies in several factors, such as the equivalent of repetition of the stimulus, the time for reverberations, and readiness in perception. A clap of thunder illustrates this principle. The origin is probably an instantaneous electrical explosion, but it is heard as a sustained roll. In a percussion instrument, such as the piano or the harp, there is an immediate drop in intensity after the first energizing of the string; but, for a complicated series of psychological reasons, we tend to hear these tones as of even loudness throughout their duration. That is, the intensity indicated by the first impact tends to carry over throughout the duration of the tone.

Sequence. The volume depends also upon the sequence of tones in terms of intensity, timbre, and spatial relationships. All the laws of contrast operate here.

SUBJECTIVE FACTORS

The experience of volume depends not only upon such physical aspects of the stimulus as those just outlined, but also very largely upon subjective factors. Among these, expectation, knowledge of the source of the sound, effort, or thought required in the production of the sound, emotional tone, such as fear or desire, and vividness of the imagination play important roles. Therefore, for purely subjective reasons, we find large individual differences in the hearing of volume, and in the same individual from moment to moment, marked changes in the flux of receptive attitude.

CARRYING POWER

From the above it follows that volume is not a specific determinant of audibility or what is generally called carrying power of speech or music. The conductor, for example, must think and direct in terms of specific factors of pitch, intensity, time, and timbre; and, of these, some in more specific terms of their variants, derivatives, and combinations, both in the performance and in the environment. Nor can he ignore the subjective factors, for example, motivation. It is not enough that the orator have great volume of voice. The volume must have certain ingredients in certain proportions in order to be heard, understood, and enjoyed.

From this skeletal analysis, which could be carried into greater detail, the significance of knowledge of volume for the performer, the teacher, and the pupil must be apparent. It is of supreme importance to the composer, the performer, the instrument-maker, and the conductor that they should know what aspects of volume are present or demanded, how they may be produced, and the various ways in which volume may be modulated. In the interest of these dynamic values in music, it is the duty of the teacher to know what is to be taught. It should be the privilege of every serious student of music to receive early reliable instruction in regard to the media at his command, the factors which he should hear, the factors which he should control, in order that he may proceed efficiently with knowledge in the mastery of each of these goals. This subject is usually treated in the field of acoustics.

The intensity required to produce tones of equal loudness varies with frequency. For instance, a tone at 5,000~ must be approximately 2,800 times as intense as a tone of 1,000~ in order to sound equally loud to the average normal ear. The intensity of each partial present in a complex tone decreases inversely as the square of the distance. The threshold of audibility is different for each frequency. Other things being equal, that partial of a complex tone which has the lowest threshold of audibility will be heard at the greatest distance. A complex sound can be heard no farther than its most persistent component can be heard alone.

12

RHYTHM

THE NATURE OF RHYTHM*

THERE are two fundamental factors in the perception of rhythm: an instinctive tendency to group impressions in hearing and a capacity for doing this with precision in time and stress. The subjective tendency is so deeply ingrained, because of its biological service, that we irresistibly group uniform successions of sound, such as the tick of a clock, into rhythmic measure. The supposed limping of a clock is often purely subjective. This is called subjective rhythm to distinguish it from objective rhythm, in which the grouping is actually marked, as in music and poetry. If a long series of quarter notes were played with absolute uniformity in time and stress, the listener would inevitably hear them divided into measures and would actually hear the appropriate notes accented. Such is one of nature's beneficent illusions.

A good illustration of this is found in a very crude way when one is lying in a Pullman sleeper and the successive beats coming from the crossing of rail joints set up a time which carries tunes that come into one's head. The rails seem, as it were, to beat the time emphatically into measures. The writer recalls once being haunted by the plantation melody, "What kind o' a crown you gwine to wear? Golden crown?" As he allowed the imagery of the melody to flow, the accentuation of the click of the rails became very prominent and satisfying as rhythm. One who is trained in observing himself may find this tendency toward rhythmic grouping in any or all his activities. Take, for example, the homely act of eating. One

* The first two sections of this chapter are reprinted with permission from the *Musical Quarterly*.[143]

who has a highly developed sense of rhythm may, even in eating soup, feel the various movements divided into measures with their artistic grouping of long intervals and short intervals, some objectively and others only subjectively marked with occasional cadences. Yet a person watching the movement might not be able to see any rhythm in the actual movements.

The objective rhythm as we find it ordinarily in prose and poetry is marked by emphasis of time or intensity, or both. Occasionally, it may be also through pitch, although that always involves intensity. It is also probable that it may come through other senses than hearing.

Subjective rhythm is more fundamental than objective rhythm and always plays a large role in the objective. This is why we find rhythm more essentially a matter of personality than a matter of objective grouping. All rhythm is primarily a projection of personality. The rhythm is what I am. For him who is not endowed with this talent the objective rhythms in nature and art are largely wasted.

While the perception of rhythm involves the whole organism, it requires primarily five fundamental capacities. The first two of these are the sense of time and the sense of intensity, corresponding respectively to the two attributes of sound, which constitute the sensory media of rhythm. The third and fourth are auditory imagery and motor imagery, that is, the capacity for reviving vividly in representation the auditory experience and the motor attitudes respectively. The fifth is a motor impulse for rhythm, an instinctive tendency, chiefly unconscious and largely organic. These five factors may be said to be basic to the sense of rhythm. Other general factors, such as emotional type and temperament, logical span, or creative imagination, are intimately woven into the warp and woof of rhythm, but we shall probably find that these are secondary to the primary and basic forces named.

We may now define rhythm as an instinctive disposition to group recurrent sense impressions vividly and with precision, mainly by time or intensity, or both, in such a way as to derive pleasure and efficiency through the grouping.

The sense of rhythm, or perception of rhythm, as thus defined, is to be distinguished from rhythmic action, an important aspect with which we are not here concerned; yet it is a complex process and involves literally the whole organism in the form of a perpetual attitude of responsiveness to measured intervals of time or tone.

To gain some insight into the actual nature of rhythm, it may be well to point out some of the things that rhythm does on the side of perception as distinguished from action, which will be equivalent to pointing out the sources of pleasure and means to efficiency in rhythm.

WHAT RHYTHM DOES

1. Rhythm favors perception by grouping. It has been demonstrated that, under happy grouping, one can remember approximately as many small groups as one can remember individual objects without grouping; for example, in listening to a series of notes, one can grasp nearly as many measures, if they are heard rhythmically, as one could grasp individual sounds if they were not heard rhythmically. This is a principle which is involved in all auditory perception. Individual sounds are grouped in measures and phrases, phrases and periods, periods and movements. The ability to grasp in terms of larger and larger units is a condition for achievement. The development of this ability results in power to handle vast numbers of sounds with ease,and this success is a source of pleasure. And that is true, not only in poetry and in music, but in our natural hearing, even under primitive conditions. Thus, rhythm has become a biological principle of efficiency, a condition for advance and achievement and a perpetual source of satisfaction. The rhythm need not be conspicuous to be effective. It need not be objective. It need not be conscious. At best it is a habit.

2. Rhythm adjusts the strain of attention. In poetry and music, for instance, the rhythm enables us to anticipate the magnitude of units which are to be grasped. This, in turn, makes it possible to adjust the effort in such a way as to grasp the unit at the strategic moment and to relax the strain for a moment between periods. Of this, again, we may not be immediately conscious, but it may be readily demonstrated by experiment, as, for example, if we should break up a measure, as in going from 2/4 to 3/4 time without warning.

Genetically, the ordinary measure in poetry and music is determined by what is known as the attention wave. Our attention is periodic. All our mental life works rhythmically, that is, by periodic pulsation of effort or achievement with unnoticed intermittence of blanks. This is easily observed in an elemental process such as hearing ability. To demonstrate it in a simple way, proceed as follows: hold a watch a distance from the ear, and then move it toward the ear till you can just hear it; then keep it in this position for two or three minutes, and observe that you hear it only intermittently. To check this, raise your finger when you hear the sound and lower your finger when you do not hear it. Do not be influenced by any theory, but act with the keenest decision for every second. You will then find the hearing and silence periods alternate with fair regularity, the periods varying from 2 to 8 or 10 seconds in the extreme. This periodicity is primarily one of attention and reaches out into all our mental processes, being one of nature's contrivances in the interest of the conservation of nervous energy.

This is a principle which is made use of in nature and in industry, as, for example, in our lighting current. The current which energizes our lamps is not, as a rule, a steady, direct current, but is "alternating," that is, it comes in pulsations, usually about 60 a second, which are frequent enough to give us the impression of continuous illumination. The rhythmic measure, then, is simply taking advantage of nature's supply of pulsating efforts of attention. And when the measure fits the attention wave, it gives us a restful feeling of satisfaction and ease. This in turn results in what is known as secondary passive attention, which is a more economical and efficient form of attention than voluntary attention. Thus it comes about that we acquire a feeling of ease, power, and adjustment when we listen to rhythmic measures because we get the largest returns for the least outlay, and the tendency to seek this assumes biological importance because it tends to preserve and enhance life.

3. Rhythm gives us a feeling of balance. It is built on symmetry, and, when this symmetry involves within itself a certain element of flexibility which is well proportioned, we have grace. Thus, when we read an ordinary prose sentence, we pay no attention to the structural form; but, when we scan the dactylic hexameter, we fall into the artistic mood, distinctly conscious of a symmetry and beauty in form, and in this sense rhythm becomes a thing in itself. Poetry may contain ideas, and music may represent sentiment; but the rhythmic structure is in itself an object of art, and the placid perception of this artistic structure takes the form of the feeling of balance under various degrees of delicate support. Children sense the rhythm of poetry before they do the meaning.

4. The sense of rhythm gives us a feeling of freedom, luxury, and expanse. It gives us a feeling of achievement in molding or creating. It gives us a feeling of rounding out a design. This sense of freedom is in one respect the commonplace awareness of the fact that one is free to miss the consciousness of periodicity in countless ways, yet chooses to be in the active and aggressive attitude of achievement. As, when the eye scans the delicate tracery in the repeated pattern near the base of the cathedral and then sweeps upward and delineates the harmonious design continued in measures gradually tapering off into the towering spire, all one unit of beauty expressing the will and imagination of the architect, so in music, when the ear grasps the intricate rhythms of beautiful music and follows it from the groundwork up through the delicate tracery into towering climaxes in clustered pinnacles of rhythmic tone figures, we feel as though we did this all because we wished to, because we craved it, because we were free to do it, because we were able to do it.

5. Rhythm gives us a feeling of power; it carries. It is like a dream of flying; it is so easy to soar. One feels as if one could lift oneself by one's bootstraps. The pattern once grasped, there is an assurance of ability to cope with the future. This results in the disregard of the ear element and results in a motor attitude, or a projection of the self in action; for rhythm is never rhythm unless one feels that he himself is acting it, or, what may seem contradictory, that he is even carried by his own action.

6. It stimulates and lulls, contradictory as this may seem. Pronounced rhythm brings on a feeling of elation which not infrequently results in a mild form of ecstasy or absent-mindedness, a loss of consciousness of the environment. It excites, and it makes us insensible to the excitation, giving the feeling of being lulled. This is well illustrated in the case of dancing. Seated in comfort and enjoyment in pleasant conversation, the striking up of a waltz is a call which excites to action. It starts the organic, rhythmic movements of the body the moment it is heard, and one is drawn, as it were, enticingly into the conventional movements of the dance. But no sooner is this done, in the true enjoyment of the dance, than one becomes oblivious to intellectual pursuits, launches himself, as it were, upon the carrying measures, feels the satisfaction of congenial partnership, graceful step, freedom of movement—action without any object other than the pleasure in the action itself. There comes

a sort of autointoxication from the stimulating effect of the music and the successful self-expression in balanced movements sustained by that music and its associations.

The same is true of the march. When the march is struck up it stimulates tension of every muscle of the body. The soldier straightens up, takes a firmer step, observes more keenly, and is all attention; but as he gets into the march, all this passes into its opposite, a state of passivity, obliviousness to environment, and obliviousness to effort and action. The marked time and accent of the band music swing the movements of all parts of the body into happy adjustment. He can march farther in better form and with less fatigue.

7. Rhythmic periodicity is instinctive. As we saw above, the grouping into natural periods of the flow of attention is a biological principle of preservative value. It is likewise true that the tendency to act in rhythmic movements is of biological value, and for a similar reason. If one does not know where to put his hand or foot the next movement, he is ill at ease and will be inefficient in the movement; but if movements may be foreseen and even forefelt, and an accompanying signal sets off the movement without conscious effort, there results a greatly lessened expenditure of energy, a more effective action, a feeling of satisfaction. Anything that accomplishes these ends in the life of a species will tend to become instinctive, to develop a natural tendency always to move in rhythmic measure; and, when our movements are not actually divided into objective periodicity, we tend to fall into a subjective rhythm. We cannot have adequate perception of rhythm without this motor setting. The bearing of this instinctive motor tendency on the perception of rhythm lies in the fact that with the motor instinct goes an instinct to be in a receptive attitude for the perception of such rhythms, both subjective and objective.

8. Rhythm finds resonance in the whole organism. It is not a matter of the ear or the finger only; it is a matter of the two fundamental powers of life, namely, knowing and acting. And, therefore, indirectly it affects the circulation, respiration, and all the secretions of the body in such a way as to arouse agreeable feeling. Herein we find the groundwork of emotion; for rhythm, whether in perception or in action, is emotional when highly developed, and results in response of the whole organism to its pulsations. Such organic pulsations and secretions are the physical counterpart of

emotion. Thus, when we listen to the dashing billows or the trickling raindrops, when we see the swaying of the trees in the wind or the waving of the wheat fields, we respond to these, we feel ourselves into them, and there is rhythm everywhere, not only in every plastic part of our body, but in the world as we know it at that moment.

This tendency to feel oneself into the music and act it out is an exhibition of the principle known as "empathy": "feeling oneself into." It may exist in a very highly developed form without the accompaniment of the other two factors involving precision in the rhythmic pattern. At the present time, we have no satisfactory way of measuring the degree of prominence of this impulse except by merely recording, as in moving pictures. But psychologically that is of little value because it is the tendency to act, rather than the free action, which is fundamentally significant. This tendency we shall probably soon be able to measure in terms of the magnitude of the rhythmic volleys of nerve impulses, which discharge into the muscles but are more or less counteracted.

9. Rhythm arouses sustained and enriching association. One need not tramp through the woods where the Wagnerian scenes are laid in order to experience the rich flow of visual association with a rhythmic flow of the music in *Lohengrin*. In most persons it comes irresistibly through free imagination. Our consciousness of pleasure in music is often a consciousness of seeing and doing things, rather than a consciousness of hearing rhythm, the tendency being to project ourselves through the sensory cue of hearing into the more common fields of vision and action.

10. Rhythm reaches out in extraordinary detail and complexity with progressive mastery. It makes use of novelty. The simple rhythms soon become monotonous, but one can find endless opportunity for enrichment by the complications of which the measure, the phrase, or the more attenuated rhythmic unit is capable. This is true both for perception and for action. A rhythmic nature tends to live more and more in the exquisite refinements and far-reaching ramifications of rhythmic perceptions and rhythmic feelings of movements, real or imagined. This power to radiate and encompass may be vastly enhanced by training in the rhythmic arts.

The sense of rhythm is like the instinct of curiosity: it takes one into wonders after wonders. Curiosity asks one question and nature asks her ten. One degree of rhythmic perception acquired becomes a vantage ground from which we may approach higher levels, and each of these in turn traversed leads to higher vantage grounds, level after level, vista after vista. They need not be objective. Nor need we be conscious of them as such. It is a state or organization into rich meaning.

11. The instinctive craving for the experience of rhythm results in play, which is the free self-expression for the pleasure of expression, or, as Ruskin puts it, "an exertion of body and mind, made to please ourselves, and with no determined end." It makes us play, young and old. It determines the form of play, in large part. Through play it leads to self-realization by serving as an ever-present incentive for practice. In music and poetry we play with rhythm, as it were, and thereby develop it in expansive and artistic forms.

This inventory of the sources of pleasure in rhythm is fragmentary and inadequate, but it should at least accomplish two ends. It should dispel the notion that the perception of rhythm is a simple mental process or action and should make us realize that, to the person who is endowed with this gift in a high degree, it is one of the great sources of pleasure, not only in music and art, but in the commonplace of humdrum life. To a person who is not so endowed, this role of rhythm may be no more concretely patent than the omnipresence of color is to the color blind.

INDIVIDUAL DIFFERENCES IN MUSICAL RHYTHM

There are three basic factors in the capacity for rhythm: (1) the rhythmic impulse to action, (2) the cognitive capacity, and (3) the motor capacity. Many variants of each of these may of course be recognized.

The instinctive impulse to express rhythmic grouping. In studying the rhythmic talent of a one-year-old child possessing highly developed rhythm, we made the following observations: In listening to a rhythmic two-step on the phonograph she approached the instrument with much interest and sat clapping her hands in correct time with the music without any prompting or suggestion. A waltz was then substituted for the two-step, and she immediately picked up the ¾ pattern. We then held her by her hands so that she stood lightly on the floor but could not move her hands and then she marked time with her feet. To determine her further resources, hand and foot action were eliminated by placing her on all fours. In this position she immediately shimmied with full bodily expression. She had the rhythmic impulse. She "had rhythm." It was plainly untutored and executed with abandon and full swing. She seemed to live herself into the music.

Of course, children differ markedly in this respect, and for very different and complicated reasons. We see this sort of exhibition in response to music, which is a form of inceptive dance, in all stages of primitive life. The free expression of this sort tends to be attenuated or repressed through the forces of maturation and culture. It is the outstanding characteristic of spirituals and revival singing but is thoroughly suppressed in the more dignified church service. It finds rich development in dramatic action, not only in music but also in the more refined arts of singing and playing.

The sense of rhythm. What we have called the sense of rhythm is the capacity for hearing and recalling rhythmic patterns with precision in time. It may also be regarded from the point of view of intensity in the manner of precision of accent. This capacity can be measured accurately by employing a graded series of musical patterns from simplest to very complex and determining what is the largest pattern an individual can hear and identify correctly. There are very large individual differences in this capacity in a normal community of individuals, and experiments have shown that this capacity is a fairly fixed constant and is elemental to a considerable degree in that it does not change greatly with age, practice, or training.

Motor rhythmic capacity. This is the capacity for expressing rhythmic patterns in music with fine discriminative action. It underlies all skillful phrasing, both of voice and of instrument.

The natural capacity for this may be measured before musical education has been undertaken. It consists of determining, under experimental conditions, what degree of precision the individual can show in tapping out rhythmic patterns, either by imitating standard patterns or by setting up his own patterns in metronomic time.

There are various forms of standardized apparatus for this purpose. *R. Seashore*[158,159] first standardized this measure.

It is often stated that great accuracy in the hearing and the performance of rhythm is not of much consequence because there is such great irregularity and license in the rhythm of even the best music. This notion is based on the assumption that rhythm should occur in metronomic time. The musician, however, knows that his artistry lies not in maintaining a rhythmic pattern in even time, but rather in the hearing and making of artistic deviations in the pattern. This is a far more strenuous demand than a demand for the setting of the pattern in even time. It is the delicate varying of pattern interpretations that puts life into the music.

PSYCHOLOGY OF RHYTHM

Perhaps more experimental work has been done in the last fifty years on the psychology of rhythm than on any other musical feature. Space does not permit us here even to summarize and interpret the findings. In recent years, *Ruckmick*[114] has compiled comprehensive bibliographies on this subject. Instead of attempting to summarize the psychology of musical rhythm, the subject is so divided that it will be discussed in concrete terms under the heads of Voice, Chap. 20; Violin, Chap. 18; and Piano, Chap. 19. Sufficient work material in the form of performance scores and phrasing scores is furnished in these chapters. The subject is treated more fully in the researches from which these illustrations were drawn.

While rhythm is a conspicuous feature in music, it is also a dominant element in nearly all phases of our daily life. The term should, however, be restricted to grouping in accordance with our definition above, to the exclusion of mere periodicity. It is very common in scientific circles to speak of mere periodicity as rhythm. The tick of a clock, for example, is periodic, but it is not rhythmic unless it is made so by the subjective grouping of the listener. Biologically, mere periodicity serves many of the purposes that rhythm serves in human perception and action. But mere periodicity in music has no rhythmic significance. Even a chain of four exact 1-second measures without regard to the internal structure would never make rhythm in music, nor would it in speech or in dancing. It is the internal organization of the pattern that makes rhythm in the rhythmic arts and it would tend to clarify language if, in the sciences and industries, the term were restricted in this manner. Mere periodicity would never make dancing beautiful. The rhythm in dancing must represent grace, versatility, surprise, balance, organization.

We hear much about rhythm in typewriting, where reference is made only to constant speed. Rhythm plays a very important role in this activity, in that it aids development of group perception and group actions in organized patterns adapted to the individual capacities. The same thing is true in the industries, where skill takes the form of gradually developed organized rhythms which are adapted to the natural capacity of the individual workman.

In this sense of organized grouping of perception or action, rhythm furnishes the backbone structure of all sports and games of grace and skill, even the humdrum of the common laborer. It is a dominant factor in the organization and facilitation of control; witness the Negro chopping wood or "working on the railroad," even setting rhythmic tunes to the accompaniment of his strokes. But whether the rhythm is consciously present or the rhythmic impulse is suppressed by demands of culture and efficiency, rhythm is one of the foundation structures in all motor skills. Perhaps the poet may find a suggestion here for picturing even the humdrum of life as involving sweet music if one but has the mind to hear it and feel it in empathy.

It is interesting to note that, as in music, the rhythm is not necessarily set up by the objective situation, but always represents an active organization on the part of the performer. In sports and industries it is more necessary that this rhythm should take objective form. However, it may be in very large part purely subjective rhythm and yet may play its biological role.

13

LEARNING IN MUSIC

THE ordinary procedure in teaching and learning music is shamefully wasteful because known laws of learning are not applied. The teaching of musical notation, ear training, and sight reading in the public schools could be vastly improved by a simple application of a few principles now applied in other subjects. The same is true in acquiring techniques of skill in performance, in the memorizing of repertoires, and in the acquisition of knowledge about music. Psychology of music therefore presents a challenge and a service to teachers and students alike.*

The learning process in music involves two primary aspects: acquisition and retention of musical information and experience, and the development of musical skills. Both of these are included in the common use of the term "memory"; thus, we have conscious memory, which is the making available of stored information and experience, and subconscious or automatic memory, which is a phase of habit, such as is exhibited in all the various types of musical skills in performance.

Musical memory is a talent which is inherited in vastly different degrees, the differences being greater for this special capacity than for memory capacity in general; one student may have more than a hundred times the capacity of another for learning music. Yet this ability, both in the gifted and in the nongifted, is capable of an astonishing amount of improvement by training. Training in the art of learning can accomplish wonders.

---

* This chapter is an adaptation from the author's Serviceable Memory, in *Psychology in Daily Life.*[136]

Psychology has furnished more experiments on problems in learning than in any other field. Volumes of material bearing on this subject are now available and are being applied in various fields of learning. Instead of summarizing the facts established by experiment, I shall put the most fundamental findings in the form of a series of simple rules for learning music and will state these rules with utmost brevity and clearness, for the purpose of motivating students of music in the effort to establish right habits of learning.

TWELVE RULES FOR EFFICIENT LEARNING IN MUSIC

(To the pupil)

Learning anything is an act which must be performed by the learner. It cannot be done for him by the teacher. The only thing a teacher can do is to assist in creating favorable conditions by motivation, supply of materials, and general guidance. The first essential then in facing any learning problem is to place the responsibility where it belongs, namely, on the pupil. This principle is violated by pupil and teacher alike in much of current instruction which seems to rest upon the assumption that it is the function of the teacher to hammer something into a pupil who is sometimes not only passive but resistant. Let us, therefore, place the responsibility on the pupil who wishes to learn, recognizing that it means work, pleasant and successful work, on the part of the pupil, and that the responsibility for this cannot be thrown upon the teacher.

1. Select your field of interest. Select as your object of study that in which you have a genuine interest, for which you have natural aptitude, and which you consider worth learning. Make this a real object to be attained at the sacrifice of many other interests. If music cannot qualify for you on the three grounds of talent, interest, and personal value, you should, perhaps, avoid it except insofar as musical instruction is a routine part of your education. In music, select first a general field and within this field from stage to stage a specific aspect or content which you desire to master. This is merely deciding what you are to do when entering upon a new enterprise. Knowing exactly what is to be learned is the first stage of mastery and making a selection on the basis of good reasons makes the work economical, effective, and pleasant.

2. Intend to learn. This does not mean an occasional or sporadic intention but a firm decision to give continuity of effort until mastery is attained. Occasional intention is ruinous because the exception tends to destroy what has been attained. Teachers say, "Give attention, concentrate, apply yourself." The present rule throws the full responsibility upon you for really intending in a responsible way to reach your goal as a matter of your own choice. If it is not your personal choice, you should, perhaps, avoid the pursuit. It should, however, be remembered that some things are learned for their own sake, and others, for example, reading, are pursued as tools for the attainment of higher things. The intentions that count in life are habitual. Therefore, make your intention a habit and suffer no violations of that habit. When the intention to remember has become a habit, you will have the feeling of ease, mastery, and joy of achievement.

3. Trust the first impression. In wrestling, shooting, photographing—in all acts of skill—success comes to the one who most effectively throws his best energies into a single stroke of effort. In learning something, make a deliberate and deep first impression and then trust that. Instead of repeating the impression, repeat the recall or memory. At a given moment you have selected a specific thing in music that you wish to learn. You approach it with the habit of intending to master it, and you will save enormous time and effort if you now trust the first impression, instead of looking or listening in a blank manner, expecting to get it another time. Trust the first impression and make this deeper and deeper by practicing recall instead of reimpression.

This is analogous to the taking of a picture. If you have selected your object, determined to photograph it, and timed your exposure properly, you may get a permanent picture from the first impression; repeating the impression will result in a blur. This principle is opposed to the rote method by which the learner simply grinds away blindly, thinking that something will be ground in.

When you take up a new selection, make a rapid survey of its general characteristics to note what is familiar and what are new features. Observe or perform the first new feature deliberately, intending to make this first impression adequate and permanent, repeating it in recall, or from recall, as often as is necessary to deepen this first impression; but be determined not to go back for a second impression. Then take the successive new features in turn in the same manner until the whole selection is mastered. This being done, the individual units can be woven together. Again let us say, practice each unit, bind the successive units together, but always by recall and not by repeating impression. Such is the practice that counts. Trust the first impression and your memory will serve you well.

4. Classify: learn by thinking. Thinking is meeting new difficulties with deliberation and solving them. If it is a new fact, a stroke, a phrase, a difficult fingering, note its relation to what you already know or can do. Recognition of this relationship is the bond that ties the new to the old, which is the act of learning. Intelligent learning consists largely in effective classification. Therefore, fit each new experience into its relationships to what you already have; that is, classify it deliberately with great precision and with as full meaning as possible.

The botanist can recognize and recall thousands of plants because he has the habit of seeing relationships. One plant is like another in this and that respect; therefore, it belongs to the same class. Instead of remembering the thousands of individual plants, the botanist remembers them by types and relationships, each within the class to which it belongs. So it is in music. Note the relationship of the new experience, classify it in the first impression, and it will be yours. For this reason, the first impression should be very deliberate and should be lingered upon until the details and character of its meaning are adequately recognized. To the student who is accustomed merely to grind away, it is difficult to realize what a short cut to learning this principle furnishes. It is the key to most of the systems of memory training which have been famous from time to time in the past.

5. Cultivate concrete imagery. We see, hear, taste, touch, or smell an object in its presence; we may recall it and see, hear, taste, touch, or smell it in mental image. For example, last night I heard a song; at this moment I can close my eyes and hear it, noting in great detail the characteristics of the rendition. Full, vivid, and accurate mental imagery is one of the most outstanding characteristics of a musical mind. It is this that enables the musician to live in a tonal world. He occasionally hears or performs music, but far more frequently images it either in recall or in anticipation.

Now our rule in making the first impression is to note details that aid in classification so that they come back faithfully reproduced in the mental image. This concrete and faithful imagery is most essential in the first recall, immediately after the first impression, but imagery is closely related to fantasy and fantasy is one of the best aids to memory in that it gives us striking, interesting, odd, and lasting impressions which aid in recall. Tie the mental image of each impression to the next by making a sort of concrete story as you go along. By this method it is possible for a person of average memory to learn a list of 50 or 100 words after a single hearing so that they may be repeated in the correct order.

I asked someone to call out slowly 10 words which apparently had no connection. He gave me the words "boy," "grass," "glass," "pike," "scissors," "ventilation," "bird," "nickel," "fury," and "gear"; and this was the way my first impression was met and strengthened by concrete imagery. As the words were recalled I had this experience:

Boy—I see a little barefoot boy
Grass—walking in the tall grass;
Glass—the stalks of grass crackle like glass under his feet:
Pike—therefore he is glad when he sees the open pike.
Scissors—His little legs clip like scissors,
Ventilation—and his lungs get good ventilation,
Bird—for he flies like a bird
Nickel—and swings his nickel-plated rod
Fury —like fury
Gear—because he is now in gear with nature.

Thus, you see, to recall the words in the proper order I had only to recall my story woven into concrete imagery. Sometimes the more ridiculous, funny, unnatural, the association, the better a bond it will be. Any relationship that is striking becomes a good bond.

Teachers of children often use devices to arouse this play attitude; but the gift of doing this well is a personal one, and you should cultivate your own type of imagery as a tool in learning. As a matter of fact this is the way we learn in daily life. You remember Mr. Jones because he made you think of a bulldog, or Mr. Smith because he made you think of a peacock. At the time, you see the bulldog and the peacock in concrete mental imagery.

6. Build larger and larger units. At certain advanced stages we learn by wholes, but the best rule for learning in general is to learn one small specific thing at a time; then weave these larger units together, and so on, until the task is completed. In doing this you acquire the power to learn in larger and larger units. Take the analogy of learning to read. The child first learns to see individual letters, to associate these with sounds, to weave the sounds into words, the words into phrases, the phrases into clauses, clauses into sentences, sentences into paragraphs, paragraphs into the topic as a whole. As he learns to read, reading becomes easier because he reads in larger and larger units. This is exactly parallel to sight reading in music, to the performing of music, and to the interpretation of music.

7. Practice only by recall. This was implied in rule three but is so important that we must let it stand out in a rule by itself. If you build in small units in which the first impression is trusted and immediately recalled in vivid imagery, a progressive mastery of such units should enable you to practice what has been learned from memory without looking it up again or being retold. Doing this is the test of whether or not you are trusting your memory. Memory is like a friend; trust him and he will be true to you. This rule requires a careful planning and a well-sustained policy in order that you may not have any difficulty in practicing by recall instead of by impression.

8. Rest economically. So far our rules force the concentration of effort in doing a thing incisively in the first instant. Such effort cannot be long sustained; but it carries its own reward and more in that, when your effort has been efficiently concentrated in successful attacks, you will have accomplished in a very short time what the happy-go-lucky methods would take a very long time to do, and you are therefore entitled to rest.

Rest should be distributed throughout a learning process so as to occur in short periods after each small unit that is mastered and in longer and longer periods in proportion to the size of the unit that is mastered. Thus, instead of practicing a selection by the rote method for two hours, work by spurts, allowing yourself complete relaxation after each unit, and you will have accomplished your task in but a small fraction of the hour, will have had periodic relaxation, and will have the remainder of the period for entire freedom. The ability to do this is an art which not only saves time in learning but develops those traits of personality in which you show yourself master of the situation.

Many a music student becomes a nervous wreck from ill-adjusted study methods in the violation of this rule. Many a student becomes disgusted with music because he cannot learn by dull drudgery. The command to rest is fully as important as the command to work in effective learning, and in general we say, "Work while you work, and play while you play."

9. Recognize what is learned and express it in action. Recognize your friend and he will recognize you; cut your friend and he will cut you. Recognize the thing once learned as it functions in your life and keep it alive; be slovenly and negligent about its daily role, and it will cut you.

When, as a child, you learned to walk, the best way of retaining that skill was to walk. So when you have acquired a skill of insight, knowledge, feeling, action, or interpretation of music, keep it alive in action. Do not merely think about it. Treat your music as a good friend; speak to him, work with him, play with him, laugh with him, do something for him. Let music function in your life.

10. Review in cycles. Certain types of knowledge, skill, facility, and efficiency need to be reviewed systematically. This is well recognized in the organization of teaching of arithmetic in the grades. A certain process is repeated at higher levels at larger and larger intervals by the practice of recall or performance. In such review, the essentials should stand out progressively more clearly. In any account of learning, we acquire a lot of incidental accretions in matters of no consequence. One condition of memory is the power to forget the nonessential or irrelevant. The cycle of review should tend to eliminate these and let the permanently valuable stand out in higher relief.

11. Build each new acquisition into a habit. As we grow we acquire more and more power to do things automatically. The boy who is just learning to tip his hat to ladies and elders does it laboriously, grudgingly, and awkwardly. No one is polite unless he is polite by his very nature. No one acts musically until the techniques have been shoved back into the subconscious where they take care of themselves as habits. No one can read music or play or sing until the fundamental facts and skills have been converted into habits which function without fail in progressively larger integrations. Only then can a singer sing with feeling and abandon; only then can the pianist pick up a complicated score and play it at sight; only then can the conductor inspire unified effort in the artistic playing of the ensemble.

Historically, there have been two schools of teachers: those who cultivate conscious attention on a specific element or process involved at a given stage in musical training, and those who take the opposite view and say, for example, "Sing naturally and with feeling and pay no attention to how the tone is produced." The psychological theory combines these two and says, "At the learning stage, be intensely conscious of the element involved in the particular that is to be learned, then relegate these elements to habit and in musical performance give yourself up to the situation as a whole, guided largely by a feelingful intelligence."

12. Learn at your own level. Great difficulty is involved in class instruction in music owing to the diversity of talent in a group. While this is a problem of the teacher, it is ultimately your problem to see to it that your learning effort is concentrated upon the acquisition, not of what you would have, but what is within your power of acquisition at the time. Refuse to learn what you already know, refuse to drill on what you already can perform with skill, insist upon the privilege of working at your own natural level so that the task that you undertake is neither too easy nor too hard. A kindly and sympathetic attitude of this sort will be welcomed by the teacher and will result in the enhancement of your musical training. Perhaps most frequently this will mean insistence on going back and acquiring that which was passed over too lightly in order that you may have the background for the making of further progress.

SOME SPECIFIC APPLICATIONS

(To the instructor)

If we evaluate musical instruction in the public schools in terms of the operation of these rules, we shall reveal a most shocking waste of time and effort, the formation of demoralizing habits, and the deadening of musical interest. There are notable and inspiring exceptions.

When music really lives and functions in the school or in the individual work, principles of learning, such as those just stated, may be seen to develop spontaneously and automatically, often without awareness of their existence by pupil or teacher.

My present appeal is most directly addressed to the teachers of public-school teachers in music, because they hold the key situation for the advancement of the science of their art. To make the above message concrete from the point of view of the teacher, and at the expense of repetition, let us note in particular some of the ways in which instruction may be improved on the basis of experimental psychology of learning, considering in turn notation, ear training, tone production, and sight reading.

In all these cases the first step is to place responsibility on the pupils, requiring them to read, or teaching them in an impressive way to observe simple rules or their equivalents, thus establishing a cooperative attitude. This of course will place the responsibility on the teacher for a constant, never-ceasing, and thorough application of the rules throughout the instruction. Making the student want to learn and placing the responsibility on him is the first element of successful teaching.

Notation. Make a specific list of all the items the grade pupils should know. Such a list is surprisingly small, particularly if well classified. Put it on the blackboard and have them write it down as a check list. Teach it all thoroughly as a unit at one stage. For this purpose, institute intensive competitive drill. Use memory devices; for example, a single rule by which a pupil can tell the key and the number of sharps and flats in a signature by the application of the rule. Enliven with concrete and striking illustrations.

This conquest of the whole task as a unit will drive away the notation bogey and boredom and the pupil will be spurred on by the joy of mastery from the first effort. Keep this notation alive by treating each item as a familiar fact daily. So organize instruction that the pupil is conscious of the possession of a useful tool which he employs for the personal satisfaction and achievement in actual music.

Institute cycle reviews by competitive tests at intervals longer and longer apart until the permanent retention is assured; but, if the previous rule is followed rigorously, this rule will not be needed.

Do not teach the facts after the first learning; use them, practice recall not relearning.

Last and most important, "Thou that teachest others; teachest thou thyself?" Score your instruction by these rules.

In other words, let pupil and teacher take aim, hit hard, bag the game, and enjoy the dinner.

Ear training. Point out that there are four—and only four—fundamental things to be learned in musical hearing: the hearing of pitch, intensity, time, and timbre. Unless this is recognized, the task may seem, to both teacher and pupil, endless and unreasonable.

Illustrate each of these by voice, instrument, or *Measures of Musical Talent* records to isolate each one from the musical situation as a whole and make the pupil clearly conscious of what it is that he is to hear. Give the pupil a concrete concept of each of these four characteristics, first, in isolation, and, second, in the actual musical situation. This identification well done is, in large part, the accomplishment of the whole task. Then, however, measure the capacity of each individual for these factors and give each his rating on these four measures. On the basis of this rating (note the basis) organize competitive drills in each of the four factors in turn in order that each pupil may be treated at his natural level of successful achievement and that no time be wasted in acquiring the skill he already possesses.

As we are here dealing with inborn capacities, the majority of pupils will not improve by this training after the concept of each item has been made fully clear to them at the first stage. This training is only for the refining of knowledge of what the factor is, the will to recognize it, the power of application, and the recognition of its significance, not in an improvement of the ear as such.

Do not blame the pupil with a poor ear for his low capacity; do not praise the pupil with the superior ear for his fortune. Apply the Bible parable of the talents: hold each one responsible for what was given to him.

Keep the ear of the pupil constantly alert to these four factors in all training, revealing their significance in the hearing of beauty in music. These four elements having been identified, treat in the same manner each of the complex processes of hearing, such as rhythm, consonance, melody, harmony, and movement, analyzing each into its component elements, and hold the ear responsible for discriminating identification of what is heard.

At this level of the complex processes the real ear training takes place for the musical and unmusical alike. A command of the power of concrete and telling illustration of musical elements is the gift of the inspiring teacher. The analysis and the synthetic production of rhythm, harmony, and tone quality by the pupils can be made an exceedingly interesting game.

Take moral responsibility for checking your performance in ear training by the parable of the talents.

In the language of the cameraman, encourage the pupil to spot the object, focus, snap the camera, develop the picture, and show it to friends.

Tone production. Base the training in tone production on a clear classification of tonal hearing, both the simple and the complex processes, keeping the pupil clearly conscious at every stage about what specific factor is to be mastered.

Conduct competitive drills for the mastery of one factor at a time. In actual singing and playing, use correct technical terminology and drill continually in terms of the definable, solable, and controllable factors. This is, of course, contrary to the common practice of barely dragging through the selection over and over again without becoming conscious of specific failures or successes or even knowing the names of them.

Do not drill the superior pupils on what they already can do; do not drill the inferior ones on what, after careful analysis, you are convinced they cannot do. At the most, use the superior ones to drill the inferior ones. Remember that the greatest returns from musical instruction should come from the musical pupils and you have no moral right to block their progress for exhibition purposes.

Use your constructive imagination in developing a pupil's command of voice or instrument through a conscious command of each element involved until it becomes automatic, in order that later he may have at his command a well-organized and serviceable automatism which is a condition for the expression of feeling in music.

Make tone production a part of ear training. This has a double advantage. It ties up hearing with action and furnishes most excellent opportunity for the vitalizing of both.

In the language of the coach, let us say to pupil and teacher alike, know your game, keep your eye on the opponent, hit hard, and make no false moves.

Sight reading. Sight reading is a combination of notation, ear training, and tone production and furnishes continual training in all.

Organize drills on the basis of capacity for achievement. A class may be divided into small squads for which pupil leadership is based upon capacity for command of the situation.

Pass by natural stages from the mechanics of sight reading to the singing and playing for pleasure and the preparation of repertoires. Remember that after all music is, for the great majority, an avocational interest; something that we do for the joy of doing it.

Introduce progressively the esthetics of music, always in terms of the media of tonal hearing, tone production, and sight reading, showing that the feeling of music and the expression of feeling in music are not beyond description and understanding.

Bear particularly in mind the principle of establishing habits without allowing exceptions, the principle of practicing recall instead of relearning, and the principle of measuring the task for each pupil in terms of capacity for achievement.

Make the goal of the striving the integration of skills which furnish the medium through which the musical mind may express itself with unhampered feeling.

Keep the pupil in the position of an artist who has his colors and brushes, the skill to use them, an object or ideal to paint, and expresses himself in the picture.

14

IMAGINING IN MUSIC

PERHAPS the most outstanding mark of the musical mind is auditory imagery, the capacity to hear music in recall, in creative work, and to supplement the actual physical sounds in musical hearing. This subject has received too little attention in recent years, largely owing to the extreme behavioristic attitude which ignores the existence of the mental image and partly owing to the fact that it is a phenomenon which does not lend itself accurately to psychophysical measurements. For the latter reason it is usually, but unfortunately, omitted in testing programs for the analysis of musical talent. Personally, I am, however, disposed to give it a central place and to expect the most immediate and helpful leads from an informal inventory of the use of mental imagery.

THE ANALOGY IN SCULPTURE AND PAINTING

The significance of auditory imagery may perhaps be best recognized through its analogy to the visual imagery of the sculptor and the painter. A sculptor who has no good visual imagery is a mere mechanic, modeling by measurements. The visualizing sculptor not only models from memory, often a single impression, but he sees in anticipation the expression, the type, the temperament, the "soul" which his creation is to embody. He sees in anticipation not only the model as a whole, but in terms of the minutest detail of fact or fidelity, of idealization or action. These features come to him in turn as the creation grows in his mind, often during the days and weeks before the first act of modeling or chiseling is begun.

In this wise he lives himself into his character so that the final work of art in a human bust portrait becomes not only a living and true representation of the subject, but also the embodiment of the artist's ideals—ways of conceiving, interpreting, mood, favorite snapshot of the subject in action, or responses—and as modes and models or trial sketches gradually take shape, the material shapes are critically compared and modified in adjustment to the imaged creation. The creation is first imaginal. The statue is a representation of the image, that is, the image gradually built up to represent the subject faithfully in a mood, pose, or action representing the artist's conception of his subject. At each stage the imaginal invention precedes the material treatment. The visual image is the working tool of the artist's imagination. Without it his workmanship would be condemned to mediocrity.

These same principles apply to the workmanship of the painter, and the analogy is perhaps faithful to an adequate account of creative power in music. It has been argued that some musicians do not have this power and the reply is, it has been found that some musicians are not musical. Certainly some do not have creative power, either in invention or in interpretation of music, and the absence of such power often correlates with the absence of musical imagery, just as the absence of visual imagery often correlates with mediocrity in painting and sculpture.

COMPARISON OF MUSICIANS AND SCIENTISTS

Normal individuals probably differ more in capacity and mode of the utilization of mental imagery than in any other mental capacity. I say "probably" because we have no comprehensive measurements. Of two equally intelligent normal persons, one may have the capacity to recall tones or to anticipate tones as clearly as if they were actually sounded at the moment, and the other may say with equal certainty that he cannot image any tone at all in its physical absence. Between these two extremes, normal persons are distributed on a scale showing relatively few cases near the extremes and a tendency to bunch toward medium abilities. Employing the rating scale from *The Psychology of Musical Talent*[137] in which, under certain experimental conditions the observers report as follows: 0, no image at all; 1, very faint; 2, faint; 3, fairly vivid; 4, vivid; 5, very vivid; and 6, as vivid as in perception, reports were obtained from three classes of observers as shown in Fig. 1, where the degree of vividness is indicated by the numbers at the bottom and the percentage of cases at each level is indicated at the side. In this figure, the dot-dash line represents musicians, the dash line psychologists, and the solid line unselected adults and children. Unselected adults and children proved to give the same distribution, and for that reason they are shown in one curve, but the significant thing for our present purpose is the very marked distinction between musicians and psychologists, psychologists being taken as representative of scientists. Fifty-five per cent of the musicians maintained that their auditory imagery could be as clear and vivid as in actual perception of the physical tone, and there is a tendency among all musicians to rate themselves high, whereas the psychologists, in spite of their professional training in the observation of imagery, rate themselves comparatively low. When we bear

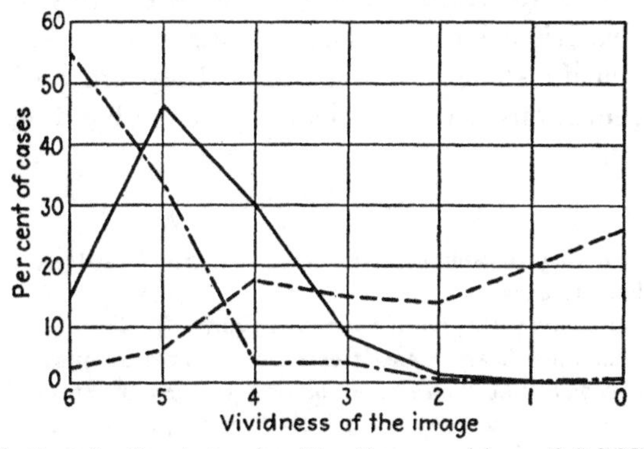

FIG. 1.—Distribution of ratings in tonal auditory imagery. (*Agnew.*[3]) Solid line, unselected adults and children; dot-dash line, musicians; dash line, psychologists.

in mind that there are inherited tendencies of capacity for mental imagery, it would seem clear that we have here a basis of selection for musicianship.

This difference in capacity for imagery has played a large role in the development of the school of psychological behaviorism, represented largely by persons in whom mental imagery plays no important role, even to the extent that many of them deny or question its reality. I have never known a highly musical-minded person to be a radical behaviorist—one who refuses to assign an important role to mental imagery.

In fact these large individual differences in capacity for mental imagery are at the foundation for the choice in vocations, and especially avocations when well considered. This difference takes live trends; for example, a person with strong visual imagery and weak auditory imagery tends to fall into activities in which his visual imagery is a distinct asset, as in graphic and plastic arts.

A study of the role of imagery in the minds of composers, as shown in their letters and autobiographies, throws much light on this situation. As evidence of this type of testimony, we may select certain expressions from the writings of Schumann, Mozart, Berlioz, and Wagner, taken as representative because of their unquestioned standing as composers. It should be borne in mind that at the time these composers wrote, the term mental images was not in current use. In fact, Galton's famous work on this subject had not yet reached their ears except possibly in the case of Wagner. They were, therefore, compelled to account for their experience in various descriptive forms based upon their immediate experience and couched in improvised terminology. In order to identify some of these terms, they are italicized in the following quotations from the gleanings made by *Agnew*.[95]

R. Schumann

From *Music and Musicians*, translated by F. R. Ritter. Second Series. London: William Reeves.

"For two long hours this motif *rang in my ears*" (p. 239).

"He who has once heard Henselt can never forget his playing; these pieces still *haunt my memory* like the recollection of a parterre of flowers" (p. 236).

"Though the *inner musical hearing is the finer one*, the spirit of realization has its rights; the clear, living tone has its peculiar effects" (p. 177).

"In the pauses of the pianoforte part *I am nearly always able to imagine* the filling out of the other instruments" (p. 180).

"I have *sung the work over* as finely as possible *in imagination*" (p. 450).

"What the mere fingers create is nothing but mechanism; but that which you have listened to when it *resounded within your own bosom* will find its echo in the hearts of others" (p. 283).

"The creative imagination of a musician is something very different, and though a picture, an idea may float before him, he is only then happy in his labor when this idea comes to him *clothed in lovely melodies*, and borne by the same *invisible hands* that bore the 'golden bucket,' spoken of somewhere by Goethe" (p. 60).

"We advise him not to write at his instrument, but to endeavor rather to *bring his forms from within* than to draw them from without" (p. 500).

From *Music and Musicians*. First Series. As above.

"I turned over the leaves vacantly; the veiled enjoyment of *music which one does not hear* has something magical in it" (p. 4).

"They will be understood by those who can *rejoice in music* without the pianoforte—those whose *inward singing* almost breaks their hearts" (p. 263).

"He is a good musician, who understands the music without the score, and the *score without the music.* The *ear* should not need the eye, the *eye* should not need the (outward) ear" (p. 63).

"In a word, the scherzo of the symphony seemed to me too slow, the restlessness of the orchestra, trying to be at ease with it, made this very observable. Yet what dost thou in Milan care about it all? And I as little, since at any moment I can *imagine* the scherzo as it ought to be played" (p. 38).

"It is a pleasant sign if you can pick out pretty melodies on the keyboard; but if such come to you unsought, rejoice, for it proves that the *inward sense of time pulsates within you*" (p. 147).

"When you begin to compose, do it all with your *brain.* Do not try the piece at the instrument until it is finished. If your *music proceeds from your heart,* it will touch the hearts of others" (p. 417).

"People err when they suppose that composers prepare pens and paper with the predetermination of sketching, painting, expressing this or that. Yet we must not estimate outward influences too lightly. Involuntarily an idea sometimes develops itself simultaneously with the musical fancy; the *eye is awake as well as the ear,* and this ever-busy organ sometimes *holds fast to certain outlines amid all the sounds and tones,* which, keeping pace with the music, form and condense into clear shapes. The more elements congenially related to music which the thought or picture created in tones contains within it, the more poetic and plastic will be the expressiveness of the composition; and in proportion to the *imaginativeness* and *keenness* of the musician in *receiving these impressions* will be the elevating and touching power of his work" (pp. 250–251).

From *Early Letters.* Originally published by his wife. Translated by May Herbert. London: Bell, 1888.

"You think I do not like your 'Idyllen'? Why, I am constantly *playing them to myself*" (p. 293).

"Sometimes I am so *full of music,* and so *overflowing with melody,* that I find it simply impossible to write down anything" (p. 81).

"But if you knew *how my mind is always working,* and how my symphonies would have reached Op. 100, if I had written them down" (p. 81).

"During the whole of this letter my 'Exercise Fantastique' has been *running in my head* to such an extent that I had better conclude, lest I should be writing music unawares" (p. 177).

"The piano is getting too limited for me. In my latest compositions I often *hear* many things that I can hardly explain" (p. 117).

Mozart

From *The Life of Mozart, Including His Correspondence.* Edward Holmes New York: Harper, 1845.

"When I am, as it were, completely myself, . . . my *ideas flow* best and most abundantly. Whence and how they come, I know not, nor can I force them. Those *ideas* that please me I retain in memory and am accustomed, as I have been told, to hum them to myself. If I continue in this way, it soon occurs to me how I may turn this or that *morsel* to account so as to make a good dish of it, that is to say, agreeably to the rules of counterpoint, to the peculiarities of the various instruments, etc.

"All this *fires my soul*, and, provided I am not disturbed, my *subject enlarges itself*, becomes methodized and defined, and the whole, though it be long, stands almost complete and finished in my mind, so that *I can survey it, like a fine picture or a beautiful statue, at a glance.* Nor do I hear in my imagination the parts *successively*, but I hear them, as it were, *all at once* (*gleich alles zusammen*). What a *delight* this is I cannot tell! All this inventing, this producing, takes place in a pleasing, *lively dream.* Still, the actual hearing of the *tout ensemble* is, after all, the best. *What has been produced thus* I do not easily forget, and this is perhaps the best gift I have my Divine Maker to thank for.

"When I proceed to write down my ideas, I take out of the *bag of my memory*, if I may use that phrase, what has previously been collected into it in the way I have mentioned. For this reason the committing to paper is done quickly enough, for *everything* is, as I said before, already finished, and it rarely differs on paper from what it was in my *imagination*" (pp. 329–330).

Berlioz

From *The Life of Hector Berlioz*, as Written by Himself in his Letters and Memoirs. Translated by Katharine F. Boult. New York: E. P. Dutton, 1923.

"If I had any paper I would write music to this exquisite poem; *I can hear it*" (p. 117).

"Two years ago, when there were still some hopes of my wife's recovery, . . . *I dreamt* one night of a symphony.

"On awakening I could still *recall* nearly all the first movement, an allegro in A minor. As I moved towards my writing-table to put it down, I suddenly thought:

"'If I do this, I shall be drawn on to *compose* the rest . . . ' With a shudder of horror, I threw aside my pen, saying:

"'Tomorrow I shall have *forgotten* the *symphony.*'

"But no! Next night the obstinate *motif returned* more clearly than before—I could even *see* it written out. I started up in feverish agitation, humming it over and—again my decision held me back, and I put the temptation aside. I fell asleep and next morning my *symphony* was gone forever" (p. 225).

"Last night *I dreamt of music,* this morning *I recalled it all* and fell into one of those *supernal ecstasies* . . . All the tears of my soul poured forth as I *listened to those divinely sonorous smiles* that radiate from the angels alone. Believe me, dear friend, the being who could write such *miracles of transcendent melody* would be more than mortal" (p. 232).

Wagner

From *My Life* (Authorized Translation). New York: Dodd, Mead, 1911.

"My whole *imagination* thrilled with *images;* long-lost forms for which I had sought so eagerly *shaped themselves* ever more and more clearly into realities that *lived again.* There rose up soon before my mind a whole *world of figures,* which *revealed themselves* as so strangely plastic and primitive, that, when I *saw* them clearly before me and *heard their voices in my heart,* I could not account for the almost tangible familiarity and assurance in *their demeanor*" (p. 314).

In these composers, recognized as representative musicians, the testimony is clear to the effect that they lived in a tonal world (auditory imagery). This tonal world is realistic, concrete, penetrating, and serviceable. They have the power to hear music in anticipation and in recall. They can select out for hearing particular tone qualities in the manner that the organist manipulates his stops. The mental hearing is frequently regarded as of larger resource and possibilities than the actual hearing. It is certainly resorted to far more frequently than the actual hearing. From the testimony, we see how they actually proceed in composing.

Although we have not collected evidence of the kind, it seems probable that, if we should take the great artists as interpreters in singing or playing, we should probably find analogous testimony; for, after all, voice and instrument give us only feeble cues to the sort of thing that the superior "mind's ear" can hear. A few quotations from letters written by recognized American musicians, secured by the author for *Agnew,*[3] will indicate their opinion as to the use of mental imagery.

"Vivid auditory imagery would seem to make the musically sensitive."

"The difference shows the degree of true musicianship."

"I consider distinct and definite auditory imagery very important. I strive to develop it in my pupils. With its development comes greater technical accuracy and better interpretation."

"Auditory imagery is a necessary factor in the higher appreciation of musical effect."

"The quality of the musician and the soundness of his aesthetic judgment depend, it seems to me, in large measure on his subjective audition."

"Significance attached to such differences depends upon whether the student has talent for composition or whether he is merely an interpreter."

"The more musical pupils have the clearer image."

"I aim at the auditory image from the start. Those having clearest imagery perform most artistically and only as they gain this ability, is music of real cultural value."

"Those who are strong on imagery memorize easily."

"Some students are more awake to musical impressions than others. Students differ in self-consciousness and the less self-conscious they are, the freer they are to hear the music mentally."

"Those who have it not should desert music at once."

"The matter of tonal imagery is a vital one in *musical training* and education. Together with the ability to *hear tones* and *sense rhythms* through the eye while looking at symbols, this power of mental hearing is fundamental and absolutely *vital in music education*, not only for the singer, the player, and the composer, but for the intelligent listener as well."

"I have laid stress with my pupils upon developing auditory imagery and urge them to study new pieces away from the piano at first."

"I consider the development of this faculty a highly important function of musical education which has been woefully neglected thus far."

"You have found probably the weakest spot in present-day musical training. I think nearly all children possess the faculty in rudimentary form, with great possibilities of development; but the *training should begin early*, and *continue throughout the entire course*. The results would be manifold: (1) more *composers* and better; (2) better *interpreters;* (3) more *intelligent listeners*, whose enjoyment of music would not only be *heightened*, but *prolonged*."

SUPPLEMENTARY IMAGERY

While the musical medium in mental imagery is the auditory image, imagery through each and all of the other senses may function in a very prominent way in music. The above quotation from Wagner illustrates his procedure of visualizing the dramatic situation as a whole, perhaps with eyes closed in a quiet room, living through the scene that is to be represented as it comes to him through all the avenues of sense. The testimony of great musicians shows them to be peculiarly capable of reliving a situation or living it in anticipation as a whole. Therefore, although supplementary imagery may not be essential, high general capacity in all mental imagery is an advantage to a musician.

But there is one in particular, the significance of which is but little understood, and that is motor imagery. In motor imagery, we act and feel the action. This is best illustrated in the case of the dream. In a vivid dream, the dreamer does not think the dream or imagine it in the usual sense. The dreamer is always the actor or an active observer of action. Therefore, when he dreams himself singing, he has all the experience of performing that comes through the kinesthetic (motor) sense; that is, in mental imagery he lives through the same sort of action that he would experience if he were actually singing. Now in imaging music in waking life, when the composer or, in rarer cases, the interpreter has an inspiration, he tends to fall into a sort of dream attitude in which he becomes oblivious to actual environment and creates within this tonal world a full setting in action.

The motor image, like the experience of action, is the raw material from which emotion is built up. The musician speaks of being able to produce the qualities just named to their general satisfaction. But a recording device attached to the piano revealed that the only two variables that had been under their control were the velocity of the hammer blow and the action of the dampers which affected the duration and loudness of the tone, and that, whenever qualitative differences were present, they were differences in intensity and time relationships.

6. The countless varieties of temporal movement are also reduced to the operation of time, with some modification by intensity. Ortmann performed experiments in which accomplished pianists gave artistic expression to such marks as "accelerando," "ritardando," "affettuoso," "espressivo," "scherzando," etc. The recording device on the piano revealed the fact that all these characteristics of musical movement were completely controlled by the two factors, the time relationships and the intensity of the tone.

7. The pianist can modify quality through controlling the time factor in three ways: the tempo and the temporal aspects of rhythmic features are determined largely by the duration between the moment of incidence of successive tones; the duration of vibration is determined by the moment of application of the dampers through the release of the key; the vibration may be continued by overholding the notes with the sostenuto pedal.

It is well known that the piano tone fades out rapidly soon after the hammer stroke; but the listening ear tends to ignore this and, instead of hearing tones as having sudden change in intensity and timbre, tends to hear the initial characteristic of the tone until the next key is struck, in spite of the fact that the physical change in the tone is very radical. For this reason, it seems to make relatively little difference whether a key is held down for the entire time assigned to it in the score. As a matter of fact, the player is often irregular and relatively indifferent in regard to the time for release of the key, especially in rapid movements. He depends on this tendency in hearing to carry over. In musical hearing, the effect of overholding the note by pedal is perhaps more evident in its modification of resulting tone quality than in the awareness of the continuation of the note or chord as such.

8. The most profound change the artist can give to tone quality comes through pedal action. By means of the sostenuto pedal tones may be carried through a series of chords after the respective keys have been released, thus producing great enrichment in the har-

moved, thrilled, heart-touched, out of himself, carried away, etc., always referring to the emotional situation created by the feeling or imaging of action. Although this has not been investigated thoroughly, case study of motor imagery will probably show that this is the outstanding characteristic of a musical temperament responsiveness to the musical situation.

LIVING IN A TONAL WORLD

From the above, it is clear that the mental image, and particularly the auditory and motor images, operates in music in the following three ways: (1) in the hearing of music; (2) in the recall of music; and (3) in the creation of music.

What a listener shall hear in music depends upon what he is, or is capable of putting into it, that is, hearing into it. Hearing is not a mere registering of sounds. It is a positive, active process of reconstruction in the mind of the listener. This may take the form of enrichment by analyzing and supplementing the objective sounds, or it may take the form of negative reaction, "hearing" elements of ugliness and countless irrelevant factors which color the interpretation of what is being heard. In the highest form of appreciative listening, we approach the attitude of ecstasy in which the actual sounds of the tones merely furnish the cues for the mental reconstruction that proceeds from the mind of the listener. To a person who is not capable of imagery, there can be no genuine music, because, like the lines in the crayon sketch, the tones by themselves, however accurately heard, furnish at the best a mere skeleton for hearing. In this lies a large part of the lack of capacity for appreciating music and the explanation of the necessity for mere formal obeisance to the social functions and amenities attaching to music.

Musical imagery is necessary in all forms of musical memory. In vivid musical memory we relive the music. The person who does not have the capacity to do so may recall in abstract terms; such as the musical notation or even the most refined logical concepts of elements in performance and musical criticism. But these are only the cold facts. He does not relive the music. He does not feel those organic responses which come from the re-reverberations of the tones in the music at the moment of the recall. He may recall the exact nature of the elements of beauty, the motif, and the forms of treatment, and give a complete account of a high order as a musical critic, but, if he does not relive it concretely, the recall is musically inadequate.

The little triggers in his autonomic nervous system which we call the glands of internal secretion are not tripped off by cold ideas; and the result is that the organism as a whole often is not thrown into effective response, which is the condition for the feeling of musical emotion. That is, the nonemotional person can recall the cold facts, but these facts are not the essence of music, the welling up of the musical emotion. The reason for this is simple enough. In the performance, it was the concourse of sounds that played upon the whole organism and stirred the musical emotions by throwing the organism as a whole into muscular tension, affecting digestion, perspiration, pose, stability, breathing, and circulation; but, if the sounds do not come back in recall, this organic reaction will be wanting, and the recall will be cold facts in mechanical array.

The image is necessary for realistic anticipation in musical thought, especially in relation to creative work. This has been amply illustrated in the above section on the testimony from composers. It may be said that all that is needed for this purpose is imagination. Now it is quite possible to have imagination that is of the pure, abstract, and cold-fact type, as in certain phases of mathematics and philosophy. Scholars in general speak freely of the operation of imagination without stopping to describe whether it has the experiential aspect of active imagery. We often speak of fantasy as if it meant nothing; whereas fantasy the world over has always been very realistic in ungovernable excursions into fancied realities. The term "imagination" in psychology designates the ideal or logical aspect of the mental act, whereas the image designates those aspects in which the idea takes on, to some extent, a live aspect of actual realization.

THE DEVELOPMENT OF IMAGERY

While the tendency to live in the world of representation which we call imagery in a vivid, precise, and indispensable manner is unquestionably an inherited trait with marked individual differences, it is equally true that, given a natural facility for imagining, it can be developed both by incidental use and by deliberate training. The development of imagery is analogous to the development of thinking where there is a natural, inherited capacity in this direction. The development consists largely in forming the habit of noting relationships which become fixed in memory so that when a situation is anticipated or recalled the image presents it in accurate and vivid detail.

In the second place, it is due to growing information, knowledge, learning, ideas, and ideals to be imaged. We say of perception that what a man shall see or hear depends upon what he is—certainly upon what he knows and wants to know, and upon his necessity of knowing it for practical purposes. The same is true of the image, but to an even greater extent, on the ground of its larger availability. The opportunity for seeing the "Sistine Madonna" is limited by conditions of travel; but, having once been seen, it becomes, in a sense, a companion in life who may be visited in the mind's eye, admired, and perhaps even embellished from time to time with ideals of beauty not actually present in the original picture. The same is true of hearing a great musician. For those musical minds who have heard him, Caruso lives not only in the knowledge about his artistic singing, but in the capacity for vivid rehearing of his song.

Development of imagery is perhaps analogous to the development of memory. With any given degree of inborn capacity there is certain possibility of improvement, and the magnitude of this possible improvement increases perhaps in geometric ratio with the quality of the inborn capacity; but, as in memory, it is by the exercise of his capacity that it grows, and the exercise is facilitated by natural ease, which is our inborn talent, and by the service it renders in life situations.

INDIVIDUAL DIFFERENCES IN MENTAL IMAGERY

A rating scale for mental imagery should be in every battery of measures of musical talent. Such a scale is found in the author's *Psychology of Musical Talent.*[137] It is different from the regular measures in that it is largely subjective. It calls for self-observation and is at the best merely a self-rating, a rating under specific conditions, which should make it rather significant. This rating is often a revelation to the person who takes it because it does show in a surprising way how different one may be from other people in this respect. One person may have auditory imagery as vivid, exact, and stable as the actual perception of the sound; whereas, another person equally intelligent may not be able to recognize any auditory imagery in his mental life.*

Types of imagination in music. Elsewhere[137] I have developed a classification of types of musical imagination in terms of which we can readily classify musicians with whom we are acquainted. Basic types in such a classification are the sensuous, the intellectual, the sentimental, the impulsive, and the motor. Any given individual may be dominantly of one of these types but ordinarily the personality represents the integration of two or more. If well developed, such a type may be called the balanced imagination.

---

* *Jacobsen*[54] has performed a series of fundamental experiments demonstrating the operation of mental imagery in purely neurological terms by what is known as the action-current technique. By this method physiological psychologists can detect and measure the flow of nerve impulses discharging from the brain into a muscle. For example, he may tell his subject, "When I say 'go' raise your right arm, raise your left arm, kick your right foot, kick your left foot." For each case his instruments will show that a certain volley of nerve impulses are discharged into the appropriate muscle. To demonstrate the neurological background for a mental image he would change the instructions as follows: "When I say 'go' imagine—don't move—but imagine clearly the lifting of your right arm, left arm, etc." In a very high percentage of cases he got the appropriate discharge of nerve impulses from the brain into the muscles that he got for the actual movement, but not strong enough to cause the actual movement. When he put the measuring instrument on the left arm and said, "Raise your right arm," there was no response in the left arm, but when the instrument was attached to the right arm the discharge occurred.

THINKING IN MUSIC

HERE we must face the analysis of a question which has been a bogey of the musical profession and the butt for scurrilous remark and generally an occasion for exhibiting ignorance about the nature of intelligence; namely, Are musicians, as a class, intelligent? Let us consider this question from three points of view: 1. Why has the question arisen? 2. What is intelligence? 3. How do musicians rate?

THE ISSUE

The question has arisen as a result of a number of outstanding aspects of the musical situation which we may note in the following:

Musical education. Until recently, musical education has been narrow, formulated and controlled from an artistic point of view alone. This has been regarded as a necessity because the highest achievements in music are often gained at the expense of sacrifice of other education. It is illustrated in the character of music scholarship, music teachers, musical degrees, musical leadership. The nonmusical world has, therefore, made the pronouncement that musicians as a class do not get the privilege of an intellectual life, do not develop sympathies with science, history, or philosophy, or marked ability in these fields. In this there is a large element of truth; but the situation is being redeemed by the modern recognition of music as a legitimate part in the academic curriculum, as it was in ancient Greece when music was recognized as one of the learned arts.

The esthetic attitude. The lifework of the musician is that of creative art. He lives in a world of images, imagination, fiction, and fancy, as contrasted with the rest of the population which, supposedly, lives in a world of facts and objects. This, again, is true and to a certain extent necessary and commendable, but there is danger of counting it against intelligent behavior.

Poetic intuition. Insofar as a musician exhibits insight and learning, he tends to develop a life of poetic intuition. It is generally admitted that great poets express profound truths often transcending the realms of science or philosophy, and that these are reached through a sort of inspiration and are expressed in figurative language, the effectiveness of which depends upon the outsider's ability to put himself in the artistic mood of the poetical situation and give reality to the prophetic and highly imaginative revelation. This is true to a certain extent and may be justly regarded as an indication of the musician's superior understanding of some part of the world in which he lives. It tends to make him lonely and to capitalize his feeling of superiority as the keeper and master of great artistic truths.

Life of feeling. Musicians as a class are of the emotional type. Their job is to play upon feeling, to appreciate, to interpret, and to create the beautiful in the tonal realm. To be successful, the musician must carry his audience on a wave of emotion often bordering on the point of ecstasy. While doing this involves intelligence and intelligent action, the medium through which he works is feeling, not factual material objects or abstract philosophies. This, again, is to a large extent necessary and to be commended. The musical mind comes into the world with an hereditary bent in this direction.

Social detachment. As a result of the above four situations, the musician is often found to be impractical, unadapted for business, industry, or logical pursuits which have social significance. He specializes so highly in his emotional control of the social group and of his own affairs that he becomes the butt of criticism from persons who regard themselves as successful in practical life, and especially in regard to science and common sense. This is one of the penalties of specialization which should be borne with patience, but hardly with pride.

Musical prodigies. It is a notorious fact that some children are born with a sort of flair for one-sided development in the astonishing exhibition of certain types of musical skill, entirely unsupported by ordinary intelligence, reason, or ability to make practical adjustments. History reveals records of musical prodigies who, from the point of view of intelligence, are correctly classified as morons. They are found in institutions for the feeble-minded and in all society, even that of the successful public entertainer. These are sports. They are rare, and yet they throw much light on the matter of musical talent and the marvelous resources that nature exhibits for self-expression.

Musical genius. We speak of a musical prodigy when music exhibits itself as a spontaneous outbreak in the life of the child and results in very exceptional achievement. We speak of musical genius when the same type of spontaneous exhibition is carried on a higher plane, even beyond that obtainable by the most highly educated. While the term "genius" may be applied to a life developed in balanced proportions, as that of Paderewski, the most conspicuous geniuses of music have been one-sided, unbalanced, and impractical. Such geniuses have appeared particularly in the exhibition of technical skill in performance, but also, though rarely, at the creative level. At the latter stage, they are analogous to the mathematical genius or the genius for invention, but they live a life of isolation which brands them as often lacking in common intelligence, in spite of the fact that their acts in their field of achievement are superintelligent.

Temperament. All the above characteristics seem to come to a focus in musical temperament which is characterized by the fact that it represents a life of impulse and feeling, extreme sensitivity and capacity for a high degree of specialization. It frequently results in frictions and clashes with the established order. The musical temperament is essential to the musical life, but it is often cultivated artificially and most of the opprobrium attached to it pertains to this affectation which may penetrate into each and every aspect of the musical life in society. *Jastrow*[55] in his *Qualities of Men* gives a masterly analysis of this problem.

THE NATURE OF MUSICAL INTELLIGENCE

In answer now to the primary inquiry, it is necessary for us to ask: What constitutes musical intelligence? There is great diversity of opinion as to the meaning of intelligence. There are scores of definitions and terms, each representing some more or less limited aspect of the function. According to *Stoddard and Wellman's*[186] most recent analysis, a person is intelligent to the extent that he is given habitually to behavior which is characterized by: (1) difficulty; (2) complexity; (3) abstractness; (4) economy; (5) adaptiveness to goal; (6) social value; and (7) emergence of originals. Let us apply these criteria to the intelligent behavior of the musician.

Difficulty. All intelligent behavior pertains to the solving of problems, not only the problems in abstract, logical situations, but all sorts of problems in daily life which pertain to effective adjustment. The capacity, will, and persistence shown in attacking difficult problems are a mark of intelligence. The more intelligent a person is, the more difficult problems he is ready and willing to tackle.

Complexity. A problem may be difficult but simple. The ability, willingness, and success in dealing with problems of increasing complexity through sustained deliberation are marks of intelligence.

Abstractness. The successful solution of problems involving increasing difficulty and complexity is characterized by the ability to deal with them in abstract symbols, ordinarily spoken of as concepts and judgments in the act of reasoning.

Economy. The ability to accomplish the most mental tasks in the least time is a mark of intelligence. Intelligent behavior is not a matter of trial and error, but consists in the economic and logical utilization of the insight resulting in premises based on previous experience.

Adaptiveness to goal. Seeing the problem, anticipating the solution, and adhering to the blue print, figuratively speaking, are marks of intelligent behavior.

Social value. Limiting the pursuit of problems to those which have social value is a mark of intelligent behavior and distinguishes it from equally difficult, complex, abstract, economic, and planned activities in all degrees of insanity or sporadic behavior.

The emergence of originals. The discovery of new and fundamental truths by a process which is verifiable is the highest achievement of intelligent behavior.

If this analysis is right, we come to the conclusion that intelligent behavior is a solution of problems of increasing difficulty, complexity, abstractness, necessity for economy, social value, and the discovery of truth. Now it is evident that these are all situations which the musician must meet to the extent that he is a rational being. Musical life demands intelligent experience and intelligent behavior in the processes of maturation, education, and the entire, serious pursuit of the art.

This intelligence is based upon both hereditary and environmental factors, and in the total population we find that there are enormous differences due purely to heredity and other differences due entirely to environment. The maturing personality is a product of both. Therefore, when we say that one person is more intelligent than another, we should take into account the raw material in the form of capacity furnished by heredity and the molding of the material through maturation in experience and training. It is a commonplace observation that a person's status in life is determined in large part by the degree and kind of intelligence. This is strikingly illustrated by elaborate statistics which came out of the mental testing program in the army.

In predicting success in musical education, we must always take intelligence into account. Thus, during the 10-year experiment in the Eastman School of Music, *Stanton*[175] employed what was known as a comprehension test. Rating on this single test has proved a very valuable index to the degree of achievement that may be predicted for the pupil, should he pursue his musical education. Any good intelligence test, however, will answer the purpose.

HOW MUSICIANS RATE

After this sketchy survey of the problem, we are now prepared to give some tentative replies to the question under consideration: On account of the emotional bent and the necessary activities in art, musicians live largely in the world of feeling and as a class have sacrificed much in intellectual pursuits for their artistic goal. Their learning is more contingent upon the feeling of appreciation and emotional action than upon facts and reasoning. Therefore, the cultivation of scientific and abstract thinking has been generally neglected in musical education. On the other hand, the musical profession makes as high a demand upon the intelligence as any other profession. Rating on intelligence as a supplement to measurement of musical talent is one of the best indices for the prediction of success in musical education or a musical career. The distribution of intelligence in musical activities is probably analogous to the distribution of intelligence in any field, such as the army, where there is a place for the corporal as well as the general.

16

NATURE OF MUSICAL FEELING

In setting out divisions, such as imagination, memory, intelligence, and feeling, there is no implication that these are separate faculties or parts of the mind. These terms simply characterize certain dominant aspects of experience and behavior as a whole. All perception involves memory, intelligence, and action; all feeling involves perception, imagination, action, etc. The organism always responds as a whole, yet in the analysis of the total response, it is convenient to isolate dominant characteristics. The most illusive of these old concepts of psychology is feeling.

Perception always has reference to the concrete, the objectively definable thinking always deals with concepts, logical and analyzable; but the affective life is scientifically less tangible and intelligible, although it may be the most violently responsive.

Fundamentally, all action in normal behavior represents either attraction or repulsion, liking or dislike, agreeableness or disagreeableness. Music deals with the feeling of agreeableness, liking, and attraction, but by contrast of the setting, it must always deal with their opposites, the disagreeable, the repulsive, and the unattractive, even if only for elimination.

DETERMINED BY CAPACITIES

Musical feeling, like all other feeling, is aroused in proportion to a certain sensitiveness to objects, either physical, mental, or ideal. A person who is sensitive to a difference of 0.01 of a whole-tone step responds to the musical situation in an entirely different affective way than the person who cannot hear any less than a quarter or a half tone. He will like or dislike only what he can hear, and the sensitive person, therefore, has vastly greater occasion for affective response to pitch than the person who is not sensitive to pitch. This is even more true in the realm of images, ideas, and emotions. Images of pitch, memories of pitch, thoughts of pitch, emotions aroused by pitch, skills in the performance of pitch, all call forth feelings of attraction or repulsion, agreeableness or disagreeableness; but the person who is sensitive to pitch has vastly greater resources in these higher mental processes than the person who is not. In other words, a person who is pitch-conscious, likes to hear pitch, is likely to build his memories, ideas, and skills in terms of this medium, but always living under the delicate balance of seeking the agreeable and attempting to avoid the disagreeable.

The same is true of the sense of intensity, the sense of time, and the sense of timbre. The degree of sensitiveness to one or all of these determines the number of objects or experiences to which he can respond affectively. The highly sensitive person lives in a vastly larger field than the less sensitive, and he is more likely to select his pursuits of life in those fields within which he has the greatest resources, the largest number of pleasures, the greatest power. This is the reason for the quite generally recognized classification of musical minds into the tonal, the dynamic, the temporal, and the qualitative. The musician may be born with superior capacity in one or more of these, and, as a result, he concentrates his interests around the use of these capacities in which he has the greatest power.

What is true of sensitivity for each of the attributes of hearing is true for each of the different sense modalities. The person with high sensitivity for color and strong visual imagery tends to find his outlets in this field and to be dominantly conscious by responses of attraction and repulsion within this field. This is particularly true in the stronger feelings, usually called emotions, which result in marked outward expression.

INTENSIFIED BY PURSUIT

Hearing and sight are the two dominant senses, followed, perhaps, by the kinesthetic sense as third in order. The artist in graphic and plastic arts tends to live in a visual world; the musician in an auditory world, though never exclusively. Affective situations and tendencies toward affective response are increased and intensified by the pursuit of a person's fortes. Thus, a musician who is of the tonal type develops more and more power of discrimination, a richer storehouse of experience, and, therefore, stronger affective reactions in music in which melody and harmony, with their vast array of variants, play the dominant role; whereas one whose forte is in the temporal field enriches his opportunities for feeling dominantly in that aspect of music.

CHARACTERIZED BY INTELLIGENCE AND MOTOR SKILLS

The limits and characteristics of the affective life of a musician are set largely by the limits of his intelligence or natural aptness in motor skills. What a person shall like or dislike depends upon the degree of comprehension that he has. This is not peculiar to music; it is true of mathematics, literature, and science. There are very few who can develop genuine enthusiasm for Einstein's mathematics. The limits of affective life are determined also by the natural capacity for developing motor skills, as in instrumental performance or mastery of voice.

TRANSFER TO OTHER SITUATIONS

Since the business of the musician is to produce, to create the beautiful, he is always beauty-conscious, or, the reciprocal, ugly-conscious. This attitude of expressiveness transfers, so that the musician is perhaps more likely than others to be beauty-conscious or beauty-expressive in relation to all other things in life, such as food, dress, and other comforts. One of the results of this is the tendency to develop irritability and oversensitiveness to all sorts of situations. The experimental work dealing with such problems is extensive but, on the whole, slushy and unsatisfactory. While it may be interesting to know what we like or dislike, such inquiries do not satisfy scientific curiosity. In Chap. 3, we laid down the criteria of scientific experiments in music. If we apply these to the semiscientific and so-called practical material in current publications on musical feeling, very little will stand the fire test.

Terms expressive of feeling are dealt with in numerous parts of this book. As far as we know, the analysis of feeling for beauty and the expression of beauty in the vibrato represent scientific procedure of the type we must look forward to and follow in the future.

It reveals quantitatively the factors that make for beauty of tone; it identifies the corresponding elements in the feeling for tone and in the expression of this feeling. It deals with scientific facts systematically, one at a time.

Analogous to this is the psychological approach to the problem of consonance-dissonance. The documenting of performance scores and phrasing scores throughout the present volume contributes vast material for the study of how to arouse agreeable feeling in music. After all, the psychology of musical feeling hinges upon the general psychology of feeling and emotion. The specialist in music cannot go far without taking this larger point of view.

17

TIMBRE OF BAND AND ORCHESTRAL INSTRUMENTS

We may best illustrate the nature and characteristics of timbre by considering quantitative descriptions of instruments in terms of their timbre spectra.

The recordings were made in an acoustically treated room which we speak of as the "live" room. This "musically acceptable" studio is a compromise between a good concert hall and a dead room. The timbres here represented embody two aspects of tone production, the instrument itself plus the room, as is characteristic of all music. The reverberations of the room play an exceedingly important role and vary significantly with many factors which it is essential to keep as constant as possible in recording.

Recent experiments show that we obtain different spectra for recordings in the dead room from those in the live room for the simple reason that here the tone is a tone of the instrument itself and is not modified significantly by the room; yet, even in a dead room, there are variable factors, such as the relation of the position of the player to the microphone. In general, the live room tends to reinforce low partials through resonance at the expense of high partials. Therefore, the true spectrum for any instrument by itself, as recorded in the dead room, shows weaker low partials and stronger high partials than in an actual music room.

It must be clearly understood that all spectra are subject to considerable variability depending upon the character of the instrument, the skill of the player, the relative intensity of the tone, the resonance of the room, and many other factors. On the whole, however, the group of tones presented for each instrument may be regarded as fair samples taken under favorable circumstances for recording in a musically acceptable room.

The tones here presented were recorded and analyzed with the Henrici harmonic analyzer (see Frontispiece) by *Dr. Donald Rothschild.* The analysis was carried through 20 partials for each tone.

The players of the bassoon, the clarinet, the flute, the oboe, and the French horn were members of the wood-wind ensemble of Bachman's band. The remaining players were soloists from the university band. Each performer played the equivalent of an arpeggio covering the acceptable range of his instrument. Each tone was played twice, once *f* and once *p*, the player being free to interpret *f* and *p* in the conventional way.

The description of instruments given in this chapter is restricted to the barest identification of the outstanding features which are shown in the spectra. A full account of the instrument would, of course, take into account historical development, the physical principles involved in the construction, various methods of energizing, the limits of variability, and many practical observations based upon actual performance, as well as upon the musical demands. Our main object here is merely to illustrate what a quantitative description in terms of timbre shows and means.

The meaning of harmonic analysis and the methods of graphic representation were explained in Chap. 8, to which we may refer for explanation of the tables and the figures in the present chapter. It will be recalled that the relative significance of a partial is expressed in terms of the height of a bar and that the decibel scale is preferred over the percentage-of-energy scale because it shows degree of perceptibility of each partial.

The frequency scale is given at the bottom. The fundamental pitch of the tone is given for its first partial. Decibels are represented on the vertical scale of 30 units. Loud tones are represented by solid bars, soft tones by open bars. The small circle indicates absence of a partial.

The first example, the bassoon, will be described in some detail, but the remaining examples must pass with bare mention, the reader being left to look in the spectra for the answers to numerous questions of his own. To supplement the nine instruments in this chapter we have further illustrations for the violin in Chap. 18.

As was explained in Chap. 8, the reading from the harmonic analyzer constitutes a table expressing for each partial the percentage of the total energy in the tone that resides in this partial. Thus in Table I for the bassoon, we see that the highest tone G 523 has but three partials in the strong tone and two in the weak. We see also that 87 per cent of the strong tone and 96 per cent of the weak tone lie in the first partial, the fundamental. On the other hand, the lowest tone, E 82, is very rich. The largest portion of energy lies in the sixth partial, and the lower partials are relatively weak.

Please note that the tables are in terms of percentage of energy, and the tone spectra in this chapter are in terms of their decibel values as in Fig. 2*b* in Chap. 8. This accounts for the difference between the tables and the graphs. Spectra like Fig. 2*a* in Chap. 8 could, of course, be made from the tables. In the tables, partials which have less than 1 per cent of the energy are not listed, but the spectra may show some of them significant.

Now let us take the concrete facts, stated numerically in Table 1 and represented graphically in Fig. 1, and see what they tell us about the timbre of the bassoon.

TABLE I. THE BASSOON

Percentage of energy in each partial

C-523	*f*:	87	9	4											
	p:	96	4												
G-392	*f*:	41	50	4	5										
	p:	84	14	1	1										
E-329	*f*:	40	29	25	5										
	p:	71	22	7	1										
C-262	*f*:	2	96	1	0	1									
	p:	5	95												
G-194	*f*:	1	88	10	1										
	p:	1	79	19	1										
E-163	*f*:	0	10	87	2	0	1								
	p:	0	12	86	1	0	1								
C-130	*f*:	0	8	58	23	10	0	0	0	1					
	p:	4	14	52	29	1									
G-97	*f*:	1	1	7	25	59	7								
	p:	2	2	4	62	25	5								
E-82	*f*:	2	0	9	6	9	49	23	1	0	0	1	0	0	1
	p:	11	3	2	16	4	42	2	1	16	1				
Partials		1	2	3	4	5	6	7	8	9	10	11	12	13	14

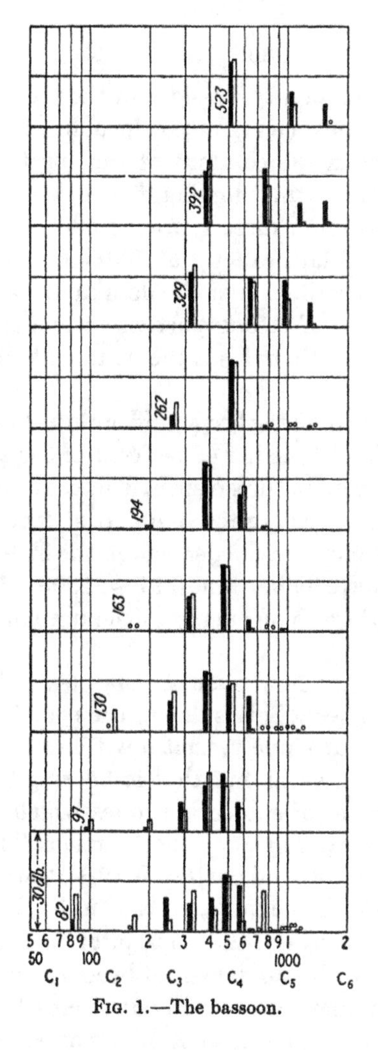

FIG. 1.—The bassoon.

THE BASSOON

1. The "bassoon quality" resides in the region of 500~, which is the dominant resonance region, or formant, for this instrument. Sighting vertically in the columns of the spectra, we see that all the long bars, representing dominant energy of the tone, tend to follow a vertical column directly above 500~ for all frequencies. None of the partials falls exactly at 500~ but it can be seen that there is a distinct gravitation of the dominant partials toward that point. This grouping of strong partials in one region is explained physically by the fact that this is the dominant resonance region of this instrument.

2. The lower the tone the less significant the low partials become. Thus the lowest loud tone has 49 per cent of the energy in the sixth partial and 23 per cent in the seventh. There is only 2 per cent in the fundamental, no energy in the second partial, 9 per cent in the third, 6 per cent in the fourth, and 9 per cent in the fifth. The same principle holds for the next higher tones, 97~, 130~, 163~. Indeed, for 130~ and 163~ there is no energy in the fundamental, that is, the first partial.

Yet we do hear the fundamental very clearly in these low tones as well as in the highest. This is due to the principle we discussed in the chapter on Pitch; namely, that low tones have relatively little energy in the fundamental, but that in hearing the fundamental is reinforced by a series of subjective tones which represent the difference tones generated by the other partials. Thus the difference between the first and second partials is 82~, the difference between the second and third is the same, and so on. Each of these generates a difference tone, always of the same pitch as the fundamental, so that the strength of the fundamental becomes cumulative. That is what makes the fundamental stand out so clearly in hearing. Other types of subjective tones operate in like manner, each according to its own formula.

3. As the fundamental pitch rises, the tone becomes thin and pure, so that for the highest three tones the dominant energy is in the first partial for the soft tone: 96 per cent in the highest, 84 per cent in the next lower, and 71 per cent in the next lower tone. In the bassoon, this is due to the fact that the fundamental for the high tones falls within the dominant resonance region of the instrument. This is characteristic of many instruments: the higher the tone

within the register of the instrument, the more nearly it may approximate a pure tone. In other words, orchestral instruments reveal more of their differences in timbre in their lower registers than in their higher registers.

4. In general, the highest partials, though few, are more conspicuous in high tones than in low tones.

5. There is an observable difference in the timbre of loud tones and soft tones for all parts of the register. Accessory noises and inharmonic elements, not here represented, are prominent in the strong tones.

Here we have answered five questions about the beauty of this musical instrument in analytical and quantitative terms. The purpose of the illustration has not been to state all observable facts but rather to create a clear picture in the mind of the reader of how characteristics of a particular instrument may be studied and described. The illustration should give us a clean-cut conception as to how the characteristics of an instrument can be defined and in what languages we can couch these definitions. Each principle that has been demonstrated suggests a variety of other principles which might be discussed if space permitted.

These dry facts may create a vivid and functional sense of familiarity with this instrument. Instead of accepting the variety of tone qualities as an irrational chaos, this line of reasoning shows how science dispels the confusion, by analyzing the tone into its component elements, which can be verified by exact measurements and described and defined in terms of verifiable concepts. This somewhat detailed description and interpretation for the bassoon is given as an example of the reading and interpretation of the data.

THE CLARINET

Here we have a picture which differs radically from that of the bassoon. The most outstanding characteristic is the dominance of the fundamental.

Voxman,[206a] who has recently made a thorough study of the quality of the clarinet tone with recordings in the dead room, has reached among others the following conclusions:

1. There is no evidence of a fixed formant as the determinant of clarinet timbre.

2. There is no consistent concentration of energy in any specific partial.

3. Both odd- and even-numbered partials exist but the odd-numbered partials predominate throughout. This predominance decreases with an increase of the fundamental frequency.

4. The acoustic spectrum for a tone of a given frequency is definitely a function of the intensity level: the louder the tone played, the more extended is the series of overtones and the greater their intensity relative to the fundamental.

5. For a given dynamic level the relative energy in the fundamental increases with frequency.

6. The lower partials in the spectrum are decidedly weaker when the recording is made in the dead room than in the live room.

7. Sonance affects our hearing of the timbre of the clarinet because this instrument is exceptionally capable of maintaining a constant wave form in a sustained tone played by an artist.

THE FRENCH HORN

The French horn has a definite resonance region, spreading from 200 to 600~. The wide and well-balanced spread of partials within this region gives the rich and mellow characteristic to the horn. It is noticeable that the dominance of this region is so strong that the fundamental is practically absent below 150~. There is no marked consistency in the distribution of energy corresponding to the basic loudness of tones.

THE BARITONE HORN

This horn has a very rich tone in the middle and the lower registers. There are two formant regions, one at 130 to 250~ and the other around 300 to 800~. The first makes the fundamental prominent in the 130, 173, and 220~ tones. The second is especially marked in the highest three tones. This wide spread of partials gives the characteristic richness of this tone, although in the highest register a pure tone may be produced. There is a tendency for the loud tones to have more energy in higher partials.

THE CORNET

The cornet gives rich tones in all registers. The first partial is comparatively weak in the 194 and 294~ tones. On the whole, the timbre remains fairly uniform throughout all registers. There is a tendency for the energy of the louder tones to be shifted to the higher partials.

THE SLIDE TROMBONE

The trombone closely resembles the French horn in that the dominant region is between 200 and 1,000~, without any evidence of sharp formants but with a fairly marked peak between 250 and 500~. All fundamentals below 200~ are weak or relatively absent. The strong fundamentals in the highest three tones indicate the peak response of the region they represent. There is no consistent shift of energy for the difference in the loudness of the tones.

THE FLUTE

The flute gives the purest and thinnest tone of all orchestral instruments. The fundamental contains 100 per cent of the energy in the highest tones and there are only five partials in each of the lowest two. This perhaps is the characteristic to which we refer when we speak of any tone as being flutelike. The pure flute timbre is best sustained in soft tones. How radical the change may be for loud tones is shown in the first two partials.

THE OBOE

The body of tone lies in the region from 600 to 1,500~. The very rich and widely spread formant around this region is what gives the characteristic of this oboe.

THE TUBA

The tuba has a resonance region between 100 and 300~. Indeed, for the lowest tone the first and second partials are practically absent, the energy lying mainly in the third and fourth. It is this region which gives the characteristic tuba tone. In the higher registers the tones are strikingly pure and, therefore, identical with tones from other instruments in their upper registers.

It is very tempting to extend this chapter indefinitely because it touches upon countless live issues in music and suggests the possibility of objective solution, classification, and description. Likewise, it is exceedingly tempting to review various issues which come up throughout this book in relation to their significance in the present illustrations, such as the relative absence of low fundamentals, the similarity of instrument and voice, and the implications for the building of new instruments. While we have attempted to simplify at every turn, we have also shown the danger of oversimplification, such as the assumption that a given wave form represents a given instrument or remains the same from wave to wave.

Aside from insight into the structure of the tone which harmonic analysis has given us, such analysis will be in the future a constant

TABLE II. THE CLARINET

Tone		1	2	3	4	5	6	7	8	9	10	11	12	13	14	15
D#-1245	*f:*	97	1	2												
	p:	94	6													
A#-932	*f:*	70	1	19	1											
	p:	70	5	24	7											
G-784	*f:*	90	3	4	0	2										
	p:	95	5	0	0	1										
D#-622	*f:*	93	0	2	1	1	3									
	p:	99	1													
A#-466	*f:*	18	0	42	1	10	0	10	7							
	p:	66	2	8	0	8	12	1	1							
G-392	*f:*	38	0	36	5	13	0	0	1	1	2					
	p:	71	1	26	0	1										
D#-311	*f:*	27	0	47	5	8	3	1	2	3	1					
	p:	93	0	6												
A#-232	*f:*	63	0	19	0	10	0	4	0	2						
	p:	73	0	15	0	3	0	2	0	5						
G-195	*f:*	67	0	2	0	18	1	9								
	p:	86	0	3	0	8	0	2	1							
D#-155	*f:*	35	0	6	0	8	0	44	0	2	1	1	0	0	1	2
	p:	77	4	7	0	5	0	7	1							
Partials		1	2	3	4	5	6	7	8	9	10	11	12	13	14	15

TABLE III. THE FRENCH HORN

Tone		1	2	3	4	5	6	7	8	9	10
B♭-466	*f:*	90	9	1							
	p:	86	12	2							
A-440	*f:*	99	1								
	p:	26	73	1							
F-349	*f:*	66	29	4	1						
	p:	94	6								
A-220	*f:*	26	31	26	5	9	2				
	p:	77	6	14	2						
F-173	*f:*	14	32	46	7	1					
	p:	10	43	36	9						
C-130	*f:*	1	19	21	48	4	5	2			
	p:	9	30	25	30	5	1				
A-110	*f:*	2	22	34	6	21	3	1			
	p:	11	34	4	25	11	9	4	1	1	
F-87	*f:*	1	43	22	19	3	6	4	1		
	p:	0	12	7	10	15	15	27	8	3	2
Partials		1	2	3	4	5	6	7	8	9	10

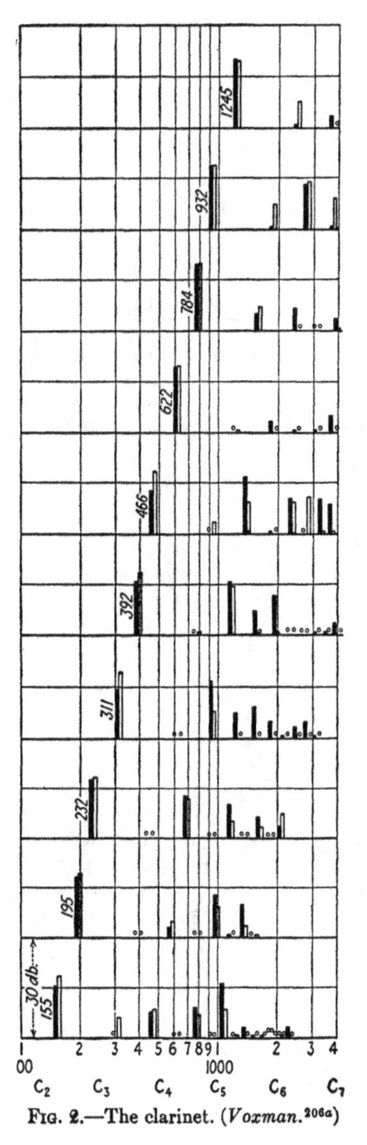

FIG. 2.—The clarinet. (*Voxman.*[206a])

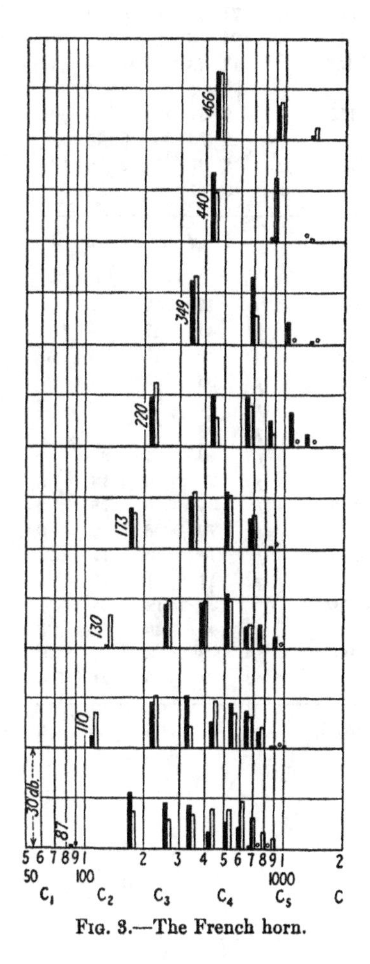

FIG. 3.—The French horn.

TABLE IV. THE BARITONE HORN

F-329	*f:*	87	11	1	1															
	p:	100																		
C-261	*f:*	10	81	6	0	2	0	1												
	p:	37	63																	
A-220	*f:*	38	5	53	1	1	1	1												
	p:	63	0	35	0	0	0	2												
F-173	*f:*	71	19	6	2															
	p:	91	6	3																
C-130	*f:*	13	13	8	42	14	8	0	0	0	0	1								
	p:	56	5	1	31	6														
A-110	*f:*	2	32	17	14	4	20	0	0	2	1	0	2	1	1	0	0	0	1	1
	p:	18	25	36	8	11	2													
F-87	*f:*	3	39	1	16	2	17	12	0	7	0	1	0	0	1	0	1			
	p:	19	17	3	1	3														
Partials		1	2	3	4	5	6	7	8	9	10	11	12	13	14	15	16	17	18	19

TABLE V. THE CORNET

F-698	*f:*	17	50	21	6								
	p:	42	48	9	1								
D-587	*f:*	10	17	34	35	2							
	p:	35	60	4									
C-523	*f:*	67	31	1	1								
	p:	88	11										
A-440	*f:*	46	7	33	8	0	2	2					
	p:	75	6	13	5								
F-349	*f:*	34	0	18	9	34	3	1					
	p:	70	8	16	3	2	0	1					
F-294	*f:*	6	13	14	52	5	1	4	1	2			
	p:	11	1	21	54	2	9	3					
B♭-232	*f:*	30	12	23	0	15	8	3	3	1	2	2	1
	p:	42	20	12	0	17	9						
G-194	*f:*	8	18	4	48	4	4	2	10	0	1	1	
	p:	3	19	21	4	20	19	2	10	0	1		
Partials		1	2	3	4	5	6	7	8	9	10	11	12

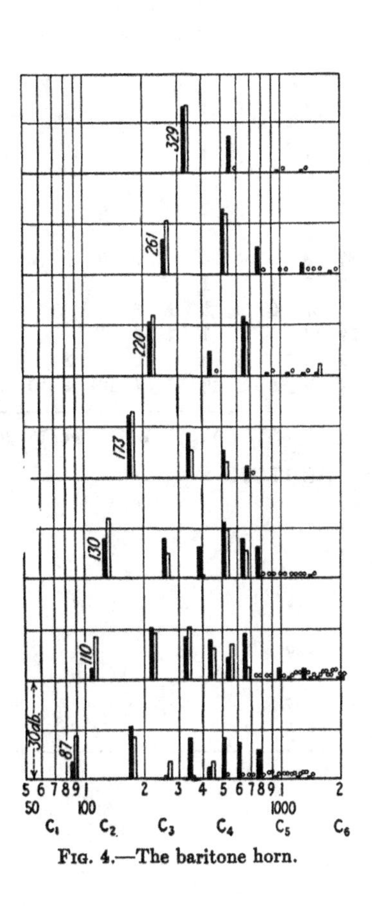

FIG. 4.—The baritone horn.

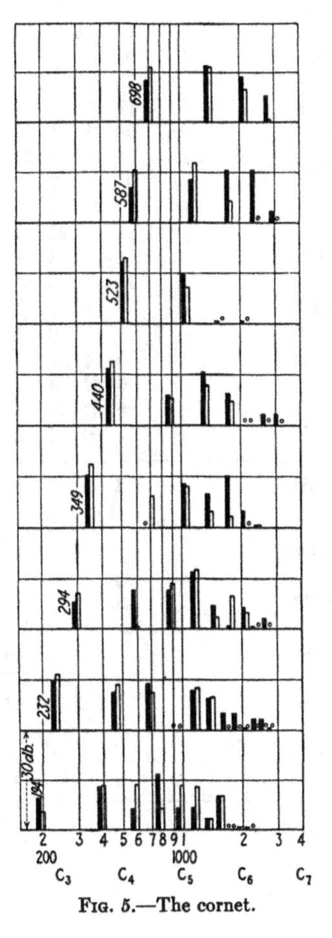

FIG. 5.—The cornet.

TABLE VI. THE SLIDE TROMBONE

Tone																		
B^b-466	*f:*	94	0	5	1													
	p:	100																
F-349	*f:*	52	20	21	5													
	p:	82	13	5														
D-294	*f:*	57	5	10	19	4	1	1	2	0	1							
	p:	94	1	3	2													
B^b-232	*f:*	8	47	32	1	1	8	1	0	0	1							
	p:	21	50	22	4	1	1											
F-173	*f:*	5	31	4	12	6	31	0	6	1	1	0	1	0	1			
	p:	26	12	25	33	0	16	2										
D-146	*f:*	1	16	1	4	7	37	8	9	1	4	0	0	0	1	0	0	1
	p:	8	29	0	14	30	10	7	1	0	1							
B^b-116	*f:*	0	14	6	21	5	4	27	0	9	5	1	5					
	p:	0	32	5	19	0	17	18	0	5	1	1	2					
F-87	*f:*	0	27	22	2	1	19	3	8	3	3	6	0	1	2			
	p:	4	20	2	0	4	14	3	0	2	12	17	4	10	4	0	3	
Partials		1	2	3	4	5	6	7	8	9	10	11	12	13	14	15	16	17

TABLE VII. THE FLUTE

Tone						
F-1397	*f:*	100				
	p:	100				
D-1174	*f:*	100				
	p:	100				
G-784	*f:*	87	11	2		
	p:	100				
B-494	*f:*	14	29	52	4	1
	p:	73	16	9	2	
G-392	*f:*	2	92	1	5	
	p:	88	5	4	0	3
Partials		1	2	3	4	5

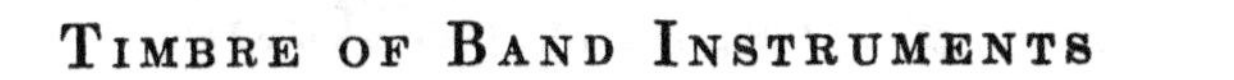

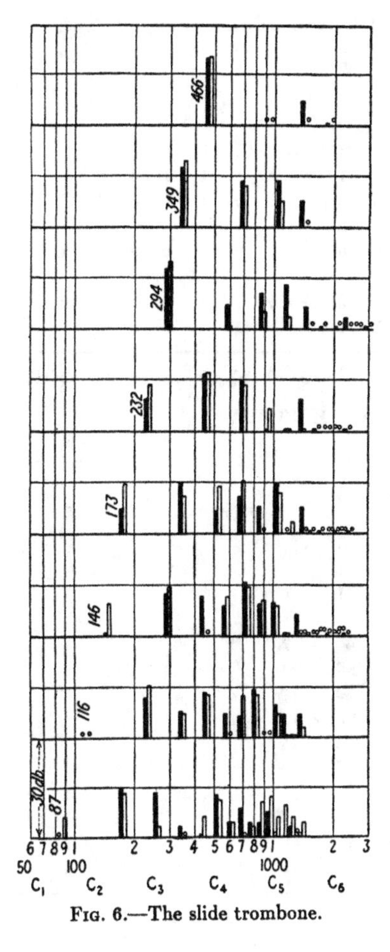

FIG. 6.—The slide trombone.

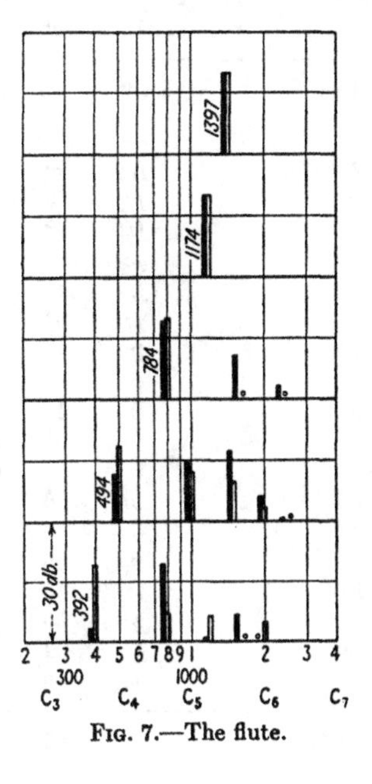

FIG. 7.—The flute.

TABLE VIII. THE OBOE

		1	2	3	4	5	6	7	8	9	10	11	12	13	14	15	16	17	18
G-784	f:	24	58	1	3	3	5	6											
	p:	26	71	2	1														
E-659	f:	3	94	2	1														
	p:	18	82																
C-523	f:	5	76	3	2	3	3	1	1	1	1	1	1						
	p:	11	35	22	1	0	15	1	2	0	1	1	6	2					
G-392	f:	4	9	37	18	3	6	2	7	1	0	1	4	3	4	2			
	p:	1	20	22	40	3	8	2	1	1									
E-329	f:	15	28	24	7	17	1	0	2	1	0	1	1	0	0	2			
	p:	22	16	27	31	4													
C-261	f:	20	6	5	32	15	3	3	3	4	1	1	3	1	0	0	1	2	2
	p:	1	11	3	36	42	2	1	0	1	1								
Partials		1	2	3	4	5	6	7	8	9	10	11	12	13	14	15	16	17	18

TABLE IX. THE TUBA

		1	2	3	4	5	6	7	8	9	10
B♭-232	f:	99	1								
	p:	100									
G-195	f:	92	6	1	1						
	p:	99	1								
E♭-155	f:	75	24	1							
	p:	83	17								
B♭-116	f:	93	5	1	1						
	p:	97	3								
G-98	f:	18	40	40	2	1	0	1			
	p:	35	42	23							
E♭-78	f:	5	60	12	17	5					
	p:	16	61	3	16	4					
B♭-58	f:	0	79	4	15						
	p:	3	87	2	5						
G-49	f:	40	6	1	15	1	28	4	3		
	p:	59	22	9	7	0	1				
E♭-39	f:	1	0	27	58	9	2	0	1	1	2
	p:	0	1	41	45	11	0	0	1		
Partials		1	2	3	4	5	6	7	8	9	10

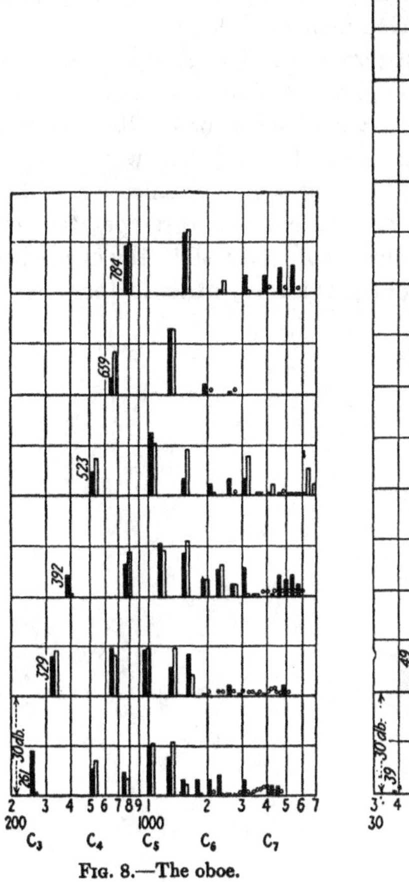

FIG. 8.—The oboe.

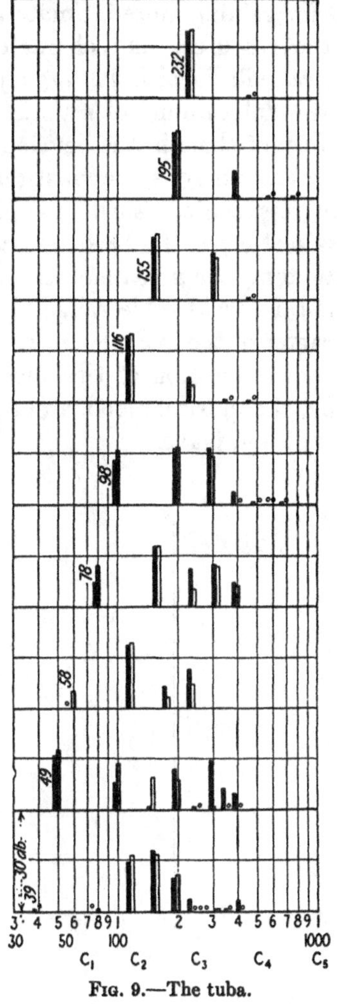

FIG. 9.—The tuba.

tool for gaining more intimate and accurate information in regard to the resources and characteristics of our instruments. Tone spectra will furnish in large part both material and measures for the determining of artistic principles of tone quality and the mastery of them in the development of skills.

In this analysis, we must remember that each individual spectrum represents a single sound wave shown as a specimen or a cross section of the harmonic constitution, or overtone structure, of the tone at a given moment, and that adjacent waves may vary within a considerable range. Among such variables would be the character of the instrument, the resonance and temperature of the room, the position of the microphone, the skill, the type of technique, the musical mood, and a great many other factors operating through the player.

18

VIOLIN

THE literature on the violin is perhaps more satisfactory than the literature on any other instrument. A good deal of it is of the character that could be included under the head of the Science of Violin Playing. However, following our precedents, we shall not attempt to survey this literature but will give a few concrete illustrations, primarily by way of the performance score.

The following topics will be treated: (1) the violin performance score; (2) the violin phrasing score; (3) comparison of two players; (4) the pitch factor; (5) the intensity factor; (6) the time factor; (7) the timbre factor; and (8) the problem of scales. The materials for the first seven sections are drawn from the work of *Small*[166, 167] and he has given most valuable assistance in the musical interpretation. The eighth section is drawn freely from the work of *Greene*.[38, 39]

TABLE I. VIOLINISTS, COMPOSITIONS, AND SOURCES OF PERFORMANCE

Violinist	*Composition*	*Source*
Busch*	*Sonata in D minor* (Bach)	Record, His Master's Voice D.B. 1422
Elman	*Air for the G string* (Bach-Wilhelmj)	Record, Victor 7103-B
Kendrie	*Ave Maria* (Schubert-Wilhelmj)	Direct
Kreisler	*Sonata in G minor* (Bach)	Record, Victor 8079-B
Menuhin†	*Sonata in C major* (Bach)	Record, His Master's Voice D.B 1370
Menuhin	*Tzigane* (Ravel)	Record, Victor 7810-A
Seidl	*Air for the G string* (Bach-Wilhelmj)	Record, Columbia 9031-M
Slatkin†	*Ave Maria* (Schubert-Wilhelmj)	Laboratory record
Small 1†	*Air for the G string* (Bach-Wilhelmj)	Direct
Small 2‡	*Air for the G string* (Bach-Wilhelmj)	Laboratory record
Small 3†	*Ave Maria* (Schubert-Wilhelmj)	Laboratory record
Szigeti	*Sonata in G minor* (Bach)	Record, Columbia 67989-D

* Hereafter only the player's name will be given, the composition as listed being implied.
† These performances have been treated the most completely.
‡ This performance was eight months after Small 1.

THE VIOLIN PERFORMANCE SCORE

Small[166] recorded photographically and studied the compositions listed in Table I by means of performance scores and phrasing

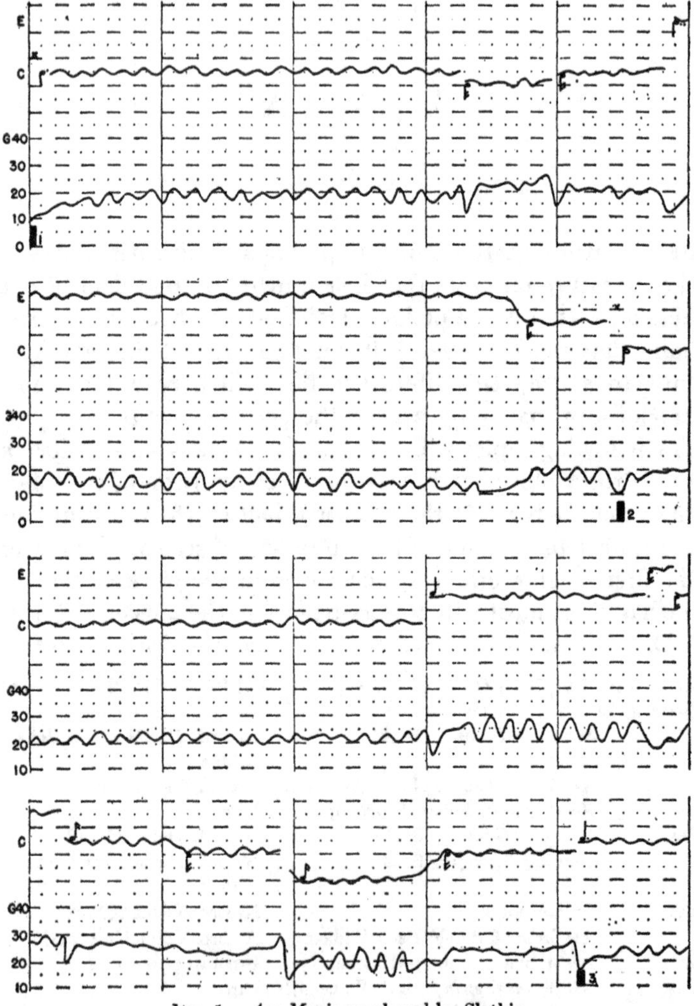

FIG. 1.—*Ave Maria* as played by Slatkin.

scores. Of these, a sample is taken from each of the two renditions of *Ave Maria* (Schubert-Wilhelmj) as played by Slatkin and Small (Figs. 1 and 2). These are placed on facing pages for convenience in comparison. The reading of the score is the same as in Chap. 4. Measures are indicated by a short vertical bar and numbered, and the actual notes of the musical score are interpolated for reference. The decibel readings shown at the left are

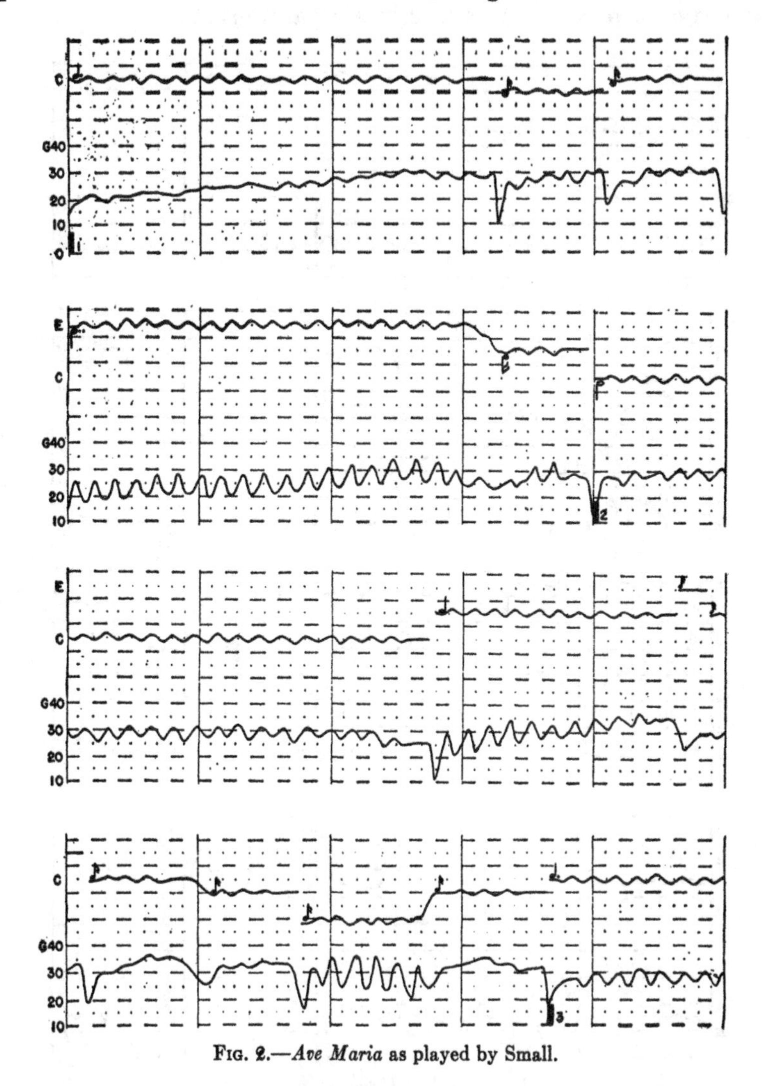

FIG. 2.—*Ave Maria* as played by Small.

not absolute but relative, in that the zero as a reference point is placed arbitrarily at the intensity of the softest note in the selection which had musical significance. When intensity is recorded from phonograph records it is clearly understood that this involves some distortion; but, in those cases, no conclusion is drawn which would be seriously affected by that distortion. These samples give complete records of performance for pitch, intensity, and time. Studies on timbre are discussed in a separate section.

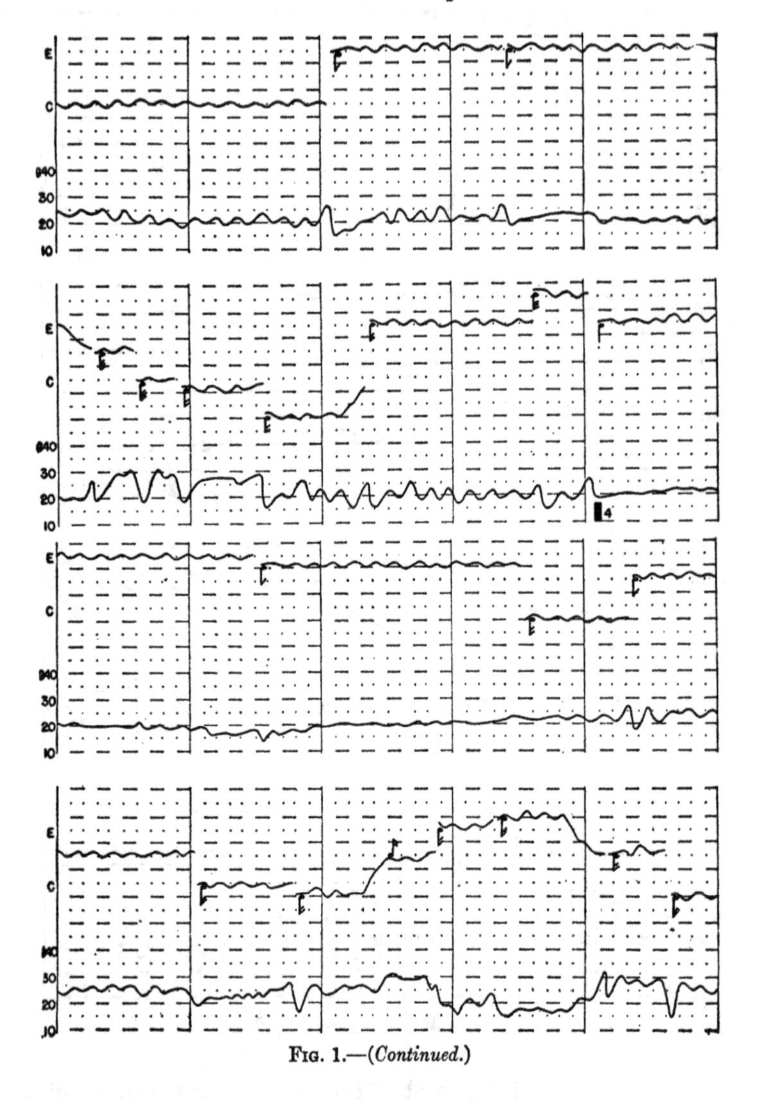

FIG. 1.—(*Continued.*)

THE VIOLIN PHRASING SCORE

The musical significance of these scores is set out more graphically in the phrasing scores (Figs. 3 and 4) for these same performance scores. This score gives an exact profile of the musical interpretation made in the phrasing. It is given in terms of pitch,

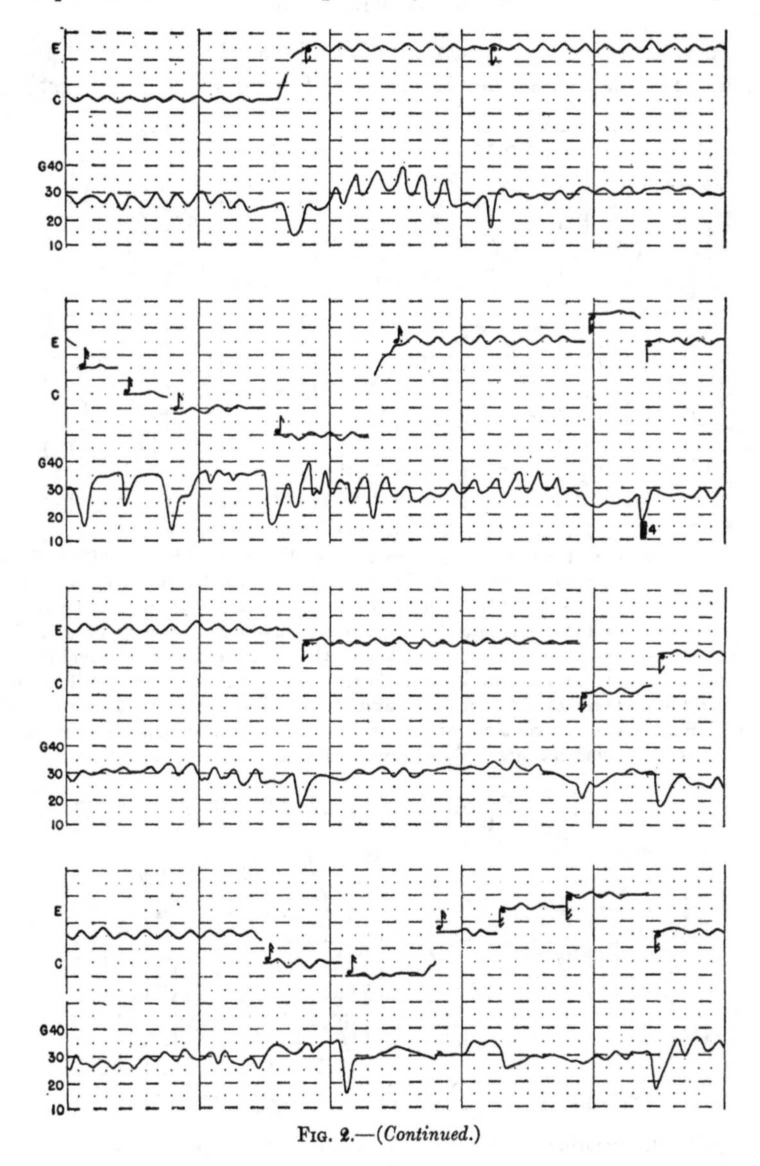

FIG. 2.—(*Continued.*)

intensity, and time; but through these media we represent all possible complex forms of phrasing except for the medium of timbre. For interpretation see the legend under Fig. 3.

COMPARISON OF THE PERFORMANCE OF TWO PLAYERS

Since these two playings were made without either player knowing about the performance of the other, it is particularly interesting

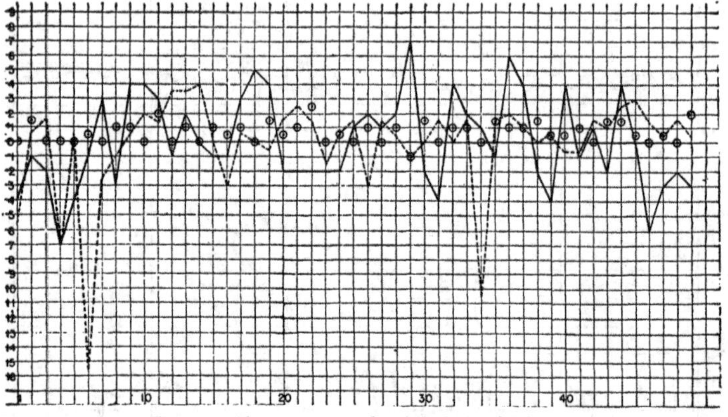

FIG. 3.—Phrasing score for first half of Fig. 1.

Pitch, intensity, and temporal deviations for the *Ave Maria* (Shubert-Wilhelmj) as played by Slatkin. Successive notes are shown on the abscissa. For pitch, units on the ordinate represent 0.1 tone, and the zero point indicates exact intonation in the tempered scale. The circles mark the mean-pitch level of successive notes. For intensity, units on the ordinate represent 1db and the zero point indicates the average of the mean intensities of the notes. The solid line indicates the mean intensity for successive notes. For duration, units on the ordinate represent 0.1 sec. and the zero point indicates exact distribution of time throughout a measure in accordance with the score. The dotted line indicates a temporal overholding (+) or underholding (−) of successive notes.

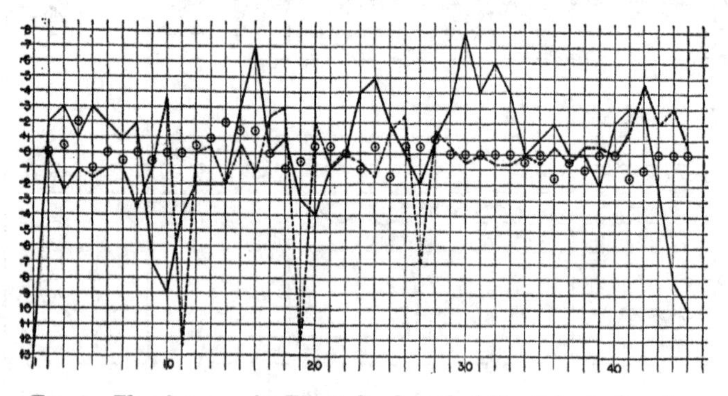

FIG. 4.—Phrasing score for Fig. 2. See legend of Fig. 3 for explanation.

to see in what respects they reveal similar characteristics and interpretations and in what particular respects they differ.

The performance scores. In comparing the performances of Slatkin and Small let us first compare item for item in the performance score (Figs. 1 and 2). We must limit ourselves to the more salient characteristics in similarities and differences. The limits of time and space prevent us from going into fine details which may be studied in the original large graphs. Let us call Slatkin *A* and Small *B*.

Both played the first note with a vibrato, the mean pitch being in true intonation. *B* stopped the vibrato for the last quarter of a second. In other respects, the vibratos are of the same type and extent. The duration of the tone is approximately the same. After the first half second *A* held an even intensity; whereas, *B* executed a crescendo of about 10 db. *A* has a fairly even intensity vibrato, synchronous with pitch and of about 5 db in amplitude; whereas, *B* has only a trace of the vibrato, and that mainly in the last half of the tone.

In passing to the second note there is a change in the direction of the bow, shown by the dip in the intensity curve in both cases. *B* has a greater dip but of shorter duration than *A*. This will be seen to indicate a characteristic difference in bowing. Both have a pitch vibrato of narrower extent on the second note than on the first. *A*'s intensity vibrato is erratic, but *B*'s seems to continue from the first note and with increasing prominence.

At the beginning of the third note there is a change of bow. Both continue the pitch vibrato, as in the second note, at less than 0.2 of a tone, and both fail to carry it to the end of the tone. These two tones, like the latter part of the first, remain at a fairly even intensity and fairly bold intensity vibrato. The characteristic difference in the change of bow again appears at the end of the third note.

At the end of the fourth note there is a glide from E to D which is similar for the two players, except that *B* shows a clearer pitch vibrato in the glide. *A* and *B* both have a bold intensity vibrato. To what this coincidence is due is not yet definitely known. However, we can say that it is probably due to some instrumental characteristic.

In these examinations we should look for agreements and disagreements and anticipate possible explanations in terms of instrumental characteristics, common difficulties in fingering, mannerisms and specific faults in performance.

In the fourth note there is a slight gap in the pitch record for *A*, owing to an incomplete recording, and *B* ceases the vibrato for the last fifth of a second. *A* increases the intensity by about 4 db; whereas, *B* remains on the same intensity level.

At the beginning of the second measure we have the same characteristic difference in dip owing to the manner of change in bow. In the first note both make a clean attack in pitch. *B* has a slightly wider vibrato, which ceases for the last 0.15 second. The intensity performance is similar. After the change of bow, both make a clean attack upon the second note. *A* plays it with a very faint pitch vibrato and *B* with an even and average pitch vibrato. *A* makes a 2 db increase in intensity, and *B* plays a crescendo of 10 db, with a progressive reduction in extent of the intensity vibrato. The increase in the intensity vibrato on this note is probably due to its proximity to the air-cavity resonance region of the instruments, which is at about C#.

The following two grace notes theoretically take time from the preceding note and differ only in that *B* carries the absence of the vibrato from the ending of the preceding note to the first grace note. Both show a drop in intensity for these two notes. Inasmuch as the grace notes are short and are played in the same bow as the preceding note, the drop of the first note in returning to the average intensity level indicates that the drop is due to moving outside of the resonance region. The time for the grace notes is taken out of the preceding notes, as is shown by the fact that the length of a quarter note in this measure is 2.41 seconds and *A* takes only 2.25 seconds and *B* 2.35 seconds, showing that the note, even with its grace notes is underheld.

In the fifth and sixth notes, following a change of bow, *A* has a more normal vibrato; *B* has a faulty vibrato. Both *A* and *B* connect the fifth and sixth notes with a continuous glide, indicating again a similar use of position change, but *B* makes a dip in intensity in the transition and executes a swell for each note. In comparison with the preceding and following notes, there is relatively little intensity vibrato.

The seventh and eighth notes, again slurred, are played approximately alike in pitch, but both players show a significant change in the intensity vibrato of the two members, and both also show an intensity rise of 4 or 5 db in the intensity level for the second note. The rise in the intensity level may be accounted for by the approach to the peak of the resonance region. The explanation of the flaring up of the intensity vibrato on the first note and its attenuation on the second may be due to some sympathetic vibrations of the free strings. The first note, A, is one octave below the open A string frequency, which means that the second partial of the present A corresponds in frequency to the open A string; whereas, the second note, which is B, has no such foundation for sympathetic vibrations in free strings.

There is not much difference in the pitch characteristic in the main body of the first note in the third measure, but *B* makes a partial glide toward the following note; whereas, *A* makes a clean release of the note, probably indicating that *A* remained in the same position while *B* shifted position. The intensity characteristics are also quite similar, there being a slight diminuendo for both *A* and *B*.

The pitch of the second note is quite similar for the players, but there is a marked difference as to both intensity level and intensity vibrato. *B* executes a swell and increases the intensity vibrato in contrast with the intensity of the note following. The difference in the behavior of intensity with change in bow at the beginning of the second and third notes in this measure may indicate a fundamental difference in the method of bow change. There is no significant difference in the playing of the third note, except that in this case *A* glides, indicating change in position, and *B* does not.

The next two thirty-second notes, played with separate bow strokes, show about the same type of treatment, both as to pitch and intensity. The intensity level for these two notes represented an increase of about 10 db for *A* and about 5 db for *B* above the level of the preceding note. The pitch of the next two notes, sixteenths, is played about the same by *A* and *B*, except that *A* runs the second note into a glide. There is a marked difference in the type of intensity change. In the character of the intensity level both have a more marked intensity vibrato in the second note. Both players show a marked intensity pulsation in the second note, as we found in the previous appearance of this *A* at the end of the second measure. *B* executes a swell in the second note.

Both make transition from the seventh to the eighth note through a partial gliding, involving a rise from the preceding note on the part of *A* and a rise toward the following note on the part of *B*, with an interruption in the change of bowing in both. This implies that *A*, in making his change in position, utilizes the finger with which he has been playing, while *B* uses the finger which will be employed in the next note.*

The phrasing scores. We may now take the data which we have just examined from the playing of Slatkin and Small and show how these scores, when measured with care with the enlarged graphs, can give us a concrete and detailed picture of the way in which each player phrased the selection.

Let us first compare the pitch, represented by the circles, beginning with the second note because the recordings for the first note in the Small graph are defective. Calling Slatkin *A* and Small *B* as before, referring respectively to graphs 3 and 4, we note the following course of pitch intonation:

A plays the second note 0.15 of a tone sharp, *B* plays it true; *A* plays the third note true, *B* plays it 0.05 sharp; *A* plays the fourth note true, *B* plays it 0.2 of a tone sharp; *A* plays the fifth note true, *B* plays it 0.1 flat; *A* plays the sixth note 0.05 sharp, *B* plays it true; *A* plays the seventh note true, *B* plays it 0.05 flat; *A* plays the eighth note 0.1 sharp, *B* plays it true.

This may suffice as a guide for the reading of phrasing through pitch. The melody is, of course, set by the composer. The player's interpretation consists in the adoption of a scale, for example, the natural scale, and then deviating from this for artistic values.

In records of this sort, which may now be readily available, we shall be able to make comprehensive studies of such remote questions as that which centers about tendency tones, both in theory and in practice. We find that certain intervals are augmented or contracted in accordance with recognized theory, that a great variety of specific deviations are dictated by the player's feeling for a particular context, that technical difficulties such as fingering,

---

* Anyone interested in further comparison will find further interpretations in the original scores in *Small*.[166,167]

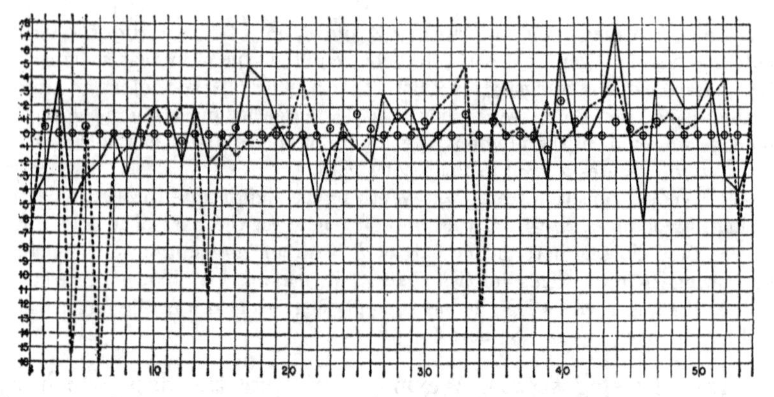

FIG. 5.—Pitch, intensity, and temporal deviations for the *Air for the G string* (Bach-Wilhelmj) as played by Small.

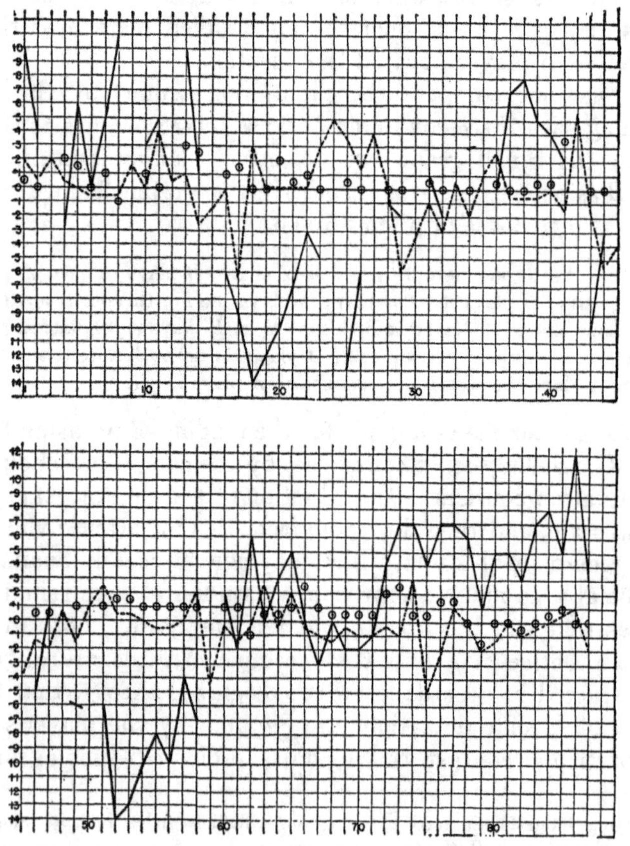

FIG. 6.—Pitch, intensity, and temporal deviations for the *Tzigane* (Ravel) as played by Menuhin. The points at which the solid line is interrupted represent the occurrence of rests as indicated by the score.

interfere with the interpretation, and that even the best of players probably make some sheer errors.

In the same manner, we may trace the comparative treatment in terms of intensity:

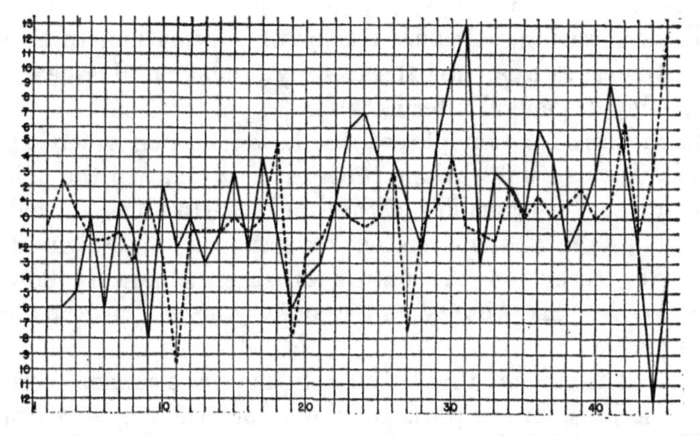

FIG. 7.—Intensity and temporal deviations for the *Air for the G String* (Bach-Wilhelmj) as played by Elman.

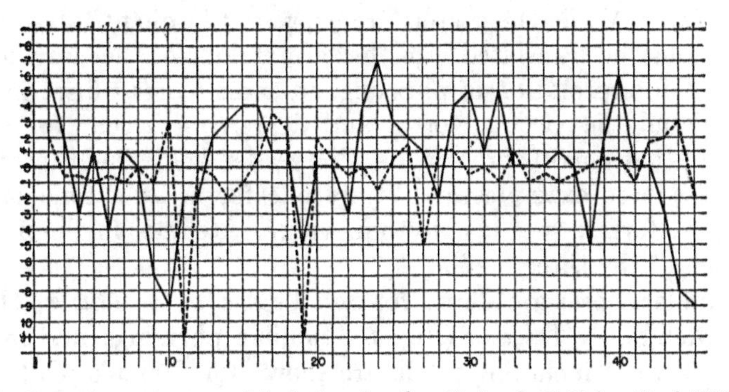

FIG. 8.—Intensity and temporal deviations for the *Air for the G String* (Bach-Wilhelmj) as played by Small (second performance).

A sounds the first note −4, that is, 4 db below the mean intensity; whereas, *B* sounds it at −13. *A* rises to −1 in the second and *B* to +2. *A* drops to −2 in the third note, but *B* rises to +3. In the fourth note *A* drops to −7 and *B* to +1. In the fifth note *A* rises to −4 and *B* rises to +3. In the sixth note *A* rises to −1 and *B* drops to +2.

Turning then to the temporal interpretation and calling underholds minus and overholds plus, in terms of tenths of a second, we find that *A* underholds the first note 0.5 second, and *B* is not recorded. *A* plays the second note +.05; whereas, *B* plays it in metronomic time. *A* plays the third note +.15 seconds and *B* −.2. *A* plays the fourth note −.7 and *B* −.1. *A* plays the fifth note in metronomic time, and *B* −.15, etc.

These phrasing scores are a mine of information. In this symbolic language, we can now discuss any fundamental issue involved in phrasing or general interpretation.

In rhythm, for example, we see how each performer expresses himself. We can put various theories of rhythm to the acid test. We can discover principles of rhythm hitherto unrecognized.

Perhaps the most interesting revelation in these figures is the light they throw on the nature of accent, showing how each player renders his primary and secondary accent in terms of time and intensity.

Thus it is evident that ultimately the performance score must be transcribed into a phrasing score for ready comparison and interpretation in musical terminology. We see here a very vivid picture of the differences in a section of the two renditions of the *Ave Maria*. While the graphs are expressed in quantitative terms, these must be translated into the terminology of the conventional musical interpretation of phrasing. In these scores we see in accurate detail the various forms and degrees of accent for phrase patterns in terms of three media. The reader would find it profitable to take these examples and study one factor at a time in their complex forms, such as rhythm, volume, tempo, in the patterns of each of the three media.

Similar scores are shown for Small's *Air for the G String* (Fig. 5) and Menuhin's *Tzigane* (Fig. 6). Similar phrasings in time and intensity, not including pitch, are shown for Elman's rendition of the *Air for the G String* (Fig. 7), which is comparable with Small's (Fig. 5) and Small's second rendition of the same selection (Fig. 8). Figures 5 and 8 furnish interesting material for comparison of the phrasing in two renditions of the same selection by the same player.

After this acquaintance with the reading and interpretation of performance and phrasing scores, we may profitably summarize Small's findings on basic issues involved in pitch, intensity, time, and timbre scores in turn.

THE PITCH FACTOR

The pitch vibrato. *Small*[166] summarizes his findings on the pitch vibrato, on the basis of the recordings listed in Table I, as follows:

Summary. 1. The pitch vibrato appears in practically all tones of the violinists studied, except on the open strings. It is typically present throughout the whole duration of a tone. These facts indicate a close similarity between the violinist's and the vocalist's use of vibrato (24).*

2. The average rate of these violinists' vibrato is 6.5 cycles per sec. with but a small range between individuals. This rate is in agreement with previous studies on violin vibrato (12, 19), and when compared with the vocalist's (24) rate indicates that the typical rates for these violinists and vocalists are the same.

3. The average extent of the vibrato is approximately 0.25 tone. This confirms previous reports (12, 19) and again indicates that the violinist's vibrato is only half as wide as the singer's.

4. Measures of regularity yield average successive cycle-to-cycle differences of 18% in rate and 10% in extent. This is essentially the same as for vocalists (24).

5. The form of the pitch pulsations is quite smooth and regular; it approximates a sine curve.

6. The rate and extent of the pitch vibrato are independent of each other, both for the individual violinists and for the group.

7. Although these measurements have yielded valid statements of sound field conditions with reference to the particular performances studied, constant caution must be used in drawing conclusions from them concerning violin playing generally and audition problems specifically. For the very reason that hearing is subject to such a variety of illusions and that a linear relationship does not exist between auditory stimulus and sensation (5), an objective approach to art, such as the present, affords a peculiar opportunity for the analysis of many technical problems which are usually obscured by the function of perception itself.

8. Implications which are significant to the understanding of the vibrato-producing mechanism are: (a) The cyclic movement of hand and arm approaches simple harmonic motion. (b) The stopping finger moves both above and below the principal pitch.

---

* Numbers in parenthesis here refer to bibliography in Small.[166]

(c) The direction of the first and last vibrato movements in a tone is not preponderantly of one kind. (d) The vibrato movement tends to persist through changes of finger and bow, and frequently through change of position.

9. A violinist's typical vibrato tends to remain the same in repeated performances of the same composition and in the performance of different compositions.

Precision of pitch intonation, mean pitch levels, tendency tones, transitions. *Small*[166] summarizes his findings on this subject as follows:

Summary. 1. The violinist deviates over 60% of the time from the tempered scale notes with deviations .05 tone or greater and over 31% of the time with deviations .1 tone or greater. The average deviation is about .1 tone. The deviations are preponderantly in the direction of sharping.

2. Some of these deviations may be due to: (a) anatomical difficulties in the necessary spacing of fingers for some intervals, (b) accidental causes, (c) use of Pythagorean or natural scale intonation, (d) the division of attention, (e) the non-linear relationship between pitch and frequency, or (f) the use of tendency tones.

3. Frequent applications of tendencies from the tempered scale were found, although their application is not invariable. The tendencies applied were for (a) the fourth degree of the scale to be lowered and the seventh raised, (b) minor and diminished intervals to be contracted, (c) major and augmented intervals to be expanded and (d) chromatically altered notes to over-shoot the alteration in the direction of the chromatic used. The percentage of possible occasions these tendencies were applied in these compositions is given in table form. The leading-tone and sub-dominant tendencies are more frequent than the remainder.

Leading-tone	*Sub-dominant (4th degree)*	*Minor and diminished intervals*	*Chromatics*	*Major and augmented intervals*
85%	80%	51%	50%	44%

4. The intonation in tempered scale intervals was found to deviate .05 tone or more over 50% of the time, and .1 tone or more about 25% of the time. Of these deviations of .05 tone or

over, 56% are in the direction of flatting. Of those .1 tone and over, 65% are flat. The typical deviation is about 0.1 tone. Intonation is slightly more accurate for intervals than for individual pitch levels.

5. The violinist interpolates certain pitch transitions between pitch levels of the score when a change in level and a change of position coincide, the object probably being to enhance the legato character of a phrase or melody. The portamenti are predominantly continuous transitions. This type of interpolation also occurs in vocal performance (24). Three types of discontinuous pitch transitions occur, verifying pedagogical theory on this subject. The average interval covered in these pitch movements is 2.5 semitones.

Gliding pitch attacks and releases as found in song (24) and speech (4) do not occur in the performances of these violinists. A typical steady-pitch-level attack and release are found in two performances.

THE INTENSITY FACTOR

Range of intensity. Figures 1 to 8 show typically the range of intensity changes. The average range of intensity between the softest and the loudest tones for all records is 21 db, with individual ranges from 14 to 26 db. The mean intensity differences between successive notes is 3.5 db. The typical range of intensity variation within individual notes was 13 db. For all violinists here studied, except Menuhin, the mean maximum intensity is in the region of middle C. This is probably due to the fact that the fundamental air-cavity resonance of the violin is just above middle C, perhaps near C#.

Change of bow. The typical drop in intensity with the change of bow is 12 db in the dead room. Other recordings, such as that of Menuhin, probably show a smaller drop on account of the reverberations in the room. Whether these drops are heard or not depends upon a large number of factors, both subjective and objective.

The intensity vibrato. *Small*[166] summarizes as follows:

Summary. 1. The intensity vibrato is present only 76% as often as the pitch vibrato in the same performances. This is essentially the proportion found in the case of singing (24, 32).

The proportion varies in individual performances from 40 to 94%.

2. The intensity vibrato is not always continuous nor does it appear throughout the entire duration of the tone in which it is found. It is frequently intermittent and sporadic.

3. The average rate of the intensity vibrato is 6.3 cycles per sec., which is the same as the pitch vibrato rate.

4. The average extent is 4.4 db, which substantiates *Reger's* report (19). The distribution of extents shows a wide dispersion.

5. The typical difference between successive cycles is 11% of the average rate and 30% of the average extent. Both intensity vibrato rate and extent, though particularly the latter, are less regular than pitch vibrato rate and extent.

6. The form of the intensity pulsations, barring superimposed secondary fluctuations, approximates a sine curve. The most common phase relationships between intensity and pitch pulsations are those of phase agreement and 90° out of phase.

7. The rate and extent of the intensity vibrato exert no significant selective influence on each other.

8. The characteristics of the intensity vibrato are very similar for the same composition played by three different violinists and for a composition played twice by the same performer.

9. The intensity vibrato probably is relatively more important in violin playing than in singing.

10. Probable causes of periodic intensity fluctuations, in addition to those already suggested (12, 19) are beats resulting from sympathetic vibration of free strings, and movement in and out of resonance regions due to the pitch vibrato.

11. The sympathetic vibrato is an intensity vibrato and exhibits the same characteristics as intensity vibrato in general.

THE TEMPORAL ASPECT

The trill. It is interesting to note that the trill in these selections, seven pulsations per second, is very near the average rate of the vibrato. Instead of even sounding of two notes of pitch indicated in the score, the violin trill closely resembles the pitch vibrato in the shape of the wave. When the interval is small and of short duration, the distinction between the trill and the pitch vibrato is largely psychological rather than physical; somehow, if we know when the trill occurs, we hear the two notes which mark the interval even in the semitone and do not hear the mean tone of the vibrato. There is a synchronous intensity change of about 5 db in the trill, the accessory note being the weaker. The accessory note is also about 25 per cent shorter than the main note.

Other temporal aspects, too numerous to mention, must be observed in the phrasing scores. In general, *Small*[166] states:

1. The violinists deviated over 80% of the time from exact note values. Half the deviations were more than .15 sec.
2. Over-holding and under-holding were about equally prevalent.
3. The average extent of deviations was approximately .25 sec. Under-holding is typically greater than over-holding and also varies more from player to player.
4. In general the longer the note duration the more liable was the appearance of a deviation. The extent of under-holding showed a tendency to be proportional to the duration of the note. Such a tendency for over-holding was very slight.
5. Temporal deviations seemed to bear a somewhat closer relationship to phrase structure of the melody than did intensity. There was also a somewhat more general agreement among the violinists in their use of temporal deviations than in their use of intensity variations.

THE TIMBRE ASPECT

The objective study of violin tones presents a most fascinating area for investigation. With the recent acquisition of adequate means of measurement, we may look for great developments in our understanding of the resources of the violin and the scientific aspects of the mastery of technique in playing.

Comprehensive studies of the violin as an instrument are in progress showing, for example, the response characteristics for all frequencies and all degrees of intensity throughout its range. Experiments are in progress in various laboratories analyzing the merits of instruments of rare value. Such findings should, of course, prove valuable in current design of instruments. The policy is to study one specific feature at a time; for example, *Horne*[53] is analyzing possibilities of modifying tone quality by the mute, varying step after step the form, the weight, and material of the mute and the relation of these to features in bowing. Mutes have grown like Topsy, topsy-turvy; but there is no longer any excuse for guesswork.

In this chapter, we can give only a single illustration (Figs. 9–12) of timbre in the violin. Here we have for comparison representative spectra from each of the four violin strings. Bearing in mind our reiterated reservations about the variability in fair samplings, we can say that here is a good illustration of what a good violin can do when well played and free from room and outside influences.

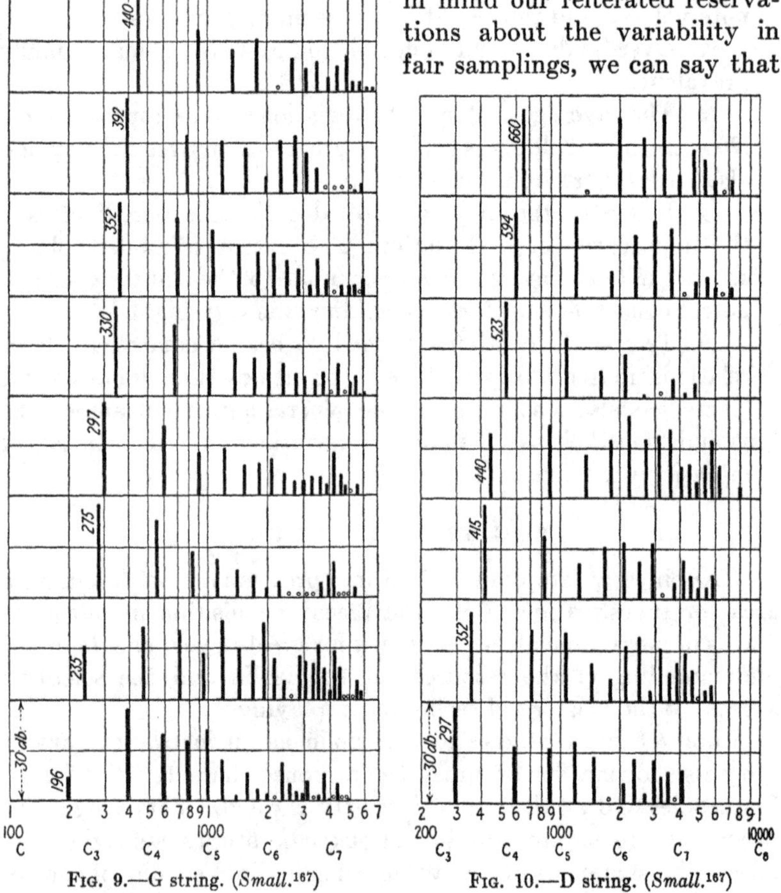

FIG. 9.—G string. (*Small.*[167])

FIG. 10.—D string. (*Small.*[167])

We are indebted to Small, sometime Eastman fellow and now a member of the staff in the faculty of the music school in the

University of Iowa, for these recordings and analyses. The recording was made in the dead room under the most reliable control conditions. These spectra, therefore, represent the actual violin timbre free from admixture of room resonance and outside disturbances. He used his own violin, an old Italian instrument made

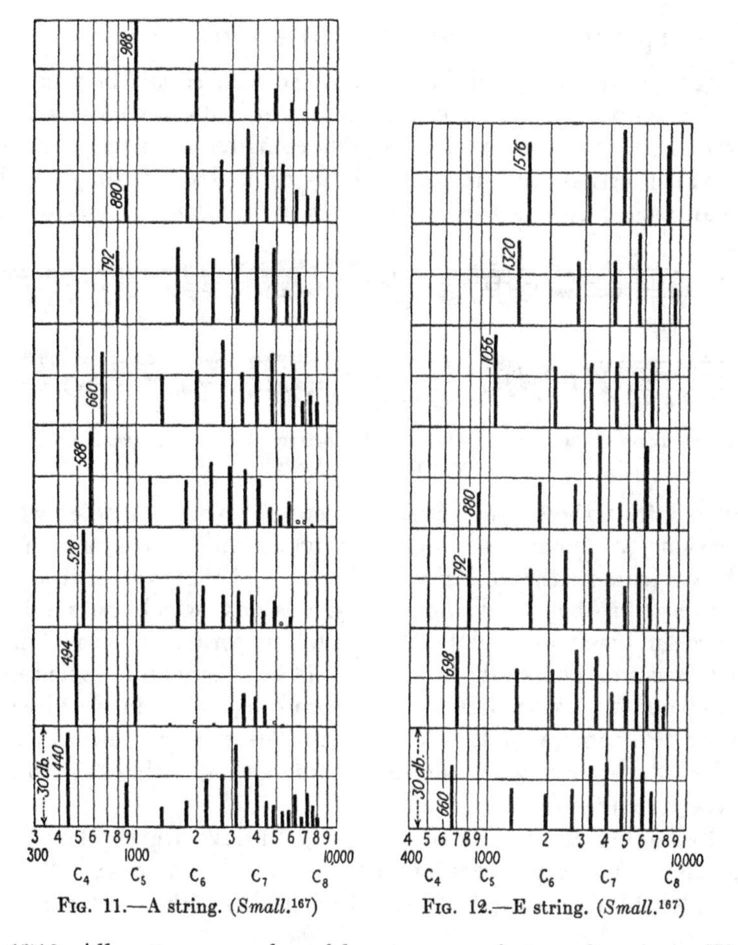

FIG. 11.—A string. (*Small.*[167])

FIG. 12.—E string. (*Small.*[167])

in 1740. All notes were played legato *mezzo forte* and up bow. The instrument was tuned to 440∼.

It is probably true that, of all instruments, the violin produces the most beautiful tone. We may see in these spectra something of the nature of this beauty. As is well known, it lies in the richness and even distribution of the partials. The "pictures" must speak for themselves, as they tell a long and complicated story. What this story shall be depends upon what questions are in the mind of the musician or scientist who interprets them. It may be a principle of physics, the solution of an historical controversy, a cue to an element in technique of playing; but to everyone it should give a striking illustration of the resources of the violin.

INTERVALS: THE PROBLEM OF SCALES

It is generally agreed that the natural scale should be preferred to the tempered scale in instruments which do not have a fixed pitch. There has been a long-standing controversy as to the extent to which artists on the stringed instruments and singers take advantage of this feature of intonation. It is also generally recognized that there are certain sequences or other factors which occasionally demand the augmenting or the contracting of an interval from its theoretical value in either of these two scales.

FIG. 13.—Score of the Kreutzer *Etude* showing passage, between the two arrows, which was played. (*Greene.*[38])

Greene[38,39] has made an extensive study which puts into a record in black and white the actual performance of violinists on this issue. The study is an analysis of 11 unaccompanied performances by six violinists.* The recordings were made directly before the camera in the dead room. The players performed as if they were playing for the radio, but without using the vibrato in the Kreutzer *Etude.*

Reliability of reading in frequency varies with the length of the note. For 78 per cent of the notes it is reliable to 0.01 of a tone; for 20 per cent to 0.02, and for 2 per cent (the shortest notes) to 0.03.

---

* The performers were Scipione Guidi, assistant director and concertmaster of the St. Louis symphony orchestra (1); Frank Estes Kendrie, professor of violin at the University of Iowa and conductor of the University of Iowa symphony orchestra (2); Arnold M. Small, concertmaster of the University of Iowa symphony orchestra (4); and Felix Slatkin (3), Ellis Levy (5), and Jacob Levine (6), members of the first violin section of the St. Louis symphony orchestra. Hereafter in this discussion the players are reported by number.

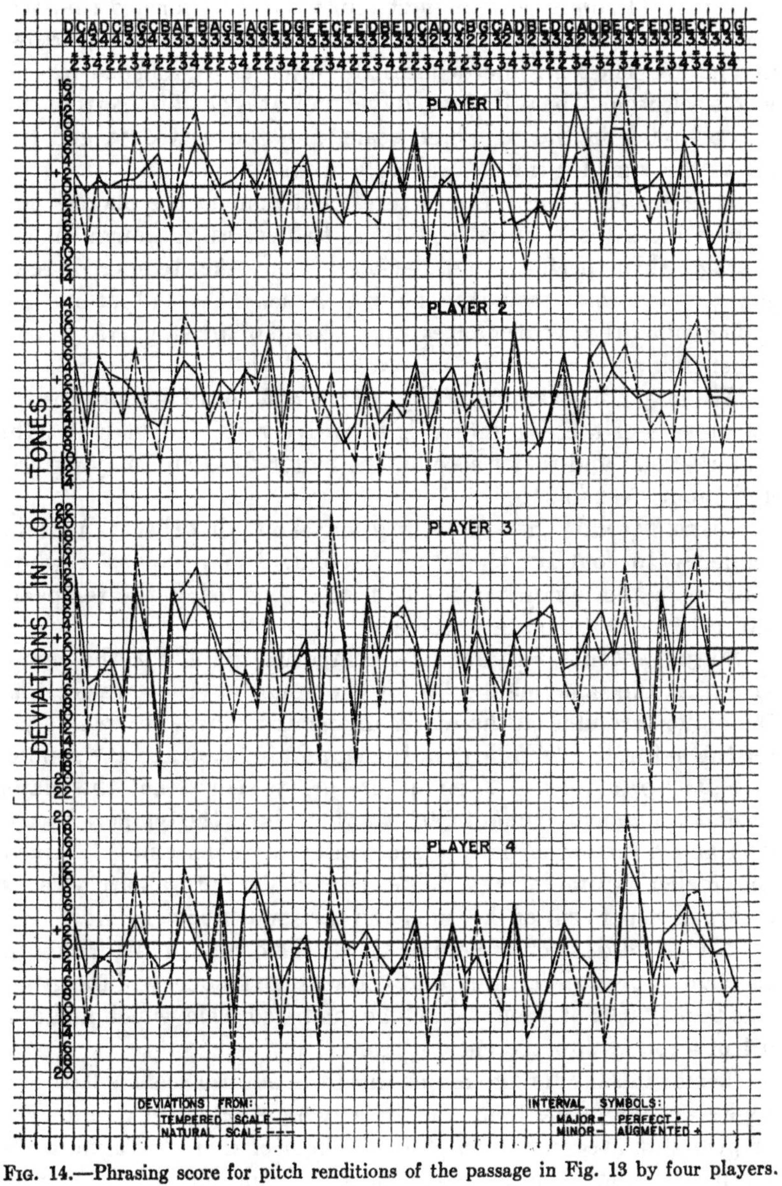

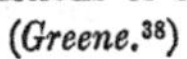

FIG. 14.—Phrasing score for pitch renditions of the passage in Fig. 13 by four players. (*Greene.*[38])

Figure 14 shows how the first four players performed that section of the Kreutzer *Etude* which lies between the two arrows in Fig. 13. The zero line denotes the pitch as established for the whole selection. The solid jagged line indicates deviations from this "true" pitch in the tempered scale, and the dotted jagged line shows the same for the natural scale or just intonation.

It is evident from these pictures that none of the players performed consistently in either of the two scales, although on the average their performance deviated from the tempered scale slightly less than from the natural scale. These situations are typical of all the performances studied, and of artistic performance in general.

We may now examine in Fig. 15 the composite findings for the six players of the five intervals intensively studied; namely, the minor second and major second, the minor third and major third, and the perfect fourth.

Minor second. The composite graph shows that there is a strong tendency to contract the minor second. The group as a whole contracted the minor seconds 0.06 of a tone below the tempered and 0.12 below the natural scale.

Major second. Reading the composite graph for the major second in the same manner as for the minor interval, we see that the major second is on the whole augmented. There are two values for the natural scale indicated, the larger at +0.02 and the smaller at −0.09 of a tone. The composite graph shows that the major second is augmented about 0.03 of a tone above the tempered scale, 0.01 above the larger natural scale interval value, and 0.12 above the smaller natural interval value. The smaller natural intervals are enlarged 98 per cent of the time, and the smaller 65 per cent.

Minor thirds. For the minor thirds the composite figure shows the arrow at −2, indicating that the average tendency of the group was to play 0.02 of a tone below the tempered scale, which makes it 0.1 of a tone below the natural scale.

Major thirds. For the major third the natural scale is 0.07 of a tone less than in the tempered. The average extent of its interval, as played, however, is 0.03 of a tone greater than its value in the tempered scale. This general tendency holds for all of the four players.

Perfect fourth. The perfect fourth was introduced as a control interval in which there should be no marked difference between the

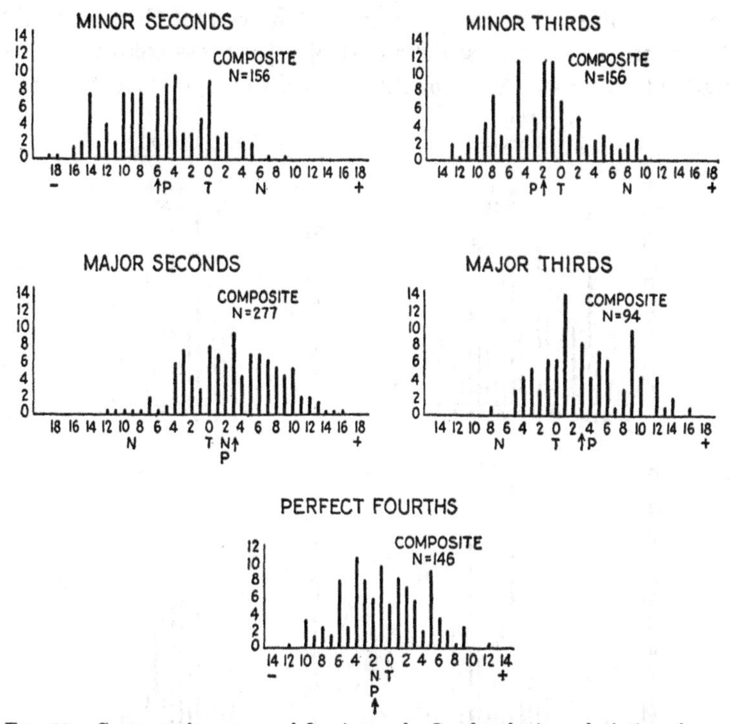

FIG. 15.—Group performances of five intervals. On the abscissa, deviations from the theoretical tonal extent of the interval in the *equally tempered* scale (marked *T*) are indicated in 0.01 tone. Cases of intervals *contracted* occur at the left, and those *expanded* at the right, of the *T* value. The symbols *N* and *P* show the direction and amount of divergence of the theoretical value of each interval in the *natural* and *Pythagorean* scales from its theoretical extent in the *equally tempered* scale. Arrows indicate the average extent of the given interval as played. On the ordinate, percentages of the total number of cases are shown.

Example: In the figure for the minor second, the natural scale value of the interval occurs at 0.06 tone from the equally tempered value, while the Pythagorean value differs from the equally tempered value by −0.05 tone. The interval tended to be contracted as compared with its natural and equally tempered values, the average extent occurring at −0.06 tone from the *T* value, and at −0.12 tone from the *N* value. Ninety-eight per cent of the cases were contracted as compared with the *N* value, while 81 per cent were contracted in relation to the *T* value. Further, the average extent of the played interval occurs at −0.01 tone from the *P* value, thus varying from it only by an amount equal to the expected error of frequency measurement. Figures for the other intervals can be read similarly. It will be seen that there are two theoretical values for the *major second* in the natural scale, and the Pythagorean value for this interval coincides with the *larger* natural scale value. Further, the Pythagorean value of the *perfect fourth* likewise agrees with the natural scale value for that interval. (*Greene.*[39])

two scale values. The composite graph shows that the extent of the interval in the natural scale is 0.01 of a tone less than in the tempered. The average extent of the interval as played is at the natural

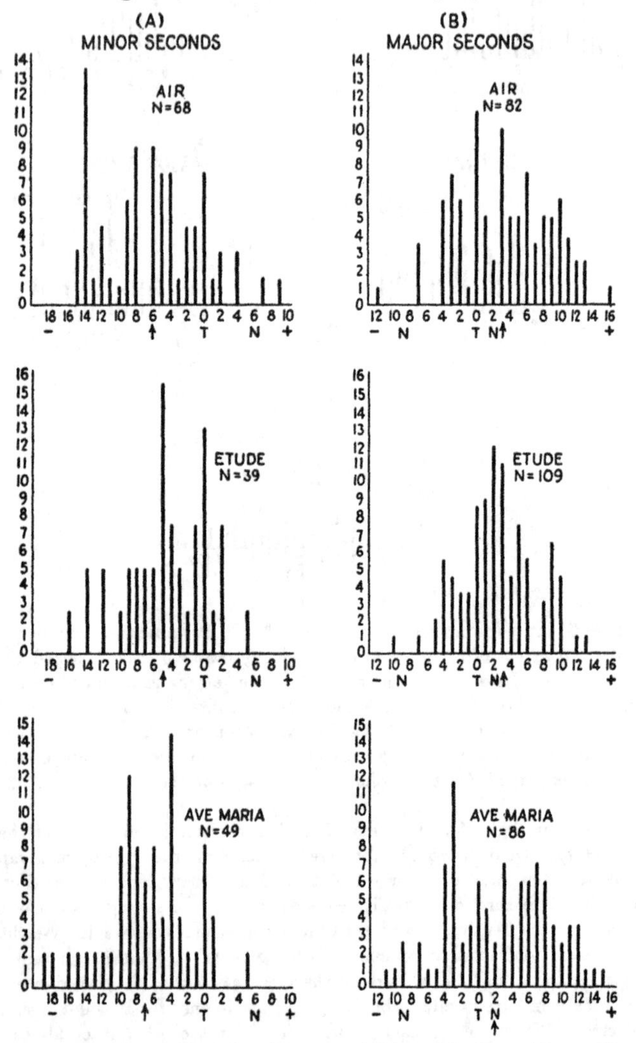

FIG. 16.—Comparison of performances in three selections. (*Greene.*[38])

scale value. There is close agreement among the different players, which indicates that this interval presents no tendency to augment or diminish, although the actual performances scatter to about the same extent as for the augmented and contracted intervals.

Comparison of three selections. In Fig. 16 there is shown the composite graph for minor seconds and major seconds in the three selections studied. While the distributions are irregular and differ in that respect, the general tendency is on the whole the same in all selections, as may be seen by observing the position of the arrow. The same principle holds true for the minor thirds and major thirds and the perfect fourth.

Direction of movement. In order to determine whether the movement of pitch up or down makes any difference, comparisons are made in all cases of upward and in all cases of downward movement for the five intervals. The conclusion was reached that, on the

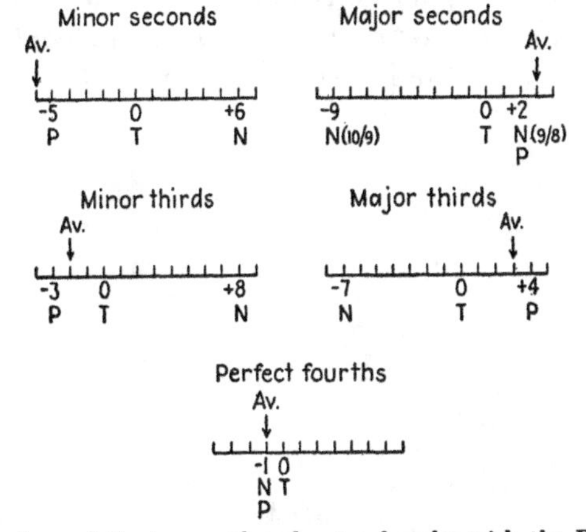

FIG. 17.—Comparison of the tempered and natural scales with the Pythagorean scale. (*Greene.*[38])

whole, there is no statistically valid difference due to movement from the lower to the higher or from the higher to the lower note in the interval.

The Pythagorean scale. The comparisons have been made between the natural scale and the tempered scale and, since a player conforms to neither of these, the question arose as to whether any other recognized scale is approximated, and it turned out that the Pythagorean scale meets the need more closely than either of the other two scales.

This is shown in Fig. 17. *P* denotes the position according to the Pythagorean scale. Again the arrow shows where the average tendency lies. Thus, for the minor second, the interval is contracted by 0.06, which makes it within 0.01 of a tone from the

Pythagorean scale and 0.12 of a tone from the natural scale. In the major second, the performance is again within 0.01 of a tone from the Pythagorean value, which is the same as that for the larger natural interval, and is 0.02 of a tone above the tempered-scale value.

The minor third is within 0.01 of a tone of the Pythagorean value and 0.10 from the natural value. For the major third the average value is within 0.01 of a tone of the Pythagorean value, 0.03 away from the tempered scale, and 0.1 from the natural. For the perfect fourth there is no significant tendency to deviate. Thus we reached the striking conclusion that the violinist, when unaccompanied, does not play consistently in either the tempered or the natural scale but tends on the whole to conform with the Pythagorean scale in the intervals here studied.

19

PIANO

THE aim of this chapter is to illustrate the application of scientific method to the study of the theory and practice of piano playing. We now have at our command adequate recording and measuring instruments, and the scientific method is beginning to express itself for various purposes; such as the purely scientific array of facts about performance on the piano, the determination of esthetic principles, the characterization of types of performance, description of individual differences, measurement of achievement, study of faults of performance, and musical criticism.

Instead of attempting to discuss the subject as a whole, we shall consider a few typical situations which illustrate the procedure and should lead to further scientific thinking on the part of the reader. The first item, piano touch, illustrates how the scientific approach clarifies thinking; the second, the piano camera, shows how accurate and permanent measurements of performance can be made; the third, phrasing, gives a short sample of the kind of facts that can be elicited from a performance score; and the fourth shows how one minute detail in technique can be analyzed into fundamental principles of operation.

PIANO TOUCH*

One is tempted to say that touch is the touchiest subject in musical circles, because we are deeply impressed with the enormous possibilities for characterizing musical artistry and expression of musical feeling in terms of this art. The current vocabulary descriptive of touch is extensive, loose, and baffling. Historically, but little

* From the *Scientific Monthly*.[134a]

effort has been made to aid the student in music by bringing order out of this chaos from a scientific point of view. However, recent scientific approaches to this subject have made progress and give assurance of the possibility of an adequate analysis, description, and terminology for many of these phenomena.* The best available book on the subject for musicians is the volume by Professor Ortmann, Director of the Peabody Conservatory of Music. It is based upon a searching analysis of historical, theoretical, and experimental evidences. His principal findings may be summarized as follows:

> The pianist has at his direct control only two of the four factors in music, namely, intensity and time. Pitch and timbre are determined primarily by the composer and the instrument.
>
> The pianist can control the intensity only in terms of the velocity of the hammer, at the moment at which it leaves the escapement mechanism, and by the action of the pedals.
>
> There are only two significant strokes on the key: the percussion and the nonpercussion. The difference between these is that the former contributes more noise to the piano tone, and the latter gives the player better control of the desired intensity.
>
> Aside from the addition of the noise, the player cannot modify the quality of the tone by the manner of depressing the key or by manipulations after the key has struck its bed except, perhaps, by a momentary partial key release and immediate key depression, damping the tone somewhat but not entirely.
>
> He can control the time factors which influence quality only by the action of the dampers either through the keys or the pedals.

In general, these facts have been known for a long time by instrument makers and leading musicians. But many musicians have failed to recognize their significance or admit the facts. Indeed, experts in various fields of acoustical science also have questioned the findings enough to justify taking the problem into their laboratories for analysis and verification. However, all the investigators have reached the same conclusion on the above points. Let us examine each of the essential factors in turn.

Insofar as it depends upon the stroke of the key, intensity (the physical fact) or loudness (the mental fact) is a function of the velocity of the hammer at the moment that it impinges upon the string. After that, the tone can be modified only by action of the dampers. The piano action for any key consists of a compound

---

* The evidence for the view here presented is largely the work of *Ortmann*,[103] of *White*,[213] *Hart*, *Fuller*, and *Lusby*,[43] and *Ghosh*.[36,37]

lever system, the purpose of which is to facilitate and control the force of the blow on the string. Let us consider the nature of the blow.

If a ball is placed on the inner end of a cleared piano key and the key is struck in the usual manner, the ball will fly from the key up against the string. Nothing can influence the velocity or the direction of the ball after it has left the key, and the ball can energize the string only at the moment of impact because, owing to the resilience of the compressed felt and the throw of the string, it bounds off instantly. The function and action of the hammer are analogous to that of the ball. The velocity of the hammer is determined by the velocity of the escapement lever at the moment the hammer is released for its flight, and the force of the blow is determined by the velocity of the hammer at the moment of impact. From this, several considerations follow:

1. It makes no difference whether the key is struck by an accelerating, retarding, even, or any form of irregular movement; the only significant thing the player controls in the stroke is the velocity of the key at the exact moment that it throws off the hammer.

This easily observed physical fact has profound significance in the theory of playing, hearing, enjoyment, and critical judgments about music. The economic aspect is not to be ignored when we consider what money is spent in trying to teach pupils to do something that cannot be done. It takes away a great deal of the glamour and grace of mannerisms in the mode of depression of the key. It reduces touch to the fundamental factor of intensity.

This should in no way detract from the resourcefulness of the instrument and the opportunity for individual expression or the indirect effects of intensity which are legion. On the other hand, it clarifies, glorifies, and reveals the extraordinary refinement that is necessary in this artistic touch. The elaborate care taken in the development of form, weight, pressure, and rate of arm, wrist, and finger movements is fully justified insofar as it results in a refined control of the intensity of the tone, but not for any independent change in tone quality.

2. The hammer is released just a trifle before the key reaches its bed. Like the ball, it has only one form of contact with the string, namely, an instantaneous impact followed by immediate rebound. The movement of the key cannot influence the hammer after it has

been released any more than it can influence the flight of the ball after it has been thrown off. Therefore, no amount of waggling, vibrating, rocking, or caressing of the key after it has once hit bottom can modify the action upon the string. The only way in which the key can further affect the string is by a new stroke of the hammer. This can easily be verified by manipulating a key near its bed and looking at the action of the hammer.

Probably the only exception to this statement is the rare or doubtful possibility that a partial release of the escapement mechanism may reengage the hammer stem so that the hammer may again be thrown against the string and a partial damping may result. However, even if physically possible, this is merely a stunt and is not attempted by artists under normal conditions of playing. Yet this fallacy plays a role in musical circles in at least three important respects. First, whenever this stunt is affected, the observable finger action serves as a suggestion which produces the desired result in the form of an illusion of hearing. Such normal illusions have a very great influence upon musical hearing. Second, in ignorance or defiance of the physical limitations, teachers often attempt to train pupils in the supposed art of this type of finesse. And third, theorists, who oppose the limitation of touch to intensity control, frequently fall back upon this phenomenon to sustain their claims. However, all well-informed musicians recognize that this feature is not important in their artistic playing. Therefore, we may ignore it in the discussion of the real factors in musical touch.

3. The pianist can produce indirectly a great variety of tone qualities, but only by his control of the intensity of the tone. Having imparted a given velocity to the hammer, the pianist is entirely at the mercy of the instrument for the determination of qualitative changes taking place in the tone, except for manipulation of the dampers. The piano is so constructed that it can produce a vast series of tone qualities, each one a function of the intensity of the tone. Each instrument has its own relatively fixed characteristic in this respect. In general, the louder the tone, the richer it will be in quality.

If we represent a series of intensities by the letters *a*, *b*, *c*, *d*, etc., and the corresponding degrees of richness and other characteristics of the quality by the symbols a', b', c', d', etc., then whenever a tone of intensity *a* is sounded, a quality a' is produced; intensity *b* for the same tone will always yield a quality b'; intensity c or any other intensity will always yield its corresponding tone quality. It is possible, therefore, to calibrate any particular piano in this way and to set up a scale of intensities which will yield approximately the corresponding scale of tone qualities. However, the situation is complicated by the fact that each instrument has its own resonance characteristics and responds differently to different chords.

This setting up of a scale of equivalents for intensity and tone quality is just what every pianist has to do empirically. Rarely is it a clearly conscious effort or scale; probably it can best be described as a relationship into which he has felt himself more or less subconsciously.

4. In 1933, *Ghosh*[36,37] demonstrated that, within a considerable range of the intensities normally functioning in music, the wave form of the vibrating string and therefore the resulting harmonic constitution remain constant. Thus, within a moderate range of changes in intensity, the player cannot modify the quality of the tone as it emerges from the string.

The qualitative changes which come with changing intensity are the result of resonance, reverberation, or damping effects of the sounding board and the rest of the piano, the thuds and rattlings on the keys, as well as the acoustical characteristics of the room. The wave emitted by the sounding board and its accessories is very much stronger than the wave emitted from the string and therefore becomes dominant in hearing. The wave form that impinges upon the ear is an amplification and modification of the wave form emitted by the string. This principle applies to all other musical instruments.

At the present time artists regard inharmonic and percussion accessories to piano response as legitimate and essential contributions to tone quality. Is it possible that this attitude may change? We are facing an era of radical change in the nature of music. It is difficult to predict what will happen to concepts of piano playing. Several factors must be taken into account.

1. The piano of today, the manner of its use, and the tastes and habits of hearing are determined in large part by the heretofore existing mechanical limitations to construction of the instrument. This piano quality involves a variety of thuds, rattlings, raspings, and various other forms of noise which are utilized for musical

effect and add pronounced characteristics significantly to the tonal elements, especially in the louder intensities. It is, to a considerable extent, in the impurities of tone that we differentiate instruments.

2. It is now possible to construct a synthetic-tone instrument in which we may include any desired sound quality, periodic or aperiodic, and therefore eliminate any of the present characteristics which may be redundant or undesirable.

3. In such an instrument, it is now possible to introduce a vast variety of tone qualities which we have not been able to produce with our present instruments. We must, therefore, consider the possibility of thinking of the future of music in terms of instruments in which the characteristics are not due to the limitations in mechanical construction, but are the deliberate choice, the result of invention and discovery of entirely new tonal complexes for musical satisfaction.

4. It is a matter of history and psychology that likes and dislikes, tolerance and intolerance, artistic cravings and urges, are matters of development contingent upon the tendency to make the best of what we have, the biological tendency toward new habit formations, and the inherent artistic merit in innovations.

These situations the piano shares with all other instruments. Conservatism tells us that there will be no sudden change, but insight into the nature of the situation tells us that the change will be radical and that it must of necessity be in the interest of higher levels of musical achievement with new problems for the composer, the performer, and the listener.

Is it probable that the electrical flute, clarinet, trumpet, or violin will introduce new satisfaction in the purity of harmonic factors, so that we can dispense with the noises which at the present time give us the characteristics of the instrument? We may venture to answer that these new resources in electrical instruments will vastly enrich our world with harmonic tones and will "chasten" or replace many of our present instruments, but there may always be an artistic demand for inharmonic elements, and other noises and percussion features.

5. Pianists have fairly clear concepts of characteristics of tone quality, such as harsh, brilliant, mellow, full, singing, round, shrill, dry, metallic, steely, brittle, shallow, poor, ringing, clear, velvety, bell-like, jarring, and strident. *Ortmann*[103] performed an experiment in which a number of distinguished artists participated and were

mony through the gradual overlapping and fading of antecedent tones. Refinement in the use of this medium is an outstanding mark of artistry.

In the use of the *una corda* pedal the artist has a choice of striking one, two, or three strings. Two effects result. The softer felt tends to dampen partial vibrations of the string and the remaining string or strings vibrate in sympathetic resonance. A combination of such tones obeys precisely the same laws as tones produced without pedal although the basic tone-complex is altered. The action of the soft pedal involves, of course, purely the factor of intensity.

9. The great tonal resources of the piano as an instrument lie in the richness of tone produced by the possibility of playing one or many keys, with or without pedals, and thus utilizing both harmonic and melodic progressions. But these are as a rule set in the score by the composer, and the possibility of legitimately introducing variants and ornaments not so indicated is limited.

10. It is, of course, recognized that the pianist has many devices for changing the quality of tone by freedom in the use of intensity or in time. For example, tone coloring is a very conspicuous feature in artistic playing, but it ordinarily means that the pianist strikes the notes in the chord with different force and thus can produce varying resonance effects from the same chord. Likewise, there are considerable resources in the variety of uses of the pedals, as to both time and intensity. The pianist has various devices by which he can get sympathetic vibrations and modulate overtones. There are also many ways of enhancing subjective tones which may play an important role, clearly modifying the perceived tone quality, and we must not overlook the vast array of illusions which have qualitative significance. Last but not least, there is the power of suggestion.

11. The artist may legitimately think and perform with tone quality as his objective and consciously control his touch in terms of tone quality. Likewise, the listener may regard tone quality as the primary factor and think of intensity as a secondary and even unrelated factor. But the fact remains that, in general, the only way in which the pianist can produce qualitative changes is through dynamic and temporal changes, and then only within the limits set by the characteristics of the instrument.

12. It follows from these considerations that a fairly adequate record of musical performance can be made by recording the veloc-

ity and time of the hammer blow and the action of the dampers. With a given composition and a given instrument of which the characteristics are known, we can describe the essentials of artistic performance on the piano in terms of the artist's command and use of these factors.

The Iowa piano camera is built on this principle. It registers the performance in minute and serviceable detail in a permanent photogram. This can be transcribed into a scientific performance score, in terms of which objective analysis of the significant tonal features of the rendition may be made.

The purpose of this analysis has been to pave the way for a synthesis. In acoustics we have analyzers which may dissect any rich tone into its component partials; conversely, we have synthesizers which can take all known partials of any rich tone and reconstruct the original single sound wave. On this analogy, it is here suggested that the principle which justifies our reducing a rendition to its two operating media justifies our assuming that, by reversing the process, we may derive all the salient elements in the performance from an adequate record of these two media. Such matters as phrasing, personal interpretation, the principles of art involved, errors, idiosyncrasies, and exhibitions of skill are embodied in such a piano-camera record.

THE PIANO CAMERA

We have just seen that, of the four factors in musical performance, pitch, intensity, timbre, and time, two, pitch and timbre, are determined by the piano. Therefore, only intensity and time need be recorded to obtain an adequate statement of piano playing. The Iowa piano camera* was designed to record these two factors. It has proved remarkably simple to operate, reliable and adequate in the musical situation. It gives a photographic record of the beginning, duration, moment of ending, and relative intensity of each note in an entire selection played under normal conditions.

Figure 1 is a sample of the photographic record, actual size, covering 0.68 second. The vertical lines show time in 0.04 second and can be estimated to within 0.01 second. Each horizontal white track represents a key on the entire keyboard. The dark horizontal

---

* This camera has been described briefly by *Tiffin* and *Seashore*,[202] and in technical detail by *Tiffin*.[198]

bands are due to the inner framework of the piano, but they aid in the identification of the keys. For each note, the length of the white space *B* is proportional to the time necessary for the hammer to move through the last 12 millimeters before striking the string. The length of the bar *A* gives a similar measure of the time necessary

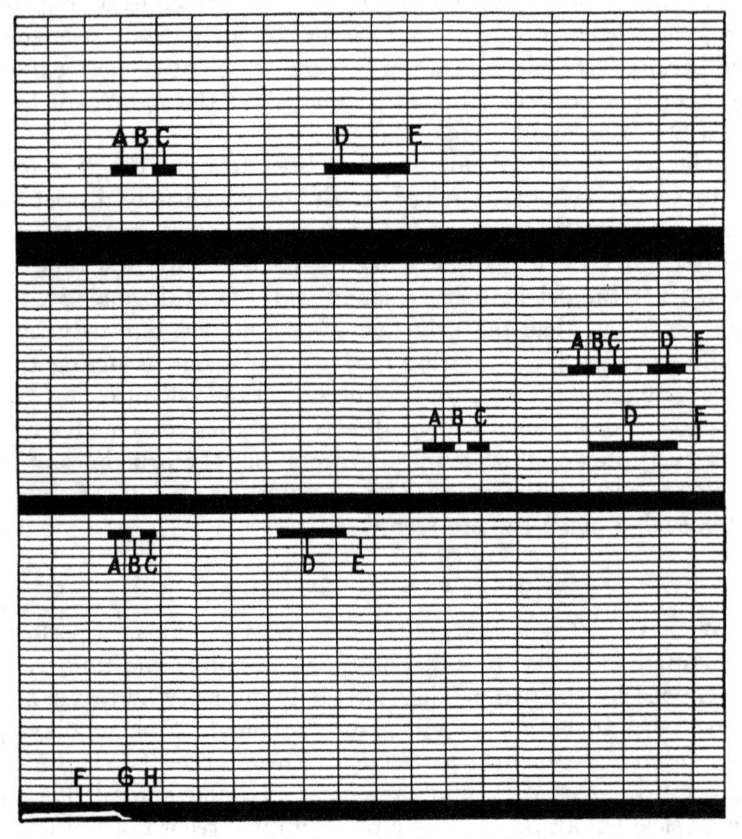

FIG. 1.—Drawing from actual photogram taken with the Iowa piano camera.

for the hammer to travel the preceding 12 millimeters. Thus, $A + B$ gives the time for the movement of the hammer through the last 24 millimeters before striking the string. From the duration of *B* or the duration of $A + B$, the velocity of the hammer and, in turn, the force of the impact and intensity of the resultant tone near the beginning of the tone may be determined. The dark bar following this shows the time of retreat of the hammer from the string, and this, together with the white bar following, gives the length of time that the key was held. For the duration of the white bar the hammer was free from the strings, but at the end of that time the strings were damped by the return of the key. The end of the last black bar indicates the complete return of the key, and shows the time necessary for it.

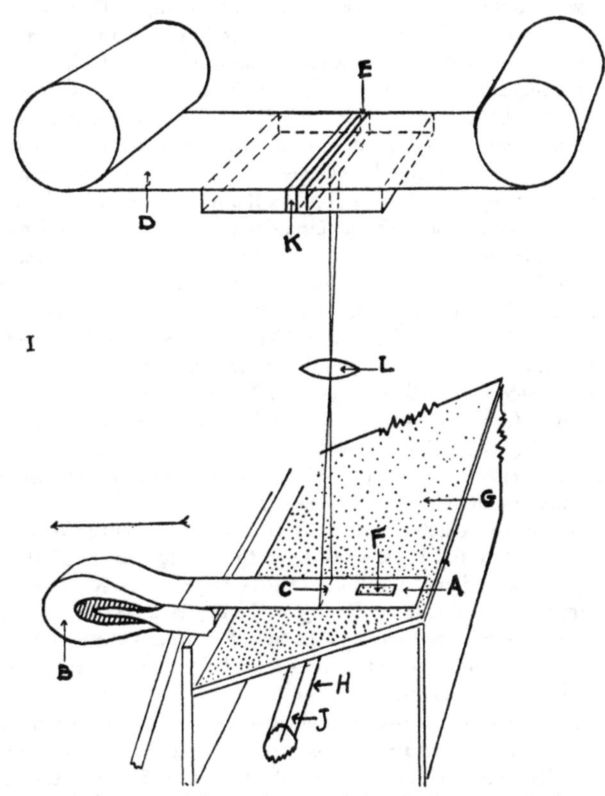

FIG. 2.—Schematic drawing of the mechanism of the piano camera. Explanation in text.

The pedal action is represented by the white line at the base, showing that the pedal was free preceding the chord, that it was put into action in time to sustain this chord, and that it was held in so as to cover the next note.

The mechanism by which this record is obtained is illustrated diagrammatically in Fig. 2. A light strip of balsa wood approximately 7 centimeters long and 7 millimeters wide is glued to the tail of each hammer in the piano. The top of the piano is raised and a lens focuses the region *C* of the tail *A* on the film *D*. This film is Eastman No. 1 recording paper, 4 inches wide. An electric motor draws this film through the camera at a rate of 12 centimeters per second. The film is exposed to the bank of hammers below only through the narrow slit *E*. As any key is depressed, its hammer moves forward in the direction of the arrow, and the hole *F* in the balsa-wood tail passes the region *C* which is focused on the film. Directly below the tails is a cylindrical electric light bulb *A*, approximately 2 inches in diameter, and 4 feet long. The filament of this bulb, *J*, which is a single long loop of wire, is directly below the point of photography *C*. As the hole *F* in the tail *A* moves forward, the region *C* (which is focused on the film *D*) is momentarily lighted from below. The result of the passage of the hole *F* is that a short bar is photographed on the moving film. This is the bar *A* in Fig. 1. The total length of the balsa-wood tail is such that, when the hammer strikes the piano string and produces the sound, the tail has just passed the region *C*, again allowing this region to be lighted from below and thus photographing another distinctive mark on the film. At this point in the movement of the hammer, two marks have been photographed on the film, one caused by the hole *F* passing the region *C*, and one caused by the end of the tail passing this region. Since the film is being drawn through the camera during this process, it is obvious that the faster the hammer is moving, the shorter will be the distance between the two marks photographed. The hole *F* is placed 12 millimeters from the end of the tail. Hence the record of velocity is secured during the last 12 millimeters which the hammer travels before the string is struck. It has been shown by *Hickman*[49] that the velocity of a piano hammer during the last 12 millimeters of its movement before striking the string is practically constant. Thus, since the intensity of the tone is determined only by the velocity of the hammer, the record gives a serviceable indication of the relative intensity of the tone.

The piano is so constructed that as soon as the hammers have struck their respective strings, they fall back away from the string. However, they do not quite fall back to the original position until the key is released. The position in which the hammer actually stays, as long as the key is depressed, is just enough in advance of its normal position that the hole *F* is within the region *C*. Hence, as long as the key is depressed, light passes from below through the hole *F*, making a narrow line on the moving film.

The procedure outlined above is duplicated for every hammer in the piano, for the lens *L* serves to concentrate a picture of the entire bank of hammers on the 4-inch film. Each hammer has its own pathway on the film, and the beginning, ending, duration, and intensity of the tone contributed by each hammer may be studied separately.

Although the film moves at a fairly constant rate, a time line is employed to insure accuracy in the measurements. A neon tube is exposed to the film through a slit as long as the film is wide and 0.5 millimeter in width. This slit is adjacent to the slit *E*. The neon tube is connected to the secondary of an induction coil, and a 25∼ electrically driven tuning fork is placed in series with the primary of the coil. a 2-volt direct current being used. This arrangement photographs 25 parallel lines per second, each line extending across the width of the film.

The movements of the damper pedal also are recorded on the film. A lever arm, mechanically controlled by the damper pedal, is mounted in the piano on one side of the bank of hammers. The movements of this lever arm are photographed while the record is taken and show partial or incomplete damping as well as the extreme positions of the pedal. A similar record may be made for the other pedals.

The camera is surprisingly simple and inexpensive. It imposes no restrictions upon the player and does not interfere with routine use of the piano in the studio.

Thus it is seen that all time factors, the moment of incidence, the duration, and the moment of cessation of each tone, are measured directly in 0.01-second units on the tracing for each key and the damper pedal.

The intensity of the tone is measured in terms of the rate of impact of the hammer as expressed in millimeter units of the section *AB* in the photogram. These units are converted into decibel readings of 17 steps. Each step represents approximately 2 db, thus giving a range of 34 db.

THE PIANO PERFORMANCE SCORE

The photogram of the type in Fig. 1 is a complete chart in itself, but, for detailed analysis and publication, this photo record is transcribed into a musical performance score as in Fig. 3. A movable scale in the form of a plat of the piano keyboard is laid vertically across the record (Fig. 1) in front of any note that is to be read. The bass end of the scale is at the top and the treble at the bottom in this figure. By this means we find that in this photogram the top note is E in the bass clef and the other note in the same dichord is E_4 in the treble. The note following is $G_3\#$, and the last note is B_2.

To represent the facts in musical notation, we utilize the conventional staff and substitute bar graphs for the conventional musical notes (Fig. 3). Thus the three bars represent the three notes just named. The position in the staff indicates the pitch of the note.

The vertical lines show time in 0.04-second units. The dotted slanting line is interpolated to show the degree of asynchronization in the first chord. The left end of a bar indicates the exact moment that the hammer struck the string. The length of the line indicates the time that the key was held down, allowing the strings to vibrate unhampered by action of the pedal. The line between the two clefs denotes the pedal action, full line meaning pedal not in action, absence of line, full pedal, and the dotted line, transition, or "half pedaling." Here the pedal is pressed in time to catch the vibration of the dichord and is held to cover the following note.

The relative loudness of each note is indicated by the number above each note. These are arranged in a scale of 17, in which 1 denotes approximately the softest note which can be played with musical significance, and 17 the loudest.

Any musician can read this score at sight and note the actual time and intensity values insofar as they are musically significant. The pitch and timbre factors are fixed by the structure of the instrument and the composition, except as modified by the damper pedal. This pattern score is so constructed that, when advantageously reduced, it can be printed as a musical notation and does

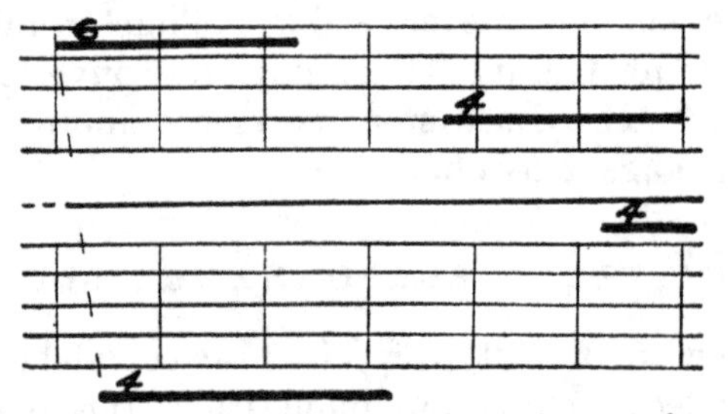

FIG. 3.—The photogram of Fig. 1 transcribed into the musical pattern score.

not require much more space than is required for the conventional score. A sustained example of the form and use of the piano performance score is given in the following section.

SECTION OF CHOPIN NOCTURNE NO. 6

In order to illustrate the nature and significance of this pattern score in a specific case, let us consider one of the hundreds of problems that come up in the subject of phrasing. Figures 5 and 6 are performance scores for the standard score shown in Fig. 4. *A* in Fig. 5 and *B* in Fig. 6 are professional pianists playing the same selection with instructions to give their best personal interpretation of the passage. Each was kept ignorant of the performance of the other.

With the description given for Fig. 3 above, the reader may now compare these pattern scores with the performance score, item for item. This comparison might be made with three purposes in view; (1) gaining familiarity with the relation of the pattern score to the standard score and skill in reading the former; (2) a comparison of the performance of the two pianists as to technical skill and personal interpretation; and (3) examination of a single element in the interpretation in detail.

The comparison of the pattern score with the standard score should be made in accordance with the interests of the reader and

FIG. 4.—The chorale section of Chopin's sixth nocturne. (*Henderson.*[46])

in terms of natural questions that may arise, such as the method of representing pitch, time, intensity, pauses, measures, chords, synchronization, release of keys, pedal, tempo, timbre, sonance, tone quality, crescendo, diminuendo, rubato, and accent. All these and many other features are clearly indicated in the performance score. With these mastered, the performance score of one player may be compared with a standard score in terms of any of the data just mentioned.

FIG. 5.—The musical pattern score of the chorale section of Chopin's sixth nocturne, as played by pianist *A*. (*Henderson*.[46])

The way is then paved for comparing the two performance scores item for item. To write out a detailed comparison of these two performances in full on the basis of the facts in hand would require a volume. The reader should therefore select in turn for comparison such features as he would regard as most significant: for example, what known principles of interpretation are illus-

FIG. 6.—The musical pattern score of the chorale section of Chopin's sixth nocturne, as played by pianist *B*. (*Henderson*.[46])

trated? What types of devices are used to attain certain artistic ends? What types and degrees of deviation from metronomic time and even intensity are employed? What manifest faults in skill may be found? Are there any personal idiosyncrasies? What are the outstanding features of merit in the interpretation given by each? What surprising features or media are here used for effect in phrasing? How is tone quality modified by the use of the sostenuto pedal? How often does emphasis on the accented beat occur through intensity or through time or other means?

When these and other questions have been answered after serious examination of the facts, the reader may be ready to sit down and attempt to reproduce one of the performance scores on the piano, interrupting the performance from point to point to "hear out" the significance of a particular variant in the phrasing. To illustrate the procedure, we may ask and answer in detail one question: By what devices does the player give emphasis to the accented note in the measure?

The reader may think at once that the accent is made by playing the note louder, but the score will show that this is seldom the case. The composer has determined emphasis in large part by his choice of harmonic elements through such means as the repetition of identical measure patterns, pitch placement, and position of cadences. In this selection, the first of these plays a very important role: one pattern (a half-half-half measure) appears nine times in the statement and ten times in the restatement of the theme. Pitch emphasis may have functioned in six beats. The role of the cadence is more marked in phrases than in measures.

Let us see first what role intensity plays in emphasis on the accented beat. In the majority of cases, the accented note is not played with greater intensity. It is a matter of coincidence that pianists *A* and *B* each play the first note in the beat louder in only 19 per cent of the 31 measures. But some of these measures were the beginning of phrases and serve the purpose of phrasal separation rather than, or in addition to, measure accent. If these be eliminated, there remain only 6 per cent for *A* and 12 per cent for *B* with undoubted intensity accent. These figures would be altered somewhat if we take into account the note preceding the accented note because of the crescendo or diminuendo. One might expect a half note to be struck harder than the quarter note for the purpose of maintaining a sound, but there is no evidence of this in the performance score.

This fact, that intensity is not essential to accent, was confirmed by measurements on phonograph records of performances by

Cortot (Victor 6063-B), Rachmaninoff (Victor 6731-B), and Paderewski (Victor 6234-B), making due allowance for lack of fidelity in the phonograph record. For all players, the same principle operated also in the secondary accent; that is, the third beat in the 4/4 measure. Very rarely was the secondary accent achieved through increasing intensity of that note in comparison with the unaccented note following.

It is quite possible that the above finding may be due to some extent to the character of the selections studied. The stressing of measures as, for example, in the march or the bolero, may call for overt physical stress on the accented notes.

But how shall we account for this relative absence of physical intensity and accent? It is a fair guess that it is due to the fact that the compositional structure suggests the beat unit, and subjective rhythms, for both the player and the listener, carry out the scheme. This presents a most interesting problem in the psychology of music, namely, what features attributed to the performer are really due to the subjective contribution of the listener? Countless instances might be cited in accordance with the laws of empathy and suggestion.

But time is always a rival of intensity in giving accent. Stress may be obtained by lengthening a note or delaying its entrance. This is a well-known fact in classical poetry. *Schramm*[117] has shown that it is largely true also of English poetry, and *Harold Seashore*[155] has found the same to be true in artistic vocal music. In quarter-quarter-quarter note measures pianist *A* shortened the second unaccented note from 2 to 18 per cent in 66 per cent of the cases, and *B* shortened the second note in every case (from 2 to 26 per cent). In the half-quarter note measures, *A* invariably lengthened the quarter note in relation to the half note (4 to 28 per cent), and *B* lengthened it 5 to 32 per cent in 88 per cent of the cases. However, this lengthening of the note accented cannot all be attributed to measure accent. There are many compositional and other factors that call for the relative lengthening of an accented note, such as the feeling of finality at the introduction of a phrase or the melodic quality between long and short notes.

Delayed entrance of the first accented note occurred in 80 per cent of the cases for *A*, and 90 per cent for *B*. The determination of the cause or the nature of this delay and the principles operating in it are too involved to be discussed here. In some, intensity plays but a slight role in emphasis on the accented beats in the measure; time is more frequently important, as to both length of the note and delay of the accentuated note. Can it be that objective emphasis by the player, either by strength or duration of the note, is comparatively secondary in value to the compositional emphasis which the musical listener "feels into" the measure subjectively? That is a matter for profitable speculation, but the facts just cited stand out in the black and white of the performance score. There is no doubt that both player and listener hear the accent.

These findings do not lighten the task of the player or reduce his vast range of achievement through the control of time and intensity. They do, however, complicate his problem when he realizes that he not only has to take account of his physical control of time and intensity but also his control of the subjective factors which psychologically are very real, tangible, and constant. Here the distinction between intensity as the physical fact and loudness as the resultant mental fact becomes very real and important.

SIMILARITY IN STATEMENT AND RESTATEMENT

The two parts of this chorale are, of course, quite different in the actual score (Fig. 4). Yet there is a surprising similarity in the interpretation given by phrasing as is shown in Fig. 7. For each artist the upper section records intensity; the lower, time, with the duration of the notes indicated between them. The fidelity in the temporal equivalence is most striking. On account of the chorale style, the intensity phrasing is not so significant. Regarding primarily the temporal phrasing, we have here proof of the possibility and perhaps even desirability of securing identical musical effects or messages in typical statements and restatements of music regardless of the difference in notes.

CONSISTENCY OF INTERPRETATION

As a second illustration of the significance of a performance score, we may consider some questions in regard to an artist's possibility of interpretation of a musical selection. It is fully recognized that any artist can give a great variety of interpretations, and it is not desirable that he should have just one, but when we consider what a large number of factors enter into a given interpretation, it is interesting to inquire about the extent to which a given interpretation can be repeated. Each artist has his own mode

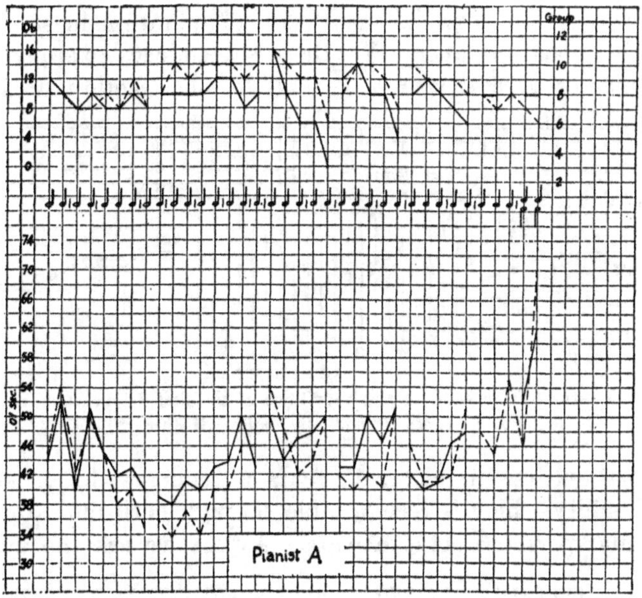

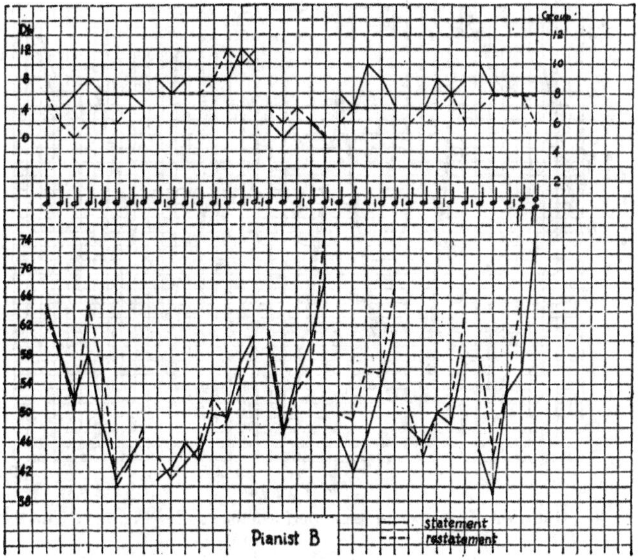

FIG. 7.—Relative duration of melody notes and the corresponding relative intensity values. (*Henderson.*[46])

of interpretation. This he may vary ad infinitum in accordance with his moods and fancies. Yet there is a tendency to apply certain principles or give the same general feeling reaction to a given

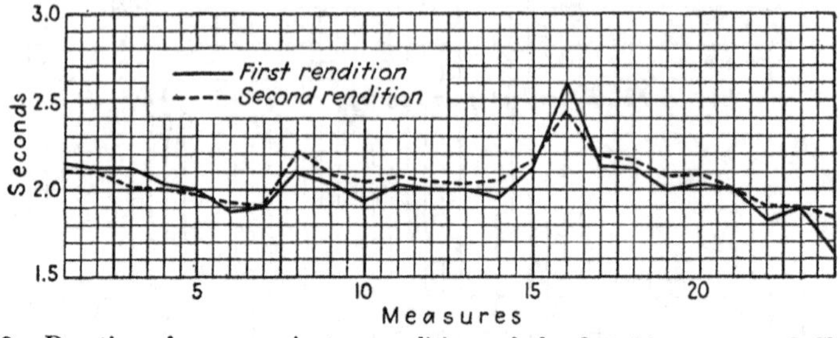

FIG. 8.—Duration of measures in two renditions of the first 24 measures of Chopin's *Polonaise*, op. 40, no. 1, by Bauer. (*Skinner.*[165a])

composition. Furthermore, there is a tendency to develop an individuality which is recognizable through both limitations and particular personal achievements. Suppose we ask the question,

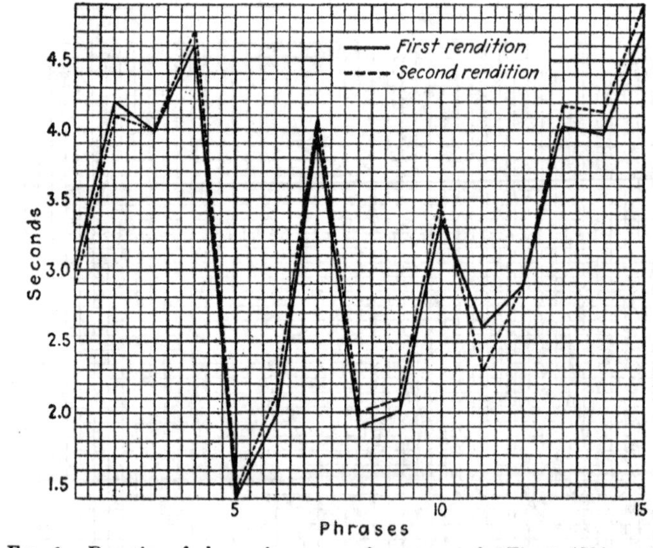

FIG. 9.—Duration of phrases in same performance as for Fig. 8. (*Skinner.*[165a])

how accurately can the artist repeat a given interpretation if he should try to do so?

Two artists, Harold Bauer and Philip Greeley Clapp, took part in this experiment and recorded samples of performances from

Beethoven, each repeating a given interpretation two or three times. One of the first considerations in attempting to apply scientific method to musical interpretation is that we must be satisfied to fractionate and deal with one item at a time. In terms of these performance scores, we could indulge in an extended discussion as to the exact nature of the interpretation. Let us consider only one, the element of time, and of this only two aspects, the duration of the measure and the duration of the phrase. Many other aspects of time are involved, such as the distribution within the measure or within the phrase, principles operating in determining the duration of tones, the use of time for emphasis, mode of pedal blending, in fact any temporal aspect which is significant for a musical interpretation.

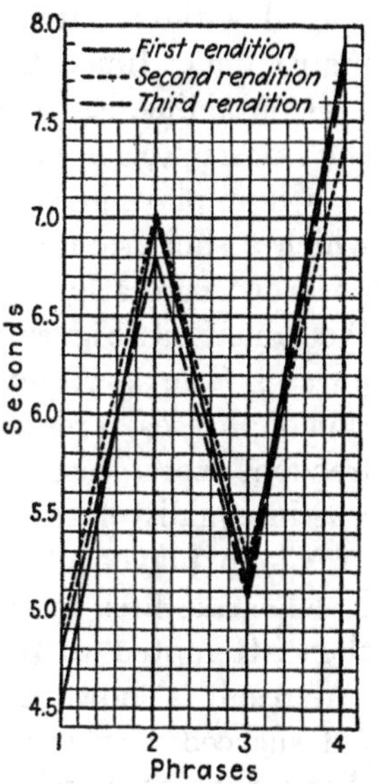

FIG. 10.—Duration of the first 4 phrases in three renditions of the first 4 phrases in Beethoven's *Sonata*, op. 57, by Clapp. (*Skinner.*[165a])

Figure 8 shows the duration of the first 24 measures in two successive renditions of Chopin's *Polonaise*, op. 40, no. 1, as played by Bauer. The first rendition took 49.1 seconds and the second, 49.7. It will be observed that there is remarkably close correspondence in that the curves have to agree

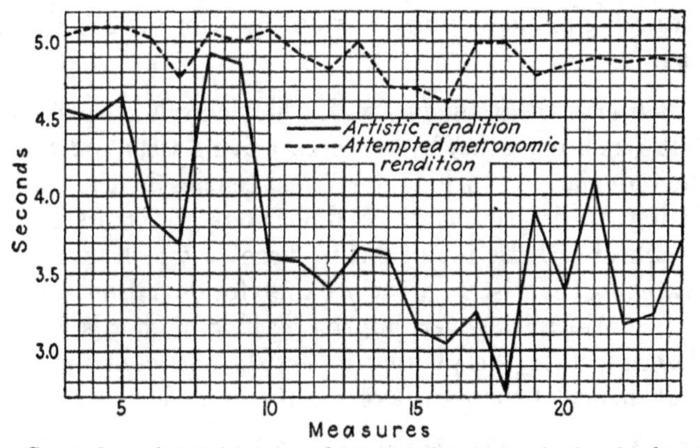

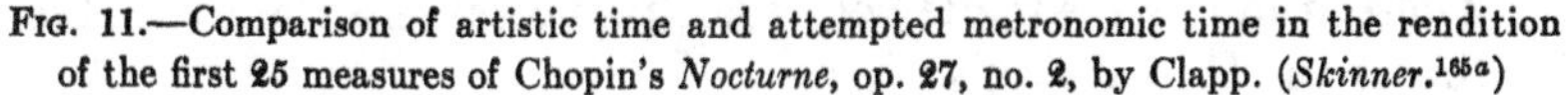
FIG. 11.—Comparison of artistic time and attempted metronomic time in the rendition of the first 25 measures of Chopin's *Nocturne*, op. 27, no. 2, by Clapp. (*Skinner.*[165a])

for the entire 24 measures. It is clear, of course, that if he had played without interpretation, simply reproducing the score in metronomic time, these graphs would have been a straight horizontal line. Figure 9 shows the consistency of interpretation in the same selection in terms of phrases.

Clapp played a selection from Beethoven's *Sonata*, op. 57, from which a short sample was taken to show to what extent his temporal interpretation would be consistent in three performances of the same unit. Figure 10 gives the record in terms of the length of phrases. The agreement of the three performances, as to the duration of phrases, is remarkably close, particularly in view of the great freedom expressed in the interpretation. The duration of measures was in equally close agreement.

Clapp played a section of Chopin's *Nocturne*, op. 27, no. 2, in which he first gave his normal interpretation by phrasing and then attempted to play the same in uniform metronomic time. The result is shown in Fig. 11, in which we see that the artist did not succeed very well in playing in metronomic time. The curve shows that there is a tendency to be influenced by motives for interpretation.

In this manner, the study of consistency in interpretation could be extended to comparisons of time and intensity in themselves and in their interrelationships, which give expression to musical feeling and values.

ASYNCHRONIZATION OF CHORDS

In studying piano playing, *Vernon*[206] set for himself the following tasks:

> To observe the frequency with which chords are played out of perfect synchronization by representative artists and the extent of their deviation: to look for consistencies in the manner of deviating; to determine which deviations are errors and which the result of esthetic intention; to discover which musical situations are most consistently the occasion for deviation; and finally, to induce principles governing the playing of chords which shall be descriptive of the playing of artists and contributory to a general theory of the nature of beauty in music.

These studies were made before the piano camera was available, by the use of Duo-art rolls.

The prevailing attitude of teachers is to demand exact synchronization, as a general rule. This is expressed typically by *Kullak*,[67] who says:

> In particular, the strictest simultaneity of all co-incident beats must be maintained and an anticipation by the left hand, which so easily becomes a habit in accompanying, resolutely suppressed. As in the drawing the line must be sharp, not blurred, the rhythmic entrance too must fall on one and the same point, and the clearest accuracy prevail throughout the interweaving threads of tone.

A second attitude is expressed by *Johnstone*,[56] who stresses the same point but admits an exception:

> In playing chord passages, watch that both hands strike exactly together and that all the notes of the chord are played simultaneously. . . . In playing a chord of which one note is a melody note, let the finger which plays the melody note drop more rapidly and an almost imperceptible shade earlier than the fingers which play notes of the accompaniment in the same chord; thus the melody will have the stronger tone.

A third point of view, which we do not find clearly set out in literature, but observe in practice, is to the effect that interpretation may use chord rolling,* or may delay or advance a particular note or notes as an element of musical touch for emphasis or clearness of perception, or enrichment. This practice is not based upon recognized rules, but seems to spring from a liberal attitude toward the use of deviations as a means of feelingful expression in the artistic mood. This view is in harmony with the main theory of the present volume, to the effect that beauty in music lies largely in artistic deviation from the exact or rigid.

It is generally recognized, of course, that deviations do occur, and the question then arises as to whether they should be regarded as errors or we should seek to discover in them principles of artistic interpretation. We may look for both. Regarding the situation from this point of view, psychological analysis leads us to expect three types of deviations from the exact synchronization. These are

---

* The present discussion has nothing to do with chord rolling or similar effects when indicated in the score.

(1) those which represent a recognized principle; (2) those types which come about entirely unconsciously and automatically through the operation of musical feeling in such a way as to pro-

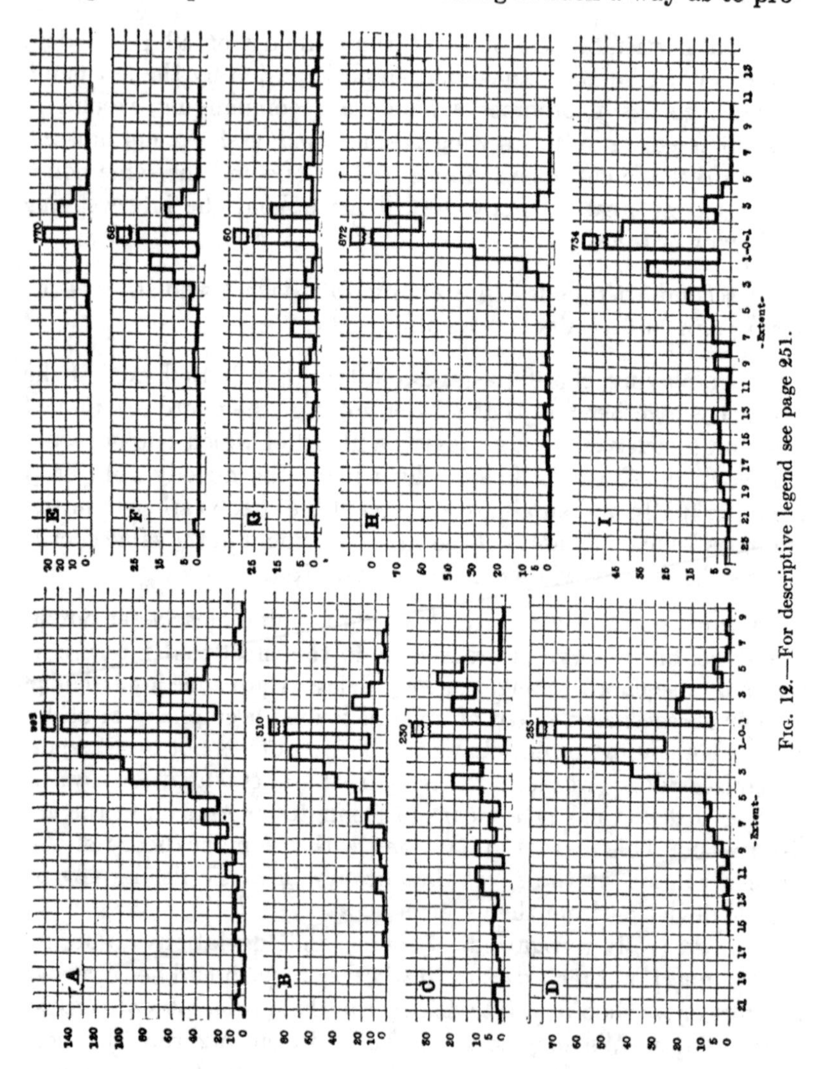

FIG. 12.—For descriptive legend see page 251.

duce effects of esthetic value without knowledge of why or how it was done; and (3) deviations which may be classified as errors. Errors are roughly of two considerably overlapping kinds: first, mere evidence of lack of skill, and, second, those due to musical impediments in the way of playing, such as difficulty in fingering, separation of the chord in the two hands, different rhythms in the two hands, intervals of more than an octave, and chords with many notes. Many of the errors in the latter class are readily recognized by knowledge of the presence of particular impediments. However, we have no satisfactory means of drawing a sharp line to distinguish between errors and artistic principles.

The question arises at once as to how much variation from synchronization we shall count as a deviation. Even the best artist cannot be absolutely exact. Our first disposition was to make a generous allowance, for example, one or two hundredths of a second, but when Vernon investigated this experimentally by measuring how small differences in time deviation musical observers could detect in asynchronous chords, he found musicians who could hear a deviation of 0.01 second from one note to another. According to this, the required interval was larger in proportion to the lack of time sense and of training of the observer. This made it necessary to assume that many musicians probably can hear deviations from exact synchronization as fine as 0.01 second in actual musical performance; and, since this was the unit of measurement, it was decided to include for the present purpose all deviations this large or larger, without assuming that the smallest difference is perceptible to all.

Our knowledge of individual differences, of course, assures us that what degree of deviation shall be heard, whether as an error or

---

FIG. 12.—*A*. Entire *Sonata Pathétique*, op. 13, rolls 5691–4, 5703–3, 5711–3; 18031 chords.

B. (Bauer) first movement, op. 13, grave and allergo con brio, roll 5691–4; 845 chords.

C. (Bauer) second movement, op. 13, adagio, roll 5703–3; 451 chords.

D. (Bauer) third movement, op. 13, allegro, roll 5711–3; 536 chords.

E. (Bachaus) first movement, op. 13, grave and allegro con brio, roll 79650; 849 chords.

F. (Hofmann) *Moonlight*, op. 27, no. 2, adagio sostenuto, roll 6101–6; 135 chords.

G. (Paderewski) *Moonlight*, op. 27, no. 2, adagio sostenuto, roll 6929–8; 136 chords.

H. (Hofmann) *Polonaise Militaire*, op. 40, no. 1, allegro con brio, roll 7620–6; 1043 chords.

I. (Paderewski) *Polonaise Militaire*, op. 40, no. 1, allegro con brio, roll 6140–0; 923 chords.

In all these figures, frequency of occurrence of a deviation is indicated on a scale in terms of per cent, the scale being divided into units of 0.1 per cent at the left of the figure; the amount of deviation from synchronism is indicated in terms of 0.01 second at the base of the figure. The zero, or no deviation, column is, of course, proportionately long. This column is broken, and the number at the top gives the per cent of chords in the entire selection which were synchronous, leaving the reciprocal percentage to be distributed among the deviations which are classified to the left as anticipations and to the right as delays.

as artistic effect, varies among individuals within very large limits. It also varies with the complexity of the chord, the tempo, and other factors.

With all these qualifications in mind, we may now compare some outstanding artists. Figure 12 tells one phase of the story. Since all the graphs in Fig. 12 are drawn to the same scale, namely, in terms of per cent, the form and size of the figures furnish us a true objective picture of the characteristics of each performer on this one specific aspect, the number, magnitude, and distribution of deviations from true synchronization.

At a glance, we see that each performer differs materially in his utilization of this device. Conversely, each figure shows to what extent each performer plays in exact synchronization. Assuming a high standard of proficiency among these artists, differences such as those indicated may possibly be attributed to the attitude that each artist takes toward the utilization of this device.

It also is noticeable that the utilization of this principle varies for the same artist in different selections, and that a given selection reveals a common tendency among artists; the *Moonlight* adagio brings out more than twice as many deviations as the *Polonaise Militaire*. More detailed studies show also that the same artist varies his deviations in repetition of similar measures, phrases, and larger units.

After preliminary study of these performances, Vernon drew up a set of 26 principles which he thought theoretically should function in the asynchronization of chords. In terms of these, he undertook a statistical analysis of all the performances to determine the validity of each proposition. Some were confirmed, others were found partly observed, and for some no evidence was found. Any musician who has attempted to state in black and white why he treats the chord in a given way will realize that this was a bold venture in view of the fact that most of the asynchronization is not done according to rules but is a spontaneous expression of feeling values. In this statistical study Vernon excluded the rolling of chords indicated by the composer. His findings may be generalized in the following statements:

1. Various causes for asynchronization lie in mechanical difficulties.
2. A considerable percentage of the smaller deviations probably may be regarded as errors.

3. A number of the specific principles may be subsumed under the general principles that notes may be brought in singly to facilitate perception.

4. Another group may be subsumed under the principle that chords may be played with a temporal spread for the sake of emphasis.

5. Chords may be spread for the purpose of softening a sharp contour, especially in legato movements, in *tempo rubato,* and other musical forms requiring softening of contour.

With the technique now available, this problem is open for extensive and intensive investigations which are certain to throw much light upon the nature of artistry in piano playing.

20

VOICE

SINGING

THE psychology of singing falls naturally into three large divisions, as it deals in turn with the singer, the song, and the listener. This chapter will be devoted to a study of the song, as represented in the musical pattern score.*

If a musician were asked to give a complete account of every detail that he, as a trained musician, had heard in a given song, his account at best would be extraordinarily laborious, and even then inadequate. In the performance score, however, we have a relatively complete record of everything that happened in the song, involving a multitude of details that the musician never hears.

In the study of this score, our first task is to see in accurate detail exactly what the physical features are in the song pattern as rendered. After one is familiar with these features, the real study of the score must be made in terms of musical theory, musical interests, musical skills, and everything else that has meaning for the musician. It presents a long and rich story which we must leave each musician to construct for himself.

A complete description of a song would involve (1) the quantitative statement of the physical features in the rendition as revealed by measurements on sound waves; (2) the relating of these to the musical score; (3) the discovery of principles of artistic expression; (4) the application of musical theory in evaluating the performance; (5) the identification of the faults in the rendition, either real or

---

* This chapter is based almost entirely upon the researches of Dr. Harold G. Seashore, working as Eastman fellow in the psychological laboratory. The student of singing will find it worth while to pursue in detail his original report.[155]

apparent; (6) an evaluation of the performance in relation to musical form and esthetic norms and ideals. The musical pattern score presents concrete data on all these issues. What we can hope to accomplish in this chapter must, therefore, be limited to an introduction to the technique of the interpretation of songs, especially as represented by items (1) and (2).

At the first inspection of the musical pattern score, the reader will be surprised by the constant and relatively gross deviation of the pattern score from the original musical score. Children delight in a demonstration with the microscope on the fingernails. Take a well-manicured, clean fingernail, and, to the naked eye, it looks smooth and presents a beautiful edge; put that nail under a high-powered microscope, and what to the naked eye had seemed smooth and graceful now appears jagged, irregular, rough, and ugly. Applying this analogy to hearing, we find that the unaided ear, like the unaided eye, has marked limits in sensitivity and, therefore, does not detect the countless deviations in tones which tone photography brings out in astonishing detail. We shall see in this score a great many elements in performance which the limits of hearing and artistic demands have normally smoothed over as a result of the complexity of the musical situation, the rapid movement of the tones, the sporadic nature of errors, and ignorance about artistic principles which operate.

The performance score gives us for the first time a real insight into specific features of the act of singing. The conventional musical score, which is a message from the composer to the singer, leaves the artist great latitude for interpretation and the exhibition of musical skills. The performance score, which we have sometimes called the pattern score, is a record of how the singer actually performed. It is a tool of investigation, a graphic picture in detail.

TABLE I. THE SINGERS AND THEIR SONGS

Singer	*Voice*	*Composition*	*Source*
Baker	Contralto	*He shall feed His flock* (*Messiah*)	Record, Victor 4026
Crooks	Tenor	*All through the night*	Record, Victor 1558
Homer	Contralto	*Calm as the night*	Record, Victor 6703
Kraft (1)	Tenor	*Drink to me only with thine eyes*	Direct
Kraft (2)	Tenor	*All through the night*	Direct
Marsh	Soprano	*Come unto Him* (*Messiah*)	Record, Victor 4026
Seashore	Soprano	*Come unto Him* (*Messiah*)	Direct
Stark	Tenor	*Ave Maria* (Bach-Gounod)	Direct
Thompson	Basso	*Phosphorescence* (Loewe)	Direct
Tibbett	Baritone	*Drink to me only with thine eyes*	Record, Victor 1238

This chapter will furnish a certain amount of study material with directions to the reader for actual work in this type of analysis at first hand. A few songs are given here *in extenso* so that they may

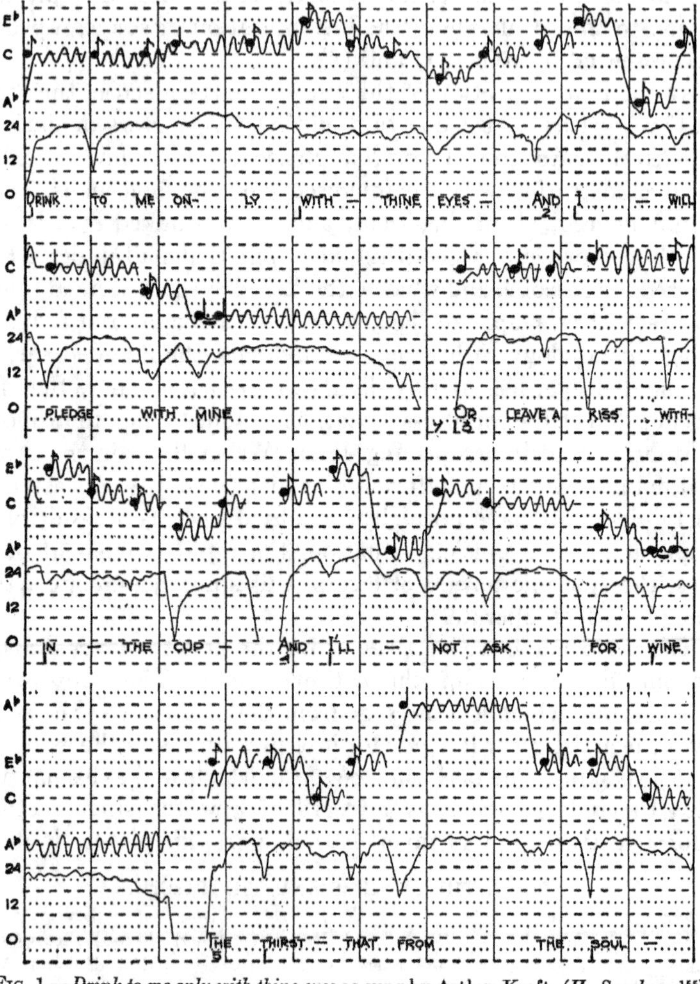

FIG. 1.—*Drink to me only with thine eyes* as sung by Arthur Kraft. (*H. Seashore.*[155])

be used as working material from several points of view in this and in other chapters.

Table I is a list of the singers with their songs which *Seashore*[155] studied intensively. The main analysis is based primarily upon Stark's rendition of the *Ave Maria* (Fig. 1, in Chap. 4). There are two songs by the same singer, Kraft (1) *Drink to me only with thine eyes* (Fig. 1) and Kraft (2) *All through the night* (Fig. 2). There are two men singing the same song, *Drink to me only with thine eyes,* Tibbett (Fig. 3, in Chap. 4) and Kraft (Fig. 1). There are also

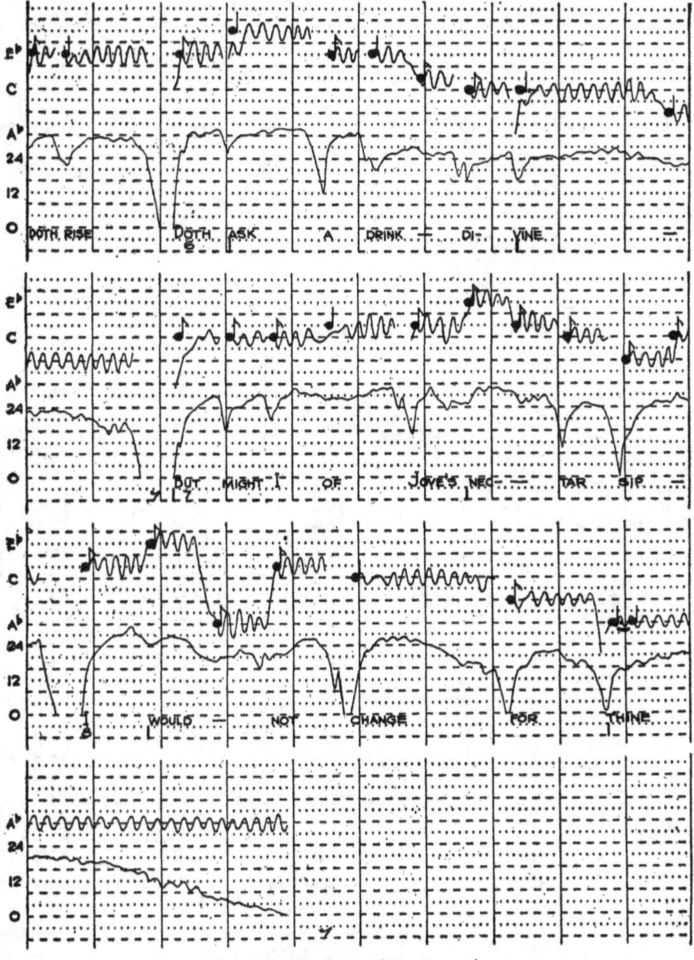

Fig. 1.—Kraft 1.—(*Continued.*)

two women who sang the same song, *Come unto Him,* from the *Messiah,* one a professional singer, Marsh (Fig. 3), and the other an amateur singer, Seashore (Fig. 4).

The serious student of music will take the assignment here suggested and compare the performance of each of the different singers on each topic which comes up for observation, insofar as time and specific interests permit. By this inductive method the analysis will

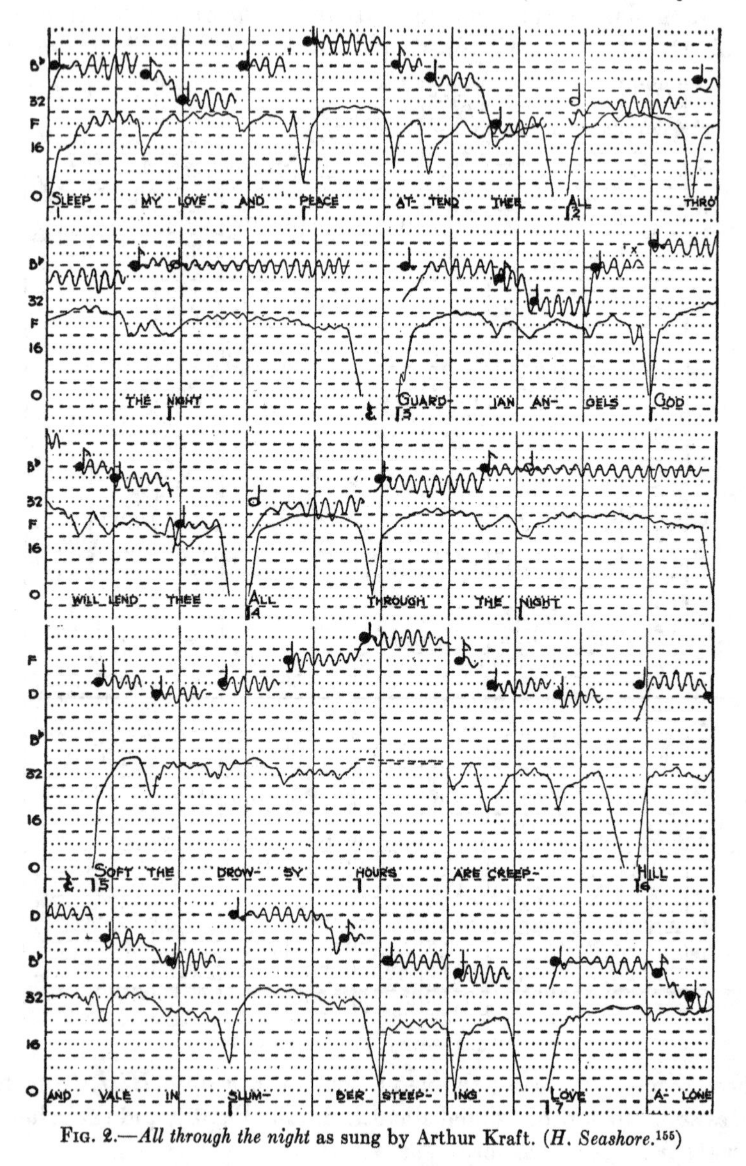

FIG. 2.—*All through the night* as sung by Arthur Kraft. (*H. Seashore.*[155])

bring out with extraordinary detail and realism the musical issues under consideration. This material will, of course, furnish a splendid starting point for the discussion of what the ear actually hears and what the musician thinks he performs, and may be compared with the study of violin (Chap. 18) and piano performances (Chap. 19).

We recall that the score is divided into half steps indicated alternately by dotted lines and dash lines. If a note was steady and in perfect pitch, the graph would be a straight line on one of these interrupted lines. Any deviation from the true pitch is shown by proportionate deflection above or below the true-pitch line. The distance between two adjacent dash lines represents a whole-tone

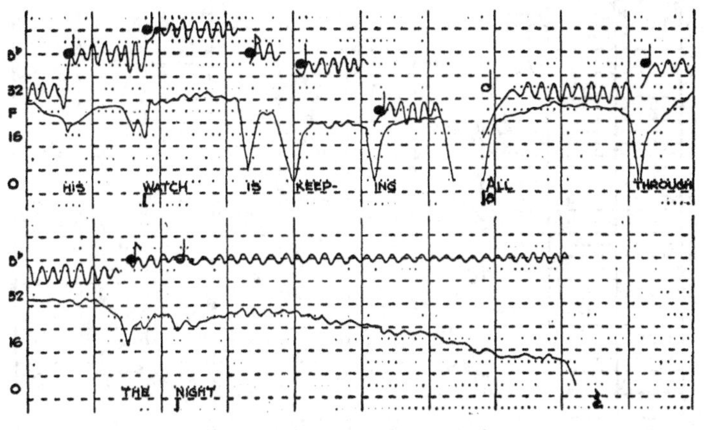

FIG. 2.—Kraft 2.—(*Continued.*)

step, and, therefore, the distance between a dotted line and dash line is a semitone. The measurements are in terms of a 0.01-tone step, and we shall use that terminology. The musical notes which are interpolated are not part of the photographic record but are inserted merely as an aid in comparing this pattern score with the original musical score. Each dot and dash represents 0.1 second. The vertical bars mark off seconds, and the short heavy bars at the bottom mark off the measures.

THE TONAL ASPECT: PITCH

General trends of intonation. In order to show how the most salient features of the pitch score in these songs may be read, we may suggest the reading for the first page of the *Ave Maria* (Fig. 1, Chap. 4) as sung by Stark.

The song is in the key of F. The first note on the syllable *A* was approached from below, rose above the mean pitch, and then remained on true pitch for a little over 3 seconds. The *ve* began in true pitch, but rose to about a quarter tone

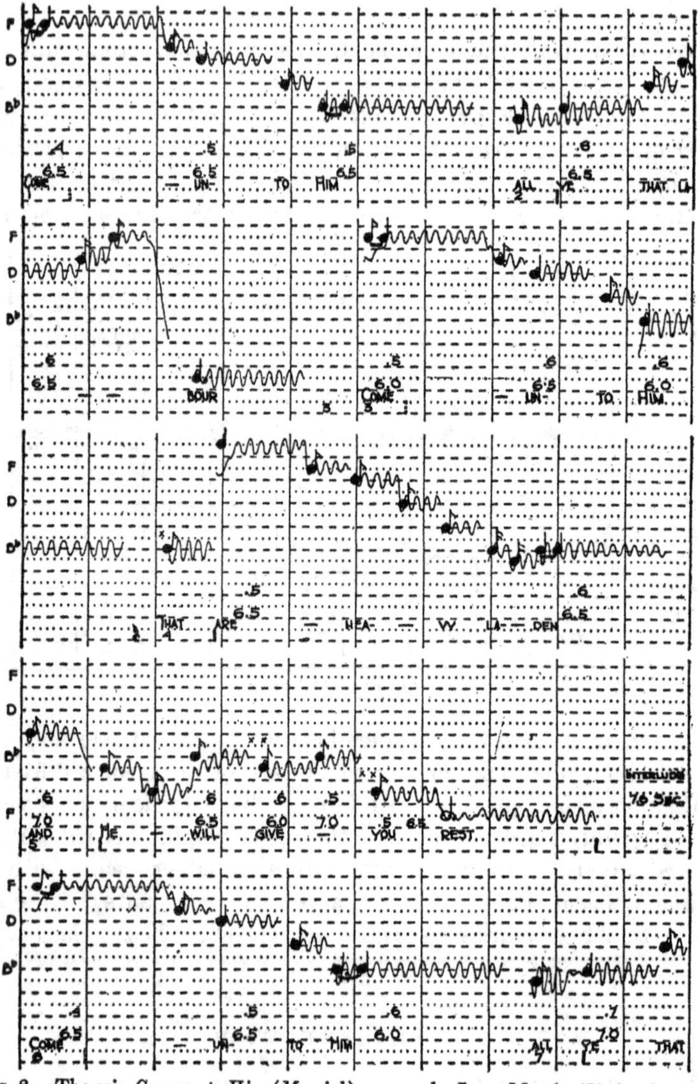

FIG. 3.—The aria *Come unto Him* (*Messiah*) as sung by Lucy Marsh. (*H. Seashore.*[155])

sharp for three-fourths of the note. The *Ma* was touched but lightly on two vibrato cycles, followed by an upward glide on the third cycle. The *ri* was begun a trifle flat, but after three cycles rose to true pitch, and remained true up to the portamento to the second note on the tie; it then flirted with this note on two wide cycles and glided upward until it was continued on the syllable *a* in true pitch throughout this note. After a breath-pause the note on *gra* was attacked by

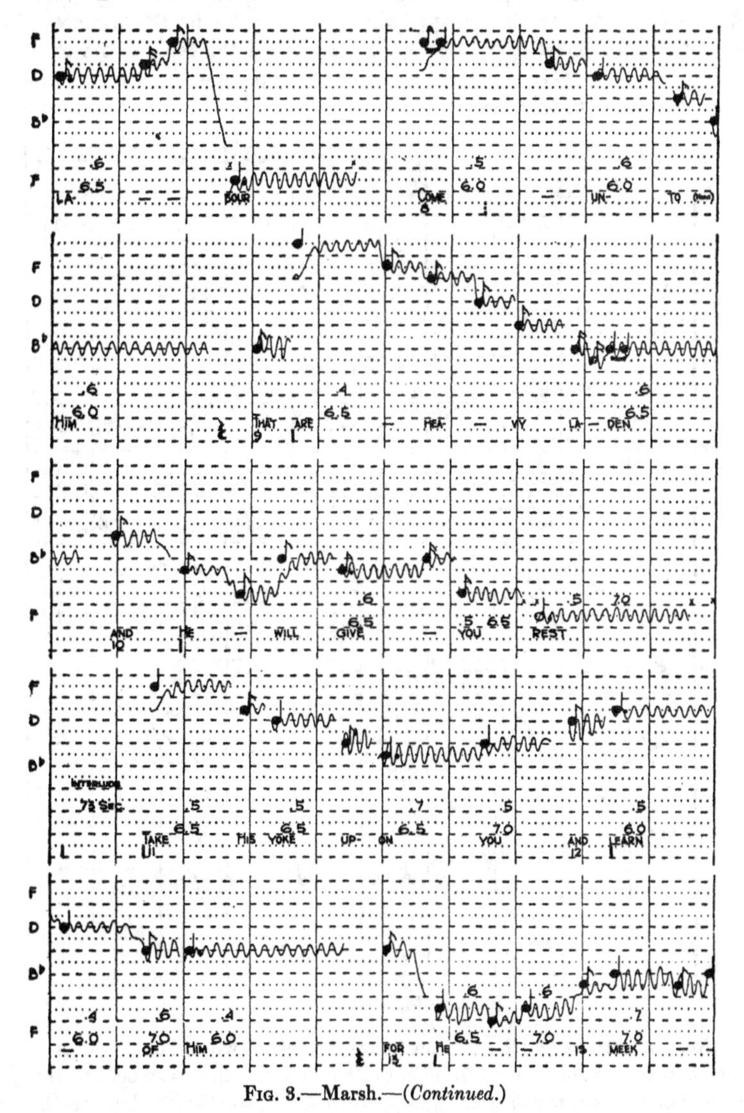

FIG. 3.—Marsh.—(*Continued.*)

a two-tone rising glide, followed by two cycles slightly flat, reaching the true pitch about the third cycle, from which there was a gradual flatting followed by a gradual return to true pitch, the portamento to the second note of the interval being considerably overreached. The movement from the flatted second note on the tie continued on the next two notes, *ti* and *a*, under a relatively even upward glide in which the true notes were only touched by the crest of the very wide vibrato cycles. *Ple* was sung on approximately true pitch for the first note of the tie, and only the crest of the vibrato cycle reached the second note of the tie from which a downward glide carried it to the true pitch of the note on *na*, which was then sung on approximately true pitch.

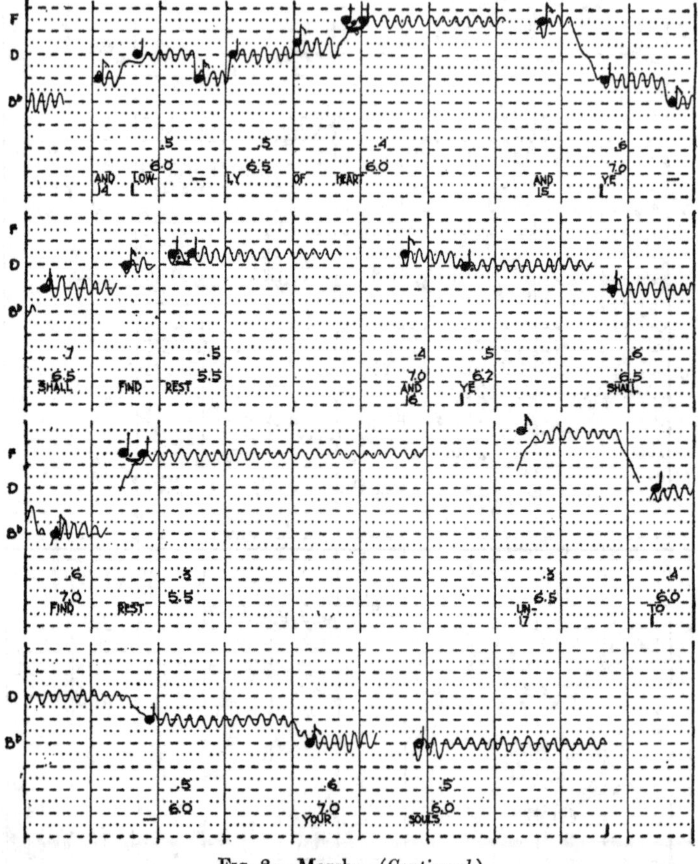

FIG. 3.—Marsh.—(*Continued.*)

After a breath pause, the note on *Do* was attacked two and one-half tones from below and rose leisurely for 0.7 second to true pitch, which was held to the glide on the second note, which was slightly overreached, so that on this and the next two notes, *mi* and *nus*, we have a parallel to the three notes at the end of the fifth measure. Both notes for the tie on *te* were sung flat but a half tone short. The note on *cum* was attacked flat but was held on true pitch after the first two cycles. The first note in the ninth measure reached the true pitch in three cycles,

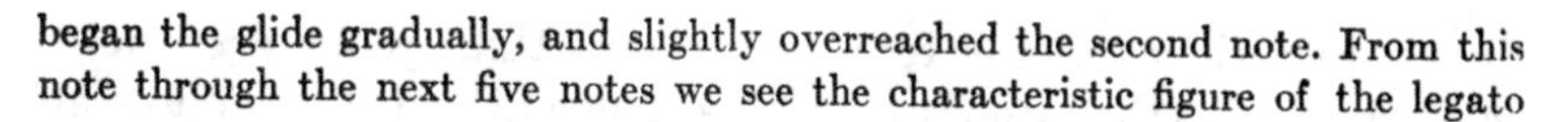
began the glide gradually, and slightly overreached the second note. From this note through the next five notes we see the characteristic figure of the legato

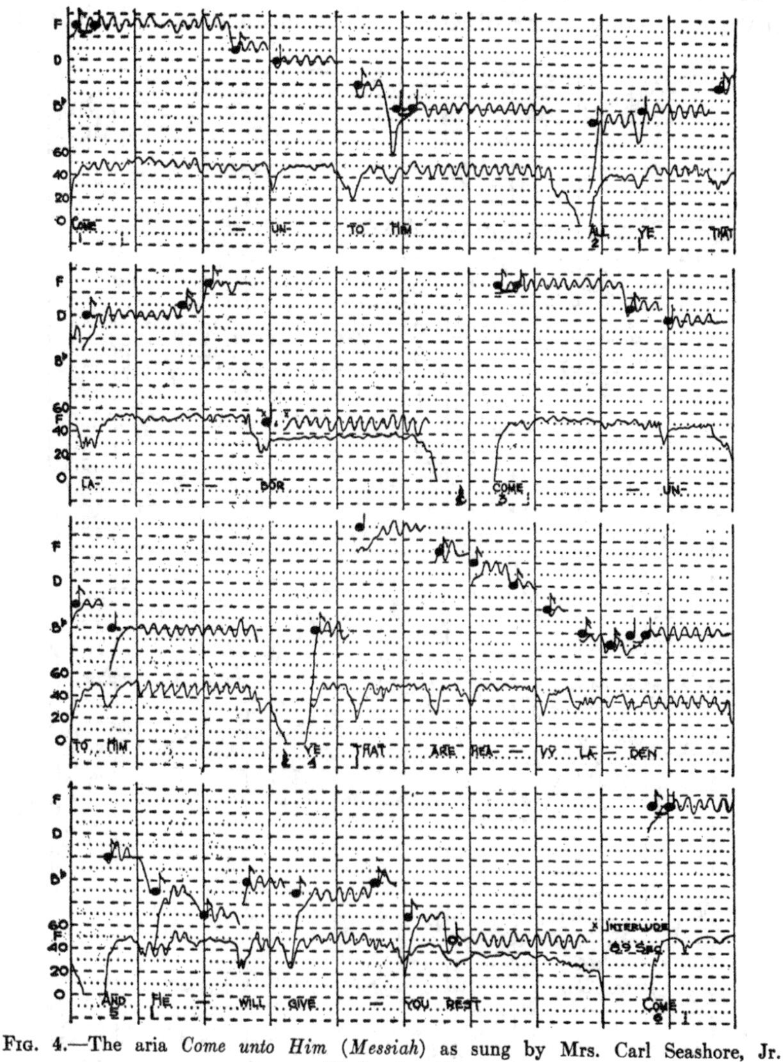

FIG. 4.—The aria *Come unto Him* (*Messiah*) as sung by Mrs. Carl Seashore, Jr. (*H. Seashore.*[155])

movement, that is, the notes lose individuality and are blended in a gliding, relatively smooth inflection which constitutes a natural unit.

With this guide in the interpretation of intonation, the reader should proceed throughout the rest of the song, noting carefully the characteristics of the tonal movement throughout each note. In such analysis the intonation of this song will reveal the following features, among many others: (1) The mean pitch, which is the

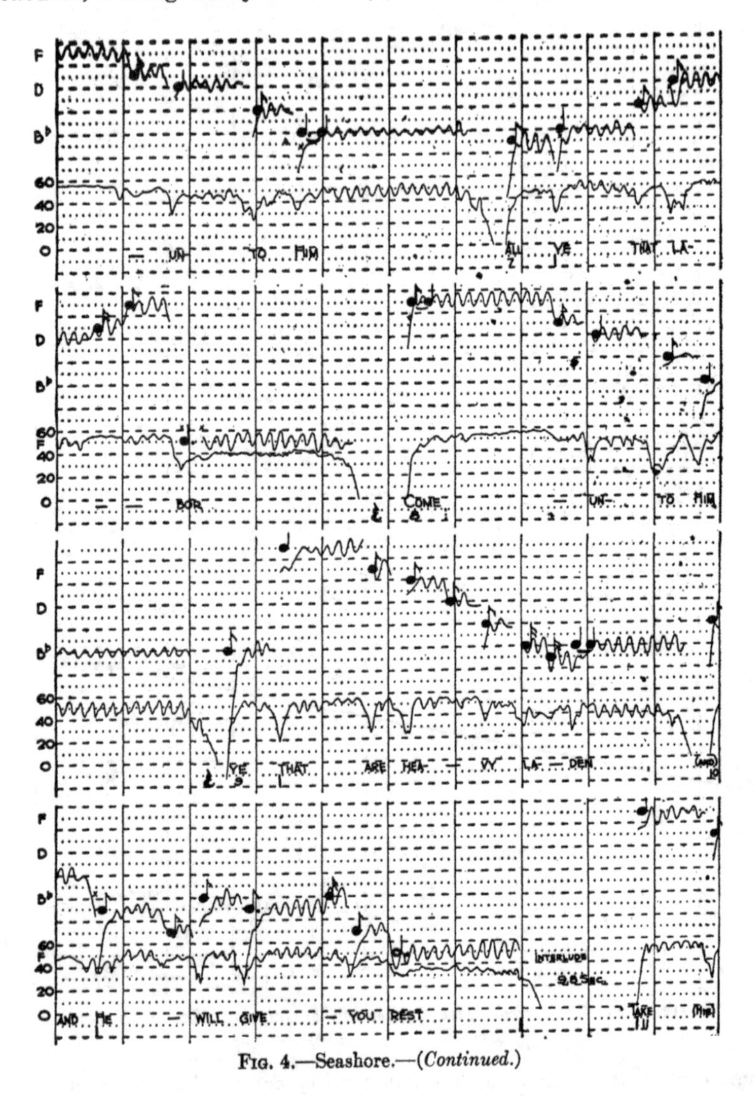

FIG. 4.—Seashore.—(*Continued.*)

actual pitch heard, tends to correspond with the true pitch of the musical score. (2) The mean pitch is, however, frequently flatted or sharped to a surprising degree. This is more characteristic of short than of long notes. Long notes tend to begin slightly flat and are gradually corrected as if by hearing. (3) The tones in the upper and lower registers are sung with equal accuracy, but there is relatively

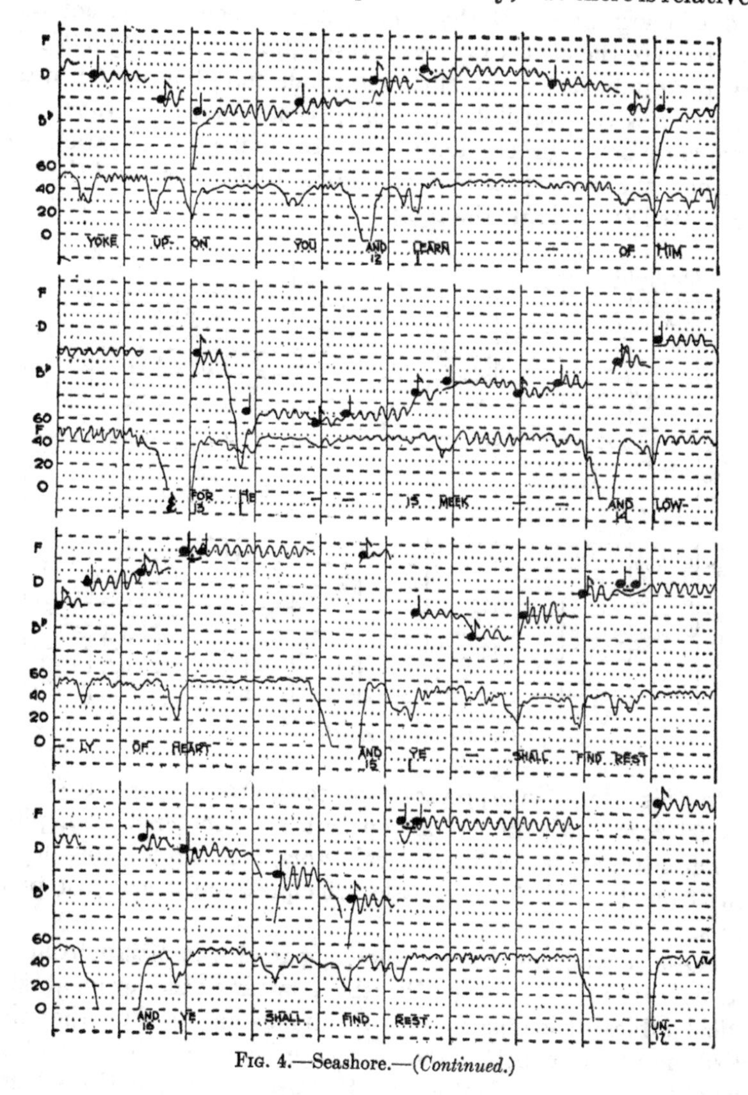

FIG. 4.—Seashore.—(*Continued.*)

more flatting in the upper and lower registers, and there are more sharped tones in the middle register. This is contrary to the common notion that flatting occurs primarily on high notes. (4)

The movement through the body of the tone may be characterized as level, erratic, rising, or falling. Of the 107 notes, 48 were sung level, 37 rising, 6 erratic, and 9 falling. The rising inflections seem to be due in large part to the legato attack, in which the characteristic sharp rise of the attack tapers off through a diminishing flat up to the true pitch. (5) In the phrasing, small units tend to fall into a more or less graceful inflection unit, rising, falling, upward bend, downward bend, or circumflex. (6) In analogous situations for phrasing, the same types of liberties tend to be taken, and the type is repeated throughout the song.

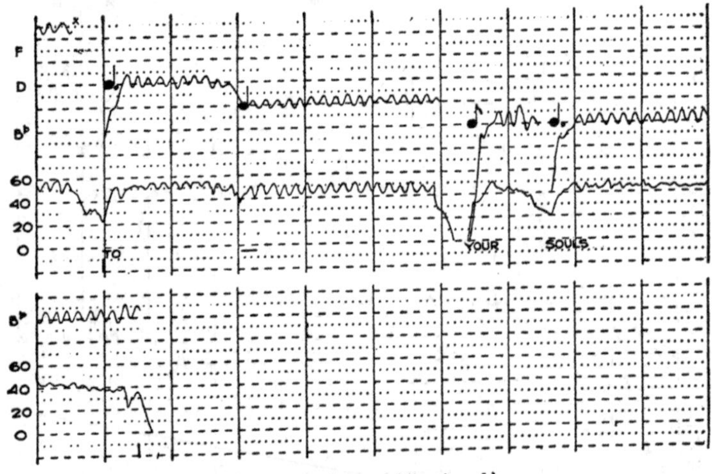

FIG. 4.—Seashore.—(*Continued.*)

In this literal interpretation of the pattern score itself, the musical reader will find numerous other characteristics of pitch intonation; some indicating typical errors, others indicating deviations from true pitch on artistic principles, and some just plain errors.

These revelations, though shocking to the uninitiated, should not condemn this singer. On the contrary, the original statistical tables of comparisons with famous artists show that this artist maintains a better than average level of achievement in each of these matters of intonation that are revealed by the pattern score.

Sharping and flatting. The issue as to sharping and flatting assumes new proportions and new phases in the light of these performance scores. All the singers show some surprisingly large deviations from true pitch. Some of these undoubtedly have esthetic value in phrasing and harmonic balancing. On the other hand, the larger deviations we find could not occur except under cover of the vibrato.*

Here we may inject a poser: Why should a musician perform in the conventional intervals? The music may demand an augmented or a diminished interval. The soloist can and does take advantage of a license which, if better known, might become an esthetic rule.

These deviations from true intonation are tolerated by the listening ear for the reason that only when the listener is highly trained and in a critical mood does he hear these deviations from the exact and rigid. But, of course, the main justification lies in the fact that beauty lies in artistic deviation from the rigid, and the legato movement is perhaps a striking example of this type of tonal license. Indeed, a rigidly true intonation without vibrato would be uninteresting and intolerable in the singing voice.

The pitch vibrato. In judging the merits or demerits of a singer, we must take into account primarily (1) the extent, (2) the regularity, (3) the form, and (4) the rate of the pitch pulsation.

The average extent of the cycles in the first song is 0.48 of a tone, that is, practically a semitone. This happens to be the average extent for the best singers of today. Sixty-five per cent of the extents fall within 0.1 of a tone from this average with a standard deviation of 0.14 of a tone. The wave form is relatively smooth, which is characteristic of a good, trained singer.

The rate of pulsation is 6.5 cycles per second, with a standard deviation of 0.6. The average rate for good singers is 6.3 with a standard deviation of 0.7. Eighty-three per cent of the cycles fall within 10 per cent of the average.

The extent of the pulsation is slightly larger (7 per cent) for the short tones than for the long tones. The rate of pulsation is approximately the same for long and short tones. The extent is slightly larger for the low tones than for the high or medium tones. The rate is approximately the same for high, medium, and low tones. There are no marked disturbing characteristics. The extent, the regularity, the form of pulsation, and the rate may be characterized as being typical. In summary, Stark's vibrato is about the average for good artists now on the American stage.

The following questions, among hundreds of this kind, are answered in these performance scores and can be observed by

* There is an instrument, called the "theremin," which is played by waving the hands in front of its antennae. If played without the vibrato, the intonation is intolerable because it is rarely true; but with the vibrato the mellow tone carries a satisfying accuracy in pitch.

detailed and critical observation. It is suggested that the reader find his own answers from firsthand study of the scores and then compare them with the summary embodied in Chap. 4.

1. How generally does the pitch vibrato occur in these songs?
2. What is the average rate of pulsation?
3. What is the average pitch extent of the pulsation?
4. How does the pitch vary from vibrato cycle to vibrato cycle?
5. How does the vibrato vary in pitch from tone to tone and within the same tone?
6. Is there any correlation between the rate and the extent of the pitch vibrato?
7. What is the relation of rate and extent of pitch vibrato to low, medium, and high pitch?
8. What is the relation of rate and extent of pitch vibrato to soft and loud tones?
9. What is the relation of rate and extent of pitch vibrato to long and short tones?
10. Does the vibrato vary with sex?
11. How does the pitch vibrato vary in two artists' versions of the same song, or two versions of the same song by the same artist?
12. How does the pitch vibrato appear in attacks, releases, and portamenti?

This list of questions is merely a fair sample. The author has listed over 200 such questions and many more may be added from the point of view of particular interests. It could be extended several times over. The answers to all except those which pertain to timbre are in the score.

In evaluating the four most significant traits of a good singer, *Bartholomew*[6] names the vibrato as one. In running through the score and observing this feature alone, it will be noted that the vibrato is present on all notes; that the shape of the pulsation is fairly smooth, taking the form of a sine curve; that the rate of pulsation is fairly constant; that, as a rule, the pulsation is present in the portamento;* and that the actual beginning, and particularly the termination, of a note is modified by the way in which it falls into phase with the vibrato cycle.

Precision of intonation in the body of the tone. A careful study of the above samples raises serious questions about the extent to which exact intonation is practiced and the large number of factors

* This is not evident at first sight for the reason that the up and down glides tend to obliterate the waves in the line; but from a geometric point of view, each line bend in the sweeping line actually represents a vibrato wave.

which have to be taken into account in judging intonation. Take, for example, Fig. 5, enlarged from the score of the first song, and Fig. 6, enlarged from Kraft. In the first figure we must ask: What was the pitch of the first tone? If the salient pitch were heard as one, it would be represented by the horizontal line. If the salient pitch were carefully discriminated, it would take the shape of the slowly rising line. What was the pitch of the second note? The third note? The fourth note? Parallel these questions in the second line. It is shockingly evident that the musical ear which hears the tones indicated by the conventional notes is extremely generous

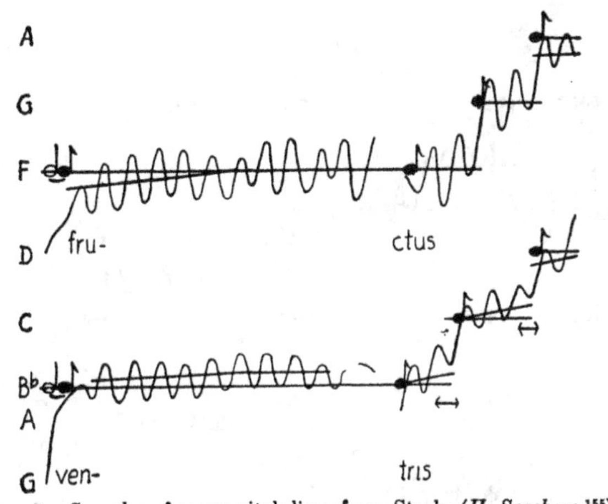

FIG. 5.—Samples of mean-pitch lines from Stark. (*H. Seashore.*[155])

and operates in the interpretative mood. Compare this principle for the various singers, and you will see that the matter of hearing pitch is largely a matter of conceptual hearing in terms of conventional intervals, and the vibrato and glides are means of covering up faulty intonation. If the last two notes in each of these samples were sustained straight, without vibrato, but a trifle sharp or flat, they would not be tolerated; but, with this artistic license which the vibrato introduces, the faults tend to be covered up by an illusion which results in gracefulness. It is interesting to compare Figs. 5 and 6 to see how common principles tend to crop out.

It is obvious that the singers never remain for as much as a tenth of a second in true pitch as a physical fact. They hover around it through the vibrato and other sources of deviation. However, it has been shown that the pitch we actually hear is approximately the mean between the crest and the trough of the vibrato cycle. This we call the mean pitch, as distinguished from the true pitch indicated by the keynote of the accompaniment.

All the characteristics of artistic deviation in the intonation of a single note of course apply equally to the singing of intervals in harmony and melody.

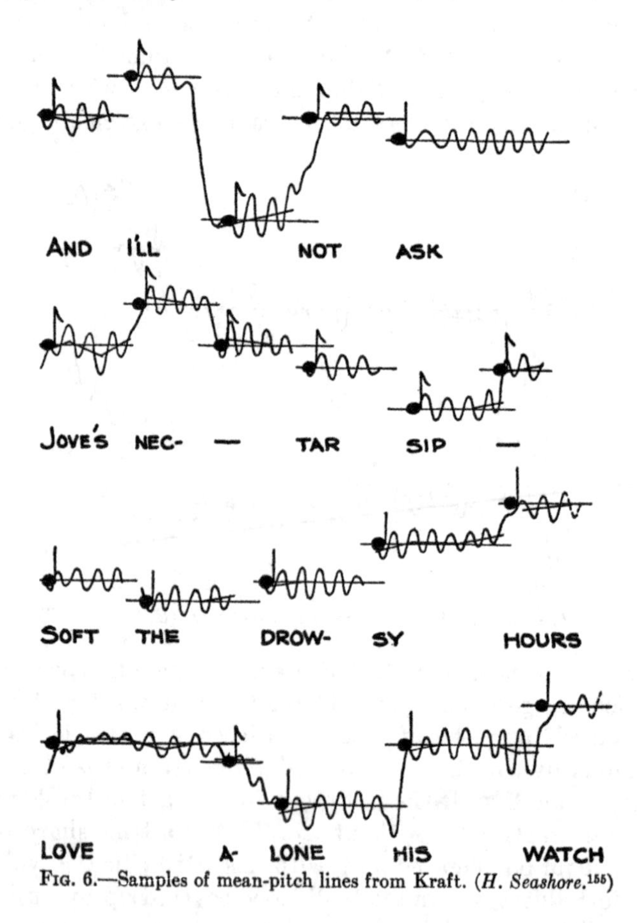

FIG. 6.—Samples of mean-pitch lines from Kraft. (*H. Seashore.*[155])

Accuracy of intonation in attack, release, and portamento. The portamento, gliding attack and release are examples of factors which influence the effectiveness and agreeableness of the tone movement characteristic of this song. The songs here studied are all in the legato style. In the group we find that 40 per cent of the intertone transitions take the form of portamento, 25 per cent of the tones are attacked with the gliding inflection, and only 35 per cent show an even attack. In the gliding attacks, 97 per cent are rising, quite irrespective of the melodic lines. This rising glide is especially associated with the opening of phrases. Figure 7 shows four characteristic types of rising glide. The longer the tone the more likely there is to be a gliding attack. The average duration of the attack in these songs is 0.2 second. The average extent of the rising glide is about 0.9 of a tone.

About half the tones in these songs end with a level release followed by a pause; about 40 per cent end in the portamento glide. Our performance scores give vivid illustration of the various types and possibilities.

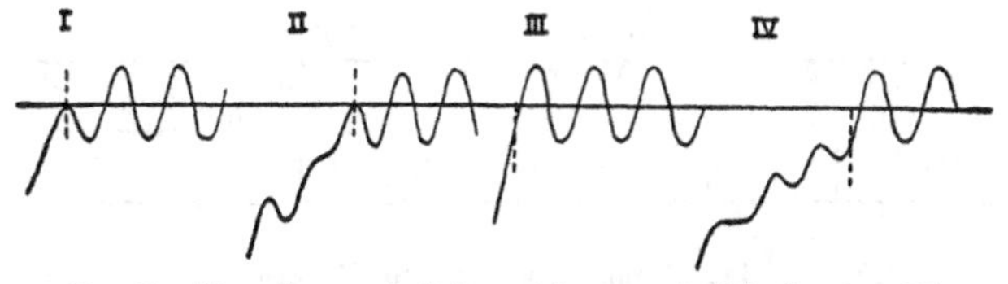

FIG. 7.—Type forms of gliding, rising attack. (*H. Seashore.*[155])

Is the gliding attack or release to be condemned? Of course, there is much slovenliness in singing, and that is to be condemned. But there is ample evidence in experimental studies to show that glides are an important medium for softening the contour of the tone by such artistic deviation from even attack or release. The pitch glide has its parallel in the gliding form of the intensity in attack. There are also physiological reasons for a rising form of both pitch and intensity in that the tone has to be "built up." The early form of the Hammond organ brought out this principle in a striking manner. The "clean" attack of the tone was disagreeable. *Larsen*[72] has devised a means of "softening" the attack by a modulator which makes pitch and intensity come in gradually in every note.

The portamento is, of course, a feature of the interpretation contributed by the singer, although it is called for on principle in legato style and partly in the score.

It may occur for any size of interval up to the octave. However, incident to melodic movement, the large majority of portamentos are for small intervals. Portamentos are, as a rule, shorter than glides of the same extent, owing in large part to the rapid movements in small intervals. The average duration for these portamentos is about 0.15 second. The wider intervals require greater duration of the portamento. It tends to appear in transitions involving changes in vowel and in the articulation of semivowels, transitionals, voiced and nasalized stop consonants, and voiced fricatives. A singer glides from one vowel to another or to a diphthong. Figure 8 shows six types of portamentos. It will be observed that in good singing the transition is always a function of the

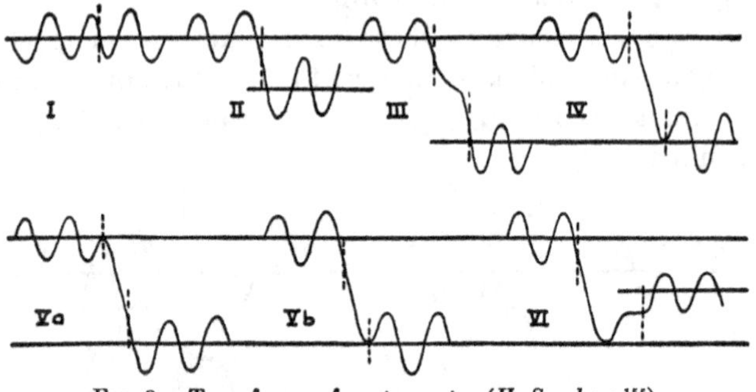

Fig. 8.—Type forms of portamento. (*H. Seashore*,[155])

vibrato, which serves to lengthen or shorten the note or the transition, according as it fits into the vibrato cycle.

THE DYNAMIC ASPECT: INTENSITY

The exact description of the dynamic aspects in singing is complicated by many factors. As has already been pointed out, we have no nomenclature in musical notation which is discriminating or detailed. The performer has no objective check by which he can judge right or wrong in intensity. The measurement in the laboratory is complicated by the fact that the reverberations in the room, the position of the singer, the position of the listener, the point at which the record is made, and many other factors of that sort greatly modify the intensity that shall be performed, heard, or recorded. Since phonograph records distort the intensity in various ways, no intensity record is shown for the last three songs, those which were made from phonograph records.

Yet there are many fundamental facts exhibited in these performance scores which throw light on the actual nature of the dynamic interpretation in these songs. The reader will profit most by careful review of the performance scores of the first four songs for the answers to the following six comprehensive questions in turn:

1. What is the dynamic pattern of a tone as to attack, sustaining, and release?
2. What are the typical group patterns, as in beat, measure, phrase, or sentence?
3. What is the characteristic range of intensity inflection for each singer?
4. Is there any correlation between intensity and pitch level?
5. What are the characteristics of the intensity vibrato as to the frequency of occurrence, extent, rates, regularity, and synchronization with the pitch vibrato?
6. What individual differences in types of intensity inflection are discernible?

Since intensity is the principal medium for phrasing, we look to the picture of the intensity movement for the complete account of the character of the phrasing as affecting accent, measures, phrases, and musical sentences in the true physical aspect. By this means we may make a comparison with the theoretical meaning or phrasing and a comparison of types and interpretation in repeated units of the same selection as well as of interpretation of the same selection by other singers.

The intensity score. Intensity is indicated in 4 db steps at the left. The zero is set for the softest tone that occurs in this selection, probably about 40 db above the threshold of hearing.

In the *Ave Maria*, there is a crescendo from 0 to 20 db; there is a weak, but even, intensity vibrato throughout all but the first 0.5 second.

After an inceptive breath pause the intensity rises to its previous level, and then follows a decrescendo of 12 db, but the vibrato has practically disappeared. In the third note the intensity rises again to the original maximum and is without vibrato. Let the reader sing these three notes and observe the natural tendency to follow this pattern, which, it will be observed, has great esthetic value.

The fourth note is maintained fairly steadily at 16 db for 2 seconds. From there, there is a slight sagging, apparently in anticipation of and in sympathy with the downward portamento of the pitch. It carries a fragmentary vibrato. In the last note of the phrase there is a fairly marked intensity vibrato. Since the intensity is one of the two principal media in artistic phrasing, we have in this graphic representation of the dynamic values a perfect picture of the type of phrasing accomplished by the artist. In the second phrase there is a gradual swell from the just audible up to a new maximum of 9 db louder than in the corresponding note of the first phrase, with a downward glide through the second note of the tie to zero for a breath pause, from which the intensity rises parallel with the arpeggio in pitch and drops to zero, giving the notes on *ti* and *a* the appearance of separation and light touch. The next note rises gradually to 19 db, which is maintained until it dips on the portamento, returns to nearly the same maximum, and then falls gradually to zero in the pause.

The curve for the note on *Do* resembles the curve for the note on *gra,* rising to the same maximum height and diminishing gradually through the tie. On the following *mi* and *nus,* we have a contrast with the above movement on *ti* and *a,* in that the two short notes are not separated from the preceding note at the beginning and there is no rising intensity with the rising pitch, undoubtedly due to the sequel which calls for a soft tone of 8 db only on *cum,* the last syllable. The intensity vibrato is intermittent.

So much for the verbal legend for the reading of the score. From here on, the reader may proceed throughout this and the other selections without the verbal aid. After that has been completed, a review of the score in perspective gives a set picture of the dynamic phrasing which should be verified by each reader in terms of his musical knowledge, personal experience, and interests.

Tonal power. In comparing the dynamic values of tones, it is conventional to speak of the highest intensity reached within a tone as representing its tonal power. Thus we may speak of the average range of an artist's tonal power; the average range for 10 concert singers was 20 db. There is a correlation of, $r = 0.61 \pm 0.05$ between rise or fall in intensity and rise or fall in pitch; *i.e.,* as pitch rises or falls, intensity tends to rise or fall. In terms of "power," we describe dynamic phrasing, as in beat, measure, accent, crescendo, or decrescendo. This is because we must use some specific point in the intensity of the note for comparison, and the highest peak is what we are likely to hear as the intensity of the tone.

Figure 9 is an illustration of one of numerous ways in which singing may be characterized in terms of tonal power as just defined. In Tibbett and Kraft (1), we see a marked contrast in the dynamic interpretation of their song. We see also how Marsh and Seashore differ in their interpretation. Crooks and Kraft (2) are in closer agreement. Kraft's range of power differs significantly in his two selections. In other comparisons, the difference in the character of the song must be taken into account.

The intensity vibrato. An intensity vibrato is present part of the time. It is very significant that it shows the same general type of intermittence and irregularity for all the singers here studied. It may be discerned 50 to 75 per cent of the phonated time, but it has an even rate and extent only about half that time. For the more constant periods it has an average extent of about 5 db; this makes it far less prominent perceptually than the

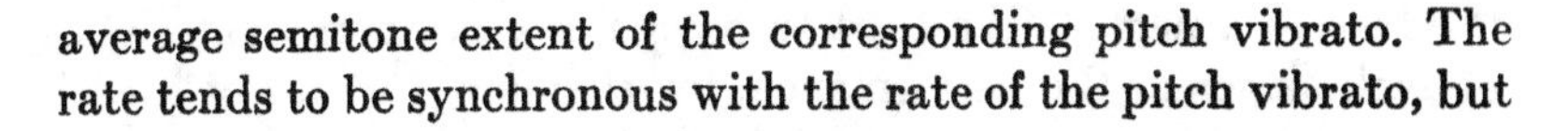

average semitone extent of the corresponding pitch vibrato. The rate tends to be synchronous with the rate of the pitch vibrato, but

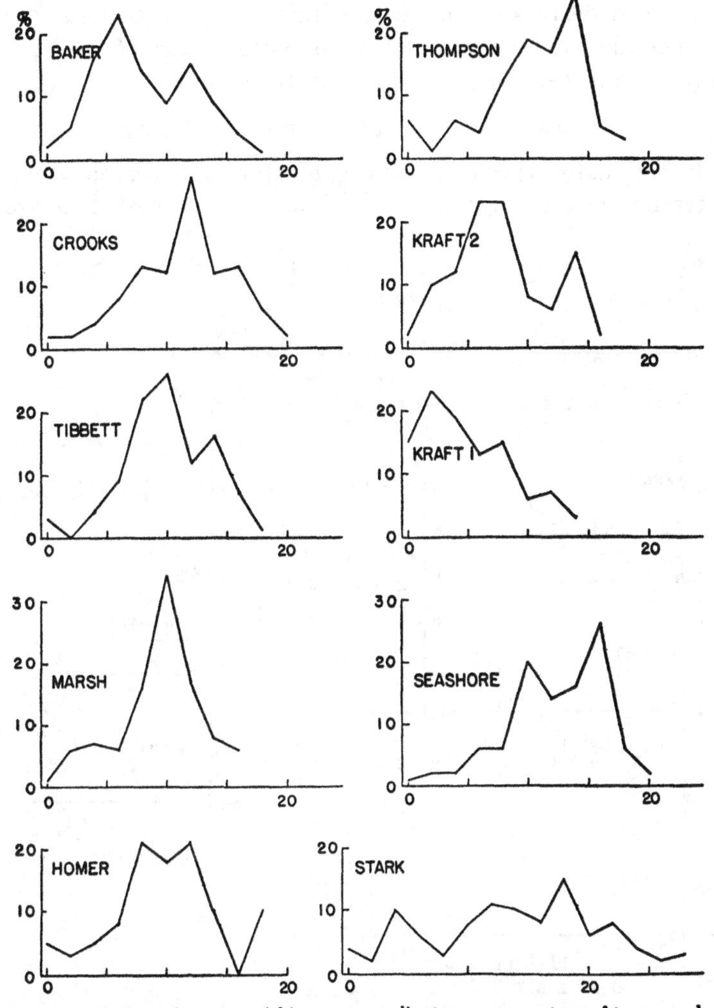

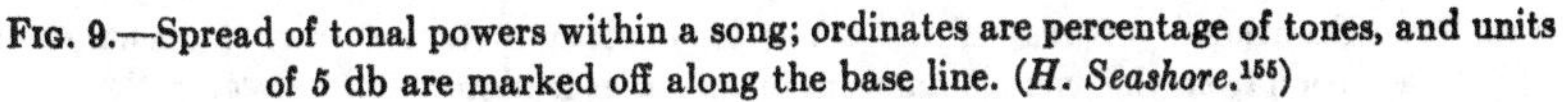

FIG. 9.—Spread of tonal powers within a song; ordinates are percentage of tones, and units of 5 db are marked off along the base line. (*H. Seashore.*[155])

there is great diversity in the phase relationships. The average rate is about 6.5 pulsations per second, 4 and 10 being the extremes.

If we are now familiar with these songs, we may have a feeling of familiarity analogous to what we experience after having seen the face of a person. We tend to recognize certain characteristics of each singer in the performance, for example, the use of breath pauses, the sharpness of the attack, the tendency to strike an even level, or to decrease or increase within the phrase. These things in songs are like the mannerisms or peculiarities of the voice in speaking, and here they are shown in the concrete.

THE TEMPORAL ASPECT: TIME

Functionally, the temporal organization is observed primarily in tempo, meter, rhythm, and phrasing. The last two are of

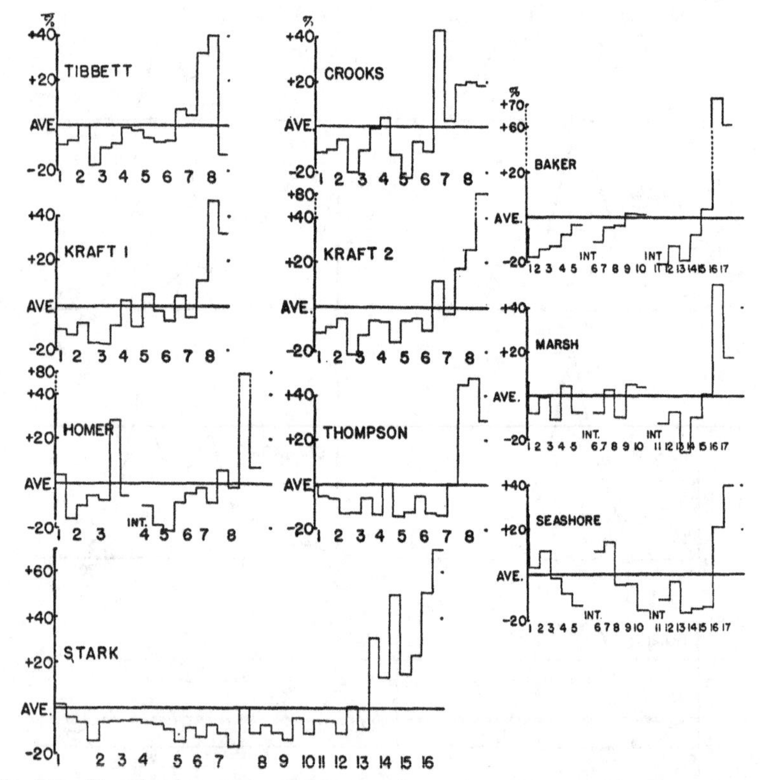

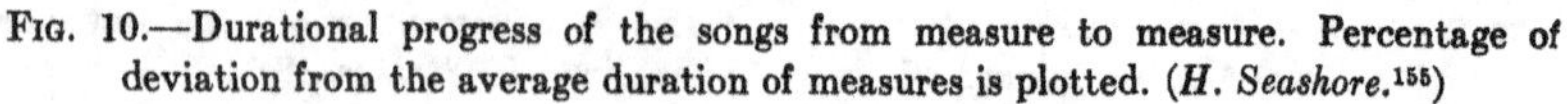
FIG. 10.—Durational progress of the songs from measure to measure. Percentage of deviation from the average duration of measures is plotted. (*H. Seashore.*[155])

primary importance psychologically and will be considered separately.

Phrasing. At this point we may restrict our interest to the acquiring of a ready command of time values as represented in the performance score. This will be facilitated by the reader's attempt to answer the following questions on the basis of a direct inspection of the scores:

1. How are the temporal aspects of tempo, beat, meter, rhythm, and phrasing represented in the scores?

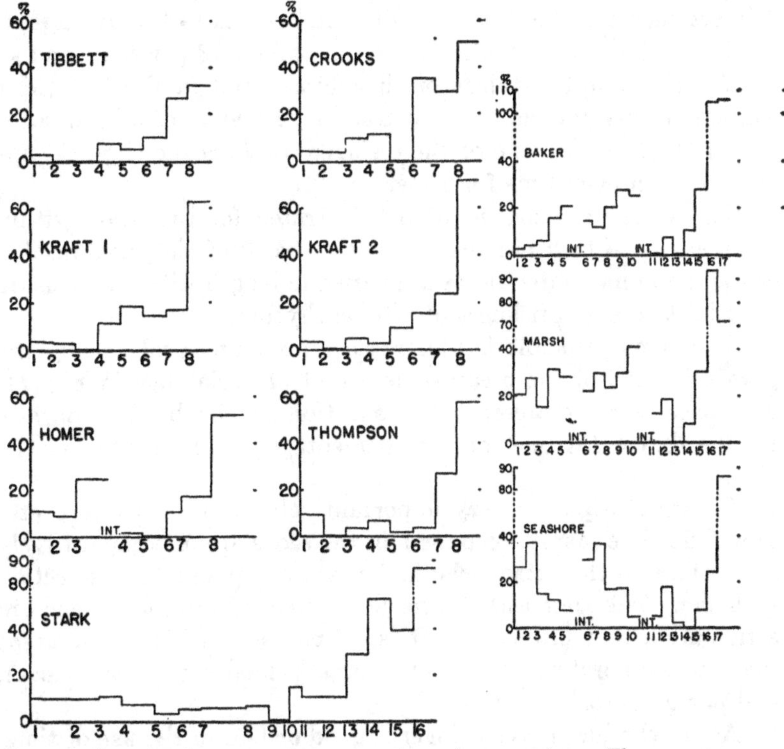

FIG. 11.—Durational progress of the songs from phrase to phrase. The percentages are calculated from the duration of the briefest phrase as the base. (*H. Seashore.*[155])

2. What types of deviation from the musical score in time are observed?
3. What types of pauses may be observed?

In studying these temporal phenomena we must distinguish clearly between the objective time and time as heard. The two are far from parallel; that is, we do not hear time as it really is. There is a vast mass of normal illusions of hearing involved, partly owing to incomplete perception but perhaps more frequently to esthetic values.

Of course, nobody sings in time indicated by the notes. Take, for example, variations in the length of the measure, as shown for the 10 singers in Fig. 10. If each measure were allowed the same duration, the result would be represented by the straight line marked "average"; this is not the case. The singer's interpretation is accomplished by artistic deviation from this average. Thus, Tibbett shortens the first two notes and comes to the average in the third, then shortens the fourth note about 18 per cent, and so on, for the first two-thirds of the phrase, and in the last third emphasizes his phrasing by a marked lengthening of all measures except the last. In none of these singers is there the slightest approach to an even time for a measure.*

The same principle might be illustrated for the beats within the measure, which are the foundation work of the rhythm. Accented and unaccented notes are varied in length within a measure in order to create briskness of artistic rhythm.

The same principle is illustrated on a larger scale, using the phrase instead of the measure as a unit of variability in Fig. 11. The base, zero, represents the duration of the briefest phrase. Points above this line indicate percentage of lengthening in the phrase.

Pauses also play a very important role in musical interpretation. The time marks for pauses in the score are of comparatively little value to the artist, who makes various pauses in connection with personally felt esthetic needs as well as for convenience in articulation and intonation. It is, of course, strikingly apparent that the temporal value of notes is greatly modified by the release, and portamento.†

As to whether a given singer is good or bad in the use of time, there are two ways in which we may judge: (1) by statistical treatment of analogous features in the performance of great singers and (2) by our own feeling as to what seems to be agreeable or disagreeable in temporal expression. The latter is, of course, our almost universal resource, but is fallible and inadequate.

* "Inc" in certain graphs indicates that the reading was incomplete, or interrupted at that point.

† The word "tempo" may be used in two meanings, as illustrated in Figs. 10 and 11. It may mean the average time as represented by the straight line, or it may mean the continually modified time from moment to moment, as shown by the rising and falling line in the graph. We may call the former tempo and the latter modified tempo. Even tempo is rarely desired outside of large group performance.

TIME AND STRESS: RHYTHM

The interpretative aspect of singing lies almost entirely in the field of phrasing, and the medium of phrasing is primarily rhythm. Table II gives a skeletal cue to the type of factors which must be considered in discussing rhythm in artistic singing. The items listed under performance in each of the four heads can be repre-

TABLE II. AN INVENTORY OF FACTORS IN RHYTHMIC EXPRESSION IN SINGING

(*From H. Seashore*[156])

I. Duration (time)
  1. Composition
    a. Note and rest values: the note pattern
    b. Meter: the measure pattern
    c. Phrase: the verse pattern
    d. Tempo: the song pattern
    e. Words: meter, phrasing, synchronization
    f. Accompaniment: coordination with melody
  2. Performance
    a. Time stress: over- and underheld tones
    b. Progressive shifts: rubato, accelerando
    c. Special effects: arrhythm, syncopations
    d. Words: scansion, phrasing, synchronization
    e. Accompaniment: synchronization, tempo
II. Loudness (intensity)
  1. Composition
    a. Symbols: *pp*, *ff*, *cresc.*, *sfz.*
  2. Performance
    a. Intertonal dynamics: stress, crescendo, phrase
    b. Intratonal dynamics: contour within tones
    c. Words: scansion by intensity stress
    d. Accompaniment: augmentation of voice stress
III. Pitch (frequency)
  1. Composition
    a. Melody: tones favoring accent
    b. Phrase: cadence, repetition, contour
    c. Words: speech, singing melody, coordination
    d. Accompaniment: melody, arpeggio, chords
  2. Performance
    a. Ornaments: vibrato, grace notes, figures
    b. Transitions: attack, release, portamento
    c. Words: effect upon pitch accuracy, transition
IV. Tone quality (wave form)
  1. Composition
    a. Words: mood, meaning, 'color,' alliteration
    b. Accompaniment: piano, orchestra, organ
  2. Performance
    a. Vowel: inter- and intratonal quality
    b. Articulation: consonants, pauses, clarity

sented in pattern scores. Rhythm is often thought of in terms of accent and duration of the tone; but the situation is vastly more

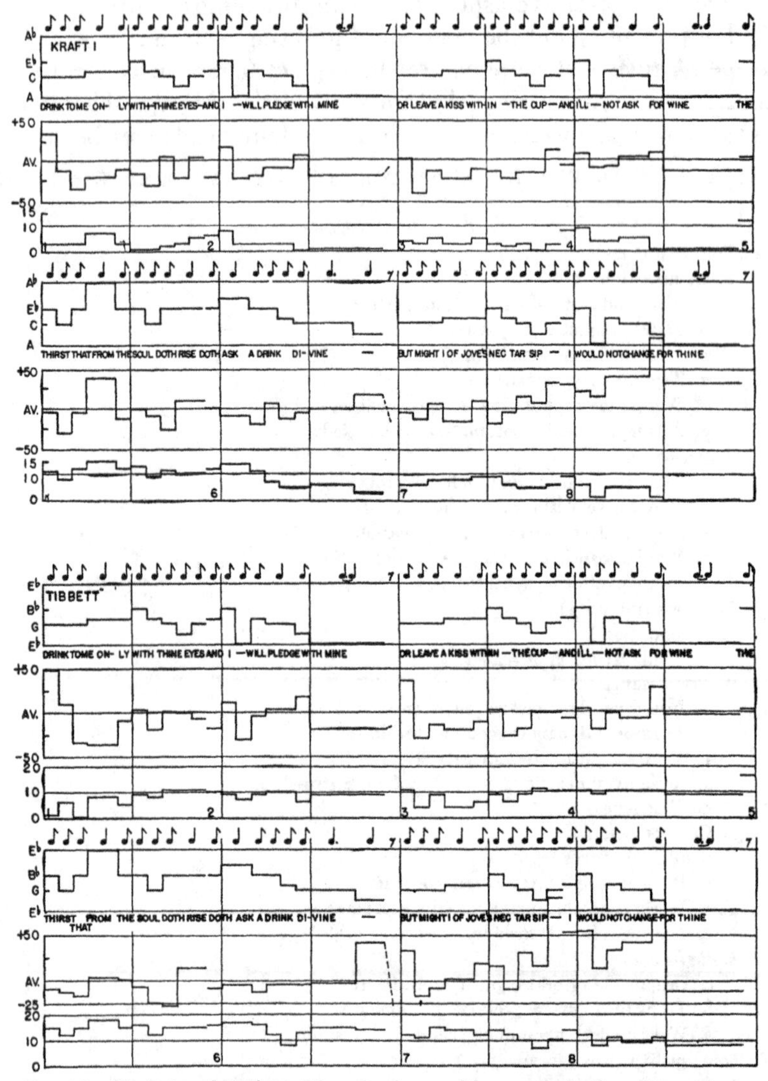

Fig. 12.—Kraft 1 and Tibbett. The role of several factors in rhythm. Top to bottom: pattern of note-length, melody, words, relative duration, tonal power, phrases. Vertical lines indicate measures. (*H. Seashore.*[155])

complicated. Instead of speaking of accent and length of tone, the psychologist favors the use of the term "rhythmic advantage." A note has rhythmic advantage, if it is strong, or disadvantage, if it is soft. It has advantage, if it is long, disadvantage, if it is short. But there are many other factors acting singly, in combination, or in opposition. These may occur in each of the four attributes of sound: pitch, intensity, duration, or tempo of the tone may give advantage or disadvantage to rhythmic emphases.

Figure 12, which is an analysis of sections from Kraft (1) and Tibbett, gives graphic illustrations of how these factors occur and work together. The top line for each unit gives the time values from the musical score. The next line graphs the rise and fall in pitch. The next line gives the words. The next gives the fluctuation in time value, that is, overholding or underholding the note. The last unit gives the emphasis caused by intensity. Let us follow analyses of the graphs made for Kraft (1) and Tibbett.

The first phrase consists of two measures, less one eighth note; all the notes, as seen in the top line, are eighth notes, except the quarter note on the second beat of the first measure. The melodic curve is level for the first three notes, rises a half step for the remainder of the measure, ascends a whole step on the beat note of the second measure, and then descends by half and whole steps to a low tone on *eyes*, which is then continued a step higher to end the phrase on the same pitch as it began. The words are self-explanatory. It is seen that the first tone, *Drink*, was overheld almost 35 per cent and that the next two were relatively much shorter; *to* and *me* not only were shorter than the equally valued note of *Drink*, but were relatively shorter than the average eighth note. In other words, the tempo of the phrase was accelerated.

On-ly with, also, were relatively underheld, but they formed a little pattern of rubato of their own. The second note of *with*, an eighth note, again was not given its relative time. Apparently this time was given to the syllable *thine*, which is important to the meaning of the lyric. Interestingly enough, the first tone of *eyes*, in an accent position, was again hurried so that it was relatively underheld, not only with respect to the average, but also to its neighboring tones. The phrase closes on the second tone of *eyes*, which apparently was retarded a little to give finality, although even here the value was just about the average of all eighth notes.

In the intensity graph at the bottom, the tonal powers of the first three tones were the same, 3 db above the smallest tonal power in the song, which is the zero level of the graph. The syllable *on* was accentuated by increased tonal power, but on *ly*, an unaccented tone, the power subsided. The lowest tonal power in the phrase was found in the accented syllable *with*. Following this, there was a steady increase of powers to the last tone of the phrase.

Articulation can be studied in the syllables, although such a study is incomplete because not all syllables were given distinct articulation; some consonants were passed over in portamento glides. The articulation in the portamento is not as distinct as the articulation of the opening vowel or consonant after a pause.

Also, it is not shown here which attacks were level and which were gliding; it is quite clear that a long gliding attack after a pause will have some articulatory rhythmic advantage. The main contribution of the graphs is the parallel portrayal of relative pitch, time, and tonal power.

These facts are, of course, all present in the original performance score but are here isolated for facilitation of observation. It is well worth while to make a detailed comparison of renditions given by Kraft and Tibbett, item for item. No one assumes that two singers should sing the same song alike, or that even one singer should repeat the same song in the same manner. But it is interesting to see how many interpretative factors must be inherent in the music itself to bring about the very numerous agreements in the rhythmic flow.

The exhibit of repeated rhythmic patterns within the same selection is very significant. It is worth while to review the various scores with this one objective in view. The temporal pattern is repeated in several phrases, giving a very clear illustration of how the composition demands phrasal patterns and how the pattern is repeated in successive phrases, often quite in disregard of melody.

In the *Messiah* arias, of Marsh and Seashore, the first five phrases are repeated in the second five with only one small change in the tenth phrases. Otherwise, for each singer we have five rhythmic, melodic, and lyrical patterns, each done twice. Furthermore, in the aria *Come unto Him*, phrases 1, 3, 6, and 8 are identical.

Consider the first phrase, *Come unto Him*. Both Seashore and Marsh sang this expression with cup-shaped patterns of relative time; Seashore's repetitions were more uniform. Phrases 2 and 7 were done differently by the two singers, although each singer was consistent with herself. The difference between the two singers was in regard to the tones on *la* and *bor*. Seashore overheld the dotted eighth note, which is the first note of *la*, while Marsh chose to effect the climax of her retard on the final tone *la*, an eighth note just preceding the drop of an octave to *bor*. Marsh's version was more arrhythmic.

Marsh did phrases 4 and 9 reasonably close to strict and uniform time, except that in the second rendition, phrase 9, she shortened both of the sixteenth notes rather excessively. Seashore's pattern is much more interesting as far as durational organization is concerned. The curve represents an accelerando-ritardando-accelerando pattern of tempo. Each time she favored the anacrusis note opening the phrases by lengthening it; then she favored the primary accent slightly by curtailing the following eighth note. On beat 2, the tertiary accent, she introduced a slight accent of relative duration; the next two notes were underheld, and then she overheld the sixteenth note which is the secondary accent on count 3, giving it not only a small durational stress, but also making the brief note more perceptible.

In the final phrases of each division, 5 and 10, Marsh showed great uniformity. Marsh overheld the anacrusis *and* in each case to open the phrase and then favored the *He* on the primary beat by overholding it in relation to the second tone on the same syllable. The tones on *give* in each repetition, being a tertiary accent on count 2, are important from the textual standpoint; they were, therefore, held considerably longer than if in strict time. However, the general retard of the phrase led up to the *you* in an unaccented position just preceding the long tone with *rest*.

Seashore stressed the meaning by accentuating *He* in the second repetition, phrase 10, and in both cases syncopated by oversustaining the second tone of *give*. She closed the phrases accelerando.

Five variables in rhythm. In the above analysis, it has been possible to take into account five variables in rhythm: (1) the note length, which is set in the composition; (2) relative overholding or underholding of a note in time; (3) the rise or fall in melody; (4) tonal power or intensity; and (5) pauses.

For each of these we may recognize double advantage, simple advantage, indifference, and disadvantage. For example, if a note is relatively overheld with respect to both of its neighbors, it has double advantage; if it exceeds only one neighbor, it has simple advantage; if it is equal to its neighbors, there is indifference; and if it is underheld, it has rhythmic disadvantage. Each of these five factors may operate singly or in combination with other factors. Thus, a long note may also be overheld and have an advantage of rise in pitch and increase in tonal power, either in a primary or secondary accent. Two or more variables may act in opposition, thus tending to cancel the rhythmic stress. In transitions a tone may have rhythmic advantage from a pause of over a half second or by initiating a gliding attack or long portamento.

THE QUALITATIVE ASPECT: TIMBRE AND SONANCE

Timbre refers to the quality of a tone at a single moment and, as we have seen, is measured in terms of the form of the sound wave. But tone quality also takes into account sonance, which embraces the rapid change of the character of the tone in timbre, pitch, and intensity, whether artistic or erratic.

Timbre. The various objective scores presented in this chapter show nothing about timbre. It is fully recognized that this fourth factor in singing is by far the most important characteristic of voice, but it is also the most complicated factor. It is not want of material or technique, but want of space that prevents treatment of the timbre of the voice in the scores here analyzed.

The best mode of complete representation of a tone is that employed for Fig. 4 and similar figures in Chap. 9. The spectrum for each sound wave is placed on a slanting base to represent the complete overtone structure of a 500 ~ tone lasting one second. We should have to represent 500 spectra in this manner. A simple figure of such proportion would require a large page!

The practical thing to do in studying voice is, of course, to take "fair samples" to the extent that time and space may permit. That is what we have done in Chaps. 8, 9, and 17, in which the general principles of timbre are discussed.

For practical purposes in the description of the timbre of a voice or in the comparative study of voices, it is quite feasible to make compact sampling of a voice with due regard for variations with pitch, intensity, time, phonetic element, and location of the sample within the tone. When principles of these variables are standardized, we shall be able to add to each objective performance score a general picture of the way in which the particular voice conforms to recognized principles and supplement this by pictures of specific peculiarities, good or bad, in the exhibition of timbre.

Sonance. To determine the exact quality of a singer's voice in a given situation, we must also take into account the phenomena of sonance. These are amply illustrated in the entire performance scores for the singers here presented, as to pitch, intensity, and time. Among the basic factors which must be considered are a full and quantitative statement of the characteristics of the vibrato, both artistic and erratic, for pitch, intensity, and timbre, all shown in the performance score. Likewise, the stability or instability of the tone in terms of intensity, both artistic and erratic, is a determining factor of sonance, principally as affecting roughness or smoothness of tone.

Space will not permit a verbal description of the very detailed comparison that can be made, but with the experience gained up to this point, each reader may now indulge in these comparisons to his heart's delight, observing first the gross resemblances and differences, and then going into details from note to note, from esthetic principle to esthetic principle, and thus gain a very rich basis for the comparison of singers and for a deeper realization of what any one singer actually accomplishes.

This chapter has undoubtedly proved to be a severe assignment for study. It is well adapted for such purposes, and can be made a constant reference whenever any principle of singing is under discussion. The student may be sent to records of this kind to obtain original qualitative statements on the issues involved.

We now have gained a bird's-eye view of the factors with which we may deal in a complete analysis of artistic performance in voice. The serious student has been confronted with a very heavy task, on the one hand, in attempting to isolate each of these facts and, on the other hand, to integrate them into a complete picture of tone quality. From this, there should follow a discriminating use of terms, a deepened insight into actual resources of what constitutes a voice, the development of the musical ear of the discriminating listener, and musical criticism. It is in terms of this approach that we must build the science of voice, musical esthetics, and the scientific foundations of training in the art of singing.

21

PRINCIPLES OF GUIDANCE IN MUSIC*

MODERN organized efforts in the direction of occupational guidance of the young take three forms—education for general culture, vocational training, and avocational training. The vocational guidance is of leading interest in the public mind—the problem of placing each youth in the occupation for which he is best fitted. But avocational guidance is coming to be recognized; first, because we are confronted seriously for the first time in the modern world with the problem of educating for leisure—how to spend spare time; and second, because in the arts we find the most marked exhibitions of talent or lack of talent, and the pursuit of the arts is and should be far more of an avocational nature than vocational. This is particularly true of music. The real emphasis needs to be laid at the point of educational guidance, whether it be for vocation or avocation. If the educational guidance is well done, the other two will take care of themselves.

The aim of this chapter is to present in rapid review a general picture of the present status of educational guidance in music, setting forth underlying principles, safeguards, and objectives. It will be restricted to a consideration of the discovery, the evaluation, and the guidance of musical talent and will not touch upon the problem of means of education or outlets for the trained.

---

* This chapter is essentially reprinted with permission, in part from *School and Society*[119a] and in part from the *34th Yearbook of the National Society for Experimental Education*.[120] It dovetails with the next three chapters, which give more specific accounts of psychological guidance in music.

THE PROBLEM

Music is the most universal art, but the outlet for a professional career is relatively limited to four fields, namely, those of composer, conductor, virtuoso, and teacher.

The highest form of musicianship is that of the composer, who represents superior creative power that is very rare. The conductor is the supreme interpreter and represents the greatest versatility, together with the power of leadership. The virtuoso is the winner in a severe struggle for survival. He represents a very small percentage of those whose ambitions lie in that direction and is often regarded as a technician with a limited outlook on the larger aspects of music. The teacher is the pedagogue and may or may not possess musical talent.

The talent required for each of these four groups is radically different; the necessary education is different; the resultant personality is radically different. Differentiated guidance toward these fields is, therefore, of the greatest importance, as it involves not only questions of expensive preparation, but, what is more important, the making or breaking of human hearts in success or failure. Yet, from the point of view of public education, it is relatively unimportant, because all these vocations together comprise less than 1 per cent of the normal population that craves musical guidance.

The problem of guidance in public schools, therefore, becomes primarily one of guidance toward the appreciation of music and self-expression in music for the joy of expression in itself. That is a problem of educational and avocational guidance, whether it be for the various degrees of amateur performance or for the general appreciation of music.

The outlets and media for expression in this large area of the musical life embrace all conceivable forms of music from the most primitive beat of drums through the countless varieties of instruments, the various gifts of voice, the power of dramatization, and the various functions and roles in the service of music in the health and the life of the home, community, church, and art.

It is, therefore, clear that musical talent is not one thing; musical education is not one thing; and the effective functioning of music in the life of the people is not one thing. Hence the problem of guidance becomes extraordinarily complicated; yet it is full of undreamed-of possibilities.

In the popular mind, a person is either musical or nonmusical, just as he is supposed to be either sane or insane. The fact is that we are all more or less sane and all more or less talented; it becomes a question of degree, kind, and value.

Musical talent is not one thing, but a hierarchy of talents as varied, as interrelated, and as dependent upon soil, environment, and inherited traits as is the vegetation of the forests. There are oaks and poplars, annuals and perennials, flowers and thorns, luscious fruits and pernicious weeds; so in the musical organism and its function, there is vast diversity. Yet in the kingdom of art, as in the plant kingdom, there is law and order in the relationships. As in the plant kingdom, the seed is always there. But what kind of seed is it? What chance does it have of coming to foliage and fruitage through the operation of natural laws and planful cultivation?

This concept of variety, intricacy, and vastness of talent, however, does not discourage the scientific approach to its analysis; because musical talent has its taproots, its modes of branching, rebranching, and enfoliage, and there is a possibility of establishing classifications and making quantitative measurements which may have a wide sweep of application. This faith in possibilities springs from the psychological laboratory where the scientist is satisfied to fractionate the problem and deal intensively with one issue at a time.

The scientific approach is, however, represented by a very small minority of those who are engaged in guidance or will be so in the future. This could not be otherwise in view of the scientific prerequisites in training for that point of view. It is no discredit to the ordinary teacher or musician that he or she does not have it.

Fortunately the situation is relieved by nature's provision for survival. In the vast majority of cases, the question of prognosis is not raised, but the child is thrown into the musical situation, and, if he has it in him, he may come out happily; but at the best, this process involves enormous waste in the field of musical nature. At the present time, by far the best and most universal test that we have of musical talent is achievement. Small children are thrown into the musical situation, and, if the character of achievement is watched intelligently, there is not much fault to find with that procedure; it is safe, although wasteful.

PAVING THE WAY

Among the significant steps which have been taken in the solution of this problem, we may note the following:

1. The idea that it can be done. The development of the idea that we can measure musical traits and can base reliable educational guidance thereon is a natural outgrowth of the testing movement of this age. On this point we are still at the very first stage of experimental procedure and readiness to accept in principle the idea that a musical education can be guided by the measurement of talent.

2. Instruments and methods. The gradual building up of measuring instruments and methods, the standardizing of both of these, and the establishment of norms is the first step in the constructive program. Here, again, we are just at a beginning, but the achievements of the last twenty-five years are encouraging and rapid progress is being made.

3. Validation. The next step has been to validate the standardized measures to show that they actually measure what they purport to measure, that they differentiate talents which are functionally significant in music and which can be shown to predict characteristics of success or failure. We have come to use the term "measure" in this program as distinguished from "test" wherever the thing that we are measuring is a specific capacity, such as absolute pitch, rather than a general ability.

4. Capacity versus ability. The demonstration of a tendency toward relative fixity and stability of inherited mental traits is furnishing the fundamental basis for a guidance program. Aside from this idea of the tendency toward relative fixity of mental or organic traits—the natural and favorable outlets in certain directions and the inhibitive and blocking tendencies in other directions, from whatever cause—the guidance program would have little significance. Our only problem would be how to educate those equally educable. For the purpose of distinguishing relatively fixed from relatively changing traits, we use the terms "capacity" to denote the former and "ability" to denote the latter. There is no sharp line to be drawn between these two, but countless practical distinctions are possible, significant, and essential to a testing program. The attempt to differentiate for practical purposes between what constitutes relatively fixed individual traits and what traits are educable and remediable is important; because on this principle the work of guidance is differentiated, on the one hand, into the organization of training and, on the other, into remedial work for specific objectives.

5. The magnitude of individual difference. It has long been recognized that some children are musical and others are not musical, but it remained for the testing program to demonstrate by quantitative measurements the enormous magnitude of these differences and, therefore, the corresponding significance for educability. When we can say on quantitative measurement, as we can, that this girl has ten, fifty, or a hundred times the capacity for a certain type of achievement in music than her equally intelligent sister has, the situation takes on a grave phase; and, when this difference can be verified with a high order of precision as often as desirable, it demands that one stop and ponder. Such demonstrations are being made daily now where talent measures are in vogue and the findings tend to hasten the adoption of a guidance program.

6. Aim. The educational objective which underlies all scientific guidance is that it is the function of the educator to keep each child busy at his highest natural level for successful achievement in the field for which he has reasonable aptitude and in which he will find a reasonable outlet for self-expression, in order that he may be happy, useful, and good. We have not yet reached more than a verbal acceptance of this undeniable principle in either music or general education; but it is our inevitable goal. The main thing that is blocking its acceptance is the lack of an acceptable and thoroughgoing guidance program as a part of the educational system.

7. The vitalizing of common sense. Considerations like those just mentioned have injected a most astonishing vitality and responsibility into the demand for the exercise of common sense on such matters. Countless means already available to the intelligent observer are coming to be utilized in the absence of exact measurement and to interpret scientific facts where available. Common sense is, therefore, rapidly assuming a new role in musical and educational circles.

This is by far the greatest good that has come out of the testing movement because we have known and we do know quite enough in a discriminating way without the use of accurate measurements; the principal consideration is the will to act upon what we do know and can observe. This will has been strengthened by the experimental revelation of the enormous extent of individual differences, the relative fixity of these differences and the radical far-reaching significance of these differences for happiness and success. The social and educational breakdown in the craze which we have lived through in the last half century, tending to demand that every girl should play the piano and all children in public schools should be taught the same music, lends great encouragement to the use of sense and reasoning in educational guidance. But this will not prevail unless an adequate testing program is maintained.

8. **The teacher's self-examination.** Many years ago the music teachers' national organization carried on its letterhead the motto, "Musical education in the public schools for every child at public expense." When the association became conscious of the magnitude of individual differences in musical talent this motto was changed for a time to read, "Musical education in proportion to his talent for every child in the public schools at public expense." This marked a new insight and a vantage ground in the evaluation of music in the public schools.

About that time I wrote in the last chapter of *The Psychology of Musical Talent*[137] the following challenge to teachers in the public schools, asking each teacher to take an inventory of his theory and practice bearing on this issue with the challenge that he clarify his own thinking and satisfy his own conscience in regard to whether or not he was doing the child justice by the manner in which he adapted the training to the nature of the child. I quote here merely the nine questions which were elaborated in that chapter.

1. Do I fully realize the magnitude and significance of individual differences in my pupils?
2. Do I believe in giving each individual pupil in music an opportunity commensurate with his actual capacity and aptitude?
3. Do I actually, in practice, give my pupils an opportunity to grow, each according to his talent?
4. Do I keep the pupil always at the highest level of successful achievement?
5. Do I justly praise or blame the pupil?

6. Do I rightly identify the retarded child? (The gifted child who is retarded by the school lock step?)
7. Do I motivate my work for each individual?
8. Do I help my pupil to find himself?
9. Do I take into account the individual as a whole—bodily, social, intellectual, moral, esthetic, and religious?

REMINISCENT INCIDENTS

A few years ago, when we were organizing the new active movement for scientific study in child welfare, an interesting incident occurred in a hearing before a legislative committee. The argument had been made that we should show as much interest and exercise as much intelligence in the care of our children as we do for our cattle through the application of scientific findings. One stately senator stood up and, in a mood of self-adulation, said, "As for me and my family, we are willing to trust Mother Nature," to which the retort came from one of his colleagues, "You wouldn't trust Mother Nature for your cow, or your sow, or your mare!"

Another incident is now apropos. When my first son was born, there was a sewing society that held a meeting across the street, and it is reported that the pastor's wife had exclaimed, "That poor Seashore baby!" In response to this, ears were pricked and queries came, to which she replied, "His father is a psychologist."

I grow reminiscent. In the early days of the Yale laboratory I noticed that visitors coming in had an unconscious tendency to put their hands to their heads, which I interpreted as a protective reaction.

At a meeting of the Music Teachers National Association, the music supervisor of one of the largest school systems in the country, who had made a low score on certain measures of musical talent, took the floor and with great gusto and assurance asserted that these measures are not significant because he had made a low score, to which it was my pleasure to solicit his response to these questions: "In what field are you proficient as a performer? What creative work have you done in music?" and similar questions, to which he replied that throughout his career his energies had been thrown into the direction of musical administration, from which the audience drew the conclusion that he was a successful business manager in music, and musical talent or no talent was not much of a consideration in his success. He should have been tested for business ability rather than music.

A professor of violin, who was visiting the laboratory, somewhat in an attitude of defiance dropped into a class and took the test for sense of pitch. He brought it to me with considerable pride as if to say "That is what your pitch test does." He had fallen down and made a wretched record on account of a negative attitude. Looking at the record, I took the bull by the horns and said, "Either you are a failure as a violinist or you can improve that record. Will you do me the honor to take the test once more?" He did, and came out at the top.

One of my first experiences in talent testing was the analysis of the ability of a brother and two sisters. The occasion grew out of the fact that the older sister had been having about 10 years of musical training without making progress and the other two children, without much attention to education, were making splendid progress through spontaneous and voluntary efforts. I found that the older sister was radically lacking in fundamental capacities, whereas the other two children were highly gifted. The action upon my findings by the parents, a minister and his wife, was to send the older daughter to the New England Conservatory of Music in order that she might be able to keep ahead of her brother and sister.

A young man of twenty-one, who had spent years of study for a professional career in music came to us for guidance, and the examiner was astounded to find that on the sense of consonance he made a negative record of 100 per cent; that is, all his answers were wrong. This finding was so interesting that I made a thorough study of the case, principally in the psychopathic hospital, and found that it was a case of dementia praecox showing itself in characteristic attitude of negativeness which accounted for his reactions to consonance and his failure up to date in his career. His perfect consistency gave him the highest rating in consonance in the light of his negativism.

PRINCIPLES OF MEASUREMENT AND GUIDANCE

1. Measurement fundamental. Educational guidance in music should be based upon measurement—the measurements of specific musical talents. A program of that sort must not ignore such considerations as intelligence, will to achieve, traditions and desires of the family and teachers, economic status and outlets, competition and aspirations for a career in other directions, and health, each of which may play a very important role in determining success or failure in the educational process. On all of these issues, relevant data may be collectible. In other words, although measurement of talent is the prime consideration, this measurement must not stand by itself but must be supplemented by and made in the light of the total situation and all available sources of relevant information. The objection of current *Gestalt* or configurational schools, given to specific measurements, is a very superficial and passing fad, because the moment they reach the stage of needing verifiable facts they must become discriminating and specific.

2. Guidance on measurement progressive. The guidance should, under the best circumstances, be a progressive one, beginning with the earliest observation of infant behavior exhibiting musical aptitude, and determining each successive stage in the organization of the musical education from time to time, as the actual situation for critical choice presents itself, beginning with the second year of infancy and continuing up through the final finishing touches upon training for a musical career of the most talented.

Mental development tends to move in cycles with successive and passing periods of dominant interests, urges, and exhibition of resources. We must, therefore, insist upon a progressive adjustment which shall take all these into account. Failure on this point has been one of the most grievous errors in vocational guidance up to date. It has been well illustrated in sectioning students on the basis of ability in classwork, which we may say has been more or less of a failure if based upon a flat assignment and a marked success when based upon progressive evidences of capacity for adjustment. Nevertheless, there are critical turning points at which we must make a decision, as, for example, in using examinations as a basis for admission. But the point is that the result of such decision and further analysis of capacities should follow at all turning points throughout the period of growth and training.

Making the guidance progressive removes all danger of becoming fatalistic because, if the thing is done wisely from stage to stage, the wisdom of such scientific inventory of capacity in progress to achieve will become more apparent. This point is of fundamental significance, because there is a popular notion that the educational guide in music says, "You be a musician," or "Be not a musician," and thus with one stroke makes or unmakes the future of the aspirant. Educational guidance is just the opposite. It is primarily the determination to utilize every type of information of the most authentic sort that will apply to a clarification of the next turn in the course.

3. The negative aspect of musical guidance. It is very important to distinguish between the negative and the positive aspects of musical guidance. The human being is equipped with marvelous resources, most of which remain unrecognized and undeveloped. The presence of unusual ability or talent, however, tends to express itself in urges or cravings for self-expression through a given channel. The well-defined presence of such urge in spontaneous self-expression is the best lead that can be offered. On the other hand, tradition, social tendencies, and many other conditions create a demand for a certain type of esthetic development often revealed in the expressed wish of parents. Although this may be unwise, it should receive adequate consideration. In both cases, the function of the guide is to throw the floodlight of his investigation upon possible obstacles in view, in order that the subject may not be tripped without warning. His position is analogous to that of a physician who attempts to ward off deterioration and disease, or of an attorney who warns against the traps of the law, or of the musical artist who warns against the dangers and pitfalls in a musical career. In other words, the guide in music will recognize the countless types of outlet possible in music and the countless possibilities for finding the equivalents of music as an artistic outlet in other fields.

When once the individual is to launch on a program, presumably in harmony with his nature and the facilities of his environment, it is the function of the guide to find out if there are any obstacles in his way, whether physiological or psychological, economic or social, hereditary or environmental. Thus the prevailing tendency of vocational guides to say, "Be this," or "Be that," should be discouraged in order that the choice of a field may rest upon natural and permanent dominating interests and impulses. Whether it be for vocation or avocation, the educational guide in music must, therefore, have at his command an adequate and analyzed conception of what capacities operate in a given type of musical situation in such a way that he can take his talent chart and weigh the evidence on the whole for or against a given musical venture and give specific and verifiable reasons for it.

4. The positive aspect of musical guidance. As implied in the term "negative," the procedure just described is protective and often results in the discouragement of expressed desires. There is, however, a very important positive function of talent measurement, namely, the dragnet survey of talent which can be made for the purpose of locating in the schools, quickly and early, evidences of outstanding natural gifts in music. Surveys continually reveal extraordinary findings of musical gifts in children who are not in the least aware of having such a gift and who might pass through life without giving any evidence to society of having such resources. This is in the main the justification of talent surveys in public schools, but when once discovered, the principle of negative or protective guidance should apply to the further guidance of talents so discovered.

Another positive aspect of musical guidance lies in the deliberate selection of a particular field in music on the basis of talent analysis. A pupil may have a great gift for music and yet lack some specific qualification in certain aspects of music. The gifts for voice or for instrument are largely different, and the gift for expression through different instruments may also be specific. Here, it is the function of the guide to give positive advice as to what avenue of musical expression the student should follow on the basis of talent analysis. This has its application in large scale in the assignment of instruments, especially where these are furnished at public expense. Thus, the talent-analysis program in the public schools is essentially a positive program: a program for discovery of the gifted and for placement within the musical fields. In this matter, it may well be looked upon as an element in a program of conservation of natural resources and economy in musical education.

5. Aim qualitative rather than quantitative. Educational guidance in music is not merely for the purpose of determining whether the child or youth is musical or unmusical, but rather to determine into which of the various musical hierarchies the individual will best fit so that after a general training in the fundamentals of music, his energies may be wisely directed into voice, instrument, or theory and within each of these fields into a particular avenue for self-expression for which he may get clearance papers on the basis of careful analysis of capacity and forethought.

Educators often make the mistake of regarding music as one thing, blissfully ignorant of the enormous divergence in outlets and opportunities that pass under the name of music. On the basis of such ignorance, the common demand of educators today is, "Is the child musical or not musical?" A "Yes" or "No" answer to that question is of very little significance unless it should be emphatically in the negative. Some of the most pitiful failures in musical careers are not due to lack of musical ability but to a misguided effort, as when the lyric singer attempts to become an opera star or vice versa, when a highly gifted pianist attempts to become a violinist for which he may not be fitted, or when one whose natural outlet is in musical performance enters the field of creative writing. Fortunately, nature often takes care of such adjustments through natural cravings; but a critical review of the personnel in the musical world on this issue reveals disheartening results of misplacement which could have been forestalled by modern guidance at early stages.

6. The whole man. Like the craze of parents for developing precocity, the blind onrush among educational guides today is often too narrow in the follow-up of a specific talent. Measurement should always be evaluated in relation to the man as a whole; all guidance should be made, not only with the objective of developing the whole man, but by giving special recognition to marked capacity for achievement in fields other than music, in order that there may be a wholesome development of the artistic nature of the individual as a whole, finding outlet in various arts, and that the artistic nature may not become top-heavy. The exclusive cultivation of a marked talent has often proved the ruin of the individual as a person, in relation both to himself and to society. Musicians and educational examiners interested primarily in music must, therefore, hold themselves responsible for this larger view which demands that, while high specialization may be encouraged, it should be planned in relation to its effect upon the bodily, intellectual, moral, social, esthetic, and religious nature of the individual as a whole.

7. Discovering by doing. Talent measurement will be of little value unless it is followed up in the plan of progressive guidance by a system of putting the talent into practice. Findings of talent measures are often negated by the results of formal instruction and drill of a purely mechanical order which becomes repressive of initiative. To aid us in "finding" him, the individual should immediately be encouraged to participate and do the things indicated by his talent chart, in large part on his own initiative and stimulated by the progressive revelations of his powers to achieve.

In this respect dramatics in the public schools have developed talent perhaps more successfully than music because the individual is given an opportunity to show what he can do and, through such encouragement, gradually develops and exhibits new powers not previously observed. Thus we find in the utilization of voluntary and competitive extracurricular exercises which stimulate the individual into enthusiastic self-expression not only a necessary sequel, but often a good substitute for further measurement.

8. Remedial work. Since a testing program reveals impediments to progress which may be of a remediable order, the measurement of talent loses its effectiveness if remedial work is not supplied to remove these impediments by treatment or reeducation. The value of that is illustrated in the field of speech, in which our freshmen are given a thorough analytical examination for speech defects and are then immediately thrown into sections for corrective work in which remediable speech defects are eradicated in very short order and thus give the individual a new sense of self-respect, power to command through speech, and stabilizing of personality. Without such follow-up work, the determination of speech defects would be of no significance. The situation is analogous in music.

SOURCES OF ERROR IN GUIDANCE PROCEDURES

The way is paved, the movement is afoot, and high expectations are afloat. I trust that the present note will not be propaganda for unwarranted enthusiasm and wild onrush in this field of endeavor, because it is fraught with many dangers. Some of these errors should be pointed out specifically and boldly; and, in the light of these, reasonable tolerance, willingness to do the best we can from stage to stage, and perseverance should be cultivated.

1. Faulty techniques of measurement. Those who have done their best work in the construction of tests and measures for capacity and ability for achievement are the first to recognize that we are yet in the experimental stage, that our measures are not always adequate for the serious purposes to which they are applied, that while they are statistically reliable, they may not predict individual achievement, and that the effort to use them on the part of people who cannot afford the best often involves the use of dangerous substitutes. We cannot hold out hope that this source of error will not be entirely overcome because the more inadequacies of instruments and methods we eradicate, the more new ones we discover in the process of refinement of technique. Yet progress is very gratifying, and practical educators are right in saying that we should use the measures progressively available with due caution in tempered and frank admission of their frailties.

2. Untrained guides. Speaking of the practical situation, particularly in the public schools today, we are suffering from necessary and unnecessary use of untrained guides. "God protect me against my friends, I can defend myself against my enemies," is the prayer of pioneers, themselves doing reliable work in the field of guidance.

There is a tendency to overestimate quantitative data obtained under more or less artificial conditions. This often results in failure to apply what common sense dictates. Justice often miscarries by the experimenter's failure "to use his head," and to this is added the very common absence of the use of hypotheses and penetrating interpretation of the fact measured in the light of intimate knowledge of the field of activity, which is the objective.

We are passing through a craze for physical measurements, mental measurements, and statistics, and have not yet in large numbers reached the stage of comprehensive and mellow insight and reserve. Granting that serviceable facts may be determined, we still face large dangers for the application of these facts. Intelligence, for example, may be a good index to a stenographer, but in industrial offices and clerical units it is not a prime consideration, and selection on that basis often leads to unreasonable turnover. A high order of intelligence is needed mainly in the secretarial position.

This principle applies to music. For one, a high order of creative imagination may not be necessary; for another, we can dispense with a fine sense of pitch; and for another, with a high sense of rhythm. On the other hand, such factors as musical memory, musical ideation, and musical imagery may be cultivated to a relatively high degree, even with a low native capacity.

Guidance on measurement requires knowledge and often some degree of proficiency within the field, as, in this case, music. But it also requires training in the art of measurement. The guidance program often fails because it is done either by a mere musician or a mere psychologist. We are marking time in the development of persons in responsible positions who combine these two qualifications in the persons of psychologists in music, who not only know measurement in music, but have a sound and mature social, moral, and educational outlook. After all, there is an easier remedy, and that is the sympathetic cooperation of specialists in the two fields, psychology of measurement and music, and in this lies the real hope of the future.

3. Improper attitude of the subject. We never secure reliable measures of capacity unless we have the full cooperation of the subject in an effort to achieve at his best. A common source of error in all mental tests is the negative or indifferent attitude of the subject. While the test in itself may be fair and significant for a life situation, the negative attitude of the subject, a general emotional blocking, or a lack of the will to achieve may lead to erroneous rating. Great ingenuity is needed in the development of testing effectively to take the individual in a cooperative mood and off guard as to his inhibitions. The competitive attitude is essential. This would be greatly facilitated if measurements were made only where there is a specific purpose to serve and intention to follow up, so that the pupil realizes the timeliness and the personal value of the test to himself.

4. Inadequate verification of low ratings. In measurements of this kind by rather rigid psychophysical methods, cheating being eliminated, a high record may always be counted as reliable somewhat in proportion to the excellence; but it is the low records which are subject to the largest number of sources of error. Therefore, when a record which counts against an individual is found, for example, in the lowest third of a normal group, it should always be verified with the best of ingenuity and care in order to make sure that the impediment indicated is really there. This requires patience and time, which are often wanting. It is a general rule of measurement and guidance that the lower the rating on a significant capacity, the more thoroughly the verification should be made; and taking the cue from this lead, the more intensive the investigation for related factors should be.

5. Inadequate sampling. Another large source of error is the failure to secure fair sampling. Often the experimental situation exhibits merely a measure of the tester's lack of insight into the situation. It is a pity that "we do not know what we do not know."

In the conduct of a testing program, a vicious example of this is the use of one or two measures of musical capacity and pronouncing on that basis for or against a musical education. The adequacy of sampling, of course, becomes important to the extent that the test is to be of critical significance.

The principle of fair sampling can be best safeguarded not by attempting to measure everything that may be involved, but by limiting the decision or the finding to the specific factor that has been measured. The significance of this the tyro does not understand and the enthusiasm of the educational guide often overrides.

We must always guard against the pertinent taunt that the examiner may not be measuring the ability of the subject, but rather his own inability to give a fair test.*

6. Failure to distinguish between capacity and ability. It is one thing to discover a low rating; quite another to determine its cause and, therefore, its bearing. The bare fact of low rating is of relatively little significance unless the real cause is revealed in the process of organizing the measurement. Herein lies one of the most difficult tasks in the mental testing program of today. Failure on this point is also one of the main reasons for generous testing and the very meager and inadequate follow-up work which is a common curse today.

The crucial question that must be answered at each turn is this: "Is this low rating remediable or is it not?" While musicians have always recognized the significance of the "gift" of music, the practical attitude in the teaching profession has been that music lessons are a remedy for all. In this attitude we recognize both humanitarian and economic motives, but back of both is the lack of a vital recognition of the limits of educability.

7. Failure "to do something about it." This takes two forms: failure on the part of the student to follow advice, and failure on the part of the teacher to base training upon the nature and extent of talent. It all comes back to this principle of recognition of individual differences: It is the function of the teacher to keep the pupil busy at his natural level of successful achievement.

---

* When the Yale psychologists reported that they had been able to show that apes can use abstract concepts, such as the value of money, how to barter, how to hoard, and how to cooperate—all so-called "higher" mental processes—a famous scientist remarked, "There it is; never before has the ape had a fair chance. Instead of testing the animal, we have been testing the testers' ability to set a fair test."

22

MEASURES OF MUSICAL TALENT

My earlier work, *The Psychology of Musical Talent*,[137] dealt specifically with the analysis of the musical mind with reference to a possible guidance program. While the present volume does not duplicate or replace the earlier manual, it does present a great deal of new material gathered in the last twenty years to supplement it on this issue. The reader will have gathered in preceding chapters a mass of facts and principles which have a bearing on the present situation. This chapter will therefore be restricted to a mere appraisal of this procedure in the light of reports and experience.

WHAT CAN WE MEASURE?

In a suitably equipped laboratory, we can measure a hundred or more specific features, each of which will throw light on the nature and extent of a person's musical talent. These may bear on heredity, native capacity, acquired ability, ability to learn, as well as character, rate, and amount of achievement. They may deal not only with sensory and motor capacities, but also with the higher brackets of ability in the complex musical situation.

The first problem, then, that confronts the musical guide is to determine what the immediate issue is in the analysis of a given individual, how far the analysis should be carried, and, in the light of varied outlets for musicians, what field of music is regarded as the goal.

In general, we may say that in all cases the first step should be the measurement of basic capacities, each of which measures receptivity for one of the four musical avenues, namely, the tonal, the dynamic, the temporal, and the qualitative. In addition to these, immediate memory, a sense of consonance, tonal imagery, and intelligence should be measured. The instrumental needs for this battery are met for the purpose of group testing by the Seashore *Measures of Musical Talent.* This battery should be accompanied by case histories and auditions. Twenty years of experience with this battery have established and validated its significance for the purpose of a general dragnet survey.

What further measurements should be made will depend upon the facilities available, the seriousness of the inquiry, and the nature of the goal. Among facilities, we should mention laboratory equipment and a technically trained examiner. Emphasis should, however, be laid on the latter; since, if a musician has once developed a concrete analysis of the musical mind, he can achieve many of the objects of guidance without instruments, so long as he understands what specific factors to observe and their significance.

A young person who contemplates a serious program in training for a musical career should, wherever possible, submit himself for analysis in a well-equipped laboratory by a trained psychologist in music.

PRINCIPLES INVOLVED IN THE ELEMENTARY BATTERY OF MEASURES OF MUSICAL TALENT

Many years ago, I adopted the term "measures" instead of the word "tests" in order to distinguish these experiments from the ordinary paper and pencil tests which deal with unanalyzed situations. The word "measure" implies standardized procedure in accordance with laboratory principles.

These measures introduce two fundamental principles into the psychology of music which were discussed in Chap. 3. The first of these is the laboratory point of view that measurement deals with a specific factor which is isolable under control. This is the first principle of pure psychology. For example, instead of asking the question, "Can this child hear music?" we ask, "Can he hear pitch?" "Can he hear loudness?" "Can he hear time?" "Can he hear timbre?" "Can he hear rhythm?" "Can he hear tone quality?" Each of these can be isolated for measurement; and, when we have the result, it is recordable, repeatable, verifiable, and predictive. What is true of hearing has its parallel on the side of performance as represented by skills. We do not ask, "Can he play?" But we ask, "Can he play a tune in time and in rhythm?" "Can he phrase?" "Can he produce good tone quality?" Such questions have their parallels at the higher levels of imagination, memory, thought, and feeling; although the higher and, therefore, the more complicated the process becomes, the more it tends to resist analysis. The second maintains that the practical conclusion drawn shall be restricted to the factor that has been measured. Thus, if we measure the sense of pitch and we find that the record made is in the 99 centile, the conclusion is not that the child is musical, but that he has an extraordinary sense of pitch, that he is superior in one of the scores of talents essential to musical success. He may be utterly incompetent in other talents. This is the first principle of applied psychology. Amateur guides in music are gross sinners through violation of this principle. Indeed, adherence to this principle at any cost is the supreme safeguard of scientific guidance. The bold and positive guidance in an unanalyzed situation is, of course, condemned on this principle, if such guidance makes any pretense to being scientific. In the light of our postwar experience, both of these principles are radical departures from current testing programs but seem to gain practical recognition and will undoubtedly stand as foundation principles in applied psychology, whenever principles of scientific measurement are to be utilized.

When a considerable number of specific measures is used as a battery we can begin to generalize with reference to the efficacy of the battery in proportion to the adequacy of the sampling, but always with reservations in accordance with the principle of applied psychology just stated. If the ranks in a fair sampling of capacities which are essential to success are all low and have been verified, a general negative prediction may be safe; whereas, if some or all are high, reservation must be made for determination of other factors which may be equally crucial signs of success. For high rating in music, numerous other factors must be considered, such as resources, conflicting interests, the will to achieve, and especially the power of application and of hard and continuous work.

This laboratory point of view, therefore, does not assume, as has often been charged, that the mere existence of a given number of good capacities will make a good musician or that a low rating in one or more capacities is necessarily discouraging. Nor can this point of view be charged with being atomistic without at the same time denying the possibility of psychological measurement. Indeed, this type of measurement has done more than anything else in the laboratory to enrich and deepen our insight into the integrated and functional character of the musical personality.

CRITICISMS OF THIS APPROACH*

The application of these principles meets criticism from several points of view. Some theoretical psychologists will say it is atomistic and point out that genuine talent is not the sum of specific talents. The psychologist in music accepts and is really the sponsor of the idea that the total talent is not the sum of specific talents. He maintains that talent is, indeed, an integrated whole, but that we get truer and deeper insight into this integrated whole by employing the scientific method of fractionating, that is, by observing one aspect at a time.

Others point out that it is futile to make specific measurements, because, according to our theory, there are scores and scores of specific capacities that are integrated in the hierarchy of musical talent as a whole, and only a small number of these can be measured in a given case. The answer to that criticism is that it would be unscientific to maintain that anyone would ever have the time or the ability to measure everything, even in such basic principles as laws of gravitation, permeability, or heat. The value of selected measures hinges upon whether or not they are of a basic character; for example, there are countless aspects of rhythm in music, many of which could be isolated and measured as such, but one basic capacity for all rhythmic performance may be a genuine sense of rhythm. Likewise, there are hundreds of varieties of hearing of pitch, but the measure of the sense of pitch is basic for all.

Another criticism comes from the clinical psychologist who maintains that real insight and true interpretation are gained only by a study of the total personality in the total situation. There is truth in that contention, but the criticism is met by the fact that it is possible to measure a specific capacity during performance in unhampered musical mood, and in every respect in the actual musical situation. In measuring capacity for performance in singing at the present time, the singer performs in an

---

* From *Yearbook*.[120]

acoustically treated music room in which there are no instruments present other than a microphone (of which he may be quite oblivious); but from that microphone there are made simultaneously phonograph records and records from three or four cameras operating simultaneously in such a way that from these records every detail of the performance as a whole, or at any moment in the performance, may be reconstructed with high order of precision. There the singer performs in the musical mood and in the musical situation, but the instruments analyze and set forth the elements involved.

Other critics say that if we limit ourselves in this way, we will know so infinitesimally little about the total musical mind that it may be of doubtful value. The answer to that is that such humiliation is true but wholesome. Awareness of the fact that you have only a small sample of measures makes you correspondingly cautious and restricted in your application. The musical guide must be profoundly conscious of how little he knows of the possible mass of talent. The practical teacher wants a wholesale judgment; the psychologist refuses to give that and simply says that such and such facts are known and may have such and such bearing on the problem.

Another criticism is that measures of talent do not enable us to predict, because development of talent is merely a matter of training. This a psychologist would simply deny.

PURPOSE OF THE PHONOGRAPH RECORDS AND SUPPLEMENTARY PROCEDURES

In designing these measures, there were several purposes in view: (1) to measure native and basic capacities in musical talent before training has been begun, and, therefore, to make them independent of musical training; (2) to measure one specific capacity at a time; (3) to make the procedure available for group measurements; (4) to simplify the use of instruments; and (5) to save time.

Each of these objectives set up certain restrictions on procedure. In the original manual,[125] it was stated thus:

These measures of musical talent comply with the following conditions: they are based on a thorough analysis of musical talent; they are standardized for content that does not need to be changed; they give qualitative results which may be verified to a high degree of certainty; they are simple and as nearly self-operating as possible; they are adapted for group measurements; they take into account practice, training, age, and intelligence; they have a two-fold value in the concrete information furnished, and in the training and pleasure gained from the critical hearing of musical elements.

RELIABILITY

With these advantages, which have been accurately established, certain disadvantages are evident. These are due mainly to two factors, namely, adaptation for group measurement and timesaving. Both result in the lowering of reliability. In order to cover the entire range of talent in an unselected group, as in surveys, it is necessary to have the range of the testing material wide enough to include all from the best to the poorest, for example, 0.01 to 0.5 of a tone. This virtually shortens the test because it is effective for those only who are near the threshold; for example, in extreme cases, if a person can hear the finest of 10 steps, then his success on larger steps does not contribute to the measurement. Likewise, if he can respond only to the largest difference, the smaller steps do not contribute to the measurement. In the first case, the test would probably be reliable and significant. The second would call for further analysis. In the first case, the test should be repeated with laboratory instruments in which at least 100 trials are made on the smallest step or smaller steps if so indicated. This would lead to a very high order of reliability. Further testing in the case of the other extreme should take the form of search for possible sources of difficulty, such as subjective or objective disturbances, ignorance of the factor involved, and many other elements of procedure, the object here being to discover why this absence of the sense of pitch exists rather than its exact extent.

The known reliabilities must always be kept in mind in making interpretations, and it should always be understood that, if time and facilities are available and the case is important, the measurement should be done with high precision laboratory instruments. This might greatly increase the reliability. In the group test, the reliability for the sense of pitch in the eighth grade is about 83, but, when this same test is made with tuning forks on the actual threshold, the reliabilities will run in the high nineties. The same applies in principle to all the other measures. Full statistical determinations of the reliability of these measures is reported by *Larson.*[74]

The merits of our principle—that specific capacities can and should be measured with a high degree of reliability—should therefore be judged in the light of exact measurement rather than in the makeshift of a short group test. This is true for all of these six measures. The less than maximum obtainable reliability published is, therefore, not due primarily to the phonograph records, but to the fact that the procedure is a short group test.

THE BASIS FOR RANK ORDER

There is another fundamental difference between group testing and testing the individual by laboratory instruments. In the former the results are expressed in terms of centile rank on the basis of norms established for adequate sampling of unselected groups. This has the advantage of showing how a given individual varies from other individuals in an unselected group on a scale from 1 to 100. It also has the great advantage of making it possible to express all the different measurements in the same terms.

In the laboratory procedure, however, the measurement is made in terms of the threshold of discrimination, that is, the just noticeable difference. This has many advantages from the point of view of experimental procedure and these records can, of course, be transformed into centile rank order if a sufficient number of cases are available for statistical treatment. Thus, a person who can hear a difference of one vibration at the standard of international pitch will probably receive a centile rank of 97 or 98.

THE USES OF THESE MEASURES

It is interesting to note that the basic measures of musical talent have been used and are further suitable for a number of purposes outside of music or musical guidance purpose.

Racial characteristics. Anthropologists have adopted these measures as standard procedure in a battery to determine racial characteristics in anthropological investigations wherever the musical characteristics of a race or a primitive group are being studied. Four rather extensive investigations of differences between Negroes and whites have been published, each covering a different type of situation. Of these, the most interesting is that by *Davenport* and *Steggerda,*[15] in which a comparison of three groups was made, namely, pure black, brown, and white, all found in the same locality. *Johnson*[55a] measured 3,300 American Negroes. *Murdock*[100a] measured 500 Hawaiians, divided into eight racial groups. *Garth*[30a] made an extensive comparison of Indians and whites in Western schools. *Mjoen*[99,100] made interesting comparisons between Lapps and Nordics in the Scandinavian countries and other races in central Europe. *Peterson* and *Lanier*[106] have conducted extensive measurements on white and Negro college students and children in the public schools, with careful attention given to conditions of environment. In all these cases, the measurements were made in terms of the Seashore *Measures of Musical Talent*. Fragments of other investigations from remote parts of the earth have been reported.

In general, it may be said that this type of measurement is suitable for anthropological studies and is likely to be enlarged and refined on a considerable scale. However, the present indications are that normal individuals in different racial groups or on different cultural levels probably do not differ markedly in the basic capacities represented by these measures. This supports the theory that we are here measuring fundamental capacities of modern man, the type of capacities which are but little modified by his environment or cultural development at the present stage of evolution. However, it has been shown that, in analogy with the age and intelligence differences, measurements in a given environment do bring up significant differences; but, before we attribute these to basic capacities, we must eliminate all social and environmental factors which may act as deterrents to an approach toward a physiological threshold.

Heredity. Such studies as those by *Stanton*,[174] *Mjoen*,[100] and others offer new approaches to this branch of science. General suggestions referring to the utilization of this technique are found in another chapter.

Where systematic surveys are made in the public school system extremely valuable material on heredity will accumulate bearing upon the distribution of talents in family relationships.

Surveys. Numerous surveys have been made by these measures for various purposes; such as, comparisons of the best residence district with the poorest, children of foreign birth with those of American birth, children in the city with those in the country, and culture levels in two radically distinct country communities. These have been used in evaluation of a standard musical course in terms of the distribution of talent, showing that the prevailing course requirements are utterly unreasonable for children below average capacities and superficial for students of high capacities. They have been used for comparison of band, orchestral, and chorus members with unselected groups, the distribution of talent in relation to training, the distribution of talent in relation to theory courses, the distribution of talent in relation to intelligence, training, and age, and the comparison of normal and feeble-minded.

Speech talent. It has been shown that the talents herein mentioned function in speech very much as in music. This comes out most strikingly in clinical psychology of speech, in which it is frequently shown that defective speech is due to an absence of ear-mindedness, and often a specific defect may be traced to lack of a basic capacity in hearing.

Skillful occupations. It has developed that many skillful occupations depend upon the presence or absence of one or more of these basic capacities. The most striking illustration of this was the capacity required for the listeners who were employed during the war to locate submarines, airplanes, and ground tunneling. During the war, submarines were located by a device which depended upon the keenness of the ear and certain aspects of hearing. We had the pleasure of demonstrating that in squads of 30, which had been selected by physicians as qualified listeners, it was possible to show by use of these measures that 1 person out of 30 may locate the direction of the deadly craft within an accuracy of 1 degree, while another listener might not do better than 10 degrees, and that different men in the squad would vary within these extremes. The significance of this in terms of human life and property can hardly be overestimated. This method of selection had just been adopted when two things happened: (1) the armistice and (2) invention of an instrument which made an adequate record photographically and, thus, replaced the listener.

Some general comments. It has been suggested frequently that the measures should be cast in terms of distinctly musical material. I do not regard the efforts which have been made in this direction as successful. In a test program of this kind, we should stay as far as possible away from anything that involves musical training and experience, if we wish to predict success on the basis of talent.

The measures have been rightly criticized as not being absolutely elemental. It should be our goal to make our tests as elemental as possible. A certain amount of allowance will, however, always have to be made for development of general capacity for observation.

The principles involved in these tests are such as to cultivate a discriminating and rigidly critical attitude toward a test situation. While the records are relatively "foolproof," the valid use of them demands a certain type of knowledge about the nature of the mind and of talent in particular, some experimental technique, and at least a critical judgment in regard to the practical application to the musical situation. Cold water is a good thing, but it is often dangerous.

ANALYSES OF TALENT IN A MUSIC SCHOOL

ORIGIN OF THE EASTMAN SCHOOL EXPERIMENT*

SOME years ago, I consulted Mr. Abraham Flexner with reference to the possibility of securing the support of a Foundation for a sustained experiment to introduce and validate my Measures of Musical Talent in a city school system, having in mind a city like Baltimore, Chicago, or Los Angeles.

His response was, "Why not take a music school instead of a public school system? A new music school has been started in Rochester and, if you don't mind, I will call up the president by long distance and ask if this new music school would be interested in the experiment." The reply came immediately inviting me to a conference, which was held the next day, with the result that I was invited to take personal charge of the experiment.

Since I could not consider this personal offer, an agreement was made inviting my first assistant, Dr. Hazel Stanton, to take the position as psychologist in the music school, with the assignment of introducing and administering these measures and other means that might become available for the purpose of discovering and analyzing talent in the music school. It was distinctly understood that this was to be an experiment and that the school would provide its best facilities for the attainment of our goal.

* Reports on the Eastman experiment have been published from time to time by Dr. Stanton and her associates. These are all summarized in her volume *The Measurements of Musical Talent*[176] from which the bulk of this chapter is freely drawn by kind permission of the author. The section on the origin of the experiment is from my editorial foreword to that volume.

This invitation from the Eastman School and the selection of Dr. Stanton proved to be strategical, timely, and appropriate. The selection of the school was most fortunate because it is one of the few music schools which are not entirely dependent upon tuitions and which, therefore, can afford to exercise a rigorous selection of pupils. It also was fortunate that Mr. George Eastman sponsored the project, authorized it, and took a deep personal interest in its furtherance up to the very last days of his life.

For the successful culmination of the experiment, however, we owe most to the sympathetic and wise administration of the present Eastman director, Dr. Howard Hanson. He had cordial support of his policies from President Rhees, who formally authorized the experiment.

The selection of Dr. Stanton proved fortunate also on account of her indefatigible devotion to a rigorous technique, her acquaintance with music and musicians, and her very extraordinary persistence and meticulous care in the conduct of the work.

To the casual observer, the procedure, though novel, was regarded as a part of personnel routine. It was more than this in the eyes of Mr. Eastman, President Rhees, Dr. Hanson, and the writer—it was an experiment of which we now have an adequate record covering a period of more than 10 years. The outcome of the experiment is an evaluation and validation of these measures, together with a critique and refinement of experimental procedure which deserve careful study on the part of all who are interested in the measurement of musical talent whether in a music school or elsewhere.

In this general report on the Eastman experiment, Dr. Stanton has restricted herself to the specific purpose of evaluating the *Measures of Musical Talent* as a battery in itself in the actual musical situation, quite apart from any other aspects which are involved. The monograph contains a statement of her personal point of view, her techniques, her rigorous control of the procedure in measuring and evaluation of the measures as tools in themselves.

The problem with which she deals has been treated in many other ways by other persons. Other methods of validating have been utilized; the problem of inheritance has been dealt with from several angles; numerous methods of utilizing the measures in practical procedures have been reported; various critiques of the method of administering the tests have developed. The most valuable use of the measures has been in connection with auditions on the part of competent musicians. An attempt has been made to weight the measures in connection with the particular types of music and instruments.

These *Measures* are not in themselves an adequate measure of musical talent as a whole. They are merely a selected battery of measures of specific talents in which a certain degree of capacity is essential to success in music and in which a certain degree of incapacity is often the basis for failure in music. For the purpose of validation, which is the aim of this monograph, the author had to determine the significance of guidance on these *Measures* alone. She has validated them in their own name, as it were, as one of the useful tools which may be employed in scientific musical guidance. But that does not imply that they should be employed in a mechanical way without other aids. They are but one of the tools in a system of adequate guidance. However, on account of their basic nature, measures of this type should constitute the first concrete information with which all serious guidance in music should begin.

PLAN AND PURPOSE OF THE EXPERIMENT

From our point of view, the purpose of this experiment was to validate the *Measures of Musical Talent* under as nearly ideal conditions as could be obtained in a music school. We found that it was possible to provide for this by giving the testing program such a place in the program of administration and guidance that neither faculty nor students would look upon it as an experiment, but would regard it as an essential part of a modern administrative program. It was recognized that ultimately the tests were to be a regular part of the admission machinery and constitute a basis for the individual guidance of the students after admission.

The testing program consisted of the administration of five of the *Measures* recorded on phonograph records, namely, pitch, intensity, time, consonance, and tonal memory. These were supplemented by a subjective test of tonal imagery, an intelligence test, and a case history.* The tests were given as the first step in

* The comprehension test was not introduced into the series until 1928, the sixth year. The rhythm test was introduced in the third year, and the test on imagination was dropped in the sixth year.

the admissions program of all students, including both children and adults. In order to validate the records before using them as a basis for admission, they were given under standard conditions and studied for the first two years, without actually using them as a basis for admission, the main purpose being to determine success or failure of those for whom an unfavorable prognosis had been made. A classification was gradually built up, and in terms of this prediction of success or failure, the tests were made before the student had had an audition or had been admitted. These records were placed in the hands of the director, but they were carefully guarded throughout the 10-year experiment so that the teachers should not be influenced or biased by these predictions. The experiments were conducted with most meticulous care by Dr. Stanton herself, and, after they had been made a basis for admission, she was included in official conferences with the admission officers in regard to the interpretation of these records and later with the director in regard to the organization of study programs, selection of instruments, etc.

CLASSIFICATION

For a given test, a centile scale was adopted as follows: the highest 10 per cent, A, or superior; the next highest 20 per cent, B, or very good; the next 20 per cent, C+, or high average; the next 20 per cent, C−, or low average; the next 20 per cent, D, or poor; the lowest 10 per cent, E, or very poor. For each individual, a chart of his profile was made in terms of centile rank (see Fig. 1). However, since a single classification had to be made for the purpose of prediction, a cumulative key was adopted, grouping various types of profiles under five heads: Discouraged, Doubtful, Possible, Probable, Safe, as shown in Table I. For a full classification of types see *Stanton*.[176]

TABLE I. THE CUMULATIVE KEY OF TEST COMBINATIONS

$N = 978$

Discouraged		*Doubtful*		*Possible*		*Probable*		*Safe*	
C+	E	B	E	A	E	A	C−	A	A
C−	C+	C+	C−	B	C−	A	D	A	B
C−	C−	C+	D	B	D	B	B	A	C+
C−	D	C−	A	C+	A	B	C+	B	A
C−	E	C−	B	C+	B				
				C+	C+				

The first letter is the classification of the talent profile; the second letter, the classification of the comprehension test.

REPRESENTATIVE PROFILES

These are actual cases from applicants for admission to the school. They set forth graphically an inventory of some of the

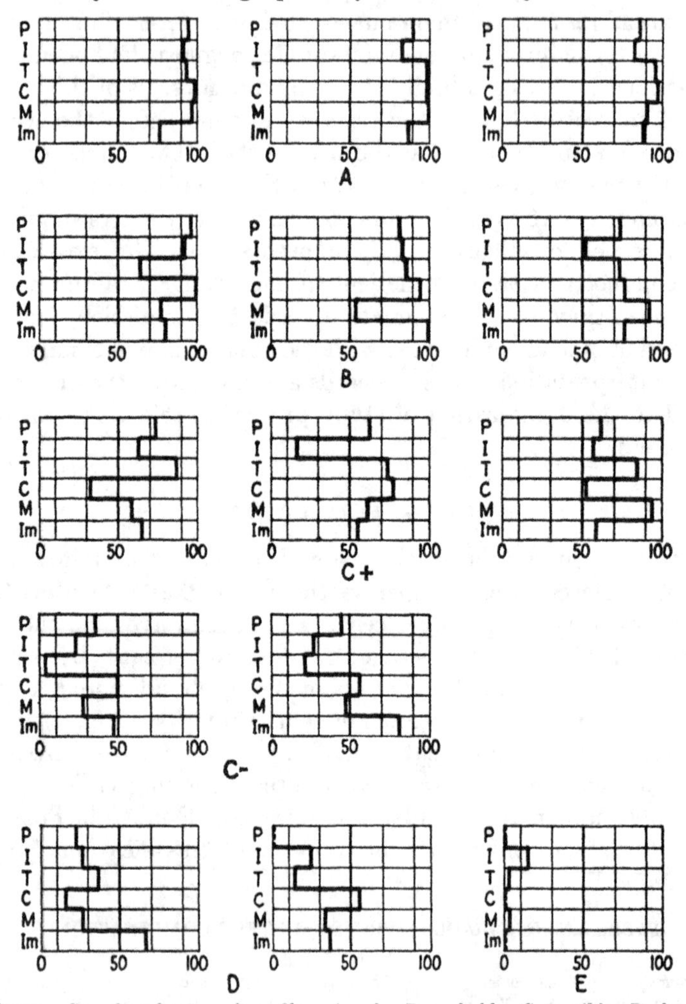

FIG. 1.—Samples of types of profiles: *A*, safe; *B*, probable; *C*, possible; *D*, doubtful; *E*, discouraged. Ratings in intelligence are not given in these charts; but ratings in musical imagery are. The labels at the left are the first letter for each of the respective tests. (*Stanton.*[176])

assets and liabilities of the prospective pupils. It does not require much imagination to see their far-reaching significance. Talent has its "ups and downs." A chart that may be satisfactory for one purpose may not be so for another. For example, a low sense of pitch disqualifies the player for stringed instruments; or, a low sense of

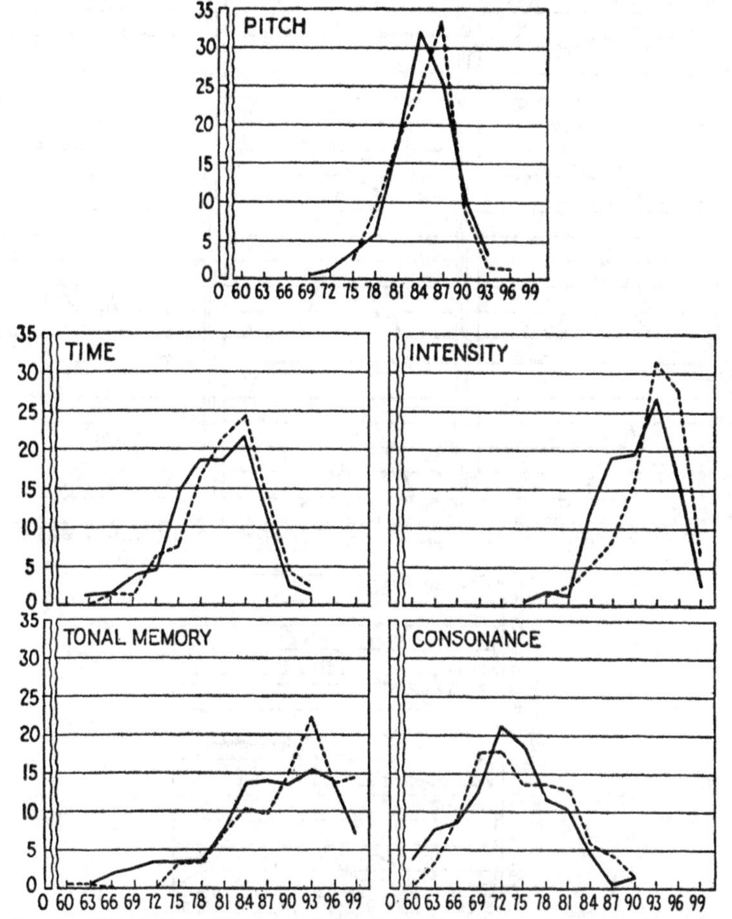

FIG. 2.—Distribution of Test 1 (solid line) and Test 2 (dotted line) raw scores in five measures with a 3-year interim between measurements. $N = 157$. The ordinates represent the percentages of cases; the abscissas, the midpoint of each three-unit step in raw scores. (*Stanton.*[176])

intensity disqualifies for the piano. That is, we cannot go only by centile rank; we must take into account the internal structure of the profile, the case history, and the audition.

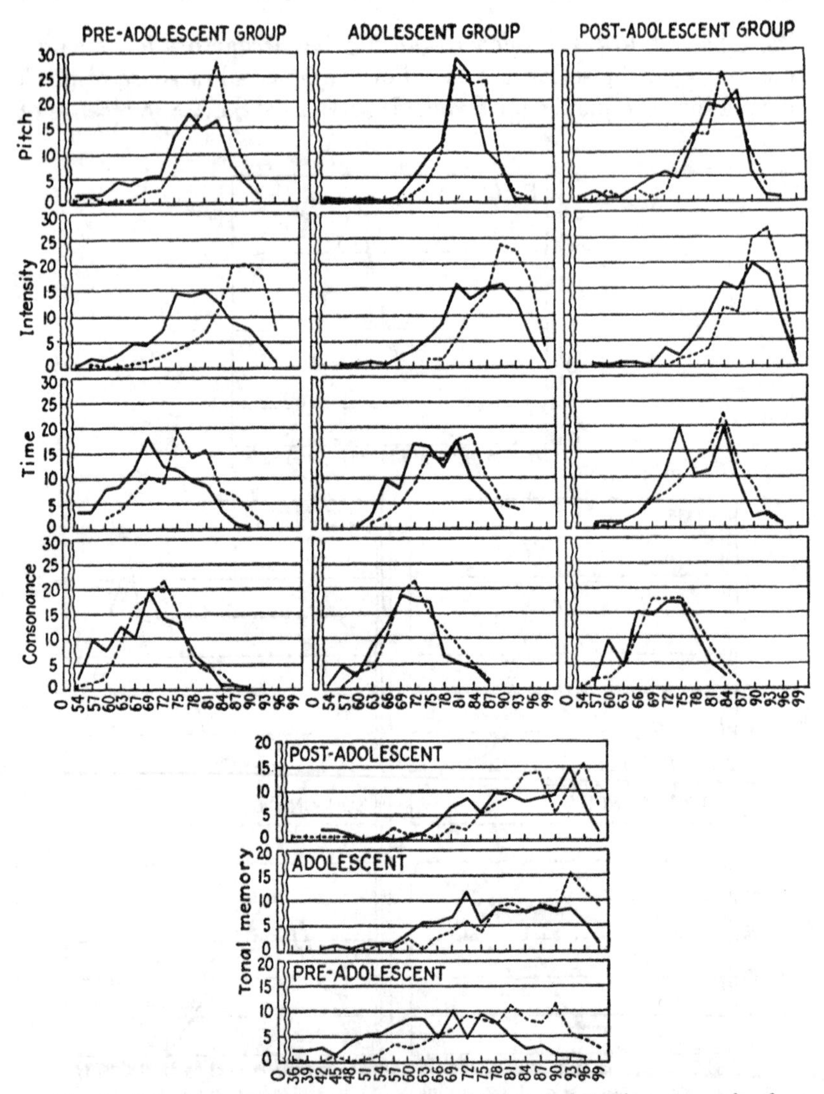

FIG. 3.—Distribution of Test 1 (dotted line) and Test 2 (solid line) raw scores for three groups in five measures, with a 3-year interim of musical training between measurements. The ordinates represent percentages of cases; the abscissas, raw scores. (*Stanton.*[176])

STABILITY OF THE CLASSIFICATION

To determine whether or not the classification thus made in the way of prediction before admission had be correct, Stanton periodically retested the pupils who were admitted. Figure 2 shows the result of the retest of 157 adults after three years of progress in musical education. For the group as a whole, the degree of talent seems to be about the same, with minor exceptions. Figure 3 shows that, with minor but more significant exceptions, especially in intensity, the same evidence of stability in the charts holds for children as for adults. There is not so much change in children as we might have expected with maturation.

RETESTS OF ADULTS AND CHILDREN

These facts substantiate the assumption that when the measures are given under controlled conditions by an experienced examiner, the physiological threshold can be reached in the first test to such a degree that there will be little appreciable variation in a second test. These facts contribute to the idea that the measures tend to be elemental.

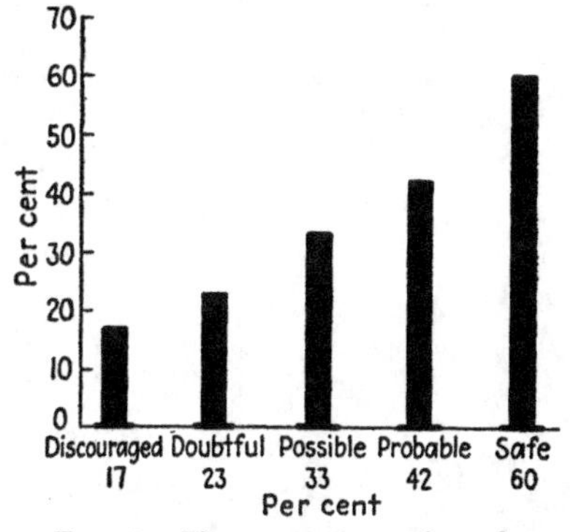

FIG. 4.—The percentage of students graduating within 4 years in each of the five groups. This covers 565 entrants in four successive classes in the university music school. (*Stanton.*[176])

BEARING ON SUCCESS IN THE COLLEGE MUSIC COURSE

Figure 4 gives a realistic picture of the significance of these tests at a glance. It shows to what extent the tests alone predict success in completing a four-year college course in music in the standard time. When one considers how many other factors must be taken into account for success, the showing for this measuring tool in itself is remarkably good. Sixty per cent of the "safes" graduated. How many of the remaining 40 per cent lost, because of economic or social reasons, a good job, early marriage, a hit on radio or in the movies, laziness, sickness, postponement of a date—

any one of a score of other impediments? So far as talent alone is concerned, the "safe" may well be regarded as 100 per cent safe.

The same principle applies, but in decreasing order, with lower ranks. Since the objective test record is the only factor taken into account, it is evident that relative lack of capacity, as here measured, is a rigid deterrent which must be taken into account in planning musical education.

If, instead of measuring in terms of success in graduation from college, we should be able to measure the progress of music in the life of these people, either in a professional career or in avocational or social value, we should get a much stronger picture. It would favor those whose "windows of the soul" were open to music. For an adequate account of the experiment the reader must turn to the comprehensive report.[176]

24

ANALYSIS OF TALENT IN THE PUBLIC SCHOOL

THE LINCOLN EXPERIMENT

FOR many years the public schools in Lincoln, Nebraska, have had a reputation for high standards of achievement in music. *William Larson*,[75] at the time in charge of the instrumental instruction, performed the following experiment to determine the significance of talent in the choice of instruction for instrumental music and in the advancement in the opportunities offered in the school orchestras.

He took during the same year four groups: A, B, C, and D: A, the group of first-year students in instrumental music, 125 members; B, the junior high school preparatory orchestra, 30 members; C, the junior high school advanced orchestra, 31 members; and D, the high school advanced orchestra, 50 members. At the beginning of the year, he gave each of these students the six Seashore *Measures of Musical Talent* and made a study of the principles of selection which operated to determine progress in instrumental music.

The general conclusion reached can be stated in general terms as follows:

Group A, admission to courses of instruction in instruments is unselected. The average percentile rank of all these measures for this group was 52, when 50 represents a theoretical average for all students. This is a fairly well-known phenomenon and is interpreted partly in the diversity of motives which operate in making music a desirable subject, such as the popularity of the instructor, the school reputation in contests, the desire of parents, and, of course, most of all the ignorance of the significance of talent. As a consequence of this heterogeneity of the group, the instruction in the first year is seldom of such a nature as to operate strongly in favor of selection.

Group B. For the junior high school preparatory orchestra, there is no significant selection in terms of talent measures. The average rank on these measures was 49. This is, of course, the result of the absence of any standard requirement for admission to this orchestra and the adaptation of the first year's instruction to all levels of capacity insofar as possible. There was also an element of negative selection in favor of Group C.

Group C. This group shows a marked selection in terms of the talents measured. This is undoubtedly due to the actual survival in the previous year's work and higher demands recognized for admission to this orchestra, although the admission was not based in any respect on other evidence of talent and achievement in previous years. The average rank for all the measures in Group C was 66.

Group D. The advanced high school orchestra again showed very marked evidence of selection above the preceding year, the average rank for all the measures being 73.

Thus, there is evidence that various factors operate in the selection of talent in a four-year opportunity for training, so that for each year more and more talented pupils are admitted to the privileges of instruction on the basis of previous achievements and interests. Larson considered carefully to what extent this rise in talent could be attributed to training and arrived at the conclusion that it was principally due to natural selection rather than training.

These figures for Group D are significant in another respect. They show that the highest orchestra is not made up entirely of highly talented students. If it were, the average for the group could be in the 90's instead of 73. One naturally asks how many of the students in this school will die with all their music in them undiscovered and not functioning. It is also interesting to ask how many of the gifted students in music were also highly gifted in other arts or disciplines and were, therefore, diverted from training in music. At any rate, we have here a fairly clear picture of what actually happens in a public school.* The next question is, can we improve upon this situation?

THE ROCHESTER SERVICE

After reviewing the experiment in the Eastman School of Music, Mr. George Eastman said, "You have rendered our school a great and permanent service. You have saved large sums of money and have rendered a humanitarian service to these pupils. But that is largely negative; is it not possible to do something more positive?"

"Yes," I replied. "That is the great future of talent selection. When a music psychologist is placed in the public school system with the sole charge of attempting to discover, analyze, and certify talent which may be discovered by dragnet tests, analyzed by case histories, and verified by auditions, we shall be doing the positive thing in the public schools. We can then not only inform the talented of their valuable possession, but we can give them privileges in the public school musical activities in proportion to their capacities for achievement, and, as a result of their achievement and in the light of talent analyses, these pupils may be recommended to the best music schools."

The most effective operation of this principle is, perhaps, to be found in Rochester, N. Y. Such a system is now in operation and may be briefly summarized. When the pioneer work in this field was undertaken, Dr. Ruth Larson, in charge of this work, was highly qualified, and has perhaps had the best opportunities and the best encouragement of anyone in this country, for this specific work. In a personal communication, she kindly outlined the character of her work, after the first two years of experience in the position as follows:

PROCEDURE IN THE GUIDANCE PROGRAM

1. *The placement of instruments.* The instrumental department has a large number of musical instruments as a result of very generous gifts by philanthropists of the city. Also, practically all the schools of the city own instruments. These instruments are placed with the more musical children through the aid of the psychological tests.

---

* Virtually the same experiment was repeated by Larson in the school system of Iowa City, Iowa. The outcome was a verification of the Lincoln findings in principle.

2. *Recommendations concerning the purchase of instruments by parents.* More and more, parents are requesting psychological tests before purchasing instruments for their children. Upon request, after the test appointments, conferences are held with the parents, and in the light of information that has been acquired concerning the child and his talent, suggestions are made as to the kind of instrument for which the child seems best equipped.

3. *Segregation of instrumental classes.* Contrary to ideas that many have had on the subject, it has been demonstrated that there is more incentive for the majority of students to work at their highest level when they are in a homogeneous group. It is a mistake to place the less talented student in classes with the more musical students. Instead of the highly gifted students acting as an inspiration to the less talented ones, it tends to discourage them. Nor is it beneficial for the talented children; the competition is not so keen, and they are not taxed to their best efforts. Therefore, children of like musical capacities are placed in the same classes whenever the schedules will permit.

4. *Cooperation with the music teachers in the study of unusual cases.* Close attention is given to students who are reported as having early indications of unusual musical aptitude. These children are studied and then given the benefit of special opportunities for musical development whenever possible.

5. *Check on accomplishment.* A report of grades for all students receiving instrumental instruction is filed at the psychology of music office. These reports are studied, and in case the report varies decidedly from what might be expected from the student's talent chart, an investigation is made in an attempt to discover reasons for this discrepancy. If the trouble is due to a lack of application, irregular attendance, or some other personal indolence, the student is informed that in order to take advantage of free musical instruction provided by the board of education, he is expected to progress at a rate in conformance with his capabilities. This pertains equally to those who own their instruments and to those who are using school instruments. This general check on the relation of talent to progress cultivates a higher level of efficiency in the classes.

When there are interferences that hinder the student in making good progress, and it is necessary to recall the instrument, it is placed in the hands of one of the numerous applicants of high talent on the waiting list, preference being given to those with the highest talent ratings. In this group of high talents may be found many who do not have the means to purchase an instrument but must wait an opportunity for the use of a school instrument or help from some other source.

6. *Cooperation with various organizations interested in child guidance.* Students are often referred to the music psychologist by such organizations as the Children's Service Bureau, Visiting Teachers Department, Special Education Department, and various members of the Child Study Department for a consideration of their musical aptitudes, with a view to the significance the development of musical talent might have in the readjustment of these special cases.

7. *Limitation of instrumental classes through talent testing.* It is recognized that the teaching of music is expensive. A psychology of music program attempts to help conserve resources for their most profitable use. Although it is the general policy to adopt a positive attitude with an endeavor to help and guide the child in music, it is necessary to protect the school and the teacher by refusing to recommend the lowest type of talent for instrumental instruction.

Although the present program concentrates on work with the instrumental department, numerous opportunities come for service in other branches of school music. . . . Thus, an influence has incidentally carried over into another department of school music. The vocal teachers also send students to the central test room, sometimes for the consideration of recommending further study beyond high school as a vocation, or for an understanding of why a student with a voice of excellent quality is not capable of singing in time or tune in the vocal ensemble classes. These are but examples of services in other branches of school music.The growth in the demands for the psychology of music service is taxing the present facilities, and the enlargement of the program to include other branches of school music, where it can be just as serviceable, is in process.

Since greater emphasis is being placed on the importance of musical development at an early age in school, greater opportunity is offered for guidance through psychology of music at this critical time. . . . The testing of musical talent at this level has the advantage of obviating an expensive and inefficient trial-and-error sifting for those inherently equipped for achievements in music.*

THE TRAINING OF TEACHERS AND SUPERVISORS

In another publication[120] I have made the following recommendations on (1) the training of teachers and supervisors and (2) on the organization of a guidance program in the public school:

> The training of teachers in the art of the analysis and adjustment for talent is the first great need in the realization of the goal for musical guidance on a large scale. That the burden falls first upon the teacher in the classroom becomes evident when we realize that the commonest evidence of talent is, and always will be, the character of performance in the early stages. To appreciate this, requires a rather highly organized technical training in the job analysis of the musical situation, the talent analysis of the child, and the actual organization of progress in training on the basis of these two sets of information.
>
> We are, however, not sanguine enough to regard it as reasonable to expect that of all music teachers. The demand, therefore, presses chiefly upon supervisors who themselves understand the situation and have the power to command the few who can cooperate in this service. The immediate responsibility for awakening interest in the possibilities of the art of music falls upon the training institutions for music supervisors. It is incumbent on them to share some of the time for methods of teaching with expert training in music guidance. Before this is done, no claim can be made for the application of science to the art of teaching music.

THE ORGANIZATION OF A GUIDANCE PROGRAM FOR THE PUBLIC SCHOOL

> A guidance program calls for systematic observation in auditions, measures of achievement, and measures of talent. In the ordinary musical situation natural selection operates at an enormous sacrifice, more or less through chance survival.

* In the April, 1938, number of the *Educational Music Magazine*, Mr. Charles H. Miller, the supervisor of music at Rochester, gives a report on the operation of this program during the first ten years. In this he confirms the principles just stated and gives additional interesting suggestions.

Auditions. To obviate this waste and to discover and direct talent, the scientifically trained teacher or supervisor will organize a systematic procedure that may informally be called auditions. It will be in the hands of a competent person who can move unobtrusively in the actual musical situation and observe and record specific evidences of the presence or absence of talent, in a cumulative record that will facilitate guidance. This auditor will, of course, get most leads from the teacher and thus furnish every teacher an outlet for influence in this service.

We teach too much; we drill too insistently; we inspire too little. A distinctive place in the training program should be assigned to auditions. When this is done by a qualified person, much of the routine teaching and drill work can give place to spontaneous self-expression and self-direction, and the problem of motivation will be solved. If asked how to reduce the budget in the music department, that is the method I would pursue. Early discovery, systematic record, and the assurance that merit will be rewarded will furnish the greatest drive that can possibly enter into the musical life of the school. A social and competitive program in which the student is encouraged to live in an atmosphere of self-expression and service in music is extremely valuable in the revelation of talent.

This audition service should, of course, be responsible for the organization and conduct of all measures of achievement, and it is now a well-established fact that the timely and adequate measurement of achievement is an effective tool in the organization of instruction. Achievement tests may often take the form of actual competitive performance. More emphasis should be placed on evidence of self-direction, self-motivation, and self-criticism than upon mere passing grades on routine instruction. The early documenting of specific abilities exhibited in performance is very valuable.

Surveys. As measures of musical talent progressively standardized, validated, and made available in inexpensive, safe, and reliable form, surveys may be conducted in various ways. These surveys should serve two primary purposes: (1) the discovery of outstanding and perhaps unrecognized talent of various kinds; and (2) the identification of persons seriously lacking in talent. They should never be undertaken except where there is a deliberate and effective intention to follow up. Tests of this kind should be of such character that their use will be fully justified by the teaching-value alone in making the music population conscious of the existence and significance of specific aspects of music.

The most profitable all-city survey would be in the fifth grade, and the second survey if undertaken should perhaps be in the eighth, for obvious reasons. A more specific and immediately profitable use of surveys is in the progressive organization of music units, such as orchestras, bands, choruses, highly specialized organizations, and individual instruction. Here the analysis of measures of musical talent should be a fixture in the procedure, and every student should know exactly how he rates in this and that.

Remedial work. Remedial work should play an important part in the organization program in the ordinary course of instruction and musical activity. The pupil faces an unanalyzed situation and may show marked defects of which he is not aware. Our demand for analysis and measurement of specific elements in performance favors the development of a system of remedial work that may be undertaken to great advantage. Many a singer who flats has simply fallen into a bad habit and can be whipped out in a few minutes of intensive attack, if there is an adequate sense of pitch. The same is true in each of the basic capacities, such as volume control, time, rhythm, and tone quality. There are now instruments available by which a person can test, check, and correct his faulty performance in a very short time, and to a very high degree. Such procedures make the pupil conscious of the defects he has. Most of the faults and defects may be attributed to sluggishness on the part of both pupil and teacher in the discovery of error. The scientific method will act as a whip. The need of this is, of course, most notoriously exhibited in the matter of the control of tone quality. Instead of thinking loosely in general terms of good and bad, the pupil should be made conscious of his specific weakness and the ways of remedying it.

In a sense, the guidance program should always be of a negative and protective character. At every turn, the pupil should be encouraged to follow his natural urge. The musical guide will then analyze the situation to determine whether the choice is wise and in accordance with natural talent. This advice favoring a protective attitude rather than a positive and directive attitude is essential to the scientific approach. The ordinary guide is far too ready to direct the future of the pupil on the basis of superficial evidence.

Appreciation of music is not primarily a problem of guidance. It is rather a problem of providing facilities, motivation, and, best of all, forms of participation that make the pupil feel that music is in him and of him, because appreciation is ultimately a form of expression.

25

THE INHERITANCE OF MUSICAL TALENT

THE NATURE OF THE INHERITANCE OF MUSICAL TALENT*

FAMILY pride, musical and social history, investments in musical education, the making or breaking of a career, hinge upon an adequate evaluation of talent; and talent, by definition, is an inherited trait. The world talks glibly of it in high praise and in deep disparagement, often without a glimmering of scientific insight or discriminating attitude. The concept of inheritance must have a place in a psychology of music.

Musical talent probably lends itself better than any other talent to the investigation of the laws of mental inheritance because it does not represent merely a general heightening of the mental powers, but is specifically recognized as a gift which can be analyzed into its constituent elements, many of which may be isolated and measured with reasonable precision. The inheritance of musical talent may, therefore, be studied, not only for itself, but also for the bearing that it has on the inheritance of mental traits in general.

Yet, in approaching this problem, we are forced to face certain complexities which tend to make the work difficult and may at first seem insurmountable. Frank recognition of these is, however, the first step in scientific procedure. The more of such facts we discover early and take into account, the more permanent will be the

* A considerable part of this chapter is drawn from the author's article on this subject in the *Musical Quarterly*.[122]

value of our labors. In this chapter, I shall try to point out some of these elements in the situation and make a general forecast as to procedure.

As we have seen, musical talent is not one but a group of hierarchies of talent. The musical person may be distinguished in voice, in instrumental performance, in musical appreciation, or in composition; each of these is an independent field in which one may gain eminence without giving evidence of marked ability in the others. Then, within each of these large avenues of musical life, we find numerous independent variables. Voice, for example, is a physical capacity which may be distinguished in volume, register, range, and timbre, all quite independent variables and not necessarily associated with the musical mind.

Scope of inheritance. We have inherited every element of what we are or can become as human organisms. We develop from this inheritance stock through the operation of environment. Environment is selective in that (1) it permits the outcropping of certain latent capacities, for example, walking, talking, or laughing, and suppresses masses of other latent capacities by failure of opportunity for functioning; (2) it furnishes training and opportunity for exercise in acts of skill, both mental and physical; (3) it favors specialization, for example, in music, art, and leadership; (4) it holds out rewards and goals which heighten achievement at the sacrifice of other talents, and *Hirsch*[51] says:

> Much of heredity's contribution to the individual is either not in evidence at all or only partially active at birth. For this reason it is often wrongly assigned to training, to learning, or to conditioning. We refer to such vital characteristics as intelligence, verbalization, walking and motor and mechanical abilities. These are innate capacities and could never be "acquired" or "learned" if they were not potentially present at birth. Their functioning, it is true, is contingent upon neural and muscular structures, but these latter are merely an aspect of the infant's entire psychophysiological maturation, which is genetically pre-determined.
>
> Too much emphasis cannot be given to the truth that an infant's functional characteristics, and traits, and patterns of behavior during the first few weeks of life are but a fraction of its psychobiological and psychological nature. The rate at which its fertile latencies develop so that they function and become

"behavior," is also largely a matter of inheritance. For a "maturational sequence" is more significant than training. . . . Not only are many hereditary contributions inactive at birth, or yet during infancy, but much if not most of our hereditary natures never function, never become actualized either in overt behavior or in our consciousness.

Four branches. On the sensory side we have recognized four branches of talent content as heard, namely, pitch, time, intensity, and timbre, each forming a main division of approaches to musicianship. Each one of these capacities runs as an independent branch, not only in sensation, but through memory, imagination, thought, feeling, and action. Each branch of this family tree throws out similar clusters of capacities. For example, the power of imagery, creative imagination, emotional warmth, and logical grasp, tend to appear in all four of these channels. In the investigation of inheritance, we must, therefore, abandon the plan of merely counting persons musical or unmusical and patiently settle down to the isolation and observation of isolable traits.

Capacity versus achievement. The investigator of inheritance is not interested primarily in the degree of achievement attained, which is usually a circumstance of fortune or misfortune in environment; he has to do exclusively with the valuation of inborn capacities. Skill or achievement is significant for inheritance only insofar as it gives evidence of native capacities. It is manifestly unjust to attempt to trace musical inheritance only in distinguished achievement in music. Wherever we find achievement, we count it as evidence of capacity; but we must employ ways and means of rating undeveloped capacities fairly in comparison with capacities which have been given natural outlets for development into achievement.

This point of view is fundamental and must be taken seriously. So long as we rate the presence of musical talent in terms of musical achievement, we shall be dealing mainly with the superficial, sociological, and pedagogical phenomena of opportunities and scope of musical training or with the effect of inhibiting circumstance on the spontaneous self-expression in music.

Investigation of inheritance has been made possible for the first time by the introduction of methods of psychological examination in which we can discover, measure, and rate the existence, kind, and extent of natural musical capacities, quite independent of age (beyond infancy), training, or musical performance. Most of us die "with all the music in us," but modern methods enable us now to observe and record the extent to which capacities are present quite apart from their evidence in a musical life.

The normal mind versus the genius and the defective. The normal mind is musical, and the normal body is the instrument for adequate expression of music. As we have seen, whether or not the person with a normal mind and body shall distinguish himself in music is largely a matter of circumstances in the way of opportunities for development and absence of suppressing forces.

Investigation of heredity naturally centers first on what is thought to be most tangible types of cases, that is, on the one hand the genius and on the other the defective. But this distinction is not so simple as it might seem at first to be, for musical genius may be of very many kinds, many of which are due to unrelated causes. Thus, we may have the genius in composing, in performing, or in interpreting music; one quite independent of the other, and in each genus of these a variety of species. Likewise, musical deprivation may be due to faulty hearing, inadequate association, inferior intelligence, and, within each genus of these and similar categories, there may be various species, many of them entirely unrelated. We shall, therefore, not find much comfort in thinking of the genius or the defective as representing peculiarly tangible cases, for we shall be compelled to deal with specific factors in analyzed concepts.

The normal mind is the average mind. But such average does not represent a single dead level for all the various human capacities. Thus, the two cases, *A* and *B*, here represented in talent charts on the basis of the measurement of talents listed, may be regarded as typical of "average" musical minds, yet they are radically different. It is not illuminating to call them "normal."

What is here illustrated in musical capacity is equally true for other capacities in human endowments. This is only saying in other words, "We normal people are so different." If, for example, we rank capacities on the scale from 1 to 100 per cent, we may find the so-called "normal" endowed with a superbly high faculty in one capacity and in another, equally important, markedly defective; in one he may rank 99 per cent, and in the other 2 per cent. There is nothing gained by speaking of this as representing the average; each one must be considered by itself.

We shall, therefore, be compelled to narrow our concept of normal and defective to the designation of these in terms of specific and isolable talents upon which musical achievement must depend. When this is done the popular distinction of genius, normal, and defective loses its significance, just as the term "insanity" has come to be merely a legal term, while the physician deals with specific causes and symptoms of mental diseases and finds all sorts of interweavings between sanity and insanity.

Genius and impulse. We should distinguish between the talented person and the genius. The most distinctive trait of the musical genius is the fact that he finds in music a dominant interest, is driven to it by an impulse, burns to express himself in music. He is driven by an instinctive impulse or craving for music which results in supreme devotion to its realization. The talented person, on the other hand, gives evidence of unusual powers which may or may not be motivated by an instinctive impulse. The talented person tends to manifest specific skills while genius actually generalizes, creates, thinks in a large whole. To view genius merely as a talent is to view the waterfall in terms of measures of water or height, instead of regarding it as water in action, falling, working, entrancing. The imposing manifestation of eternal grandeur in the graceful folds of the giant veil of water is a reality. But there would be no fall were there no gorge, quantity of water, or height of shelf. The functioning power is implied in the structural composition. So, in music, the impulse to live the life of music owes its existence to the high possession of other musical talents. In laying the foundations for a scientific study of heredity, we may, therefore, content ourselves with describing the waterfall in terms of the shape of the gorge, the quantity of water, and the height of fall; that is, in terms of capacity for sensing, executing, imagining, remembering, thinking, feeling music, including with these the instinctive urge for self-expression in music.

Urge without talent. In literature and art, it is a well-known fact that we often find people desperately devoted to their art, that is, drawn by a dominant impulse to a given art objective, who never achieve and who are finally spotted as hopeless. Although a vital index, the impulse itself does not make the genius and may be a misleading guide.

Versatility and plasticity of the human organism. In stressing the classification in terms of inborn capacities as distinguished from developed skill or achievement, we must not neglect the equally important fact that the limits of achievement depend on the relationship of one capacity to another; and that inferior and medium capacities in some factor may constitute adequate support for excellence in some dominant capacity; and some capacity may be utterly lost without interfering prohibitively with the function of another. For example, one may be stone deaf, and yet be a superior composer if he has had normal hearing at some period of his life; but though he be a genius of musical intelligence and lack creative imagination, he cannot create music.

The resourcefulness of the human organism is marvelous. Recently a one-armed man won the national honors in marksmanship in various forms of shooting with gun and rifle. A one-legged man became a rope dancer. The war cripples are astonishing us in many directions by their performances after loss of parts of the body. The same is also true mentally, since the mind is more complicated and plastic than the body. Therefore, it requires great insight to distinguish real achievement reached after the overcoming of handicaps from the possession of talent. Such achievement, under handicap, is favored in music by the fact that the material of music is manifold and the avenues of expression are abundant. A person without a voice may play; a person lacking sense of tone may excel in the rhythmic aspects of music; a person lacking the sense of time may dwell in the tonal aspects; a person lacking emotion may excel in the more abstract processes of composition and musical criticism.

Now, in all such cases, it will be necessary to deal with specific gifts, either unusual excellences or marked absence of excellences, and in all cases to rate natural capacities as distinguished from the acquired skill or ability.

This point of view throws a flood of light on the analysis of likes and dislikes, character of performance, and character of creation in music. Thus a distinguished singer was found to be inferior in the sense of pitch, and in this was found the explanation of the fact that she had failed in several roles of music before she hit by chance upon the role of folk songs, in which she appeared in solo and in which she, without apparent extravagance, makes use of the artistic liberties which the folk singers take with their melodies. She has a beautiful voice, wide compass, and very effective support, from a dramatic point of view, in a graceful body and a beautiful face, so that appeal to the eye dominates the esthetic appeal of the tonal message.

Persons who lack a sense of time or a sense of intensity are common in musical circles. The relative absence of feeling, imagination, or intellect in persons who have attained distinction in music is a notorious phenomenon. Many persons prominent in musical circles perform in a certain mechanical way and are always pronounced unmusical by the connoisseur; the voice lacks life, the rhythm is mechanical, the tone is cold. In any investigation of heredity, we may have to call such highly trained persons unmusical on the basis of rating in natural capacities.

Attitude of the artist. We can apply mental tests to rate the capacities of soldiers under military command, and the youth must accept the consequence of the rating, whether it be favorable or unfavorable to his military career. In the schools, there has now been established a variety of systems of tests by which the "gifts of nature" in the pupil are thrown into relief for the guidance of the educator, and children are coming to look upon the intelligence quotient, mathematical rating, and the learning curve as matters of routine, which they regard with the same complacence as they view their measures of height, weight, and lung capacity. The prospective musician in the music school is eager to secure her talent chart as a basis for the organization of her course, the identification and analysis of encountered difficulties, and the forecast of prospects in a musical career.

But when we attempt to follow up the individuals in a family of musicians, with all its collateral branches, we encounter prejudices, fears, scruples, and other negativisms. There is in the very warp and woof of the musical temperament an attitude of mind which, by its very esthetic glow, is opposed to cold scientific procedure with particulars. This aloofness of the artist is also partly justified by the fact that the necessary procedure for the investigation of musical inheritance is yet crude and has not become a part of the common stock of well-recognized custom.

Absence of established biological theory. This reserve is further supported by the barren situation in regard to established biological concepts of the physical mechanism in the inheritance of mental traits by transmission through the germ plasm. There must, for some time to come, be a patient procedure by "trial and error" in an attempt to try out the best working hypotheses now available.

We have but little precedent for the application of Mendelian principles to mental traits. But, from the point of view of modern psychology, the prospect of drawing analogies from related experiments in plants and animals is very hopeful. Indeed, that is the only logical and economic way to proceed. We may accept as a general working basis the Mendelian hypothesis and proceed to ascertain what determiners in the germ plasm function for musical talent; which are dominant and which recessive; which musical dispositions are carried on the same determiner, and which are carried on determiners charged with nonmusical factors, etc. In psychology, this will be virgin soil.

Practical significance. If it should prove possible to identify heritable musical traits, as we believe it is, and if the laws of the operation of this inheritance should become common knowledge, it is conceivable that the gain for the development of artistic resources would be as far-reaching in consequence for musical art as knowledge of such laws is proving to be in conservation of favorable traits and the elimination of unfavorable traits in animals and plants. And this may all come about without any eugenic infringement of the rights and finer sensibilities of esthetic man in human evolution. Yet the greatest gain through studies in musical heredity will survive mainly in an increase in our knowledge and appreciation of the nature, the resources, the limits, the significance, and the value of this precious gift of music as we appraise it daily in home, school, and society.

The discarding of the literature on musical inheritance. The above facts, and many others like them, prove conclusively, to those acquainted with the literature of the subject, that we can get little or no help from the nonscientific works now extant on the inheritance of musical talent. The mass of musical biography and autobiography has sprung up in terms of loose and utterly unscientific concepts. True, when we adopt a scientific terminology, it may be possible to go back and identify specific factors in compositions, published musical criticism, and a variety of other objective evidence of the presence of similar traits in successive generations of certain musical families. This was illustrated in our study of musical imagery in the biography of great musicians in Chap. 14. But it will be difficult to determine how much to attribute to nature and nurture respectively. Even then, it will be like counting only the ships that come in, for we can get but scant information about the musical nature on the maternal side. The male musical genius has often come from a mother whose extraordinary talent has passed undiscovered until it appeared in the career of a son. To trace inheritance we must count all the members of a family of blood relations, including certain collaterals, and attach as much significance to the rating of talent which has found no outlet for expression as to that which has found expression. This has not been done in musical biography because biography deals primarily with achievement.

Even in the few biometric studies of traits in which musical inheritance has been taken into account, the data obtained and the technique developed are of little value because none of them deals with specific capacities. To those who are not trained in the technique of individual psychology or biometric experiments, this discarding of the contributions of the past may seem sweeping and even arrogant; yet such is the process of clearing away the rubbish before breaking ground for a scientific venture in this field.

The experimental method essential. "Where there is no experiment there can be no science." Scientific investigation of musical talent had to wait for the appearance of the scientific psychology of music. Only in comparatively recent years have we seen the beginning of such a science. This science is still restricted to laboratories and other technical activities and has not yet invaded musical thought to any considerable extent. It is still in the inceptive stage, and the investigator of heredity must, therefore, content himself with a few aspects of musical talent which have been reduced to experimental control. In view of the considerations mentioned above, we must now deal tentatively with such aspects as can be isolated, measured, and described with precision. To the investigator it is no sacrifice to abandon the hope of tracing the inheritance of musical talent as a whole. He prizes the opportunity of dealing with one specific capacity at a time.

BASIC APPROACHES NOW AVAILABLE

Among the measures on specific factors of musical talent now available for use in quantitative procedure, I would mention the following:

The basic sensory capacities. Beyond question, the first thing to do is to measure quantitatively the four basic capacities, namely, the sense of pitch, the sense of intensity, the sense of time, and the sense of timbre. For these we have standards of procedure, instruments, and norms available. Each of these represents a primary branch in the fourfold fork of the trees of musical talent; each should be followed further into its branching. The measurement of these four factors will reveal the actual psychophysical capacities for the hearing of music because all musical sounds are perceived in these four forms. Since measures of the sense of rhythm and the sense of consonance are not adequately indicated by any one, or any combination, of these four, they should be added to the battery.

The basic motor capacities. Singing and playing as such are not suitable measures of inherited traits, except insofar as great distinction has been attained, because these abilities are so largely the result of training and opportunity. Certain physical measurements on structure of organs of voice and hand may be significant. As corresponding to those of the basic sensory capacities, four basic motor capacities may be used, namely, the control of pitch, the control of intensity, the control of timbre, and the control of rhythm. For each of these we have techniques and instruments.

Musical imagery. While we relive and create music through images in all the senses, two of these are characteristic of musical life and essential, namely, auditory imagery and motor imagery. We must determine auditory imagery because it is in terms of this that we relive music in the nature of sounds which we have once heard and express new music in creative imagination. Motor imagery, that is, the subjective sensory experience of action in association, is also a basic factor because it is the taproot of emotional expression and is really an index of musical emotion. For each of these, we have only introspective measures. Crude as these introspective measures are, they are, nevertheless, vital indices to ear-mindedness.

Memory. There are many vastly divergent aspects of musical memory in musical talent which may be measured, but, if we shall select only one for the present purpose, that one will undoubtedly be auditory memory span, that is, the capacity for grasping and retaining for a moment a group of musical sounds apart from melodic situations. This measurement is ordinarily made in terms of memory for pitch or rhythmic pattern.

Musical intelligence. Since the character of the musician is determined largely by the character of his general intelligence, quite apart from music, the first measure should be a reliable I.Q.

The rating of factors not measured. The development of experimental technique has led to clearness of analysis and critical procedure in the observation and recording of factors which cannot be put under experimental control. Such observation and rating of factors, with reasonable precision, must furnish very valuable supplementary information for aid in the interpretation of the quantitative measures. Quantitative measurements furnish abundant opportunity for the systematic recording of relevant facts when once knowledge of classification, relationships, and characteristic evidences enter into the critical judgment of the experimenter.

Among the items to be observed in examining the person, record should be kept of voice—quality, register, volume, evidences of training; general motor control—as in the shape of the hands, grace and precision of movement; and general alertness. Evidences of rhythmic tendencies, vividness and fertility of imagination, characteristics of memory, musical centers of interests, stock of musical ideas, the expression of musical feeling, temperament, and artistic attitudes when off guard, physique, health, and physical development are all significant.

Significant biographical data in the form of case history should be gathered, bearing upons triking ancestral traits, hereditary disease, social and vocational status, educational opportunities, impediments which have stood in the way of successful education and achievement, and other significant facts of life history bearing upon the factors at issue. No set form should be followed, but alertness and skill in observing the essentials are desirable.

In these matters of ratings and case history the experimenter should not fill out forms or pad records but should take the same attitude that the physician takes. The physician has in mind the generally recognized varieties of diseases and their symptoms, and in the best practice he makes a record of anything which, in his judgment, may appear to be relevant.

One factor which cannot be measured, but may possibly be observed systematically for the purpose of tracing transmission through heredity, is that of the musical impulse as shown in a natural craving for music, sustained interest in its pursuit, and a deep feeling of satisfaction in things musical. This impulse, when genuine, rests upon natural bent of mind due mainly to the possession of capacities, but also to a general artistic disposition in the form of artistic temperament. The best that we can do, at the present time, is to record all observable evidences of such a driving impulse apart from artificial stimulation and simulation. We shall undoubtedly find interesting relationships between these impulses and the power to achieve, as to both amount and kind. It is very desirable to learn to what extent such an instinctive impulse may be lost by very slight untoward circumstances in early life. It will also be interesting to see to what extent a dominating impulse of this sort is related to lack of capacities or absence of interest in other activities.

POSSIBLE WAYS OF ORGANIZING INVESTIGATION

The laws of the inheritance of musical traits must ultimately be determined by actual experiment on carefully selected matings in which the measurements may be repeated for successive generations. Such an undertaking can be fostered only by an agency heavily endowed, of a nation-wide or international scope, adopting a thoroughly standardized procedure which can be sustained for many years.

In general, it would seem feasible to follow, in an investigation of this sort, the same methods that have been followed so successfully with plants and animals; that is, to isolate and observe under experimental control, one factor at a time, in all the progeny from a given pair for a certain number of generations. There need be only one restriction in view of the fact that we are dealing with human beings; namely, that we cannot breed successive generations for this specific purpose. This, however, is not serious, because we can adopt the device of selecting from volunteers, in which the factor under control is mated in a known way, and examine them and their children and their children's mates in successive generations. Ratings through systematic observations and case histories may be kept quite complete. This is undoubtedly the method of the future. It involves not the slightest infringement upon reasonable sensibilities or proprieties; on the contrary, it should constitute a most fascinating cooperative search for truth.

A more direct procedure would be to aim at the same result by examining large numbers of musical parents with their children and taking into account the transmission of this factor, or factors, in one generation. Here we would have the alternative of spending time and effort in selecting conspicuous matings for a given capacity; or taking musical families at random and depending upon large numbers of measurements to yield reliable data. The former of these alternatives would undoubtedly be more desirable.

The most promising immediate approach is, however, to utilize material now available in the test programs of public schools by selecting marked cases of talent or absence of specific talent among children and working back from them to their parents, brothers and sisters, and other near blood relatives.

THE NATURALIST'S POINT OF VIEW

The point of view here presented is that of the naturalist. Musical life is made up of phenomena in nature all operating according to determinable laws of nature—analyzable, describable, explainable, knowable, and worth knowing.

This point of view does not conflict with the artistic and philosophical points of view, both of which regard these same phenomena from entirely different angles. The artist may, in successive attitudes, regard his life from each of these three points of view. As an artist, he finds himself in esthetic rapport with nature without and nature within—human emotion. As a philosopher, he reasons about the relations of this life of music to the life of nature as a part of beauty and truth and weaves it into his world view. As a scientist, he turns upon the same phenomena in a cold microscopic attitude; he is interested in particulars, causes, conditions, and mental laws.

This entire chapter might well have been devoted to an account of procedure and findings in a study of certain elements of inheritance in six of the foremost families of musicians in this country conducted by *Stanton*,[174] because that study marks the beginning of a new epoch in the measurement of inheritance of musical talent. Space, however, will permit only a brief mention. This investigation was a joint undertaking between the Department of Genetics in the Carnegie Institution of Washington and the Department of Psychology in the University of Iowa.

Six of America's foremost musicians were selected on the basis of their standing and rank among musicians. Each one was interviewed, musical case histories were written, and four quantitative measurements were made. The same procedure was then followed for each of the available blood relatives in each family group.

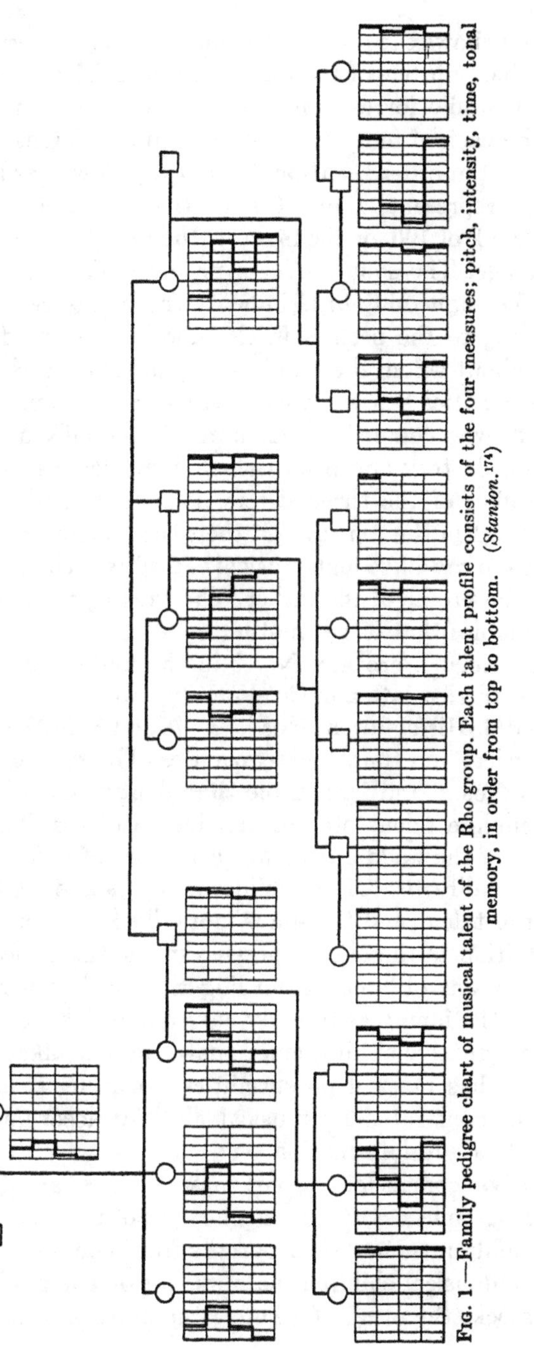

Fig. 1.—Family pedigree chart of musical talent of the Rho group. Each talent profile consists of the four measures; pitch, intensity, time, tonal memory, in order from top to bottom. (*Stanton.*[174])

Figure 1 shows the result of the measures in the form of a talent-pedigree chart for one of the foremost musical families in America. The small profile for each individual shows the rank of that individual on each of four measurements: pitch, intensity, time, and memory, in the order mentioned from top downward. The left of the square represents rank of 1, or the lowest; the right of the square, a rank of 100, or the highest; the middle vertical line represents average. The square over a profile indicates male; a circle, female. The connecting lines indicate the family relationship.

Referring to the profiles in the middle row, we find that the musician about whom the family study developed, No. 4, has high musical capacities expressed by a superior talent profile. He married No. 3, who comes from an unmusical family as known from their family history and from their low musical capacities as seen in the profiles of the three sisters, Nos. 1, 2, and 3, and of the mother, No. 1 in the top row. Of their three children, Nos. 1 and 3 in the bottom row have high musical capacities. Their talent profiles resemble the profile of the father. The talent profile of the middle sister resembles that of her mother.

The musician's brother, No. 7 in the middle row, is very talented. He married into a musical family, two of whom were tested, Nos. 5 and 6. His children, Nos. 5, 6, 7, and 8, in the bottom row, are all musical and show high capacities. The two complete talent profiles of Nos. 6 and 7 resemble the talent profile of their father. The incomplete talent profiles are due to illness. The musician's sister, last in the middle row, was a teacher of voice and of piano and a choral director. Of her children, Nos. 9 and 10, the daughter has superior talent, but the son is more like his mother.

In addition to the data expressed in the talent-pedigree chart, information was obtained regarding the musical history of each member of the family as to early environment, education, musical expression, creative ability, emotional reactions, likes and dislikes. The family has musical potentialities according to measurement and has demonstrated its musical abilities according to supplementary data and information.

Tentative conclusions from these studies are that musical parents from musical stock on one or both sides tend to have musical children; nonmusical parents from nonmusical stock tend to have nonmusical children; parents, one of whom is musical from musical stock, the other of whom is nonmusical from nonmusical stock, tend to have both musical and nonmusical children. The method of inheritance of each capacity is too complex to be known from the data at hand, but there is indication that the inheritance of musical capacities seems to follow Mendelian principles.*

Mjoen[100] and his associates in the Winderen laboratory at Oslo have made rather notable contributions to studies in race heredity in various European countries, employing in large part these measures in musical talent. On the point of heredity, he has drawn the following conclusions:

> Untalented parents never have very talented children, while very talented parents never have untalented children. The higher the average of talent in the parents, the higher is also the average of talent in the children. When there is only a slight divergence or none at all in the parents, the average talent in the children is a little higher than that of the parents. When the divergence increases the average talent in the children declines; so that in cases of great divergence in the parents the average for the children is lower than that of the parents. Accordingly, it seems that a great difference of talent in the parents exercises an unfavorable influence on the degree of talent in the children.

Another investigation of a quantitative character made with our measures of musical talent is that of *Davenport* and *Steggerda*,[15] in which a study is made of anthropological differences between blacks, whites, and browns, who have lived on the same island under similar conditions for a long period of time. While this investigation was not organized primarily for the tracing of inheritance, the findings throw much light upon that problem.

---

* The original report[174] is worth careful study. All the original records are on file in the offices of the Carnegie Institution at Cold Springs Harbor.

26

PRIMITIVE MUSIC

MUSICAL ANTHROPOLOGY THROUGH PHONOPHOTOGRAPHY

THE coming in of methods of recording and reproducing sounds from a film is one of the marvels of the present century. It enables us to live in a new world situation. When we can sit down in a theater or private studio and see the primitive savage in his native haunts at work and play, in ceremonial dance and song, the world is made smaller. Concrete situations, as seen and heard, are brought to us from all parts of the globe, regardless of distance, and may be preserved for all time.

We have marveled at the exhibition feature, at the entertainment which we enjoy in the theater, and at the possibility of collecting data for all kinds of historical purposes by this extraordinary means; but very few have realized anything of the unlimited possibilities of a scientific character that this movement introduces for music.

The tone film not only reproduces the sounds to our ears, but it presents the message also in visual form. As a record of sound waves, it furnishes the necessary raw material for physical and mathematical treatment in the interests of the science of music. The music thus reported becomes laboratory material, available as a key to the anthropological and musical approaches to all the problems involved in the origin and development of racial music. The sound film which we hear in the theater has been edited by a process analogous to the retouching of photographs. This makes it more acceptable to the ear but, to that extent, distorts the actual raw material. The original film is, however, preserved and it is from this unretouched film that the scientific studies may be made. The sound film, like the phonograph record, may be taken into the laboratory for rephotographing for the purposes of analysis as described in Chap. 2.

The moving picture industry is now ready to cooperate with scientists in the interest of making their films more "educational" and scientifically more faithful records of primitive music and speech. The first step that is necessary to take in this cooperation is to employ a musical anthropologist to go into the field as a scout and apply existing knowledge of the situation in a survey of available material. This will take two forms. First will be the determination of what is anthropologically the most significant aspect of musical culture in a selected group. The anthropologist will probably find that it represents a definite culture stage in the development of melody, accompaniment, musical instruments, ceremonial value, echo of environment, and a number of other issues fundamental to the history of music. He may then select from these the features which should be illustrated in order to show the most characteristic and significant elements in the situation. These elements may be of as good entertainment value as the hodgepodge ordinarily assembled by the professional photographer in the interests of stage playing.

In the second place, it will be the function of the anthropologist to discover and organize performing units. One of his most important functions will be to overcome the fears, prejudices, and taboos of the people in order that he may get a full and natural response from them. While the stage manager must have relatively free hands in the interest of entertainment, the intelligent good will thus established may redound to the interest of both science and music.

These two things have never been done, but producers are ready to make the venture and the way is entirely clear. If we consider the problems involved in collecting primitive music at home, such as the truly Negro music and Indian music, which is not spoiled by contact with our own, we can realize something of the importance of these two steps. What the ordinary "movies" collect is not truly Indian or truly Negro music.

Cooperation with commercial producers has another advantage. The cost of making films of this kind in remote places is very great. There is perhaps no musical scientific agency that is ready to promote expeditions by itself. On the other hand, by dovetailing with the commercial producer, the scientific interests can be served at but little additional expense and with enhancement of value to the producer. The scientist will gain his end in two ways: he will have an opportunity to get into the entertainment film materials which are truly representative of the situation portrayed; and much of this can be reworked for purely scientific purposes.

On the other hand, when the camera force is in the field and rapport has been established with the performers, it involves a matter of very small expense to have films taken which are of purely scientific character under satisfactory conditions of control. There is also a definite advantage in cooperation with the producers, an advantage which will increase in significance as producers see their way clear to do for music what they have attempted to do in historical dramas; namely, to make them scientifically accurate as materials for entertainment. The scientist will, therefore, not only have contributed to the learned tomes that issue from the laboratories and studios, but will have acted as a censor and an impresario in placing a faithful representation before the public throughout the world for amusement and enlightenment.

In recent years, we have had remarkable demonstrations of the value of pure science to industry as illustrated in the development of large research divisions of industrial organizations. Here we may look for a parallel example in the advancement of the art of educational entertainment through a science faithfully performed by research men at the critical points.

NEGRO SONGS

Before the tone film had reached its present popularity and perfection, a project for the collecting of Negro songs by means of the camera was carried out as a joint enterprise of the University of Iowa and the University of North Carolina under a grant from the Laura Spellman Rockefeller Foundation. In North Carolina, Professor H. W. Odum and his associates had made a study of Negro singers and their songs in adjacent territory; and, in the University of Iowa, we had developed a field camera for the photographing of the sound waves in the actual singing situation. Professor Milton Metfessel, then a National Research Council fellow, had charge of the investigation and published the results in a volume entitled *Phonophotography in Folk Music*,[85] containing 32 songs, presented in the pattern score. The object of this investigation was to make it a sort of feeler into the possibilities of this type of recording, the ways of establishing rapport with the desired singers, and the means of presenting the song in such a way as to be musically significant and yet couched in rigidly scientific forms and concepts.*

Manifestly a chapter of this kind at this time does not permit any adequate presentation of the characteristics of primitive music or of Negro music in particular, or even the findings in this particular project. I shall simply call attention to some of the features presented by *Metfessel* in his volume.[85] Those who are interested in the subject must go to the original for full treatment.

Ear-eye interpretation. Figure 1 is a transcript of a section from a phonograph record, Victor 20013-B, entitled *On ma journey.* This is introduced for the purpose of demonstrating the significance of eye-ear coordination in the description and interpretation of this type of music.†

The student should have this record available for use in interpreting the score and coordinating eye and ear impressions. Such use of the pattern score with a phonograph record is a most valuable

---

* Up to the time these records were made, two means, both relatively inadequate, had been utilized in collecting primitive music. The first was the direct listening of the collector, taking notes and giving an account in musical notation and verbal description of what he heard. The limitations of that procedure are obvious. A better procedure has been that of using the phonograph record. Primitive music collected throughout the world has been preserved in this form, which is now found very unsatisfactory; valuable collections are being scrapped. The gravest source of error has, however, lain in the transcription of these records by ear, which introduces countless subjective factors and limitations in the report. Some of these records may be salvaged by photographing; but, in doing so, we find serious faults in the softness of the record and the original timing of it.

† The notation is essentially the same as that with which we are familiar from the preceding chapters. The letter in the box indicates the approximate keynote. The horizontal lines of the staff divide into semitones as indicated by the notation at the left; the vertical divisions indicate time in terms of seconds; and the dashes, time in terms of tenths of seconds. The measures are indicated by the heavy bars across the section at the bottom. Below the words as pronounced by the Negro, a phonetic transcription is given in order to show the phonetic elements of the dialect. Below this, the duration of each phonated unit is given in hundredths of a second. The musical notes are interpolated to represent, from a musician's point of view, what the singer probably intended, and what a listener would probably hear. This is included with apologies, as it simply represents a musician's guess upon inspection of the score, and might be varied as to both pitch and time. It is not a part of the standard record. This score shows two of the four factors of performance, namely, pitch and time, which includes the temporal aspects of rhythm. The intensity and timbre were not recorded.

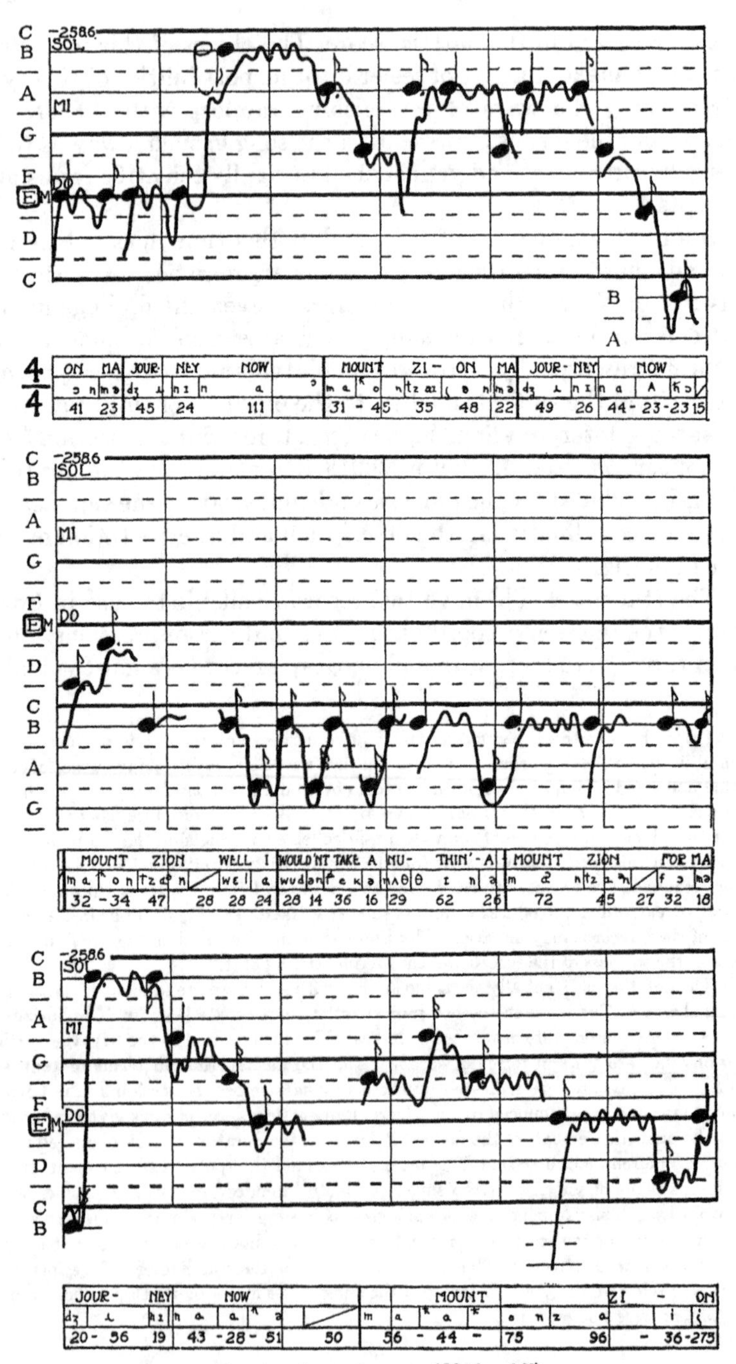

FIG. 1.—*On ma journey.* (*Metfessel.*[85])

study and teaching device in that the visual picture aids the ear in bringing out numerous features of detail which would otherwise not be heard or rightly evaluated. Let us trace the tonal movement in this pattern score.

The first note on the word *On*, for example, may be played over and over until the student can actually hear, with some precision, the attack, the vibrato, and the release, terminating in an inceptive downward dip, which is a Negro characteristic, better illustrated in the third note. The pattern of this note, the inverted cup, will be recognized as a type for this singing. The second note is barely touched, as the downward dip which leads to the attack of the third note was not voiced. The third note is most characteristic of Negro performance in its slow, sweeping attack, shortened note, and a sweeping dip before the next note, which is on the same pitch. It would be a very profitable exercise to hear this over and over again. Is the fourth note heard as suggested by the interpolated score? Or, is it heard flat, as represented by the mean of the vibrato? The tie on the fourth word again gives us the characteristic Negro pattern, a slow portamento, a shortened note on the actual pitch, and a slow, sweeping release, with vibrato present in both attack and release. This tone, being slow, may be compared with the first and the third, which are of the same general type but shorter.

The word *Mount* is sung on a tie which has two distinct pitch levels with good vibrato, the two tones being tied by a slow glide, and the second note ending in the dip. It is worth while to note to what extent one can hear the pitch and duration of these two notes correctly and differentiate them from the glide, which itself occupies as much time as the two notes. As has been shown by *Miller*, in our volume on the vibrato, the bulge in the glide is a vibrato wave, physiologically of approximately the same significance as the waves on the notes, the difference in appearance being due to the fact that it is plotted on the downward sweep.

The word *Zion* is sung apparently on two notes of the same pitch, but the true pitch of the first note is not reached on account of the slow portamento. Is that pattern heard? The word *ma* is merely flirted with, combining two principles: first, the dip from the preceding note; and, second, the tendency to hear a note which is merely pointed at, if it represents a word. The same principle is represented for the word *journey* as for *Zion*. The true pitch of the first note is not reached for the first half of the note, the two tones together forming the characteristic inverted cup-shaped pattern. The Negro license is well illustrated on the word *now*, where relatively small time is given to the indicated pitch, and the bulk of the time is given to a slow portamento with two grace notes.

In the second line the intonation on the word *Mount*, which is not really on any note but suggests the interpolated notes, is characteristic. The merest touch is given to the word *Zion*, making one syllable of it, to give time for the breath pause, which is used with great freedom by the Negro. The next seven notes illustrate admirably a characteristic of the Negro singing; namely, that the note which represents the destination is merely touched, and a large part of the time is spent in gliding up and down with ease. The syllables *nu* and *thin* reveal the shortening of the first to give room for the dip (downward sweep not voiced) before the quarter note, which gives us again the inverted cup with the pointing to the next note. The diphthong in *Mount* is sustained beautifully after he reaches it. The word *now*, reveals the characteristic approach to the first note, with what may be regarded as a grace note on the portamento and overreaching the destination for the last note. The word *Mount* is embellished with a grace note between the first and the last part, sung with a good vibrato, slightly flat. The word *Zion* (*i* being sung as *a*) gives us again the cup-shaped pattern on the diphthong and the lazy rise to the last note.

Thus, the score is found to be a mine of exact information in regard to audible, and yet seldom heard, pitch. These phrases may now be repeated to "hear out" the scale, the interval values, the feeling mode, the legato grace, the mood, and any other intonational aspect which may interest the musician or be a specific object of inquiry.

In the same manner, all the elements of time and rhythm may be checked up in hearing against the objective facts of the score. In the future, the pattern score will include the other two factors, intensity and timbre, so that sample exercises for the refinement of the hearing of dynamic and quantitative features of tones may be heard, the ear being sharpened by the aid of the eye.*

In presenting the following snatches of song, we must allow each illustration to speak for itself. Figure 2, represents the last section of the song *All my days*, as sung by the famous bass of the Hampton quartet. While this singer has appeared before learned audiences and thrilled musicians, he is still ignorant and sings by his primitive impulses with a most charming abandon. He was so lazy that it was difficult to keep him awake for the recording. The words of the song seem appropriate to the character.

His singing is characterized by a very deep voice, lazy legato movement, conspicuous vibrato, and the characteristic Negro ornaments, all of which operate to convey deep feeling. He could not sing the song twice alike, but his performance conveyed the feeling to the listener that it was one of those beautiful outpourings of soul which could not be set or formalized. His rendition keeps ringing in my ears, even to this day, as one of the most beautiful tone pictures I have ever heard.

* Incidentally, it may be suggested that this type of eye-ear exercise, with phonograph record checked against pattern score in artistic singing, presents a vast help in the shortening of ear training and the sharpening of musical criticism.

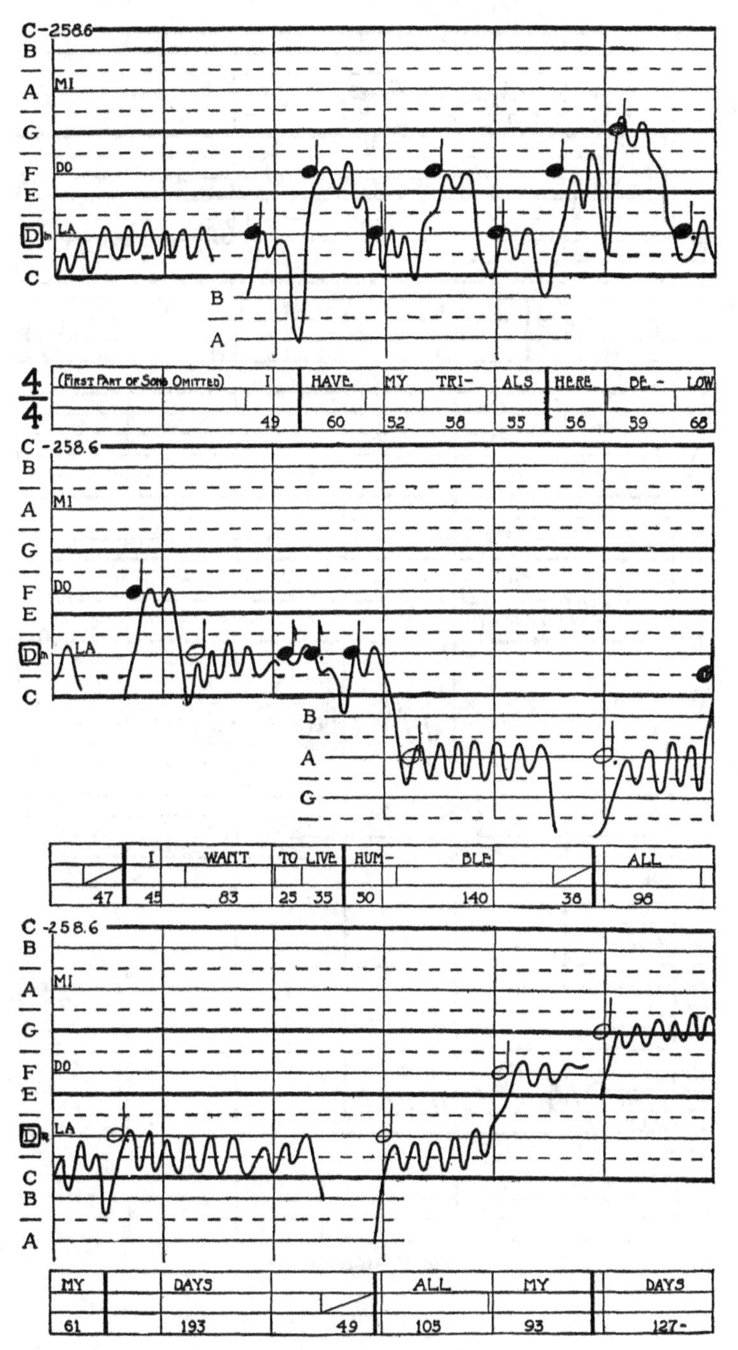

FIG. 2.—*All my days.* (*Metfessel.*[85])

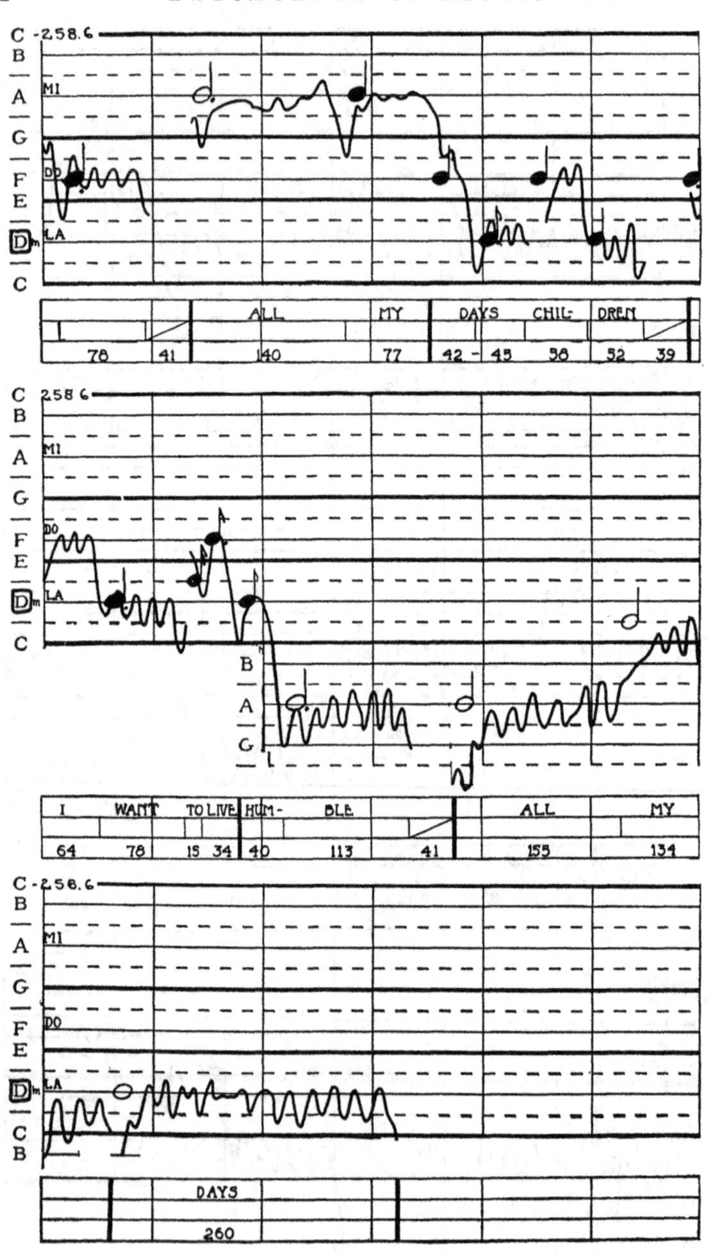

FIG. 2.—(*Continued.*)

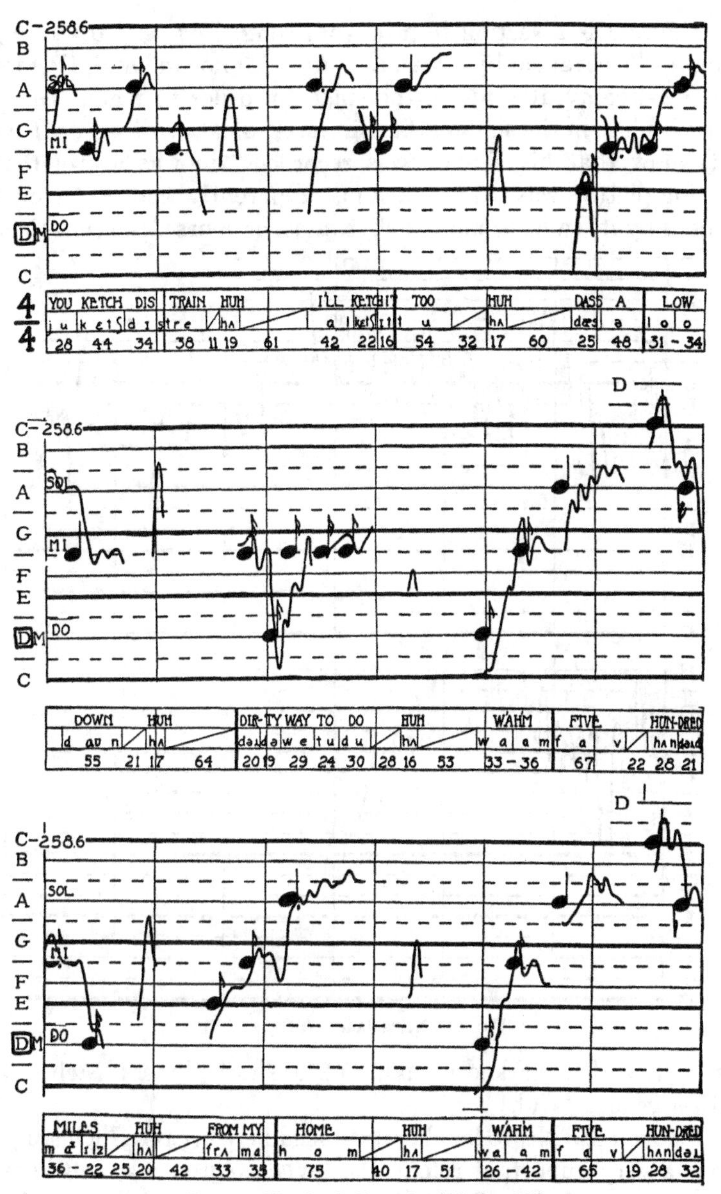

FIG. 3.—*You ketch dis train.* (*Metfessel.*[85])

Figure 3 is a section from a work song, *You ketch dis train*, as sung in the cornfield by a man at work with hoe in hand. One must see the dreamy attitude of the singer in order to realize that his spirit is more in the singing than in the eradication of weeds. He did not know that his singing was recorded. He was aware that a moving picture was being taken but apparently was not much distracted by it. In his song, the rhythm is, of course, the conspicuous

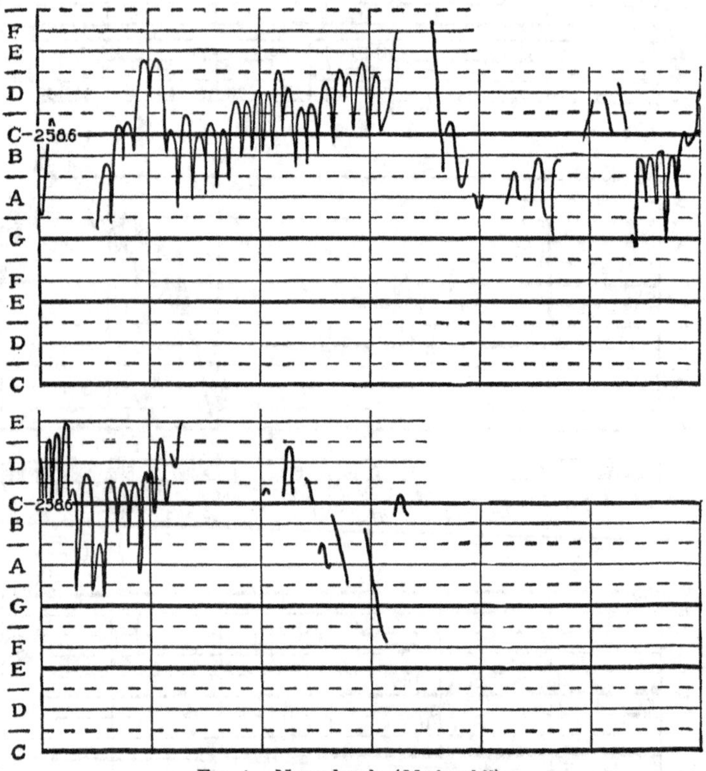

FIG. 4.—Negro laugh. (*Metfessel.*[85])

element, with a marked breaking up of short phrases, each ending with a grunt, "Huh!"

Figure 4 is a Negro laugh, introduced here because such laughter plays a very important role in the jovial Negro song, and here we have, perhaps for the first time, the preservation of a hearty laugh in Negro style.

The feelingful abandon. When our first photograph records of Indian and Negro songs were made, we were surprised at the apparent "wildness" of the singing, and we naturally had to ask ourselves, "How wild is this singing?" That led to the recording of some of our best artists for purposes of comparison. To our astonishment, these records also revealed numerous evidences of unsuspected relative license, the appearance of which made us more charitable toward the untutored savage. The reader will do well to make a similar comparison. Our volume *The Vibrato* is most revealing on this point: all good music involves great flexibility and freedom. The Negro indulges most lavishly in various forms of license, and that is one of the secrets of his resourcefulness. We make the mistake of approaching his song in terms of conventional concepts of pitch and time. That is not his approach in his natural habitat. If he knew the diatonic scale, he would probably shun it. At his best, he soars through tonal regions with rhythmic movements, sharp syncopation, and liberal frills of adornment.

Intervals. From this point of view, the moot question of intervals—favored intervals, scales, and deviations from scales, all in relation to our conventional music—gains a new significance. From our inspection of the records, it becomes clear that it is difficult to determine exactly at what pitch a note is heard or intended to be heard. A large part of the intonation is carried on transition tones. We must also realize that all American Negro singing is influenced by current music.

Certain authors have maintained that this deviation from accepted intervals is due to the inability of the Negro to sing them with tonal precision. Measures of Negro hearing, however, have shown that his ear is probably as keen in natural capacity as that of the cultured singer. He sings in his own way and likes it. The present vogue of Negro singing and the imitation of it in the music of the whites might suggest that there are other people who like the same kind of freedom and that fixed intervals are not the goal of all music.

Ornaments. *Metfessel*[85] says:

> The personal decorations of primitive folk are no more tangible than the ornaments of voice, when the latter are brought out by phonophotography. The ornaments appealing to the hearing of their fellows may now be displayed in our museums alongside the appeals to sight. Any vocal ornaments may be classified and placed on exhibit as particular patterns on the new

notation. With a phonograph record or film reproducing the music, it will be possible to hear the vocal ornaments which are pictured.

A finished tone quality is rarely found in Negro folk singing. The Negro may enjoy good tones, but he makes little effort to produce them. He is interested in the more obvious embellishments and rhythmical devices rather than in the subtle effects of beauty resulting from the relatively regular vibrato of artistic singing.

He then gives a list (Table I) of features in pitch characteristics which may be observed in these songs. A similar table might be made for the temporal aspects.

TABLE I*

1. Notes
   a. Irregular and widely variable vibrato
   b. Erratic quaver
2. Intonations (as a separate tone or in attack or release)
   a. Rising
   b. Falling
   c. Circumflex
   d. Inverted circumflex
3. Succession of notes
   a. Interpolated notes
   b. Grace notes
   c. Slow quaver
4. Succession of intonations
   a. Rising with circumflex
   b. Circumflex with falling
   c. Rising tone with rising tone
   d. Rising tone with falling tone, and vice versa
   e. The dip
5. Succession of notes and intonations
   a. Interpolated intonations
   b. Falsetto twist
   c. All intonation types in attack or release of notes

* Metfessel uses the word "note" to designate the body of a tone which rests on a recognizable and relatively constant pitch. The transition tones, including the portamento in attack and release, as well as the ornaments, he calls "intonations." The intonation and the note as a unit he calls a "tone."

The records show that in the best of these songs the vibrato is as good as in recognized artistic singers. It is, however, probably subject to larger variability and more transition forms into other pulsations, of which the erratic quaver is characteristic.

The intonations, as we have seen, come from the characteristic legato in rising, falling, circumflex, and inverted circumflex forms and include many of the embellishments of the song.

The presence of interpolated notes and grace notes, and the slow quaver, which is a pulsation midway between a vibrato and a slow, wide trill, are conspicuous.

In the succession of intonations, the most characteristic Negro ornament is the dip, which tends to come at the end of each note, and, even when not gross or conspicuous, is present in inceptive tendencies in that direction. It perhaps contributes more to the droll character of the singing than anything else.

The falsetto twist, which is a reverse of the dip and usually of a much larger extent, is an upward sweep, in which the voice breaks quickly into a falsetto. This ornament is very easily heard and is laboriously aped in imitations of Negro singing.

The Negro dialect. Instead of singing, "I heard the voice of Jesus say," the Negro sings, "Ah ray ah voice of Jesus zey." This is not mere ignorant dialect or affectation but represents a natural gravitation toward the musical vowels, especially the broad vowels in "Lawd," "doan'," "ma(my)," "ah (the)." This principle of intonation upon musical vowels is further aided by the shortening of words, syllables, and consonants, which do not lend themselves readily to this purpose.

This presentation has, perhaps, contributed but little toward the listing of facts about Negro music; but I trust it will serve the purpose of setting up a point of view guarding against sources of error, creating a sympathetic attitude toward what the Negro singer is trying to do, noting that he may be hampered by the cultured music of his day, and that such things as the spirit of Negro song or any other song are not something mysterious but are couched in concrete, observable, and recordable facts.

27

THE DEVELOPMENT OF MUSICAL SKILLS

When listeners from every part of our nation can hear the same musician at the same time in actual performance, and when the musician may stand up before us to be seen and heard in the same song for generations to come, a new type of responsibility is thrown upon the performer and his instrument. As soon as we get our breath after finding ourselves in this marvelous situation through the achievement of science in the transmission and reproduction of sound, interest is going to center upon improvement of the singer and player, of the musical instrument, of the art of teaching music and standards of artistic achievement through the application of scientific methods. Our musical instruments are far from perfect. Current scientific knowledge applied to the improvement of musical instruments is destined to cause a revolution in the means of instrumental tone production. At every turn, there will be demand for application of scientific technique for the improvement and mastery of the art of music.

The present chapter is based on the fundamental assumption that training in singing or playing involves a number of specific capacities and skills which may be identified and made direct objects of training with instrumental control in order to shorten the time of training and increase the degree of precision that may result from training.

This theory assumes that ability at any stage of training may be measured and that specific training exercises may be instituted to make the student profoundly conscious of the specific skill which he is to acquire in order that he may attain the highest degree of precision in the act in a minimum time, and that sufficient training by this method will make the act automatic, so that it shall function in actual performance without consciousness of it as a specific act of skill. That is, it gives credence to the school of music teachers which maintains that the singer should be conscious of the specific act and the means of its control at the time that the skill is acquired as an isolated act; it also gives credence to the opposite school which maintains that in the artistic attitude of singing or playing the performer should not center attention upon any of the countless specific skills involved but should enjoy the freedom of the artistic mood, all the specific skills having been automatized. In other words, one school is right at the training stage and the other is right at the stage of artistic performance. If this is admitted, there should be no conflict between the two.

This distinction between attitude in the learning stage and the attitude in artistic performance is a most fundamental and radical contribution of experimental psychology. It rests upon the application of the laws of learning in the acquisition of skills in order to furnish the tools of musical performance which, when integrated and thoroughly automatized, are thereby removed from the field of conscious effort. It thus provides an essential condition which will make it possible for the inspired composer or artist in musical performance to live his music unhampered by technique and acting spontaneously on his inspiration.

The instruments used in training are on the market and, therefore, need not be explained in detail here. Only enough will be indicated to show the general character, purpose, and principle on which they work.

In the development of musical skills by instrumental aids, our problem is again vastly simplified by recognition of the fact that we do not need many instruments. What we do need is convenient, observable methods of showing pitch, intensity, time, and timbre. From these basic measures countless complex forms of skill may be exhibited and measured. To illustrate, if we have a simple and direct way of observing pitch performance in voice or instrument, then that instrument can be used for the study of all the pitch skills. The same is true about the other three basic instruments. It, therefore, becomes a relatively simple problem to equip a music studio for the training of musical skills by instrumental aids. In this chapter only a few suggestions can be made in regard to the significance and nature of the procedure. A fundamental requirement in the selection of instruments is that the tone shall be observable immediately and in detail at the moment of actual musical performance.

CONTROL OF PITCH INTONATION

The tonoscope.[146] The tonoscope serves this purpose within a wide range of pitch intonation. It works on the principle of moving pictures, and the pitch performance may be seen immediately. If desired, it may be recorded either by the performer or by an experimenter; that is, the singer sees himself sing, the violinist sees his pitch performance. By this visual aid, he may correct his intonation and thereby refine his hearing of pitch and acquire precision in the intonation.

The tone is produced on the principle of moving pictures, and the frequency is read on the principle that when a tone corresponds to a certain frequency of dots, that line of dots will stand still, whereas, all other lines will appear as moving. The screen covers one octave and reads directly in tenths of a tone; but if a tone is steady, such as that of a tuning fork, it can be read with accuracy to a hundredth of a tone. The octave above and the octave below the one represented on the screen may be read as well as the one on the screen. The notes for the octave are indicated in the chromatic scale. For the purpose of standards to be sung or played, a phonograph record may be placed at the top of the instrument and the pitch to be reproduced is carried over a head receiver to the performer. Since this record is fixed to the tonoscope, it synchronizes the standard tone with the tone that is to be produced perfectly.*

Significant measures. In studying the sounding of a keynote, a musical scale, or an actual melody, the performer simply looks at the instrument and immediately sees the character of his performance and then has the opportunity of trying to correct or improve upon this at will. But, if he wishes to record his performance, he can obtain three standard measures which can be treated statistically in permanent form. The first of these is the average error.

---

* This instrument is marketed by the C. H. Stoelting Company, 424 N. Homan Ave., Chicago, Ill. Since the instrument is accompanied by a complete manual of instructions and suggestions for exercises, it is not necessary to go into such details here.

Suppose that he tries to sing the interval of a major third. He makes a number of trials and records the actual error in terms of hundredths of a tone. The average of a series of 10 or more trials will be a significant figure. This is usually designated as A.E. (average error). The tendency to sharp or flat is given in terms of C.E. (constant error) and the measure of reliability of the average error as well as the constant error is given in terms of S.D. (standard deviation).

Representative measures. Countless varieties of measures of precision in pitch intonation in singing and playing may be made with the tonoscope, both for the purpose of diagnosis and as material for practice and measurement of gain by training series. As a rule the experimenter should set up a measure to fit the purpose that he has in hand. However, as a unit battery of measures for general survey of ability, and as material for general practice, the following three are proposed as basic and representative of pitch control:

1. *Reproduction of a tone.* Reproduce the standard tone as heard in the receiver. When all three measures are used, only a few trials need be taken on this because the same situation is repeated in other exercises, and, if there is need for other data, this item may be taken from each of the following tests in which the standard tone is reproduced and run into a single composite score.

In all these exercises, women sing the standard tone as it is heard; namely, middle C; and men sing, as is conventional in music, an octave lower.

2. *Singing intervals.*

a. The major scale. Sing or play the major scale in C upward, beginning with the standard tone.

b. Intervals in major scale. Sing or play the intervals in the natural scale, key of C, separately, thus, do-re, do-mi, do-fa, etc.

c. Melody. Sing or play the first three measures of *America.**

3. *Fine shading of pitch.* Sing or play the small intervals as played on a phonographic record.† For beginners and average performers use the record A, which contains large intervals, 8 to

* For example, in *America* these might be the notes for the following syllables: *My*, *'tis*, *land*, *-ty*, *of*, and *sing*. This is for the purpose of facilitating reading. The singer should not know this fact. For good singers it may be desirable to take a more difficult melody such as *Annie Laurie* or *Drink to me only with thine eyes.*

† *Measures of Musical Talent*, "Sense of Pitch," No. 1A, Record 53004-D.

30 ~; for fine performers use the record B, which contains steps from 12 to 5 ~. For principles of fine shading in pitch see *Miles.*[92]

This procedure is a great improvement over the older method of having a performer simply sharp or flat a note by minimum amount. It gives an index to ability to shade the pitch by a small interval and to know the size of that interval.

The transfer of training from the tonoscope to the later musical situation. It has been shown in the University of Iowa Laboratory that training the ear by aid of the eye results in rapid improvement in correct pitch intonation and that the training with the instrument transfers to actual performance without the aid of the eye. For example, if a student takes remedial exercises with the tono-

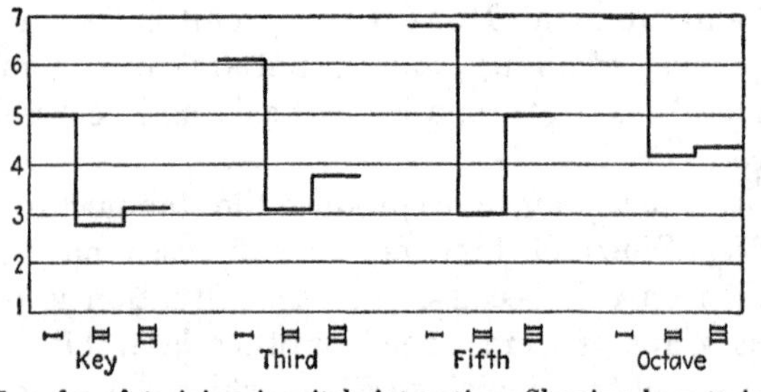

FIG. 1.—Transfer of training in pitch intonation. Showing how training for pitch intonation by the aid of the eye improves this skill and that the skill so acquired transfers to singing and playing without the instrument. (*Knock.*[61])

scope, correcting his intonation at each trial, this permanently improves the control by hearing so that a large part of the gain thus made will be retained when he sings without the tonoscope aid. Sample results for a training series are shown in Fig. 1, indicating the amount of gain in special training and the transfer of this gain to actual singing.

These relationships would vary with a large number of factors, such as the original degree of accuracy of the singer, his personal equation as a learner, the interval practiced, the relation of this to previous training, and numerous other factors. But the figure may be taken as a fair sample of what training the ear with the aid of the eye can accomplish and the significance of this for musical performance is, of course, strikingly clear as applied to accuracy of intonation in singing and, by inference, to accuracy in playing instruments in which the performer controls the pitch.

In order to show the development and findings in a specific case, Table I is presented. It is a record of the violin student who had a good ear but was reported as unsatisfactory in pitch control.

TABLE I. RECORD OF DEVELOPMENT OF CONTROL BY VIOLIN STUDENT
(pitch discrimination, percentile rank 70)

	Preliminary			*Final test*		
Average errors (*A.E.*)	*A.E.*	*% rank*	*S.D.*	*A.E.*	*% rank*	*S.D.*
Standard keynote	0.22	7	0.21	0.01	99	0.01
Scale	0.10	47	0.21	0.02	100	0.02
Major interval	0.17	9	0.12	0.03	90	0.02
Melodies	0.11	25	0.03	0.03	93	0.01
Average	0.14	23	0.11	0.02	95	0.02
	Preliminary			*Final test*		
Averages for the intervals of all exercises:	*A.E.*	*C.E.*	*S.D.*	*A.E.*	*C.E.*	*S.D.*
Keynote	0.11	.11	0.06	0.00	0.00	0.00
Second	0.13	−0.06	0.04	0.02	−0.01	0.01
Third	0.20	−0.03	0.05	0.01	0.00	0.00
Fourth	0.17	−0.17	0.08	0.12	−0.12	0.03
Fifth	0.12	−0.12	0.03	0.02	0.02	0.01
Sixth	0.10	−0.10	0.10	0.02	−0.01	0.01
Seventh	0.32	−0.32	0.09	0.01	0.01	0.01
Octave	0.05	−0.05	0.02	0.01	−0.01	0.01
A.E. fine shading test:	0.19	0.09	0.15	0.07	0.01	0.02

A.E.—Average error; *C.E.*—Constant error; *S.D.*—Standard deviation. Minus sign denotes flat.

Table I shows his average error and constant error in the preliminary record to be poor. He was then given 10 half-hour periods of training with the tonoscope, and this was followed by a final test of performance without this visual aid. He made marked improvement, and this improvement is carried over, since the final test consisted in performance on new material and without the visual aid.

One of the most significant features in training series of this kind is the fact that the correction is made very early, almost immediately, in the training series; so that the main advantage of continuing the training for 10 days in persons whose pitch discrimination is satisfactory is the fixing of the correction by habituation. In other words, inaccuracy in control of intonation is usually due to either ignorance of interval or slovenliness of the ear. Both can be corrected almost instantly under the proper spur, namely, that of seeing his actual error.

General training may be given upon the three measures described above, namely, the reproducing of a standard tone, the singing of musical intervals, and fine shading in pitch. Choice of material in these three fields may be made to suit one's taste; but in general, drill on these three fundamentals should serve the purpose of ear training and motor control. Indeed, whatever specific training is to be undertaken, it would be well to precede it with training in each of these three factors as they are indicated.

The chief purpose of these directions is to explain the method by which remedial training may be instituted: (1) for specific training in pitch control at an early stage as a part of the ear-training course; (2) for the correction of any recognized fault in singing or playing true pitch; and (3) as a means of mastering artistic deviations from true pitch.

Remedial training for specific defects. The principal faults of intonation occur in the following factors:

1. General failure to secure true pitch. Remedy: Drill on varied exercises in pitch intonation.

2. Sharp or flat of the principal tone in general or in some specific region. Remedy: Practice exercises with the tonoscope where the fault exists until the ear control has been corrected and the fault eliminated.

3. Faulty attack, mainly slovenliness in dragging gradually into the tone from above or below. Remedy: Practice by the aid of the eye until the tone can be reached in a clear-cut attack. This is a preliminary requirement to artistic deviation in attack.

4. Faulty release. The same situation applies as in attack.

5. Progressive change. Gradual sharping or flatting habitually in a sustained tone. Remedy: Practice on actual musical tones or phrases in which the difficulty occurs.

6. Specific tendencies to sharp or flat; as with a loud tone or a soft tone or with certain vowels. Remedy: Specific corrective work in actual situations.

Artistic control. When we record artistic performance of singers or players with great precision photographically, a mass of deviations in pitch intonation shows up. Many of them are, of course, merely faulty intonation due to error or incapacity in performance; but many have artistic value. One group of these represents artistic intention. Another, a much larger class, represents psychophysic tendencies for intonation of interval that are produced unconsciously by the performer but yet serve artistic purpose in the melodic situation or in the modification of tone quality. The collection and classification of samples of this latter class is a sort of natural-history procedure in the psychology of music studio and presents a very fertile field for investigation.*

Reliability and validity. The accuracy of reading will improve with practice very quickly if engaged in with well-directed and intensive effort. Taking the act as a whole, including both errors of performer and errors of readers, it has been found that a trained experimenter with good singers gets a correlation of .94, $\pm$.01 by the method of chance halves in the reproduction of a tone.

It is natural to ask what is the validity of these results in terms of relationship to accuracy in singing and playing. The answer is that each act is taken out of the actual singing or playing situation and is specific. The only question then is whether or not the performances here selected are such as actually function in music. The answer is self-evident. The ability to reproduce a standard tone, the ability to sing intervals, and ability to make fine shadings in pitch are fundamental units of action in music. But are these the most representative samples? Insofar as we know, they are. There is no end to the number of variants that could be introduced. The conventional statistical method of checking of specific measurements against somebody's judgment is not in place here.

The above presentation of the theory and the means of procedure in training for pitch intonation is offered as a model on which corresponding training exercises are built for the other three elements in tone production. A brief reference to each one may be in place.

CONTROL OF INTENSITY

But little has been done in the study of intensity control in spite of the fact that this is one of the four fundamental elements

* One important element of discipline in the type of training herein described, lies in the fact that after preliminary instructions, the student may be assigned the task of training by himself, singing or playing into the instrument and seeing immediately the error which he has to correct and thus engage in an intensive drill in self-correction by aid of the instrument. This serves two purposes. It saves the time of the instructor and creates a situation for much finer objective recognition of errors than the teacher can set without the instrument. The teacher sets a training task, and, when the student is satisfied that he has mastered that, he may present himself for checking out.

In this free use of the instrument by the student lies one of its greatest values for training. Like the piano, this instrument may be available for anyone who needs to practice and, as in the case of the piano, the student practices on exercises at his stage of learning. Wherever he is conscious of need for the measurement of attainment or guidance in achievement in the control of pitch, he resorts to this visual aid and the adequate use of this opportunity becomes a routine part of musical instruction.

in the world of musical performance, especially in the phrasing, or what is generally called "playing with feeling." One reason for this lies in the fact that for pitch and time we have absolute standards and deviations from these are readily checked and noted by teachers and performers. The need of training in this field is, however, just as great as in pitch or time. This is especially true as regards the necessity of isolating this factor and making it a special object of attack in the acquisition of musical skill. Improvement will lie largely in the consciousness of differences in intensity. The execution of the differences is different for voice and each of the instruments.

Reading of such an excellent recent book as *Klein's*[66] *Great Women Singers I Have Known* is irritating to the psychologist on account of the loose, airy, and emotional terminology that the writer uses. In all that has been written on phrasing in music, there seems to be very little embodying any scientific conception of the dynamics involved. We have the terms "loud" and "soft," and all their cognates, equivalents, and shades; but nothing is said in regard to what constitutes loudness and only a little about its mastery. The time has come for analysis of the problem into its constituent factors, the measurement of capacity and the basing of training for the acquisition of the dynamic skills in music upon these ascertained factors.

Indeed, the whole problem of dynamic aspect of the esthetics of music must be reviewed to show (1) what are the media for the expression of beauty through intensity, (2) what are the prevailing types of error, and (3) what new principles of art in this field can be discovered by the objective method. Basic to all these is the technical mastery of dynamic control.

The intensity meter. There are various forms of so-called output meters available for this purpose. The types of meters used in radio studios are serviceable for training exercises. The intensity of any sound in a particular position before the microphone is registered in terms of decibels.

Three types of exercises are regarded as basic: (1) The reproduction of a given intensity either for a single tone or for a given period of musical performance. (2) A capacity for fine shading in intensity. For this purpose the phonograph record for intensity in the *Measures of Musical Talent* may be played in front of the microphone, setting up a definite series of degrees of difference in loudness. The ability to sing or play these differences in intensity in all the pairs of tones is employed as a measure of achievement and as a means of training for skill in the control of intensity. (3) Upper and lower limits in intensity in good tone production under specific conditions. Thus, one may take these exercises to produce a good tone very softly or with maximum loudness.

CONTROL OF TIME AND RHYTHM

There are various ways of testing one's ability to keep metronomic time. The simplest way is to use a pencil as a baton and tap the time with a metronome. One can then easily hear to what extent the two clicks coincide; but, since the ability to vary from metronomic time, especially as in rhythmic phrasing, a measure of rhythmic action in phrasing is more to the point.

THE RHYTHM METER

R. H. Seashore's rhythm meter[158] is essentially a phonograph, a disk with attachments on a turntable in which contacts can be made at any points on the circumference. By this means, any particular rhythm within the period of revolution of the disk can be set up. The performer is asked to reproduce or follow this rhythm for a minute or two, tapping on a telegraph key, so as to make the telegraph click coincide with the stimulus. For rough exercises in training, mere hearing of the degree of deviation is sufficient; but, for fine work, records of the standard and the reproduction are made with a stylus on paper placed on the turntable.

The greatest value in this exercise lies in the training of the ear for precision in the hearing of a rhythmic pattern and the coordination of that with the actual performance. There is an immediate check for the ear and the eye at the time of the performance, and a particular rhythmic control can be established in a very short series of organized exercises.

TRAINING FOR PRECISION IN RHYTHMIC ACTION

In a series of experiments on remedial training in musical skills, *Henderson*[46a] performed the following experiment in the development of precision in rhythmic action. He set up a specific rhythmic pattern on the Seashore rhythm meter[158] and gave intensive training of half-hour periods for five days and recorded the measure of the performance for each day.

Figure 2 tells the story. The group consisted of nine unselected students of piano in the school of music. The numbers at the bottom indicate the days; the preliminary test is given as the starting point. Achievement is measured in terms of average deviation in the scale at the left, in which zero would mean perfect performance to within 0.01 of a second in metronomic time. The mean, showing improvement for the entire group, is indicated by a heavy line.

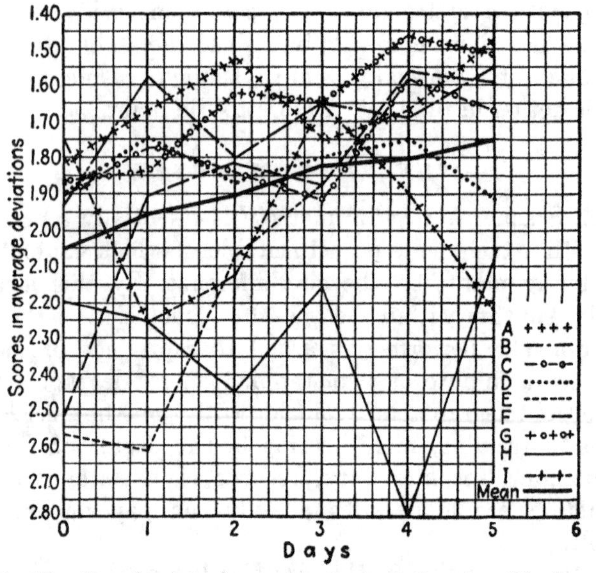

FIG. 2.—The effect of training for precision in rhythmic action. (*Henderson.*[46a])

The graph shows that: (1) They started at different levels of achievement. In this rating there is but little agreement with their classification as piano students. (2) Each had his days of ups and downs due to a variety of conditions which modified achievement. The subject represented by the lowest curve had a general reputation for being an erratic student; but in three extra days of training, she made definite progress over the fifth day's performance. (3) On the whole, the group made distinctive progress during the five days as is illustrated by the heavy line giving the mean performance of the group for each day. The curves rises from 2.50 in the preliminary rating to 1.75 in the fifth day.

One may wonder if any ordinary musical exercises on rhythmic precision in piano playing ever achieved such marked progress in so short a time. What happened in this training we may designate as a development of ear-hand coordination; but other experiments show that the most significant thing that happened was the whipping up of the ear for precision in hearing. This ability is one which, of course, transfers bodily to the playing of an instrument. That such transfer to actual piano playing took place, in both metronomic playing and phrasing, was verified in a tentative way. The student had become precision-conscious for rhythm.

CONTROL OF TIMBRE

This is a most important field for training, especially in voice, where so much depends on voice quality and knowing when to attain it. There are various forms of instruments for the projecting of the sound wave. A satisfactory instrument for this purpose is rather expensive and difficult to manage, but well worth while if training the control of tone quality is taken seriously. There are two types of instruments: one is represented by the cathode ray oscillograph, which projects the exact form of the wave on a large scale; the other is a mechanical harmonic analyzer, which shows, in a steady tone, the number of overtones present and their distribution and relative intensities. With either of these instruments, it is possible to have standard tones of recognized good quality set up as standards which the student is required to reproduce.

With the oscillograph countless exercises may be set up, for example, for the control of vowel quality, training in a particular register, or exercises in the development of a desirable performance region.

GENERAL SIGNIFICANCE OF SPECIFIC TRAINING FOR SKILLS

Throughout this volume emphasis has been laid upon the possibility and necessity of analyzing and isolating specific factors which may be studied under control. The organization of researches and the cumulative organization of discovered facts has been immensely facilitated by the recognition of the taproots and the family tree for each of the four elements of musical traits. Enough has been done to show that faulty performance is due in very large part to sluggish or inadequately critical control by the ear and that this may be improved or sharpened for any specific factor in very brief training for a specific skill. The cumulative integration of such skills in the automatisms built up in the pupil furnish a necessary control of the organism for artistic performance. Familiarity with the analysis of the constituents of the musical medium, with the pupil's fortes and faults, capacities and abilities, and with the scientific language of music places the pupil in a position of both intelligent and artistic command of the situation; and, for the teacher, all these stages will contribute toward the goal of making music teachable.

MUSICAL ESTHETICS

APPROACHES TO MUSICAL ESTHETICS

ALL fine arts are creative. In this sense, they are also practical; something is done to serve a purpose. This is eminently true of music. The composer creates, the performer re-creates and interprets, and the musical listener responds musically within the limits of his creative power. Esthetics deals with the theory of the nature of art, in this case, the theory of music. The great musicians pursue both theory and practice; but the practice far outruns the theory, because the work of genuine creation always comes from self-expression rather than through the deliberate application of rules. In the musical mood, theory must always be relegated to the subconscious through which it operates automatically, if once mastered. Furthermore, the musician's energies, both in training and in the professional life, are so deeply engrossed in the practical aspects of his work of creation, re-creation, and interpretation that he must delegate the scientific problems proper to other specialists.

Musical esthetics falls into a number of stages; primarily, physics, physiology, psychology, anthropology, philosophy, and metaphysics. Let us consider these in turn.

Music, as rendered by voice or instrument, consists of sound waves. Physics deals with the nature and the laws of these sound waves, the characteristics of their structure, and the laws of their propagation. To the musician, these facts and laws of physics are matters of common knowledge and are taken for granted. However well informed the musician may be in the science of structure and propagation of sound waves, he rightly accepts these facts on the authority of the physicist.

Physiology deals with those aspects of the human organism which are involved in the sensory and central aspects of hearing, the central and motor mechanisms for tone production, and the organic basis of musical emotion involving both the central and the autonomic nervous systems and both the smooth and the striated muscular systems. However well informed the musician may be, for example, about the function of the inner ear or the function of the adrenal glands in strong emotion, he accepts these facts on the authority of the physiologist. Indeed, current esthetics is largely physiological in theory.

Psychology aims to describe and explain musical experience and musical behavior; it investigates the nature of musical talent; it analyzes the sensory responses to music; it traces the human drives, which we used to call instincts and impulses, that crave music and find their outlet in music; it examines feeling, emotion, and musical thought processes, both functionally and structurally; it traces the development of the musical mind from infancy through maturation and training. One is at once impressed with the appalling task which this inceptive science has assumed for itself and how undeveloped the work is within this field. Yet, however familiar the musician may be with the experimental findings about the functioning of the musical mind, he looks to the psychologist for the further exploration and organization of knowledge in this field.

Musical anthropology, that is, the ethnic history of music, deals with the origin and evolution of music in the race. It treats of the development of instruments, of musical forms, and the vastly varied roles of music as progressively unfolded in rising racial cultures. This aspect of history involves a high order of scientific technique, often closely associated with archaeology. However versed the musician may be in the theories and the established facts of musical anthropology, he trusts the anthropologist, trained in music, to conduct further research.

These four aspects—physics, physiology, psychology, and anthropology—furnish scientific approaches to the theory of beauty in music and, conversely, also the theory of ugliness. It is in the light of these sciences that we may look for the progressive development of our concept of the nature and power of beauty in music. These sciences are so interrelated and interdependent that in dealing with the subject of esthetics it is profitable to treat them as a single unit. Hence, we have a tendency to speak of psychophysics, psychophysiology, psychobiology, and psychogenetics as in many respects replacing the term "psychology."

However, it falls largely to the lot of the psychologist to integrate, coordinate, and apply findings from these four specific fields. The psychologist does not restrict himself to the study of the mind but takes as his field the behavior of the human organism as a whole in the musical situation. The psychology of music, in the broad sense of musical esthetics, might more appropriately be called the "science of music." The advantage of calling it "psychology of music" is that, at the present time, it places responsibility and initiative for the work of integration which would otherwise fall for want of a sponsor. In the near future, the science of music, as such, is likely to take possession of the field in its own rights.

In like manner, we may speak of the psychology of musical esthetics, the science of musical esthetics, or possibly, merely musical esthetics.

Beyond these scientific approaches, and, indeed, long anticipating them, we have two other approaches, namely, the philosophical and the metaphysical. Man approached the problem of philosophy and metaphysics long before he acquired the tools of science. Music has its roots in the most primitive savage life and has evolved through countless culture strata. Throughout the ages the untutored primitive mind has asked: What is music? What can it do? Where does it come from? Where does it go? As philosophy has developed in modern times, its principal interest has come to center around the theory of values as a specific esthetic problem. In this, the philosophical technique has been brought to bear upon the progressively evolving concepts. These concepts are derived from three sources: (1) primitive impulses and intuitions; (2) gradually emerging scientific findings in concrete situations; and (3) working theories which are the direct outgrowth of the practice of the art.

To primitive man, music came from the gods. It was the spirits that performed. Musical inspiration was revelation. Music was an offering acceptable to the gods. Philosophers, throughout the ages, have progressively rationalized, attenuated, and modernized such impulses and hunches, which well up in all cultural levels. The spiritistic conception of music still plays a dominant role in mystical philosophy and theories of music. With the dawn of the scientific age, the philosopher turned his attention upon the concepts that crop out from the specific sciences. The critique of such concepts is a large part of the business of philosophy today. Then the philosopher must take cognizance of the more immediate experience of the musician in which he joins the musician in the immediate evaluation of experience. Philosophical criticism has tended to center on the effort to find a single unitary principle, which would account for the nature and function of beauty, and thus explain the nature and purpose of music. This, I think, has resulted in a succession of failures, and the philosopher of the future will not attempt that again.

Metaphysics deals with such things as the theory of ultimate reality, the nature of knowledge, and theories of origins. It asks, for example, What is mind of which the power of music is a manifestation? What is the nature of that knowledge of which musical inspiration is an aspect? How has the musical mind come into existence?

These are eternal questions, tantalizingly interesting, but their solution is deferred from age to age. Yet, theories on each of these issues underlie scientific approaches, although usually in purely naïve form, often an antiquated, purely materialistic, or a purely idealistic, approach to the subject.

Practically, metaphysics and philosophy proper are not separated, and they are not marked off in sharp distinction from science, on the one hand, and common sense, on the other. In fact, the historical development of any question, such as the nature of musical value, arises as the main question and soon takes on both metaphysical and supernatural interpretations. These are criticized in philosophy and gradually analyzed and clarified by scientific methods; this done, the information tends to be regarded as a matter of common knowledge or common sense.

If philosophy be defined as the best thoughts of the greatest men on the most important questions of life, then philosophy has made the largest contribution to musical esthetics and this contribution has come, in large part, from men who were at the same time musicians and philosophers. Yet, with the coming in of the scientific approach, with the techniques available for scientific investigation, and with the philosophized attitude of the scientist, the problem of esthetics has become almost entirely a problem of science. It is not likely that philosophy will make any great contribution to esthetics, for it deals with facts at second hand.

Only as philosophy and metaphysics wield the weapon of superior techniques in constructive and creative criticism will they make any vital contribution to musical esthetics. The rehashing of semi-scientific knowledge, under the name of philosophy in esthetics, has had its day. The esthetics of the past is giving way to the science of the art, both in investigation and in teaching on the subject.

Let us, therefore, make bold to attempt a rough outline of the general scheme of musical esthetics from the scientific point of view.

ESTHETICS AS A NORMATIVE SCIENCE

For the purpose of classification and description, the coming musical esthetics, which is based upon experimental science, may be divided into four aspects, namely, the musical medium, the musical form, the musical message, and the musical response. Any classification of this kind is, however, a compromise and does not represent sharp separation of parts. Indeed, there is an intricate dovetailing and overlapping among these four members. This classification, however, has an advantage over all the classifications extant in the literature of philosophers and artists in that it is based upon objectively verifiable grounds and follows the method of natural history of collecting observable and verifiable facts and arranging them in natural order.

The musical medium. The musical medium is the music proper as executed in the form of physical sounds which have their physiological and mental correlates. Esthetics accepts the scientific approach to the medium as physical, psychophysical, physiological, and psychological. Instead of assuming that millions of phenomena of musical sounds are ethereal and unclassifiable, not reducible to law and order, it begins at once to put order into chaos by setting questions to nature under control. It proceeds on the assumption that these phenomena are knowable if we have the patience and skill to search for them; it discredits the armchair procedure of merely thinking and talking about them; it distrusts traditions, vogues, hobbies, and mystical and theological hunches. Instead of beginning with the pinnacle, it starts from the ground, building its structure patiently, block by block, even realizing that the structure will never be completed. It will never give us the dreamed-of theory of beauty but will progressively enrich our insight into the nature and structure of beauty with the growing appreciation of the infinite richness of possibilities.

It begins with the classification of the physical characteristics of the sound wave and carries this classification through the physical sounds, as mediated through the physiological organism, as responded to by the psychological organism in sensory experience, and as reproduced and elaborated in memory, imagination, thought, and emotional drives in their marvelous possibilities of intricate relationships.

But let us not delude ourselves into thinking that the situation is simple or solved. If there were a one-to-one relationship between the physical sound and the mental experience or response which it elicits, our problem would be simplified. However, such relationships scarcely if ever exist. The mental process never corresponds exactly to the physical event, and it is in this situation that the real problem of the psychologist begins in the task of discovering law and order in the deviations of the mental event from the physical event. This leads us first to the staggering realization that in musical art, "All is illusion." Without the blessing of normal illusions, musical art would be hopelessly stunted. Our profoundest appreciations of nature and of art are detachments from the physically exact and constitute a synthesis through the medium of normal illusions. But the composer, the performer, and the listener all deal with the physical medium and all the theories of form and interpretation of message and response must in the long run be grounded upon a true cognizance of the nature of this medium and its possible roles.

The musical form. The musician is primarily concerned with the nature of musical form, the organization of its art principles, its development, and the theory of art objectives. Thus, musical form deals with the different genres of musical composition, the rules for composition and interpretation, and the theory as to the nature of the esthetic appeal; in all cases, how to do this and that, and the reason for it. It deals, for example, with sonata forms, with the rules of harmony in the execution of such forms, and the theories underlying and justifying these forms and rules.

The problem is primarily that of the composer; but the composer, like the architect, is at the mercy of available materials, competent workmanship, and adequate resources of all kinds. He is usually limited by the conventions, vogues, and culture levels of the day, by his mastery of techniques, and most of all, by the nature and limitations of his creative genius.

The esthetics of musical form may be reduced largely to the cumulative body of practical principles of artistic structure, the interpretation of these in terms of musical objectives, and the theory of the nature of the beauty involved. Historically, the esthetics of form is the main and almost the entire body of historical treatises on musical esthetics, and the development and validation of principles for composition represent the best contribution that the musician can make toward the scientific foundation of the art. The laws of harmony, for example, are somewhat analogous to the laws of philology, and philology is recognized in the sisterhood of sciences. To the musician, musical form is the primary issue to which the medium, the message, and the response play but a secondary role. It is in this field that musical theory has made the most notable advances; it is in this field also that the musician has held and must continue to assume larger and larger responsibility for initiative in the building of musical esthetics; it is the creative work.

The scientist, however, makes his entry into this field by critique of concepts and by reducing aspects of musical form to concrete issues which may be treated exhaustively in the laboratory for verification, criticism, and adaptation, and even for the development of new forms. Such problems as the analysis of scales, of consonance and dissonance, and of rhythm, are problems of form which may properly come up for review in the laboratory at this time.

THE MUSICAL MESSAGE

The musical message is that esthetic experience—be it feeling, ideation, impulse, craving, wish, or inspiration—which the composer in the first instance and the interpreter at the next level desire to convey to the audience through the form given by the musical medium. In the same manner, the message may be regarded as that experience or interpretation which the listener arrives at from hearing the rendition, from scanning the score, or from reminiscent memory in vivid and constructive imagination. The esthetics of the message, therefore, becomes the psychological analysis, interpretation, and explanation of the musical experience of the sender and the receiver of music, in terms of content.

Musical literature is replete with speculations in regard to the nature and origin of the musical message and the possibility and means of its transmission. Here lies the battleground for those who contend for pure music and those who argue for descriptive music. The moot question between these two camps can be settled only by a psychological analysis of the character of the musical message in the mind of the originator and the limitations upon its transmission. The award will not be in favor of one party but will give new and richer meaning to both sides.

The composer or performer who desires to transmit an experience of pure feeling places himself in a receptive mood in which the musical material takes the form that satisfies his mood spontaneously. He takes the artistic attitude, which is radically opposed to the psychological attitude; the former is the attitude of abandon in which he feels his inspiration and allows it to develop in his own organism under favorable conditions without regard for rule, meaning, or the technique of analysis. The message is to him an inspiration, a sort of surrender to pure feeling without intentional meaning. His feelings are molded in pure tone or tone experience, and the musical material and form take the shape of a stimulus for feeling of the beauty of tone in itself, aside from formal art or meaning.

On the other hand, in program music, the originator attempts to use musical figures which convey concrete ideas that serve as a sort of idol, stilt, or skeleton to which the musical feeling is attached. Such themes aim to portray moonlight, the lover, contest, the forces of nature. In addition to the feeling of pure beauty, which is of but doubtful existence, the message is supposed to convey a certain degree of objectivity intended to favor the immediacy of the experience in the listener. Thus, in the musical description of moonlight, the attempt is to demonstrate that music can be a language which conveys ideas and pictures of objects that arouse the feeling revealed in the tone conveyed in music. The shortcomings of this type of language are notorious. It is often used as a substitute for words and the real psychological justification for it is that, if the listener is eye-minded and sees the topic announced in the name of the selection or from the beginning begins to read into it any concrete situation that comes from his own mind, the feeling is enhanced by the ease with which we experience pleasure or displeasure in the actual presence of an object as distinguished from an abstract situation.

The problem of understanding and explaining the nature of the process of musical invention lies within this field of the message. How does the composer get his ideas? The answer to that question presents the most fascinating aspect of biography and autobiography of the great musicians and is one of the most fascinating in musical esthetics. The account of the birth throes of musical ideas, the ecstasy, the emotional upset, the inhibitions, the influence of world view, the effect upon personality, the outcropping of genius; such are psychological aspects in the study of the genesis of the musical message. This is strikingly exemplified in the later period of Beethoven's composition.

More commonplace aspects of the same problem are those which describe how the composer proceeds in composing. For example, does he get a spontaneous flash image, which gives him the theme or a key to the further development, and then work this out according to rule in calmer moments? Does he compose by the instrument, or does he compose every detail of the piano or orchestral score without any aid of instruments? In answer to such questions, we find an interesting key to the character of the musical genius and personality traits.

Another fascinating problem in this field is the question as to whether or not it is necessary for the singer actually to feel the emotions which he portrays. The old demand for a "Yes" or a "No" answer has lost its meaning, and in its place we now inquire as to what are the comparative bodily and mental reverberations of emotion in the musical experience and, in the portrayal of the experience, under what conditions these may vary.

The musical response. The same line of thought that has been outlined for the message applies, in a general way, to the interpretation of the response. When the heat from coal is converted into electrical energy, a large amount of energy is lost; so, when a message is transmitted from the sender to the listener, a great deal of the message is lost on the ground of inadequacy in sending, inadequacy of medium, or shortcomings in the receiver. Hearing of music is subject to vast limitations; among these are the limitations of musical talent or aptitude, musical information, musical skills, general intelligence, temperament, and countless other factors.

On the other hand, the listener may put a great deal more into the music than was originally intended or is actually present in the musical form, as, for example, the vivacious responses to primitive tom-toms or to present-day ragtime. Fundamental to this issue is the fact that there is not a one-to-one relationship between music as performed and music as experienced. The hearing of music is a response to a stimulus. It has been said that what a man shall see in a landscape depends on what he is; so in music. The ideas and feelings which constitute the response are the creation of the listener in his own image. "To bring back the wealth of the Indies, you must take out the wealth of the Indies."

Such, in brief, is the outline map of the territory covered by musical esthetics from the modern scientific point of view. The interaction of the artist and the scientist creates new situations, asks new questions, and promises new solutions. While it is hoped that the scientific approach to music may be productive of a great enrichment of our understanding and control of the power of music, it is equally true that the creative work of the musician and the enlightening interpretation and critical observation of the practice of the art will contribute greatly to the resources of science and will reverberate deeply in our philosophy and attitude toward life.

APPENDIX

(In the October, 1937, issue of the *Music Educators Journal,* Professor Mursell has set forth his point of view in regard to methods of evaluating musical talent. As his views are radically different from those presented in this volume, I take the liberty of quoting my reply in the December issue of the same journal in the hope that it may aid in clarifying the important issues involved.)

TWO TYPES OF ATTITUDE TOWARD THE EVALUATION OF MUSICAL TALENT

One attitude toward this problem was expressed in the aggressive and lucid formulation by Professor Mursell in the last issue of this Journal. Accepting the courteous invitation of the editors, I take pleasure in giving my reaction, as one of the spokesmen for the opposite attitude and theory.

His article should be before the reader in considering the validity of the arguments from the two sides on the basis of specific facts. He gives the key to his theory in one sentence.

"There is only one satisfactory method of finding out whether the Seashore tests really measure musical ability; and that is to ascertain whether persons rating high or low or medium on these tests also rate high and low and medium in what one may call 'musical behavior,' *i.e.*, sight singing, playing the piano, getting through courses in theory and applied music, and the like."

The idea seems to be this: any test or battery of tests must be validated against behavior and success in all musical situations—"musical behavior," of the types that he mentions, "and the like." If this is true, his entire argument can be maintained; if not, the whole argument based thereon falls.

Let me designate his theory as the "omnibus theory" and mine as the "theory of specifics," somewhat on the analogy of the distinction between cure-alls and specifics in drugs. Since his view was stated specifically in part against my six *Measures of Musical Talent,* now available on phonograph records, I may simplify my argument in the limited space by speaking only of the issue involved in these six measures.

1. They represent the theory of specific measurements insofar as they conform to the two universal scientific sanctions, on the basis of which they were designed; namely, that (1) the factor under consideration must be isolated in order that we may know exactly what it is that we are measuring, and that (2) the conclusion must be limited to the factors under control.

Each of these six tests purports to measure one of six capacities or abilities for the hearing of musical tones. There is little overlapping in these functions, and their isolation for the purpose of measurement has been criticized only in the case of one. In testing, we ask, specifically, "How good a sense of pitch, of intensity, of time, of rhythm, of consonance, of immediate tonal memory has this child?" The measurements are stated in terms of centile rank and may well be the first and most basic items in a musical profile which may have scores of other factors, quite independent and equally measurable. I deliberately coined the term "measure" for this type of procedure in order to indicate its scientific character and distinguish it from the ordinary omnibus theory procedure in tests.

2. They have been validated for what they purport to measure. This is an internal validation in terms of success in the isolation of the factor measured and the degree of control of all other factors in the measurement. When we have measured the sense of pitch, that is, pitch discrimination, in the laboratory with high reliability and we know that pitch was isolated from all other factors, no scientist will question but that we have measured pitch. There would be no object in validating against the judgment of even the most competent musician. We would not validate the reading on a thermometer against the judgment of a person sensitive to temperature.

3. They are subject to criticism on the ground of relatively low reliability. But it must be remembered that the phonograph records are a makeshift for the purpose of securing a dragnet group test of an unselected population in a limited period of time and without training for observation. When such requirements are made, we cannot expect high reliability. We should also note that these recordings were designed when we had no precedents to go by for this type of instrument construction and when recording was relatively inferior to what it is today. Careful revision and re-recording is forthcoming.

In actual testing it has been shown that all ratings in the upper half of the group may be counted as reliable for individual diagnosis. Those showing low ratings must always be reinvestigated before any conclusions can be based upon them. The ideal condition is, of course, to use the original measuring instruments of precision. For a responsible experimenter working with laboratory instruments testing a single subject under controlled conditions, the reliability of each of these six measures runs in the high 90's. I would, therefore, admit that the six measures at present are makeshifts but maintain that the principle of measurement for guidance involved is right and highly reliable.

4. They should not be validated in terms of their showing on an omnibus theory or blanket rating against all musical behavior, including such diverse and largely unrelated situations as composition, directing, voice, piano, violin, saxophone, theory, administration, or drums; because there are hundreds of other factors which help to determine job analysis in each of such fields.

In view of this, the ratings found in the formidable table compiled by Professor Mursell are unwarranted. I have been bombarded all these years by the omnibusists for this type of validation, but I have persistently refused action on the ground that it had little or no significance. The two experiments by Brennan in that table which emanated from my laboratory were performed during my year's leave of absence under the direction of an outsider inexperienced in testing and against my protests.

For the same reason, I have always protested against the use of an average of these six measures, or any other number of the same kind and have insisted upon the principle of a profile in which each specific measure stands on its own. Again, for the same reason, I have insisted that even the most superficial rating for selection or placement in musical training or adjustment should be based upon a careful case history and a reliable audition with the profile of measurements in hand. That has always been the procedure in the Eastman School. The experimenter works in the attitude of a physician who takes note of blood pressure, heart action, and metabolism.

It is easy to show that we cannot find a good violinist who does not have a good sense of pitch; or a good pianist who does not have a good sense of intensity, which is the sine qua non of touch. But it does not follow that goodness in these capacities alone will make a good artist.

Validation of pitch against the violinist's artistic performance in the actual musical situation would require that we correlate the sense of pitch with objective records of musical performance in *pitch intonation* or ability to hear *artistic pitch deviation* in the musical situation—not with the countless other merits or demerits that the violinist may exhibit. The same principle applies to any other scientific measure; such as the sense of intensity with artistic touch by the pianist.

5. They play a primarily negative role in musical adjustment. If a child has the urge, the facilities, and the support for a particular type of achievement in music, the purpose of these measures is to see whether or not a given measure indicates any probable impediment. Great musicians may rate low in one or more of these six, and many other equally important capacities. The musical guide must use his head and consider whether high or low record in a specific capacity has any significance in the specific situation before him.

There is, however, a positive use, as in dragnet surveys in a school system, a social center, a musical organization, or any other group in that a relatively good profile may lead to case history, further measurement, and auditions for the purpose of discovering and encouraging talent. My main point is that a good profile is not in itself a guaranty of musical success, but it may furnish a good lead and may become a basis for encouragement.

6. Their application is relatively limited in terms of the self-imposed restriction that the conclusion shall be limited to the legitimate implications of the factors measured. Such sacrifice by limitation is one of the fundamental characteristics of scientific procedure. It does not permit of wholesale solutions and, therefore, cannot meet the demands of the popular clamor for a single index or universal practical guide.

If, for example, a child makes a record of 99 on the centile scale for pitch, the conclusion is not that he is musical but that he has a very high capacity in one of the very numerous capacities which function in music. The problem of application is then to find out in what types of musical situation a keen sense of pitch discrimination actually functions; as in the hearing of pitch, in the control of pitch, and in the feeling for pitch. It may also be worth while to inquire to what extent a keen sense of pitch functions in the hearing of melody, of intervals, of harmony, and of tone quality. The guide has in hand a verifiable fact and must use judgment in determining what application is to be made of it in the analysis of a given situation.

7. They have suffered much from popular and superficial advertising and propaganda. I have often paraphrased the aphorism: The Lord protect me from my friends, I can protect myself against my enemies. Among the friends are many who assume a blanket validity of these tests on the omnibus theory and have, therefore, sold the notion on a large scale. This has also been the basis of many journalistic stunts, and there are many wrong applications made. Occasionally

my own unguarded statements should have been qualified. This difficulty lies in the fact that nonlaboratory people have been fed up on the omnibus theory.

I have here tried to state the basic issues involved in the theory of specific measures so that comparison may be made with the omnibus theory. Musical guidance is a new and very complicated procedure. I agree with Professor Mursell that we should beware of easy solutions. I am glad that he has made the cleavage in the issue so clear and that he has sounded a warning to his followers against the use of my specific measures of musical talent on his omnibus theory. It is my humble opinion that no creditable test of musical talent can be built on that theory.

BIBLIOGRAPHY

In addition to the replacing of footnote references this bibliography should be regarded as a grateful acknowledgment of indebtedness to authors and sources for material in this book. Where substantial parts of these contributions have been utilized, this is indicated by superscript numbers in the appropriate places of the text. This list should, therefore, not be regarded as a general bibliography on the psychology of music, or the complete writings of any one author on this subject, as only those sources which are most significant for the present purpose are mentioned.

Since three series of technical studies are referred to so frequently, the following abbreviations have been adopted:

For the *University of Iowa Studies in Psychology*, The University Press, Iowa City, Iowa, abbreviation: *Ia. St. Psy.*

(This series of studies is published in the *Psychological Review Monographs*, and the articles are often listed by the serial number in that publication.)

For the *University of Iowa Studies in the Psychology of Music*, The University Press, Iowa City, Iowa, abbreviation: *Ia. St. Mus.*

For the *Journal of the Acoustic Society of America*, abbreviation: *J. A. S. A.*

1. Abbott, R. B. Response measurement and harmonic analysis of violin tones, *J. A. S. A.* VII, 1936, 111–116.

1a. Acoust. Soc. Amer. Report of committee on acoustical standardization, *J. A. S. A.*, II, 1931, 311–324.

2. Agnew, Marie. The auditory imagery of great composers, *Ia. St. Psy.*, VIII, 1922, 279–287.

3. Agnew, Marie. A comparison of auditory images of musicians, psychologists and children, *Ia. St. Psy.*, VIII, 1922, 268–278.

4. Baier, Everett D. The loudness of complex sounds, *J. Exper. Psychol.*, XIX, No. 3, 1926.

5. Bannister, H. Audition, *Hand. Gen. Exper. Psychol.*, Clark Univ. Press, 1934, 880–923.

6. Bartholomew, W. T. Physical definition of good voice quality in the male voice, *J. A. S. A.*, VI, 1934, 25–33.

7. Bedell, E. H. Auditorium acoustics and control facilities for reproductions in the auditory perspective, *Bell Lab. Record,* XII, 1934, 199–202.

8. Black, John W. The quality of the spoken vowel, *Arch. Sp.*, II, 1937, 7–27.

9. Borchers, O. The timbre vibrato, *The Psychological Record* (in press).

10. Brennan, Florence. The relation between musical capacity and performance, *Ia. St. Psy.*, IX, 1926, 200–248.

11. BRENNAN, FLORENCE. A report of three singing tests—given by the tonoscope, *Ia. St. Psy.*, IX, 1926, 249–262.
12. CHESLOCK, L. An introductory study of the violin vibrato, *Res. St. in Mus.*, *No.* 1, Baltimore, Peabody Conservatory, 1931.
13. COWAN, MILTON. Pitch and intensity characteristics of American dramatic speech, Thesis, Univ. of Iowa Library, Iowa City, 1935.
14. COWAN, MILTON. Pitch and intensity characteristics of stage speech, *Arch. Sp.*, I, Suppl.
15. DAVENPORT and STEGGERDA. Race crossings in Jamaica, *Carnegie Inst.*, *Pub.* 395, Washington, D.C., 1929.
16. DAVIS, ALFRED HORACE. *Modern Acoustics*, Macmillan, New York, 1934.
17. DAVIS, H., and STEVENS, S. S. Psychophysical acoustics: pitch and loudness, *J. A. S. A.*, VIII, 1936, 1–13.
18. DENSMORE, FRANCES. *The American Indians and Their Music*, The Women's Press, New York, 1926.
19. EASLEY, ELEANOR. A comparison of the vibrato in concert and opera singing, *Ia. St. Mus.*, I, 1932, 269–275.
20. ERICKSON, CARL I. The basic factors in the human voice, *Ia. St. Psy.*, X, 1926, 82–112.
21. FARNSWORTH, PAUL R. Are musical capacity tests more important than intelligence tests in the prediction of the several types of music grades? *J. Appl. Psychol.*, XIX, 1935, 347–350.
22. FARNSWORTH, PAUL R. Comments on Duo-art as a laboratory instrument, *J. Appl. Psychol.*, XII, 1928, 214–216.
23. FIRESTONE, F. A. The phase differences and amplitude ratio at the ears due to a source of piano tone, *J. A. S. A.*, II, 1930, 260–270.
24. FLETCHER, HARVEY. Loudness, pitch, and the timbre of musical tones and their relation to the intensity, the frequency, and the overtone structure, *J. A. S. A.*, VI, 1934, 59–69.
25. FLETCHER, HARVEY. Newer concepts of pitch, loudness, and timbre of musical tones, *J. Franklin Inst.*, 220, 1935, 205–429.
26. FLETCHER, HARVEY. Some physical characteristics of speech and music, *Rev. Modern Physics*, April, 1931.
27. FLETCHER, HARVEY. *Speech and Hearing*, Van Nostrand, New York, 1929.
28. FLETCHER, HARVEY. The physical criterion for determining the pitch of a musical tone, *Phys. Rev.*, XXIII, 1924.
29. FLETCHER, HARVEY, and MUNSON, W. Loudness, its definition, measurement and calculation, *J. A. S. A.*, V, 1933, 102.
30. FLETCHER, HARVEY, and STEINBERG, J. C. Loudness of a complex sound, *Phys. Rev.*, XXIV, 1924, 306–317.
30*a*. GARTH, T. R. *Race Psychology*, McGraw-Hill, New York, 1931.
31. GAW, ESTHER ALLEN. A revision of the consonance test, *Ia. St. Psy.*, VII, 1918, 134–147.
32. GAW, ESTHER ALLEN. A survey of musical talent in the music school, *Ia. St. Psy.*, VIII, 1922, 128–156.
33. GEMELLI, AGOSTINO. Nuovo contributo alla conoscenza della struttura delle vocali, *Commentationes*, I, 1937.

34. GEMELLI, AGOSTINO, and PASTORI, GIUSEPPINA. *L'analisi Elettroacustica del Linguaggio*, 2 vols., Milan, 1934.

35. GEMELLI, AGOSTINO. Nuovi risultati nell'applicazione dei metodi dell'-elettroacustica allo studio della psicologia del linguaggio, *Estud. Rend. d. Sem. Matematico e Fisico d. Milano*, XI, 1937, 1–21.

36. GHOSH, R. N. Elastic impact of a pianoforte hammer, *J. A. S. A.*, VII, 1936, 254–260.

37. GHOSH, R. N. On the tone quality of pianoforte, *J. A. S. A.*, VII, 1936, 27–28.

38. GREENE, PAUL C. Violin intonation, *J. A. S. A.*, IX, 1937, 43–44.

39. GREENE, PAUL C. Violin performance with reference to tempered, natural and Pythagorean intonation, *Ia. St. Mus.*, IV, 1937, 232–251.

40. HALL, HARRY H. Recording analyzer for the audible frequency range, *J. A. S. A.*, VII, 1935, 102–110.

41. HATTWICK, MELVIN. The vibrato in wind instruments, *Ia. St. Mus.*, I, 1932, 276–280.

42. HANSON, C. F. Serial action as a measure of basic motor capacity, *Ia. St. Psy.*, VIII, 1922, 320–383.

43. HART, C. H., *et al.* A precision study of piano touch and tone, *J. A. S. A.*. VI. 1934, 80–94.

44. HEINLEIN, C. P. An experimental study of the Seashore consonance test, *J. Exper. Psychol.*, VIII, 1925, 408–433.

45. HEINLEIN, C. P. A new method of studying rhythmic responses of children together with an evaluation of the method of simple observation. *J. Genet. Psychol.*, XXXVI, 1929, 205–228.

46. HENDERSON, MACK T. Rhythmic organization in artistic piano performance, *Ia. St. Mus.*, IV, 1937, 281–305.

46*a*. HENDERSON, MACK T. Remedial measures in motor rhythm as applied to piano performance, Thesis, Univ. of Iowa Library, Iowa City, 1931.

47. HENDERSON, M. T., TIFFIN, JOSEPH, and SEASHORE, CARL E. The Iowa piano camera and its use, *Ia. St. Mus.*, IV, 1937, 252–262.

48. HEVNER, K. Studies in appreciation of art, *Univ. of Ore. Publication* IV. *No.* 6, 1934.

49. HICKMAN, C. N. Acoustic spectrometer, *J. A. S. A.*, VI, 1934, 108–111.

50. HIRSCH, NATHANIEL D. *Dynamic Causes of Juvenile Crime*, Art Publisher. Cambridge, Mass., 1937.

51. HIROSE, K. An experimental study of the principal pitch in the vibrato, *Japan. J. Psychol.*, IX, 1934, 793–845.

52. HOLLINSHEAD, MERRILL T. A study of the vibrato in artistic violin playing, *Ia. St. Mus.*, I, 1932, 281–288.

53. HORNE, R. Structure and function of the violin mute, dissertation, Univ. of Iowa, 1938.

54. JACOBSEN, EDMUND. Electrophysiology of mental activities, *Am. J. Psychol.* XLIV, 1932, 677–694.

55. JASTROW, JOSEPH. *The Qualities of Men*, Houghton Mifflin, Boston, 1910.

55*a*. JOHNSON, G. B. The negro and musical talent, *Southern Workman*, LI, 1927, 339–344.

56. JOHNSTONE, J. A. *Phrasing in Piano Playing*, Witmark, New York, 1913.
57. JOHNSTONE, J. A. *Touch Phrasing and Interpretation*, Reeves, London, 19—.
58. KELLEY, NOBLE. A comparative study of the response of normal and pathological ears to speech sounds, *J. Exper. Psychol.*, XXI (September), 1937, 342–352.
59. KELLEY, NOBLE. Presbycousis, *J. A. S. A.* (in press).
60. KELLEY, NOBLE, and REGER, SCOTT N. The effect of binaural occlusion of the external auditory meati on the sensitivity of the ear for bone conducted sound, *J. Exper. Psychol.*, XXI, August, 1937, 211–217.
61. KNOCK, CARL J. Visual training of the pitch of the voice, *Ia. St. Psy.*, VIII, 1922, 102–127.
62. KNUDSEN, V. O. The sensibility of the ear to small differences of intensity and frequency, *Phys. Rev.*, XXI, 1923, 84–102.
63. KOCH, HANS, and MJOEN, FRIDTJOF. Die Erblichkeit der Musikalität, *Zsch. Psychol.*, 121, 104–136.
64. KOCK, WINSTON E. Certain subjective phenomena accompanying a frequency vibrato, *J. A. S. A.*, VIII, 1936, 23–25.
65. KOERTH, WILHELMINA. A pursuit meter: eye-hand coordination, *Ia. St. Psy.*, VIII, 1922, 288–292.
66. KLEIN, HERMAN. *Great Women Singers of My Time*, E. P. Dutton, New York, 1931.
67. KULLAK, A. *Esthetics of Pianoforte Playing*, Schirmer, New York, 1893.
68. KURTZ, E. B., and LARSEN, M. J. An electrostatic audio generator, *Elec. Eng.*, September, 1935.
69. KWALWASSER, J. *Tests and Measurements in Music*, Birchard, New York, 1927.
70. KWALWASSER, J. The vibrato, *Ia. St. Psy.*, IX, 1926, 84–108.
71. LAASE, LEROY T. The effect of pitch and intensity on the quality of vowels in speech, *Arch. Sp.*, II, 1937, 41–61.
72. LARSEN, M. J. An electrostatic tone generator, *J. A. S. A.* (in press).
73. LARSON, DELIA. An experimental critique of the Seashore consonance test, *Ia. St. Psy.*, XI, 1928, 49–81.
74. LARSON, RUTH C. Studies on Seashore's "Measures of Musical Talent," Univ. of Ia. series, *Aims and Progr. of Res.*, II, 1930.
75. LARSON, WILLIAM S. Measurement of talent for the prediction of success in instrumental music, *Ia. St. Psy.*, XIII, 1930, 33–73.
76. LENOIR, ZAID D. Racial differences in musical capacities, thesis, Univ. of Iowa Library, Iowa City, 1925.
77. LEWIS, DON. Pitch: its definition and physical determinants, *Ia. St. Mus.*, IV, 1937, 346–373.
78. LEWIS, DON. Vocal resonance, *J. A. S. A.*, VIII, 1936, 91–99.
79. LEWIS, DON, and COWAN, MILTON. The influence of intensity upon pitch of violin and cello tones, *J. A. S. A.*, VIII, 1936, 20–22.
80. LEWIS, DON, COWAN, MILTON, and FAIRBANKS, GRANT. Pitch variations arising from certain types of frequency modulation, *J. A. S. A.*, IX, 1937, 79.
81. LEWIS, DON, and LARSEN, M. J. The cancellation, reinforcement and measurement of subjective tones, *Proc. Nat. Acad. Sci.*, XXIII, 1937, 415–421.

82. LEWIS, DON, and REGER, SCOTT N. Experimental study of the role of the tympanic membrane and the ossicles in the hearing of certain subjective tones, *J. A. S. A.*, V, 1933, 153–158.

83. LINDER, FORREST E. Measurement of the pitch extent of the vibrato on attack, release, and transition tones, *Ia. St. Mus.*, I, 1932, 245–249.

84. MALMBERG, C. F. The perception of consonance and dissonance, *Ia. St. Psy.*, VII, 1918, 93–133.

85. METFESSEL, MILTON. *Phonophotography in Folk Music*, Univ. of North Carolina Press, Chapel Hill, 1928.

86. METFESSEL, MILTON. Sonance as a form of tonal fusion, *Psychol. Rev.* XXXIII, 1926, 459–466.

87. METFESSEL, MILTON. Techniques for objective studies of the vocal art, *Ia. St. Psy.*, IX, 1926, 1–40.

88. METFESSEL, MILTON. The strobophotograph; a device for measuring pitch, *J. Gen. Psychol.*, II, 1929, 135–138.

89. METFESSEL, MILTON. The vibrato in artistic voices, *Ia. St. Mus.*, I, 1932, 14–117.

90. METFESSEL, MILTON. What is the voice vibrato? *Ia. St. Psy.*, XII, 1928, 126–154.

91. METZGER, WOLFGANG. The mode of vibration of the vocal cords, *Ia. St. Psy.*, XI, 1928, 82–159.

92. MILES, WALTER R. Accuracy of the voice in simple pitch singing, *Ia. St. Psy.*, VI, 13–66.

93. MILLER, D. C. *Anecdotal History of the Science of Sound*, Macmillan, New York, 1935.

94. MILLER, D. C. *Science of Musical Sounds*, Macmillan, New York, 1926.

95. MILLER, RAY E. A strobophotographic analysis of a Tlingil Indian's speech, *Int. J. Amer. Ling.*, VI (March), 1930, 47–68.

96. MILLER, RAY E. The pitch of the attack in singing, *Ia. St. Mus.*, IV, 1937, 158–171.

97. MILLER, RAY E. The pitch vibrato in artistic gliding intonations, *Ia. St. Mus.*, I, 1932, 250–268.

98. MILLS, JOHN. *A Fugue in Cycles and Bells*, Van Nostrand, New York, 1935.

99. MJOEN, J. A., and MJOEN, F. Die Bedeuting der Tonhöhenunterschiedsempfindlichkeit für die Musikalität und ihr Vertalten bei der Vererbung, *Hereditas*, VII, 1926, 161–188.

100. MJOEN, J. A. Die Vererbung der musikalischen Begabung, Alfred Metzner, Berlin, 1934.

100*a*. MURDOCK, KATHERINE M. A study of differences found between races in intellect and morality, *School and Society*, XXII, 1925, 564–569, 628–632.

100*b*. *Music Educators Journal.* (See Preface, pp. ix, x.)

101. National Association of Musical Instrument Manufacturers.

102. NIELSEN, J. T. A study of the Seashore motor rhythm test, *Ia. St. Psy.*, XIII, 1930, 74–84.

103. ORTMANN, OTTO. *The Physical Basis of Piano Touch and Tone*, Dutton, New York, 1925.

104. ORTMANN, OTTO. *The Physiological Mechanics of Piano Technique*, Dutton, New York, 1929.

105. PARMENTER, C. E., and TREVINO, S. N. A technique for the analysis of pitch in connected discourse, *Arch. néerland. Phon. Exper.*, VII, 1932, 1–29.

106. PETERSEN, J., and LANIER, L. H. Studies in the comparative abilities of whites and negroes, *Ment. Meas. Monog.*, *No.* 5, 1929.

107. REAM, M. J. The tapping test—a measure of motility, *Ia. St. Psy.*, VIII, 1922, 293–319.

108. REGER, SCOTT N. Historical survey of the string instrument vibrato, *Ia. St. Mus.*, I, 1932, 289–304.

109. REGER, SCOTT N. The string instrument vibrato, *Ia. St. Mus.*, I, 1932, 305–338.

110. REGER, SCOTT N. A history of the measurement and analysis of hearing ability (unpublished).

111. REGER, SCOTT N. The threshold of feeling in the ear in relation to artificial hearing aids, *Ia. St. Psy.*, XVII, 1933, 74–94.

112. RIETSZ, R. R. Differential intensity sensitivity of the ear for pure tones, *Phys. Rev.*, XXXI, 1928, 867–875.

112*a*. ROSS, VERNE R. Relationships between intelligence, scholastic achievements, and musical talent. *Calif. Bureau of Juv. Res.*, Claremont, Calif., 1937.

113. ROTHSCHILD, D. A. The timbre vibrato, *Ia. St. Mus.*, I, 1932, 236–244.

114. RUCKMICK, CHRISTIAN A. A bibliography of rhythm, *Amer. J. Psychol.*, XXIX, 1918, 214–218; see also XXIV, 1913, 508–519; XXVI, 1915, 457–459.

115. SCHOEN, MAX. An experimental study of the pitch factor in artistic singing, *Ia. St. Psy.*, VIII, 1922, 231–259.

116. SCHOEN, MAX. The esthetic attitude in music, *Ia. St. Psy.*, XII, 1928, 162–183.

117. SCHRAMM, W. L. Approaches to a science of English verse, Univ. of Ia. series, *Aims and Progr. of Res. No.* 44, 1935.

118. SEASHORE, CARL E. A base for the approach to quantitative studies in the esthetics of music, *Amer. J. Psychol.*, XXXIV, 1927, 141–144.

118*a*. SEASHORE, CARL E. (Autobiography) *Hist. of Psychol.* in *Autobiogr.*, Clark Univ. Press, Worcester, 1930, 225–297.

119. SEASHORE, CARL E [ed.]. The vibrato, *Ia. St. Mus.*, I, 1932.

119*a*. SEASHORE, CARL E. Educational guidance in music, *School and Society*, XLV, 1937, 385–393.

120. SEASHORE, CARL E. Educational guidance in music, *National Society for the Study of Education, Yearbook*, 1934, 385–393.

121. SEASHORE, CARL E. Individual and racial inheritance of musical traits, Eugenics, Genetics and the Family, *Proc. Int. Congr. Genet.*, I, 1923.

122. SEASHORE, CARL E. The inheritance of musical talent, *Musical Quarterly*, VI, 1920, 586–598.

123. SEASHORE, CARL E. *Introduction to Psychology*, Macmillan, New York, 1923.

124. SEASHORE, CARL E. Learning and living in college, Univ. of Ia. series, *Aims and Progr. of Res.*, II, 1927.

125. SEASHORE, CARL E. *Manual of Instructions and Interpretations of Measures of Musical Talent*, C. H. Stoelting, Chicago, 1919.

126. SEASHORE, CARL E. Measurement of the expression of emotion in music, *Proc. Nat. Acad. Sci.*, IV, 1923, 323–325.

127. SEASHORE, CARL E. The measurement of pitch discrimination, *Psychol. Monog.*, XIII, 1910, 21–63.

128. SEASHORE, CARL E. The measurement of pitch intonation with the tonoscope in singing and playing, Univ. of Ia. series, *Aims and Progr. of Res.*, II, 1930.

129. SEASHORE, CARL E. The measure of a singer, *Science*, XXXV, 1912, 201–212.

130. SEASHORE, CARL E. The musical mind, *Atlantic Monthly*, March, 1928, 358–367.

131. SEASHORE, CARL E. Natural history of the frequency of the vibrato, *Proc. Nat. Acad. Sci.*, XVII, 1931, 623–626.

132. SEASHORE, CARL E. New vantage grounds in the psychology of music, *Science*, LXXXIV, 1936, 517–522.

133. SEASHORE, CARL E. Phonophotography as a new approach to the psychology of emotion. *Feelings and Emotions* (Wittenberg Symposium), Clark Univ. Press, Worcester, 1928, 206–214.

134. SEASHORE, CARL E. Phonophotography in the measurement of the expression of emotion in music and speech, *Sci. Monthly*, XXIV, 1927, 463–471.

134*a*. SEASHORE, CARL E. Piano touch, *Sci. Monthly*, XLV, 1937, 360–365.

135. SEASHORE, CARL E. The present status of research in the psychology of music at the University of Iowa, Univ. of Ia. series, *Aims and Progr. of Res.*, IV, 1928.

136. SEASHORE, CARL E. *Psychology in Daily Life*, Appleton, New York, 1913.

137. SEASHORE, CARL E. *The Psychology of Musical Talent*, XVI, Silver, Burdett, New York, 1919.

138. SEASHORE, CARL E. Psychology in music: the role of experimental psychology in the science and art of music, *Musical Quarterly*, XVI, 1930, 229–237.

139. SEASHORE, CARL E. The psychology of the vibrato in music and speech, *Proc. Int. Congr. Psychol.*, *Acta Psychol.*, The Hague, 1935.

140. SEASHORE, CARL E. Psychology of the vibrato in voice and instrument, *Ia. St. Mus.*, III, 1935, pp. 159.

141. SEASHORE, CARL E. The role of mental measurement in the discovery and motivation of the gifted student, *Proc. Nat. Acad. Sci.*, II, 1925, 542–545.

142. SEASHORE, CARL E. Seeing yourself singing, *Science*, XLIII, 1916, 592–596.

143. SEASHORE, CARL E. The sense of rhythm as a musical talent, *Musical Quarterly*, IV, 1918, 507–515.

144. SEASHORE, CARL E. Some new instruments in the Iowa laboratory for the psychology of music, *J. A. S. A.*, II, 1930, 75–78.

145. SEASHORE, CARL E. A survey of musical talent in the public schools, Univ. of Ia., *St. in Child Welfare*, I, 1920.

145*a*. SEASHORE, CARL E. Three new approaches to the study of negro music, *Ann. Amer. Acad. Pol. Soc. Sci.*, CIL, 1928, 191–192.

146. SEASHORE, CARL E. The tonoscope and its use in the training of the voice, *The Musician*, XI, 1906, 331–332.

147. SEASHORE, CARL E. Vocational guidance in music, Univ. of Ia. series, *Aims and Progr. of Res.*, II, 1916, 1–11.

148. SEASHORE, CARL E. A voice tonoscope, *Ia. St. Psy.*, III, 1902, 1–17.
149. SEASHORE, CARL E., and JENNER, E. A. Training the voice by aid of the eye, *J. Educ. Psychol.*, I, 1910, 311–320.
150. SEASHORE, CARL E., and METFESSEL, MILTON. Deviation from the regular as an art principle, *Proc. Nat. Acad. Sci.*, II, 1925, 538–542.
151. SEASHORE, CARL E., and SEASHORE, HAROLD G. The place of phonophotography in the study of primitive music, *Science*, LXXIX, 1934, 385–487.
152. SEASHORE, CARL E., and SEASHORE, ROBERT H. *Elementary Experiments in Psychology*, Holt, New York, 1935.
153. SEASHORE, HAROLD G. Forms of artistic pitch deviations in singing, *Psychol. Bull.*, XXXI, 1934, 677–678.
154. SEASHORE, HAROLD G. The hearing of the pitch and intensity in vibrato, *Ia. St. Mus.*, I, 1932, 213–235.
155. SEASHORE, HAROLD G. An objective analysis of artistic singing, *Ia. St. Mus.*, IV, 1935, 12–157.
156. SEASHORE, HAROLD G. The relative importance of intensity and time stress in singing, *Proc. Ia. Acad. Sci.*, XXXXI, 1934, 287–389.
157. SEASHORE, HAROLD G., and TIFFIN, JOSEPH. Summary of established facts in experimental studies on the vibrato up to 1932, *Ia. St. Mus.*, I, 1932, 344–376.
158. SEASHORE, ROBERT H. Studies in motor rhythm, *Ia. St. Psy.*, IX, 1926, 142–199.
159. SEASHORE, ROBERT H. Individual differences in motor skills, *J. Gen. Psychol.*, III, 1930, 38–66.
160. SEASHORE, SIGFRID. The aptitude hypothesis in motor skills, *J. Exper. Psychol.*, XIV, 1931, 555–561.
161. SHOWER, E. G., and BIDDULPH, R. Differential pitch sensitivity of the ear, *J. A. S. A.*, III, 1931, 275–287.
162. SIMON, CLARENCE. The variability in consecutive wave lengths in vocal and instrumental sounds, *Ia. St. Psy.*, IX, 1926, 41–83.
163. SIVIAN, L. J., JUNN, H. K., and WHITE, S. D. Absolute amplitudes and spectra, *J. A. S. A.*, II, 1931, 330–371.
164. SIVIAN, L. J., and WHITE, S. D. Minimum audible sound fields, *J. A. S. A.*, IV, 1933, 288–321.
165. SKINNER, LAILA, and SEASHORE, CARL E. A musical pattern score of the first movement of the Beethoven Sonata, op. 27, no. 2, *Ia. St. Mus.*, IV, 1937. 263–280.
165*a*. SKINNER, LAILA. Some temporal aspects of piano playing, Thesis, Univ. of Iowa Library, Iowa City, 1930.
166. SMALL, ARNOLD M. An objective analysis of artistic violin performance, *Ia. St. Mus.*, IV, 1937, 172–231.
167. SMALL, ARNOLD M. Response characteristics of the violin, *J. A. S. A.*, (in press).
168. SMITH, F. O. The effect of training in pitch discrimination, *Ia. St. Psy.*, VI, 1914, 67–103.
169. SNOW, W. B. Auditory perspective, *Bell Lab. Record*, XII, 1934, 194–198.

170. SNOW, W. B. Audible frequency ranges of music, speech and noise, *J. A. S. A.*, III, 1931, 151–166.

171. SNOW, W. B. Change of pitch with loudness at low frequencies, *J. A. S. A.*, VIII, 1936, 14–19.

172. STANLEY, DOUGLAS. *The Science of Voice,* Fischer, New York, 1929.

173. STANLEY, DOUGLAS, and MAXFIELD, J. P. *The Voice, Its Production and Reproduction,* Pitman, New York, 1933.

174. STANTON, HAZEL M. An experimental investigation of musical inheritance, *Eugenics, Genetics and the Family,* I, 1923.

175. STANTON, HAZEL M. The inheritance of specific musical capacities, *Ia. St. Psy.*, VIII, 1922, 157–204.

176. STANTON, HAZEL M. Measurement of musical talent, *Ia. St. Mus.*, II, 1935.

177. STANTON, HAZEL M. *Psychological Tests of Musical Talent,* Eastman School of Music, Univ. of Rochester, 1925.

178. STEINBERG, J. C. Application of sound measuring instruments to the study of phonetic problems, *J. A. S. A.*, VI, 1934, 16–24.

179. STEINBERG, J. C. Positions of stimulation in the cochlea by pure tones, *J. A. S. A.*, VIII, 1937, 176–180.

180. STEINBERG, J. C., and MUNSON, W. A. Deviations in the loudness judgments of 100 people, *J. A. S. A.*, VIII, 1936, 71–80.

181. STETSON, R. H. The breathing movements in singing, *Arch. néerland. Phon. Exper.*, VI, 1931, 115–165.

182. STEVENS, F. A., and MILES, W. R. The first vocal vibrations in the attack in singing, *Psychol. Monog.*, XXXVII, 1928, 200–229.

183. STEVENS, S. S. The relation of pitch to intensity, *J. A. S. A.*, VI, 1935, 150–154.

184. STEVENS, S. S., VOLKMANN, J., and NEWMAN, E. B. Scale for the measurement of the psychological magnitude pitch, *J. A. S. A.*, VIII, 1937, 185–190.

185. STEWART, G. W. *Introductory Acoustics,* Van Nostrand, New York, 1933.

186. STODDARD, GEORGE, and WELLMAN, BETH L. *Child Psychology,* Macmillan, New York, 1936.

187. STOUT, BARRETT. The harmonic structure of vowels in singing in relation to pitch and intensity, Thesis, Univ. of Iowa Library, Iowa City, 1937.

188. STÜCKER, N. *Zsch. Sinnesphysiol.*, XLII, 1908.

189. STUMPF, CARL. Differenztone und Konsonanze, *Zsch. Psychol. Physiol.*, XXXIX, 1905, 269–283.

190. STUMPF, CARL. Konsonanz und Dissonanz, *Beitr. Ak. Musikwiss.*, I, 1898, 91–107.

191. STUMPF, CARL. Beobachtungen über Kombinationstone, *Beitr. Ak. Musikwiss.*, V, 3–133.

192. STUMPF, CARL. Die Unmusikalischen und Tonverschmelzung, *Zsch. Psychol. Physiol.*, XVII, 1898, 422.

193. STUMPF, CARL. Neueres über Tonverschmelzung, *Zsch. Psychol. Physiol.*, XV, 1897, 280–303.

194. STUMPF, CARL. *Die Anfange der Musik,* Leipzig, 1911.

195. TALLEY, HORTON C. A comparison of conversational and audience speech, *Arch. Sp.*, II, 1937, 28–40.

196. TIFFIN, JOSEPH. A vibrato tonometer, *Science*, 70, 1929, 73.

197. TIFFIN, JOSEPH. Characteristics of children's vibratos, Thesis, Univ. of Iowa Library, Iowa City, 1928.

198. TIFFIN, JOSEPH. Phonophotograph apparatus, *Ia. St. Mus.*, I, 1932, 118–133.

199. TIFFIN, JOSEPH. The psychophysics of the vibrato, *Ia. St. Psy.*, XIV, 1931, 153–200.

200. TIFFIN, JOSEPH. Recent studies in the science of the art of speech from the Iowa laboratory, *Ia. St. Mus.*, IV, 1937, 374–376.

201. TIFFIN, JOSEPH. The role of pitch and intensity in the vocal vibrato of students and artists, *Ia. St. Mus.*, I, 1932, 134–165.

202. TIFFIN, JOSEPH, and SEASHORE, HAROLD. Summary of established facts in experimental studies on the vibrato up to 1932, *Ia. St. Mus.*, I, 1932, 344–376.

203. TUTHILL, CURTIS E. Timbre and sonance aspects of the sustained vowel, Thesis, Univ. of Iowa Library, Iowa City, 1936.

204. VALENTINE, WILLARD LEE. *Readings in Experimental Psychology*, Harper, New York, 1931.

205. VAN DE WALL, W. *Music in Institutions*, Russell Sage Foundation, New York, 1936.

206. VERNON, L. M. Synchronization of chords in artistic piano music, *Ia. St. Mus.*, IV. 1937, 306–345.

206*a*. VOXMAN, H. The tone quality of the clarinet, Thesis, Univ. of Iowa Library, Iowa City, 1936.

207. WADA, Y. The influence of tonal backgrounds upon time-errors in the successive comparison of intensity of tones, *Japan. J. Psychol.*, X, 1935, 47–48.

208. WAGNER, ARNOLD H. An experimental study in the control of the vocal vibrato, *Ia. St. Psy.*, XIII, 1930, 166–214.

209. WAGNER, ARNOLD H. Remedial and artistic development of the vibrato, *Ia. St. Mus.*, I, 1932, 166–212.

210. WEGEL, R. L. The physical examination of hearing and binaural aids for the deaf, *Proc. Nat. Acad. Sci.*, VIII, 1922, 155–160.

211. WEGEL, R. L., and LANE, C. E. The auditory masking of one pure tone by another, *Phys. Rev.*, XXIII, 1924, 266–285.

212. WEVER, E. G., and BRAY, C. W. The perception of low tones and the resonance-volley theory, *J. Physiol.*, III, 101–114.

213. WHITE, WILLIAM. Musical instruments and acoustical science, *J. A. S. A.*, VIII, 1936, 62–63.

214. WILLIAMS, HAROLD M. An audiometric test for young children, *Child Development*, II, 1931, 237–241.

215. WILLIAMS, HAROLD M. Experimental studies in the use of the tonoscope, *Ia. St. Psy.*, XIV, 1931, 266–327.

216. WILLIAMS, HAROLD M. A note in regard to the extent of the vibrato, *Ia. St. Psy.*

217. WILLIAMS, HAROLD M. A study in the prediction of motor rhythmic performance of school children, *J. Genet. Psychol.*, 43, 1933, 377–388.

218. WILLIAMS, HAROLD M., and HATTWICK, MELVIN S. The measurement of musical development, Univ. of Ia., *St. in Child Welfare*, II, 1935.

219. WILLIAMS, HAROLD M., SIEVERS, CLEMENT H., and HATTWICK, MELVIN S. The measurement of musical development, Univ. of Ia., *St. in Child Welfare*, VII, *No.* 1, 1933.

220. WOLF, S. K., STANLEY, D., and SETTE, W. J. Quantitative studies of the singing voice, *J. A. S. A.*, VI, 1935, 255–266.

221. YASSER, J. A theory of evolving tonality, *Amer. Libr. Musicol.*, Contemp. Ser., I, 1932.

222. ZWIRNER, EBERHARD, and ZWIRNER, KURT. *Grundfragen der Phonometrik*, Berlin, 1936.

Mentioned or Quoted in the Text

INDEX TO MUSICIANS

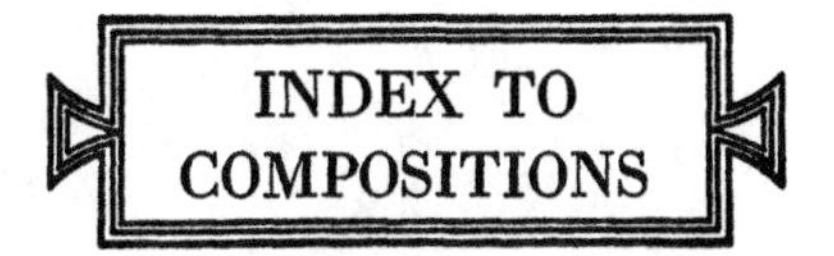

INDEX TO COMPOSITIONS

SUBJECT INDEX

A CATALOG OF SELECTED
DOVER BOOKS
IN ALL FIELDS OF INTEREST

A CATALOG OF SELECTED DOVER BOOKS IN ALL FIELDS OF INTEREST

CATALOG OF DOVER BOOKS

ALICE'S ADVENTURES IN WONDERLAND, Lewis Carroll. Beloved classic about a little girl lost in a topsy-turvy land and her encounters with the White Rabbit, March Hare, Mad Hatter, Cheshire Cat, and other delightfully improbable characters. 42 illustrations by Sir John Tenniel. 96pp. 5³⁄₁₆ x 8¼. 0-486-27543-4

AMERICA'S LIGHTHOUSES: An Illustrated History, Francis Ross Holland. Profusely illustrated fact-filled survey of American lighthouses since 1716. Over 200 stations — East, Gulf, and West coasts, Great Lakes, Hawaii, Alaska, Puerto Rico, the Virgin Islands, and the Mississippi and St. Lawrence Rivers. 240pp. 8 x 10¾. 0-486-25576-X

AN ENCYCLOPEDIA OF THE VIOLIN, Alberto Bachmann. Translated by Frederick H. Martens. Introduction by Eugene Ysaye. First published in 1925, this renowned reference remains unsurpassed as a source of essential information, from construction and evolution to repertoire and technique. Includes a glossary and 73 illustrations. 496pp. 6⅛ x 9¼. 0-486-46618-3

ANIMALS: 1,419 Copyright-Free Illustrations of Mammals, Birds, Fish, Insects, etc., Selected by Jim Harter. Selected for its visual impact and ease of use, this outstanding collection of wood engravings presents over 1,000 species of animals in extremely lifelike poses. Includes mammals, birds, reptiles, amphibians, fish, insects, and other invertebrates. 284pp. 9 x 12. 0-486-23766-4

THE ANNALS, Tacitus. Translated by Alfred John Church and William Jackson Brodribb. This vital chronicle of Imperial Rome, written by the era's great historian, spans A.D. 14-68 and paints incisive psychological portraits of major figures, from Tiberius to Nero. 416pp. 5³⁄₁₆ x 8¼. 0-486-45236-0

ANTIGONE, Sophocles. Filled with passionate speeches and sensitive probing of moral and philosophical issues, this powerful and often-performed Greek drama reveals the grim fate that befalls the children of Oedipus. Footnotes. 64pp. 5³⁄₁₆ x 8 ¼. 0-486-27804-2

ART DECO DECORATIVE PATTERNS IN FULL COLOR, Christian Stoll. Reprinted from a rare 1910 portfolio, 160 sensuous and exotic images depict a breathtaking array of florals, geometrics, and abstracts — all elegant in their stark simplicity. 64pp. 8⅜ x 11. 0-486-44862-2

THE ARTHUR RACKHAM TREASURY: 86 Full-Color Illustrations, Arthur Rackham. Selected and Edited by Jeff A. Menges. A stunning treasury of 86 full-page plates span the famed English artist's career, from *Rip Van Winkle* (1905) to masterworks such as *Undine, A Midsummer Night's Dream,* and *Wind in the Willows* (1939). 96pp. 8⅜ x 11. 0-486-44685-9

THE AUTHENTIC GILBERT & SULLIVAN SONGBOOK, W. S. Gilbert and A. S. Sullivan. The most comprehensive collection available, this songbook includes selections from every one of Gilbert and Sullivan's light operas. Ninety-two numbers are presented uncut and unedited, and in their original keys. 410pp. 9 x 12. 0-486-23482-7

THE AWAKENING, Kate Chopin. First published in 1899, this controversial novel of a New Orleans wife's search for love outside a stifling marriage shocked readers. Today, it remains a first-rate narrative with superb characterization. New introductory Note. 128pp. 5³⁄₁₆ x 8¼. 0-486-27786-0

BASIC DRAWING, Louis Priscilla. Beginning with perspective, this commonsense manual progresses to the figure in movement, light and shade, anatomy, drapery, composition, trees and landscape, and outdoor sketching. Black-and-white illustrations throughout. 128pp. 8⅜ x 11. 0-486-45815-6

Browse over 9,000 books at www.doverpublications.com

THE BATTLES THAT CHANGED HISTORY, Fletcher Pratt. Historian profiles 16 crucial conflicts, ancient to modern, that changed the course of Western civilization. Gripping accounts of battles led by Alexander the Great, Joan of Arc, Ulysses S. Grant, other commanders. 27 maps. 352pp. 5⅜ x 8½. 0-486-41129-X

BEETHOVEN'S LETTERS, Ludwig van Beethoven. Edited by Dr. A. C. Kalischer. Features 457 letters to fellow musicians, friends, greats, patrons, and literary men. Reveals musical thoughts, quirks of personality, insights, and daily events. Includes 15 plates. 410pp. 5⅜ x 8½. 0-486-22769-3

BERNICE BOBS HER HAIR AND OTHER STORIES, F. Scott Fitzgerald. This brilliant anthology includes 6 of Fitzgerald's most popular stories: "The Diamond as Big as the Ritz," the title tale, "The Offshore Pirate," "The Ice Palace," "The Jelly Bean," and "May Day." 176pp. 5⅜ x 8½. 0-486-47049-0

BESLER'S BOOK OF FLOWERS AND PLANTS: 73 Full-Color Plates from Hortus Eystettensis, 1613, Basilius Besler. Here is a selection of magnificent plates from the *Hortus Eystettensis,* which vividly illustrated and identified the plants, flowers, and trees that thrived in the legendary German garden at Eichstätt. 80pp. 8⅜ x 11. 0-486-46005-3

THE BOOK OF KELLS, Edited by Blanche Cirker. Painstakingly reproduced from a rare facsimile edition, this volume contains full-page decorations, portraits, illustrations, plus a sampling of textual leaves with exquisite calligraphy and ornamentation. 32 full-color illustrations. 32pp. 9⅜ x 12¼. 0-486-24345-1

THE BOOK OF THE CROSSBOW: With an Additional Section on Catapults and Other Siege Engines, Ralph Payne-Gallwey. Fascinating study traces history and use of crossbow as military and sporting weapon, from Middle Ages to modern times. Also covers related weapons: balistas, catapults, Turkish bows, more. Over 240 illustrations. 400pp. 7¼ x 10⅛. 0-486-28720-3

THE BUNGALOW BOOK: Floor Plans and Photos of 112 Houses, 1910, Henry L. Wilson. Here are 112 of the most popular and economic blueprints of the early 20th century — plus an illustration or photograph of each completed house. A wonderful time capsule that still offers a wealth of valuable insights. 160pp. 8⅜ x 11. 0-486-45104-6

THE CALL OF THE WILD, Jack London. A classic novel of adventure, drawn from London's own experiences as a Klondike adventurer, relating the story of a heroic dog caught in the brutal life of the Alaska Gold Rush. Note. 64pp. 5$\frac{3}{16}$ x 8¼. 0-486-26472-6

CANDIDE, Voltaire. Edited by Francois-Marie Arouet. One of the world's great satires since its first publication in 1759. Witty, caustic skewering of romance, science, philosophy, religion, government — nearly all human ideals and institutions. 112pp. 5$\frac{3}{16}$ x 8¼. 0-486-26689-3

CELEBRATED IN THEIR TIME: Photographic Portraits from the George Grantham Bain Collection, Edited by Amy Pastan. With an Introduction by Michael Carlebach. Remarkable portrait gallery features 112 rare images of Albert Einstein, Charlie Chaplin, the Wright Brothers, Henry Ford, and other luminaries from the worlds of politics, art, entertainment, and industry. 128pp. 8⅜ x 11. 0-486-46754-6

CHARIOTS FOR APOLLO: The NASA History of Manned Lunar Spacecraft to 1969, Courtney G. Brooks, James M. Grimwood, and Loyd S. Swenson, Jr. This illustrated history by a trio of experts is the definitive reference on the Apollo spacecraft and lunar modules. It traces the vehicles' design, development, and operation in space. More than 100 photographs and illustrations. 576pp. 6¾ x 9¼. 0-486-46756-2

A CHRISTMAS CAROL, Charles Dickens. This engrossing tale relates Ebenezer Scrooge's ghostly journeys through Christmases past, present, and future and his ultimate transformation from a harsh and grasping old miser to a charitable and compassionate human being. 80pp. 5³⁄₁₆ x 8¼. 0-486-26865-9

COMMON SENSE, Thomas Paine. First published in January of 1776, this highly influential landmark document clearly and persuasively argued for American separation from Great Britain and paved the way for the Declaration of Independence. 64pp. 5³⁄₁₆ x 8¼. 0-486-29602-4

THE COMPLETE SHORT STORIES OF OSCAR WILDE, Oscar Wilde. Complete texts of "The Happy Prince and Other Tales," "A House of Pomegranates," "Lord Arthur Savile's Crime and Other Stories," "Poems in Prose," and "The Portrait of Mr. W. H." 208pp. 5³⁄₁₆ x 8¼. 0-486-45216-6

COMPLETE SONNETS, William Shakespeare. Over 150 exquisite poems deal with love, friendship, the tyranny of time, beauty's evanescence, death, and other themes in language of remarkable power, precision, and beauty. Glossary of archaic terms. 80pp. 5³⁄₁₆ x 8¼. 0-486-26686-9

THE COUNT OF MONTE CRISTO: Abridged Edition, Alexandre Dumas. Falsely accused of treason, Edmond Dantès is imprisoned in the bleak Chateau d'If. After a hair-raising escape, he launches an elaborate plot to extract a bitter revenge against those who betrayed him. 448pp. 5³⁄₁₆ x 8¼. 0-486-45643-9

CRAFTSMAN BUNGALOWS: Designs from the Pacific Northwest, Yoho & Merritt. This reprint of a rare catalog, showcasing the charming simplicity and cozy style of Craftsman bungalows, is filled with photos of completed homes, plus floor plans and estimated costs. An indispensable resource for architects, historians, and illustrators. 112pp. 10 x 7. 0-486-46875-5

CRAFTSMAN BUNGALOWS: 59 Homes from "The Craftsman," Edited by Gustav Stickley. Best and most attractive designs from Arts and Crafts Movement publication — 1903–1916 — includes sketches, photographs of homes, floor plans, descriptive text. 128pp. 8¼ x 11. 0-486-25829-7

CRIME AND PUNISHMENT, Fyodor Dostoyevsky. Translated by Constance Garnett. Supreme masterpiece tells the story of Raskolnikov, a student tormented by his own thoughts after he murders an old woman. Overwhelmed by guilt and terror, he confesses and goes to prison. 480pp. 5³⁄₁₆ x 8¼. 0-486-41587-2

THE DECLARATION OF INDEPENDENCE AND OTHER GREAT DOCUMENTS OF AMERICAN HISTORY: 1775-1865, Edited by John Grafton. Thirteen compelling and influential documents: Henry's "Give Me Liberty or Give Me Death," Declaration of Independence, The Constitution, Washington's First Inaugural Address, The Monroe Doctrine, The Emancipation Proclamation, Gettysburg Address, more. 64pp. 5³⁄₁₆ x 8¼. 0-486-41124-9

THE DESERT AND THE SOWN: Travels in Palestine and Syria, Gertrude Bell. "The female Lawrence of Arabia," Gertrude Bell wrote captivating, perceptive accounts of her travels in the Middle East. This intriguing narrative, accompanied by 160 photos, traces her 1905 sojourn in Lebanon, Syria, and Palestine. 368pp. 5⅜ x 8½. 0-486-46876-3

A DOLL'S HOUSE, Henrik Ibsen. Ibsen's best-known play displays his genius for realistic prose drama. An expression of women's rights, the play climaxes when the central character, Nora, rejects a smothering marriage and life in "a doll's house." 80pp. 5³⁄₁₆ x 8¼. 0-486-27062-9

DOOMED SHIPS: Great Ocean Liner Disasters, William H. Miller, Jr. Nearly 200 photographs, many from private collections, highlight tales of some of the vessels whose pleasure cruises ended in catastrophe: the *Morro Castle, Normandie, Andrea Doria, Europa,* and many others. 128pp. 8⅞ x 11¾. 0-486-45366-9

THE DORÉ BIBLE ILLUSTRATIONS, Gustave Doré. Detailed plates from the Bible: the Creation scenes, Adam and Eve, horrifying visions of the Flood, the battle sequences with their monumental crowds, depictions of the life of Jesus, 241 plates in all. 241pp. 9 x 12. 0-486-23004-X

DRAWING DRAPERY FROM HEAD TO TOE, Cliff Young. Expert guidance on how to draw shirts, pants, skirts, gloves, hats, and coats on the human figure, including folds in relation to the body, pull and crush, action folds, creases, more. Over 200 drawings. 48pp. 8¼ x 11. 0-486-45591-2

DUBLINERS, James Joyce. A fine and accessible introduction to the work of one of the 20th century's most influential writers, this collection features 15 tales, including a masterpiece of the short-story genre, "The Dead." 160pp. 5³⁄₁₆ x 8¼. 0-486-26870-5

EASY-TO-MAKE POP-UPS, Joan Irvine. Illustrated by Barbara Reid. Dozens of wonderful ideas for three-dimensional paper fun — from holiday greeting cards with moving parts to a pop-up menagerie. Easy-to-follow, illustrated instructions for more than 30 projects. 299 black-and-white illustrations. 96pp. 8⅜ x 11. 0-486-44622-0

EASY-TO-MAKE STORYBOOK DOLLS: A "Novel" Approach to Cloth Dollmaking, Sherralyn St. Clair. Favorite fictional characters come alive in this unique beginner's dollmaking guide. Includes patterns for Pollyanna, Dorothy from *The Wonderful Wizard of Oz,* Mary of *The Secret Garden,* plus easy-to-follow instructions, 263 black-and-white illustrations, and an 8-page color insert. 112pp. 8¼ x 11. 0-486-47360-0

EINSTEIN'S ESSAYS IN SCIENCE, Albert Einstein. Speeches and essays in accessible, everyday language profile influential physicists such as Niels Bohr and Isaac Newton. They also explore areas of physics to which the author made major contributions. 128pp. 5 x 8. 0-486-47011-3

EL DORADO: Further Adventures of the Scarlet Pimpernel, Baroness Orczy. A popular sequel to *The Scarlet Pimpernel,* this suspenseful story recounts the Pimpernel's attempts to rescue the Dauphin from imprisonment during the French Revolution. An irresistible blend of intrigue, period detail, and vibrant characterizations. 352pp. 5³⁄₁₆ x 8¼. 0-486-44026-5

ELEGANT SMALL HOMES OF THE TWENTIES: 99 Designs from a Competition, Chicago Tribune. Nearly 100 designs for five- and six-room houses feature New England and Southern colonials, Normandy cottages, stately Italianate dwellings, and other fascinating snapshots of American domestic architecture of the 1920s. 112pp. 9 x 12. 0-486-46910-7

THE ELEMENTS OF STYLE: The Original Edition, William Strunk, Jr. This is the book that generations of writers have relied upon for timeless advice on grammar, diction, syntax, and other essentials. In concise terms, it identifies the principal requirements of proper style and common errors. 64pp. 5⅜ x 8½. 0-486-44798-7

THE ELUSIVE PIMPERNEL, Baroness Orczy. Robespierre's revolutionaries find their wicked schemes thwarted by the heroic Pimpernel — Sir Percival Blakeney. In this thrilling sequel, Chauvelin devises a plot to eliminate the Pimpernel and his wife. 272pp. 5³⁄₁₆ x 8¼. 0-486-45464-9

AN ENCYCLOPEDIA OF BATTLES: Accounts of Over 1,560 Battles from 1479 B.C. to the Present, David Eggenberger. Essential details of every major battle in recorded history from the first battle of Megiddo in 1479 B.C. to Grenada in 1984. List of battle maps. 99 illustrations. 544pp. 6½ x 9¼. 0-486-24913-1

ENCYCLOPEDIA OF EMBROIDERY STITCHES, INCLUDING CREWEL, Marion Nichols. Precise explanations and instructions, clearly illustrated, on how to work chain, back, cross, knotted, woven stitches, and many more — 178 in all, including Cable Outline, Whipped Satin, and Eyelet Buttonhole. Over 1400 illustrations. 219pp. 8⅜ x 11¼. 0-486-22929-7

ENTER JEEVES: 15 Early Stories, P. G. Wodehouse. Splendid collection contains first 8 stories featuring Bertie Wooster, the deliciously dim aristocrat and Jeeves, his brainy, imperturbable manservant. Also, the complete Reggie Pepper (Bertie's prototype) series. 288pp. 5⅜ x 8½. 0-486-29717-9

ERIC SLOANE'S AMERICA: Paintings in Oil, Michael Wigley. With a Foreword by Mimi Sloane. Eric Sloane's evocative oils of America's landscape and material culture shimmer with immense historical and nostalgic appeal. This original hardcover collection gathers nearly a hundred of his finest paintings, with subjects ranging from New England to the American Southwest. 128pp. 10⅝ x 9. 0-486-46525-X

ETHAN FROME, Edith Wharton. Classic story of wasted lives, set against a bleak New England background. Superbly delineated characters in a hauntingly grim tale of thwarted love. Considered by many to be Wharton's masterpiece. 96pp. 5³⁄₁₆ x 8 ¼. 0-486-26690-7

THE EVERLASTING MAN, G. K. Chesterton. Chesterton's view of Christianity — as a blend of philosophy and mythology, satisfying intellect and spirit — applies to his brilliant book, which appeals to readers' heads as well as their hearts. 288pp. 5⅜ x 8½. 0-486-46036-3

THE FIELD AND FOREST HANDY BOOK, Daniel Beard. Written by a co-founder of the Boy Scouts, this appealing guide offers illustrated instructions for building kites, birdhouses, boats, igloos, and other fun projects, plus numerous helpful tips for campers. 448pp. 5³⁄₁₆ x 8¼. 0-486-46191-2

FINDING YOUR WAY WITHOUT MAP OR COMPASS, Harold Gatty. Useful, instructive manual shows would-be explorers, hikers, bikers, scouts, sailors, and survivalists how to find their way outdoors by observing animals, weather patterns, shifting sands, and other elements of nature. 288pp. 5⅜ x 8½. 0-486-40613-X

FIRST FRENCH READER: A Beginner's Dual-Language Book, Edited and Translated by Stanley Appelbaum. This anthology introduces 50 legendary writers — Voltaire, Balzac, Baudelaire, Proust, more — through passages from *The Red and the Black, Les Misérables, Madame Bovary,* and other classics. Original French text plus English translation on facing pages. 240pp. 5⅜ x 8½. 0-486-46178-5

FIRST GERMAN READER: A Beginner's Dual-Language Book, Edited by Harry Steinhauer. Specially chosen for their power to evoke German life and culture, these short, simple readings include poems, stories, essays, and anecdotes by Goethe, Hesse, Heine, Schiller, and others. 224pp. 5⅜ x 8½. 0-486-46179-3

FIRST SPANISH READER: A Beginner's Dual-Language Book, Angel Flores. Delightful stories, other material based on works of Don Juan Manuel, Luis Taboada, Ricardo Palma, other noted writers. Complete faithful English translations on facing pages. Exercises. 176pp. 5⅜ x 8½. 0-486-25810-6

FIVE ACRES AND INDEPENDENCE, Maurice G. Kains. Great back-to-the-land classic explains basics of self-sufficient farming. The one book to get. 95 illustrations. 397pp. 5⅜ x 8½. 0-486-20974-1

FLAGG'S SMALL HOUSES: Their Economic Design and Construction, 1922, Ernest Flagg. Although most famous for his skyscrapers, Flagg was also a proponent of the well-designed single-family dwelling. His classic treatise features innovations that save space, materials, and cost. 526 illustrations. 160pp. 9⅜ x 12¼. 0-486-45197-6

FLATLAND: A Romance of Many Dimensions, Edwin A. Abbott. Classic of science (and mathematical) fiction — charmingly illustrated by the author — describes the adventures of A. Square, a resident of Flatland, in Spaceland (three dimensions), Lineland (one dimension), and Pointland (no dimensions). 96pp. 5³⁄₁₆ x 8¼. 0-486-27263-X

FRANKENSTEIN, Mary Shelley. The story of Victor Frankenstein's monstrous creation and the havoc it caused has enthralled generations of readers and inspired countless writers of horror and suspense. With the author's own 1831 introduction. 176pp. 5³⁄₁₆ x 8¼. 0-486-28211-2

THE GARGOYLE BOOK: 572 Examples from Gothic Architecture, Lester Burbank Bridaham. Dispelling the conventional wisdom that French Gothic architectural flourishes were born of despair or gloom, Bridaham reveals the whimsical nature of these creations and the ingenious artisans who made them. 572 illustrations. 224pp. 8⅜ x 11. 0-486-44754-5

THE GIFT OF THE MAGI AND OTHER SHORT STORIES, O. Henry. Sixteen captivating stories by one of America's most popular storytellers. Included are such classics as "The Gift of the Magi," "The Last Leaf," and "The Ransom of Red Chief." Publisher's Note. 96pp. 5³⁄₁₆ x 8¼. 0-486-27061-0

THE GOETHE TREASURY: Selected Prose and Poetry, Johann Wolfgang von Goethe. Edited, Selected, and with an Introduction by Thomas Mann. In addition to his lyric poetry, Goethe wrote travel sketches, autobiographical studies, essays, letters, and proverbs in rhyme and prose. This collection presents outstanding examples from each genre. 368pp. 5⅜ x 8½. 0-486-44780-4

GREAT EXPECTATIONS, Charles Dickens. Orphaned Pip is apprenticed to the dirty work of the forge but dreams of becoming a gentleman — and one day finds himself in possession of "great expectations." Dickens' finest novel. 400pp. 5³⁄₁₆ x 8¼. 0-486-41586-4

GREAT WRITERS ON THE ART OF FICTION: From Mark Twain to Joyce Carol Oates, Edited by James Daley. An indispensable source of advice and inspiration, this anthology features essays by Henry James, Kate Chopin, Willa Cather, Sinclair Lewis, Jack London, Raymond Chandler, Raymond Carver, Eudora Welty, and Kurt Vonnegut, Jr. 192pp. 5⅜ x 8½. 0-486-45128-3

HAMLET, William Shakespeare. The quintessential Shakespearean tragedy, whose highly charged confrontations and anguished soliloquies probe depths of human feeling rarely sounded in any art. Reprinted from an authoritative British edition complete with illuminating footnotes. 128pp. 5³⁄₁₆ x 8¼. 0-486-27278-8

THE HAUNTED HOUSE, Charles Dickens. A Yuletide gathering in an eerie country retreat provides the backdrop for Dickens and his friends — including Elizabeth Gaskell and Wilkie Collins — who take turns spinning supernatural yarns. 144pp. 5⅜ x 8½. 0-486-46309-5

HEART OF DARKNESS, Joseph Conrad. Dark allegory of a journey up the Congo River and the narrator's encounter with the mysterious Mr. Kurtz. Masterly blend of adventure, character study, psychological penetration. For many, Conrad's finest, most enigmatic story. 80pp. 5$\frac{3}{16}$ x 8¼. 0-486-26464-5

HENSON AT THE NORTH POLE, Matthew A. Henson. This thrilling memoir by the heroic African-American who was Peary's companion through two decades of Arctic exploration recounts a tale of danger, courage, and determination. "Fascinating and exciting." — *Commonweal*. 128pp. 5⅜ x 8½. 0-486-45472-X

HISTORIC COSTUMES AND HOW TO MAKE THEM, Mary Fernald and E. Shenton. Practical, informative guidebook shows how to create everything from short tunics worn by Saxon men in the fifth century to a lady's bustle dress of the late 1800s. 81 illustrations. 176pp. 5⅜ x 8½. 0-486-44906-8

THE HOUND OF THE BASKERVILLES, Arthur Conan Doyle. A deadly curse in the form of a legendary ferocious beast continues to claim its victims from the Baskerville family until Holmes and Watson intervene. Often called the best detective story ever written. 128pp. 5$\frac{3}{16}$ x 8¼. 0-486-28214-7

THE HOUSE BEHIND THE CEDARS, Charles W. Chesnutt. Originally published in 1900, this groundbreaking novel by a distinguished African-American author recounts the drama of a brother and sister who "pass for white" during the dangerous days of Reconstruction. 208pp. 5⅜ x 8½. 0-486-46144-0

THE HUMAN FIGURE IN MOTION, Eadweard Muybridge. The 4,789 photographs in this definitive selection show the human figure — models almost all undraped — engaged in over 160 different types of action: running, climbing stairs, etc. 390pp. 7⅞ x 10⅝. 0-486-20204-6

THE IMPORTANCE OF BEING EARNEST, Oscar Wilde. Wilde's witty and buoyant comedy of manners, filled with some of literature's most famous epigrams, reprinted from an authoritative British edition. Considered Wilde's most perfect work. 64pp. 5$\frac{3}{16}$ x 8¼. 0-486-26478-5

THE INFERNO, Dante Alighieri. Translated and with notes by Henry Wadsworth Longfellow. The first stop on Dante's famous journey from Hell to Purgatory to Paradise, this 14th-century allegorical poem blends vivid and shocking imagery with graceful lyricism. Translated by the beloved 19th-century poet, Henry Wadsworth Longfellow. 256pp. 5$\frac{3}{16}$ x 8¼. 0-486-44288-8

JANE EYRE, Charlotte Brontë. Written in 1847, *Jane Eyre* tells the tale of an orphan girl's progress from the custody of cruel relatives to an oppressive boarding school and its culmination in a troubled career as a governess. 448pp. 5$\frac{3}{16}$ x 8¼. 0-486-42449-9

JAPANESE WOODBLOCK FLOWER PRINTS, Tanigami Kônan. Extraordinary collection of Japanese woodblock prints by a well-known artist features 120 plates in brilliant color. Realistic images from a rare edition include daffodils, tulips, and other familiar and unusual flowers. 128pp. 11 x 8¼. 0-486-46442-3

JEWELRY MAKING AND DESIGN, Augustus F. Rose and Antonio Cirino. Professional secrets of jewelry making are revealed in a thorough, practical guide. Over 200 illustrations. 306pp. 5⅜ x 8½. 0-486-21750-7

JULIUS CAESAR, William Shakespeare. Great tragedy based on Plutarch's account of the lives of Brutus, Julius Caesar and Mark Antony. Evil plotting, ringing oratory, high tragedy with Shakespeare's incomparable insight, dramatic power. Explanatory footnotes. 96pp. 5$\frac{3}{16}$ x 8¼. 0-486-26876-4

THE JUNGLE, Upton Sinclair. 1906 bestseller shockingly reveals intolerable labor practices and working conditions in the Chicago stockyards as it tells the grim story of a Slavic family that emigrates to America full of optimism but soon faces despair. 320pp. 5³⁄₁₆ x 8¼. 0-486-41923-1

THE KINGDOM OF GOD IS WITHIN YOU, Leo Tolstoy. The soul-searching book that inspired Gandhi to embrace the concept of passive resistance, Tolstoy's 1894 polemic clearly outlines a radical, well-reasoned revision of traditional Christian thinking. 352pp. 5³⁄₁₆ x 8¼. 0-486-45138-0

THE LADY OR THE TIGER?: and Other Logic Puzzles, Raymond M. Smullyan. Created by a renowned puzzle master, these whimsically themed challenges involve paradoxes about probability, time, and change; metapuzzles; and self-referentiality. Nineteen chapters advance in difficulty from relatively simple to highly complex. 1982 edition. 240pp. 5⅜ x 8½. 0-486-47027-X

LEAVES OF GRASS: The Original 1855 Edition, Walt Whitman. Whitman's immortal collection includes some of the greatest poems of modern times, including his masterpiece, "Song of Myself." Shattering standard conventions, it stands as an unabashed celebration of body and nature. 128pp. 5³⁄₁₆ x 8¼. 0-486-45676-5

LES MISÉRABLES, Victor Hugo. Translated by Charles E. Wilbour. Abridged by James K. Robinson. A convict's heroic struggle for justice and redemption plays out against a fiery backdrop of the Napoleonic wars. This edition features the excellent original translation and a sensitive abridgment. 304pp. 6⅛ x 9¼. 0-486-45789-3

LILITH: A Romance, George MacDonald. In this novel by the father of fantasy literature, a man travels through time to meet Adam and Eve and to explore humanity's fall from grace and ultimate redemption. 240pp. 5⅜ x 8½. 0-486-46818-6

THE LOST LANGUAGE OF SYMBOLISM, Harold Bayley. This remarkable book reveals the hidden meaning behind familiar images and words, from the origins of Santa Claus to the fleur-de-lys, drawing from mythology, folklore, religious texts, and fairy tales. 1,418 illustrations. 784pp. 5⅜ x 8½. 0-486-44787-1

MACBETH, William Shakespeare. A Scottish nobleman murders the king in order to succeed to the throne. Tortured by his conscience and fearful of discovery, he becomes tangled in a web of treachery and deceit that ultimately spells his doom. 96pp. 5³⁄₁₆ x 8¼. 0-486-27802-6

MAKING AUTHENTIC CRAFTSMAN FURNITURE: Instructions and Plans for 62 Projects, Gustav Stickley. Make authentic reproductions of handsome, functional, durable furniture: tables, chairs, wall cabinets, desks, a hall tree, and more. Construction plans with drawings, schematics, dimensions, and lumber specs reprinted from 1900s *The Craftsman* magazine. 128pp. 8⅛ x 11. 0-486-25000-8

MATHEMATICS FOR THE NONMATHEMATICIAN, Morris Kline. Erudite and entertaining overview follows development of mathematics from ancient Greeks to present. Topics include logic and mathematics, the fundamental concept, differential calculus, probability theory, much more. Exercises and problems. 641pp. 5⅜ x 8½. 0-486-24823-2

MEMOIRS OF AN ARABIAN PRINCESS FROM ZANZIBAR, Emily Ruete. This 19th-century autobiography offers a rare inside look at the society surrounding a sultan's palace. A real-life princess in exile recalls her vanished world of harems, slave trading, and court intrigues. 288pp. 5⅜ x 8½. 0-486-47121-7

THE METAMORPHOSIS AND OTHER STORIES, Franz Kafka. Excellent new English translations of title story (considered by many critics Kafka's most perfect work), plus "The Judgment," "In the Penal Colony," "A Country Doctor," and "A Report to an Academy." Note. 96pp. $5\frac{3}{16}$ x $8\frac{1}{4}$. 0-486-29030-1

MICROSCOPIC ART FORMS FROM THE PLANT WORLD, R. Anheisser. From undulating curves to complex geometrics, a world of fascinating images abound in this classic, illustrated survey of microscopic plants. Features 400 detailed illustrations of nature's minute but magnificent handiwork. The accompanying CD-ROM includes all of the images in the book. 128pp. 9 x 9. 0-486-46013-4

A MIDSUMMER NIGHT'S DREAM, William Shakespeare. Among the most popular of Shakespeare's comedies, this enchanting play humorously celebrates the vagaries of love as it focuses upon the intertwined romances of several pairs of lovers. Explanatory footnotes. 80pp. $5\frac{3}{16}$ x $8\frac{1}{4}$. 0-486-27067-X

THE MONEY CHANGERS, Upton Sinclair. Originally published in 1908, this cautionary novel from the author of *The Jungle* explores corruption within the American system as a group of power brokers joins forces for personal gain, triggering a crash on Wall Street. 192pp. $5\frac{3}{8}$ x $8\frac{1}{2}$. 0-486-46917-4

THE MOST POPULAR HOMES OF THE TWENTIES, William A. Radford. With a New Introduction by Daniel D. Reiff. Based on a rare 1925 catalog, this architectural showcase features floor plans, construction details, and photos of 26 homes, plus articles on entrances, porches, garages, and more. 250 illustrations, 21 color plates. 176pp. $8\frac{3}{8}$ x 11. 0-486-47028-8

MY 66 YEARS IN THE BIG LEAGUES, Connie Mack. With a New Introduction by Rich Westcott. A Founding Father of modern baseball, Mack holds the record for most wins — and losses — by a major league manager. Enhanced by 70 photographs, his warmhearted autobiography is populated by many legends of the game. 288pp. $5\frac{3}{8}$ x $8\frac{1}{2}$. 0-486-47184-5

NARRATIVE OF THE LIFE OF FREDERICK DOUGLASS, Frederick Douglass. Douglass's graphic depictions of slavery, harrowing escape to freedom, and life as a newspaper editor, eloquent orator, and impassioned abolitionist. 96pp. $5\frac{3}{16}$ x $8\frac{1}{4}$. 0-486-28499-9

THE NIGHTLESS CITY: Geisha and Courtesan Life in Old Tokyo, J. E. de Becker. This unsurpassed study from 100 years ago ventured into Tokyo's red-light district to survey geisha and courtesan life and offer meticulous descriptions of training, dress, social hierarchy, and erotic practices. 49 black-and-white illustrations; 2 maps. 496pp. $5\frac{3}{8}$ x $8\frac{1}{2}$. 0-486-45563-7

THE ODYSSEY, Homer. Excellent prose translation of ancient epic recounts adventures of the homeward-bound Odysseus. Fantastic cast of gods, giants, cannibals, sirens, other supernatural creatures — true classic of Western literature. 256pp. $5\frac{3}{16}$ x $8\frac{1}{4}$. 0-486-40654-7

OEDIPUS REX, Sophocles. Landmark of Western drama concerns the catastrophe that ensues when King Oedipus discovers he has inadvertently killed his father and married his mother. Masterly construction, dramatic irony. Explanatory footnotes. 64pp. $5\frac{3}{16}$ x $8\frac{1}{4}$. 0-486-26877-2

ONCE UPON A TIME: The Way America Was, Eric Sloane. Nostalgic text and drawings brim with gentle philosophies and descriptions of how we used to live — self-sufficiently — on the land, in homes, and among the things built by hand. 44 line illustrations. 64pp. $8\frac{3}{8}$ x 11. 0-486-44411-2

ONE OF OURS, Willa Cather. The Pulitzer Prize–winning novel about a young Nebraskan looking for something to believe in. Alienated from his parents, rejected by his wife, he finds his destiny on the bloody battlefields of World War I. 352pp. 5$\frac{3}{16}$ x 8¼. 0-486-45599-8

ORIGAMI YOU CAN USE: 27 Practical Projects, Rick Beech. Origami models can be more than decorative, and this unique volume shows how! The 27 practical projects include a CD case, frame, napkin ring, and dish. Easy instructions feature 400 two-color illustrations. 96pp. 8¼ x 11. 0-486-47057-1

OTHELLO, William Shakespeare. Towering tragedy tells the story of a Moorish general who earns the enmity of his ensign Iago when he passes him over for a promotion. Masterly portrait of an archvillain. Explanatory footnotes. 112pp. 5$\frac{3}{16}$ x 8¼. 0-486-29097-2

PARADISE LOST, John Milton. Notes by John A. Himes. First published in 1667, *Paradise Lost* ranks among the greatest of English literature's epic poems. It's a sublime retelling of Adam and Eve's fall from grace and expulsion from Eden. Notes by John A. Himes. 480pp. 5$\frac{3}{16}$ x 8¼. 0-486-44287-X

PASSING, Nella Larsen. Married to a successful physician and prominently ensconced in society, Irene Redfield leads a charmed existence — until a chance encounter with a childhood friend who has been "passing for white." 112pp. 5⅜ x 8½. 0-486-43713-2

PERSPECTIVE DRAWING FOR BEGINNERS, Len A. Doust. Doust carefully explains the roles of lines, boxes, and circles, and shows how visualizing shapes and forms can be used in accurate depictions of perspective. One of the most concise introductions available. 33 illustrations. 64pp. 5⅜ x 8½. 0-486-45149-6

PERSPECTIVE MADE EASY, Ernest R. Norling. Perspective is easy; yet, surprisingly few artists know the simple rules that make it so. Remedy that situation with this simple, step-by-step book, the first devoted entirely to the topic. 256 illustrations. 224pp. 5⅜ x 8½. 0-486-40473-0

THE PICTURE OF DORIAN GRAY, Oscar Wilde. Celebrated novel involves a handsome young Londoner who sinks into a life of depravity. His body retains perfect youth and vigor while his recent portrait reflects the ravages of his crime and sensuality. 176pp. 5$\frac{3}{16}$ x 8¼. 0-486-27807-7

PRIDE AND PREJUDICE, Jane Austen. One of the most universally loved and admired English novels, an effervescent tale of rural romance transformed by Jane Austen's art into a witty, shrewdly observed satire of English country life. 272pp. 5$\frac{3}{16}$ x 8¼. 0-486-28473-5

THE PRINCE, Niccolò Machiavelli. Classic, Renaissance-era guide to acquiring and maintaining political power. Today, nearly 500 years after it was written, this calculating prescription for autocratic rule continues to be much read and studied. 80pp. 5$\frac{3}{16}$ x 8¼. 0-486-27274-5

QUICK SKETCHING, Carl Cheek. A perfect introduction to the technique of "quick sketching." Drawing upon an artist's immediate emotional responses, this is an extremely effective means of capturing the essential form and features of a subject. More than 100 black-and-white illustrations throughout. 48pp. 11 x 8¼. 0-486-46608-6

RANCH LIFE AND THE HUNTING TRAIL, Theodore Roosevelt. Illustrated by Frederic Remington. Beautifully illustrated by Remington, Roosevelt's celebration of the Old West recounts his adventures in the Dakota Badlands of the 1880s, from round-ups to Indian encounters to hunting bighorn sheep. 208pp. 6¼ x 9¼. 0-486-47340-6

THE RED BADGE OF COURAGE, Stephen Crane. Amid the nightmarish chaos of a Civil War battle, a young soldier discovers courage, humility, and, perhaps, wisdom. Uncanny re-creation of actual combat. Enduring landmark of American fiction. 112pp. 5 3/16 x 8¼. 0-486-26465-3

RELATIVITY SIMPLY EXPLAINED, Martin Gardner. One of the subject's clearest, most entertaining introductions offers lucid explanations of special and general theories of relativity, gravity, and spacetime, models of the universe, and more. 100 illustrations. 224pp. 5⅜ x 8½. 0-486-29315-7

REMBRANDT DRAWINGS: 116 Masterpieces in Original Color, Rembrandt van Rijn. This deluxe hardcover edition features drawings from throughout the Dutch master's prolific career. Informative captions accompany these beautifully reproduced landscapes, biblical vignettes, figure studies, animal sketches, and portraits. 128pp. 8⅜ x 11. 0-486-46149-1

THE ROAD NOT TAKEN AND OTHER POEMS, Robert Frost. A treasury of Frost's most expressive verse. In addition to the title poem: "An Old Man's Winter Night," "In the Home Stretch," "Meeting and Passing," "Putting in the Seed," many more. All complete and unabridged. 64pp. 5 3/16 x 8¼. 0-486-27550-7

ROMEO AND JULIET, William Shakespeare. Tragic tale of star-crossed lovers, feuding families and timeless passion contains some of Shakespeare's most beautiful and lyrical love poetry. Complete, unabridged text with explanatory footnotes. 96pp. 5 3/16 x 8¼. 0-486-27557-4

SANDITON AND THE WATSONS: Austen's Unfinished Novels, Jane Austen. Two tantalizing incomplete stories revisit Austen's customary milieu of courtship and venture into new territory, amid guests at a seaside resort. Both are worth reading for pleasure and study. 112pp. 5⅜ x 8½. 0-486-45793-1

THE SCARLET LETTER, Nathaniel Hawthorne. With stark power and emotional depth, Hawthorne's masterpiece explores sin, guilt, and redemption in a story of adultery in the early days of the Massachusetts Colony. 192pp. 5 3/16 x 8¼. 0-486-28048-9

THE SEASONS OF AMERICA PAST, Eric Sloane. Seventy-five illustrations depict cider mills and presses, sleds, pumps, stump-pulling equipment, plows, and other elements of America's rural heritage. A section of old recipes and household hints adds additional color. 160pp. 8⅜ x 11. 0-486-44220-9

SELECTED CANTERBURY TALES, Geoffrey Chaucer. Delightful collection includes the General Prologue plus three of the most popular tales: "The Knight's Tale," "The Miller's Prologue and Tale," and "The Wife of Bath's Prologue and Tale." In modern English. 144pp. 5 3/16 x 8¼. 0-486-28241-4

SELECTED POEMS, Emily Dickinson. Over 100 best-known, best-loved poems by one of America's foremost poets, reprinted from authoritative early editions. No comparable edition at this price. Index of first lines. 64pp. 5 3/16 x 8¼. 0-486-26466-1

SIDDHARTHA, Hermann Hesse. Classic novel that has inspired generations of seekers. Blending Eastern mysticism and psychoanalysis, Hesse presents a strikingly original view of man and culture and the arduous process of self-discovery, reconciliation, harmony, and peace. 112pp. 5 3/16 x 8¼. 0-486-40653-9

SKETCHING OUTDOORS, Leonard Richmond. This guide offers beginners step-by-step demonstrations of how to depict clouds, trees, buildings, and other outdoor sights. Explanations of a variety of techniques include shading and constructional drawing. 48pp. 11 x 8¼. 0-486-46922-0

SMALL HOUSES OF THE FORTIES: With Illustrations and Floor Plans, Harold E. Group. 56 floor plans and elevations of houses that originally cost less than $15,000 to build. Recommended by financial institutions of the era, they range from Colonials to Cape Cods. 144pp. 8⅜ x 11. 0-486-45598-X

SOME CHINESE GHOSTS, Lafcadio Hearn. Rooted in ancient Chinese legends, these richly atmospheric supernatural tales are recounted by an expert in Oriental lore. Their originality, power, and literary charm will captivate readers of all ages. 96pp. 5⅜ x 8½. 0-486-46306-0

SONGS FOR THE OPEN ROAD: Poems of Travel and Adventure, Edited by The American Poetry & Literacy Project. More than 80 poems by 50 American and British masters celebrate real and metaphorical journeys. Poems by Whitman, Byron, Millay, Sandburg, Langston Hughes, Emily Dickinson, Robert Frost, Shelley, Tennyson, Yeats, many others. Note. 80pp. 5 3/16 x 8¼. 0-486-40646-6

SPOON RIVER ANTHOLOGY, Edgar Lee Masters. An American poetry classic, in which former citizens of a mythical midwestern town speak touchingly from the grave of the thwarted hopes and dreams of their lives. 144pp. 5 3/16 x 8¼. 0-486-27275-3

STAR LORE: Myths, Legends, and Facts, William Tyler Olcott. Captivating retellings of the origins and histories of ancient star groups include Pegasus, Ursa Major, Pleiades, signs of the zodiac, and other constellations. "Classic." — *Sky & Telescope.* 58 illustrations. 544pp. 5⅜ x 8½. 0-486-43581-4

THE STRANGE CASE OF DR. JEKYLL AND MR. HYDE, Robert Louis Stevenson. This intriguing novel, both fantasy thriller and moral allegory, depicts the struggle of two opposing personalities — one essentially good, the other evil — for the soul of one man. 64pp. 5 3/16 x 8¼. 0-486-26688-5

SURVIVAL HANDBOOK: The Official U.S. Army Guide, Department of the Army. This special edition of the Army field manual is geared toward civilians. An essential companion for campers and all lovers of the outdoors, it constitutes the most authoritative wilderness guide. 288pp. 5 3/16 x 8¼. 0-486-46184-X

A TALE OF TWO CITIES, Charles Dickens. Against the backdrop of the French Revolution, Dickens unfolds his masterpiece of drama, adventure, and romance about a man falsely accused of treason. Excitement and derring-do in the shadow of the guillotine. 304pp. 5 3/16 x 8¼. 0-486-40651-2

TEN PLAYS, Anton Chekhov. *The Sea Gull, Uncle Vanya, The Three Sisters, The Cherry Orchard,* and *Ivanov,* plus 5 one-act comedies: *The Anniversary, An Unwilling Martyr, The Wedding, The Bear,* and *The Proposal.* 336pp. 5 3/16 x 8¼. 0-486-46560-8

THE FLYING INN, G. K. Chesterton. Hilarious romp in which pub owner Humphrey Hump and friend take to the road in a donkey cart filled with rum and cheese, inveighing against Prohibition and other "oppressive forms of modernity." 320pp. 5⅜ x 8½. 0-486-41910-X

THIRTY YEARS THAT SHOOK PHYSICS: The Story of Quantum Theory, George Gamow. Lucid, accessible introduction to the influential theory of energy and matter features careful explanations of Dirac's anti-particles, Bohr's model of the atom, and much more. Numerous drawings. 1966 edition. 240pp. 5⅜ x 8½. 0-486-24895-X

TREASURE ISLAND, Robert Louis Stevenson. Classic adventure story of a perilous sea journey, a mutiny led by the infamous Long John Silver, and a lethal scramble for buried treasure — seen through the eyes of cabin boy Jim Hawkins. 160pp. 5 3/16 x 8¼. 0-486-27559-0

Browse over 9,000 books at www.doverpublications.com

THE TRIAL, Franz Kafka. Translated by David Wyllie. From its gripping first sentence onward, this novel exemplifies the term "Kafkaesque." Its darkly humorous narrative recounts a bank clerk's entrapment in a bureaucratic maze, based on an undisclosed charge. 176pp. 5³⁄₁₆ x 8¼. 0-486-47061-X

THE TURN OF THE SCREW, Henry James. Gripping ghost story by great novelist depicts the sinister transformation of 2 innocent children into flagrant liars and hypocrites. An elegantly told tale of unspoken horror and psychological terror. 96pp. 5³⁄₁₆ x 8¼. 0-486-26684-2

UP FROM SLAVERY, Booker T. Washington. Washington (1856-1915) rose to become the most influential spokesman for African-Americans of his day. In this eloquently written book, he describes events in a remarkable life that began in bondage and culminated in worldwide recognition. 160pp. 5³⁄₁₆ x 8¼. 0-486-28738-6

VICTORIAN HOUSE DESIGNS IN AUTHENTIC FULL COLOR: 75 Plates from the "Scientific American – Architects and Builders Edition," 1885-1894, Edited by Blanche Cirker. Exquisitely detailed, exceptionally handsome designs for an enormous variety of attractive city dwellings, spacious suburban and country homes, charming "cottages" and other structures — all accompanied by perspective views and floor plans. 80pp. 9¼ x 12¼. 0-486-29438-2

VILLETTE, Charlotte Brontë. Acclaimed by Virginia Woolf as "Brontë's finest novel," this moving psychological study features a remarkably modern heroine who abandons her native England for a new life as a schoolteacher in Belgium. 480pp. 5³⁄₁₆ x 8¼. 0-486-45557-2

THE VOYAGE OUT, Virginia Woolf. A moving depiction of the thrills and confusion of youth, Woolf's acclaimed first novel traces a shipboard journey to South America for a captivating exploration of a woman's growing self-awareness. 288pp. 5³⁄₁₆ x 8¼. 0-486-45005-8

WALDEN; OR, LIFE IN THE WOODS, Henry David Thoreau. Accounts of Thoreau's daily life on the shores of Walden Pond outside Concord, Massachusetts, are interwoven with musings on the virtues of self-reliance and individual freedom, on society, government, and other topics. 224pp. 5³⁄₁₆ x 8¼. 0-486-28495-6

WILD PILGRIMAGE: A Novel in Woodcuts, Lynd Ward. Through startling engravings shaded in black and red, Ward wordlessly tells the story of a man trapped in an industrial world, struggling between the grim reality around him and the fantasies his imagination creates. 112pp. 6⅛ x 9¼. 0-486-46583-7

WILLY POGÁNY REDISCOVERED, Willy Pogány. Selected and Edited by Jeff A. Menges. More than 100 color and black-and-white Art Nouveau–style illustrations from fairy tales and adventure stories include scenes from Wagner's "Ring" cycle, *The Rime of the Ancient Mariner, Gulliver's Travels,* and *Faust.* 144pp. 8⅜ x 11. 0-486-47046-6

WOOLLY THOUGHTS: Unlock Your Creative Genius with Modular Knitting, Pat Ashforth and Steve Plummer. Here's the revolutionary way to knit — easy, fun, and foolproof! Beginners and experienced knitters need only master a single stitch to create their own designs with patchwork squares. More than 100 illustrations. 128pp. 6½ x 9¼. 0-486-46084-3

WUTHERING HEIGHTS, Emily Brontë. Somber tale of consuming passions and vengeance — played out amid the lonely English moors — recounts the turbulent and tempestuous love story of Cathy and Heathcliff. Poignant and compelling. 256pp. 5³⁄₁₆ x 8¼. 0-486-29256-8